# LABOR GUIDE
# TO LOCAL UNION LEADERSHIP

# LABOR GUIDE
# TO LOCAL UNION LEADERSHIP

Gene Daniels

Roberta Till-Retz

Lawrence E. Casey

Tony DeAngelis

A Reston Book

Prentice-Hall

Englewood Cliffs, New Jersey 07632

**Library of Congress Cataloging in Publication Data**

Labor guide to local union leadership

"A Reston book."
Includes index.
1. Trade-unions—United States—Local unions—
Management. I. Daniels, Gene
HD6508.L2 1986      331.88'068      85-19608
ISBN 0-8359-3924-3

A Reston Book
Published by
Prentice-Hall
A Division of Simon & Schuster, Inc.
Englewood Cliffs, New Jersey 07632

10  9  8  7  6  5  4  3  2  1

PRINTED IN THE UNITED STATES OF AMERICA

Why do people always wonder
whether books are any good,
without wondering whether
they are themselves
in a state to profit from them?

— Idries Shah
*Learning How To Learn*

# CONTENTS

# LIST OF EXHIBITS, FIGURES AND TABLES

# INTRODUCTION

*Labor Guide to Local Union Leadership* is about the role of leadership in the management of unions. The book comes as a partial response to a host of not-too-pleasing conditions—for union officials. Union membership continues to decline. Local union officers are failing to motivate members to even the lowest acceptable level of union activity or commitment. Union political influence is questionable in the face of single-issue politics. Collective bargaining power has increased on the side of the employer with the aid of a global economy and the transnational conglomerate. The list does not get any better. It only gets worse.

Unions have been long-time believers in leadership education. Such education can be found at permanent union education sites, such as the AFL–CIO's George Meany Center for Labor Studies, the IAM's Placid Harbor facility, and the UAW's Black Lake compound. Most unions provide staff leadership education and regional or district programs for local union officers and activists. Finally, college and university labor studies departments provide leadership courses directly to and in cooperation with unions through labor studies courses of their own.

Despite these efforts, today's local union leaders are often perceived to be failing in critical areas of union management. These officials are alternately blamed by community leaders for chasing away employers with alleged excessive wages, benefits, and work practices and accused by their bargaining units as self-seeking, dues-hunting petty bureaucrats who care little for their members and who are powerless in the face of employer ultimatums. Being asked today to run for union office is something akin to being asked to be the first officer on the *Titanic!*

Predictably, turnover of local union officers has been substantial. The outright loss of jobs and the increasing legal burden placed on union activities have resulted in only the hardiest (or most foolhardy) of individuals seeking or accepting union office. These people are asking for help. In response to these calls, union education staffs and labor educators are attempting to provide leadership education and management training that will help both old and new officers alike.

This book is a part of that effort. It is not about the history and function of unions, nor even the purpose of unions. Rather, it is about providing leadership when the situation calls for it. The purpose of this book is to provide its readers with a plan for leadership behavior and a *means* of putting this behavior to work in the management of a local union. Our goal is to help *increase leadership effectiveness* in local unions.

## II

To make sense of this book, one must understand the perspectives of its authors. Our views include our beliefs about the leadership process and unions as organizations. The authors have no proof that unions are organized as we suggest they are. Nor can we claim without reservation that the models of situational leadership presented in Chapter 1 and power management in Chapter 2 will absolutely lead to more effective union leadership. Yet we do consider the ideas proposed in this book to be of practical use to most union officials.

Our perception of effective union leadership behavior and union organization is based on *contingency* theory. Simply put, contingency theory for unions means that:

There is no single best method of union organization and leadership behavior style.

Some leadership styles and some methods of organizing a group are more or less effective than others.

The most effective union leadership style and form of union organization should result from an understanding of how the union and its leaders relate to the demands of changing internal and external environments.

What kind of organization is a union? The authors are not asking this question with the traditional answers in mind. We do not mean Robert Hoxie's "business unionism," "revolutionary unionism," "uplife unionism," or "predatory unionism." Nor are we asking for the distinction between unions as economic, service, or mutual-aid organizations. These designations are important labels and union officers should be aware of their meanings and implications. But even an understanding of these terms fails, in our opinion, to provide union officers with a rationale for effective leadership. And this is what is so desperately needed—a blueprint for action!

The authors suggest that unions are *open natural systems*. Unions are open organizations because of their constant contact with the environment. At any one time, a union's membership may be drawn from a variety of communities. These men and women represent various ethnic origins, educational attainments, degrees of economic security, and dreams. Employers may be locally based, parts of a governmental system, or tentacles of a transnational conglomerate. Legal constraints, reaching into the very heart of union existence and operation, may come as a result of local, state, and federal legislation and administrative decision making. Our economy is global, with little or no local control. Unions are constantly interacting with these aspects of the environment, as well as others. Unions are open systems.

Because of the internal complexity within unions among its members, unions can also be considered to be natural organizations. Memberships are diverse and political. Formal and informal communication networks operate side by side. Both formal and informal leaders try to attain the goals of the organization and of their own internal union interest group. Power is always present. Its master often changes and its impact is variable. As a result of this natural ebb and flow (or conflict!), much time and effort is spent just trying to maintain the organization, while organizational goals are neglected or poorly pursued. Taking together the openness of interaction with the environment and the constant state of internal change, unions can be termed as open natural systems. They require effective administration, management, and leadership to meet the demands placed on them. Again, the authors are concerned here with effective leadership behavior.

To help achieve the purpose of this book, the authors have chosen the following definition of leadership:

> Leadership is the process of influencing the activities of an individual or a group in efforts toward goal achievement in a given situation. From this definition of leadership, it follows that the leadership process is a function of the *leader,* the *follower,* and other *situational* variables . . . .[1]

We have also chosen to present Hersey and Blanchard's situational leadership theory in Chapter 1 and Brewer, Ainsworth, and Wynne's power management in Chapter 2 as a means of enhancing effective local union leadership and thereby increasing local union organizational effectiveness. The authors selected these models of leadership behavior because they allow for leadership style adaptation from situation to situation as the organization and its leaders move to meet environmental and internal pressures. It is both an understandable and practical leadership framework that can enhance the practice of effective local union management as outlined in Chapter 3.

[1] Paul Hersey and Ken Blanchard, *Management of Organizational Behavior: Utilizing Human Resources,* 4th ed. Prentice-Hall, 1982. Englewood Cliffs, N.J., pp. 10-11.

III

This book has four units divided into twelve chapters. Unit One contains three chapters setting out the authors' framework for increased union leadership effectiveness. Unit Two consists of three chapters outlining areas the authors feel are particularly challenging to local union leaders. To be sure, there are critical concerns not presented in Unit Two; however, we believe that, if the challenges presented in this unit can be met head on, any successes will assist in other critical problem areas as well. There are four chapters in Unit Three. These chapters serve as informational and administrative learning areas aimed at increasing personal leadership and management skills. Finally, in Unit Four, Chapter 11 brings the varied aspects of our book together in one chapter by presenting an in-depth view of how a local's grievance handling system can be enhanced through better management and leadership. The last chapter of the book is on stress. The authors conclude the book with this chapter because we believe that an effective leader is also one who prevents the ravages of burnout and continues to serve the local.

Chapter 1, "Union Managers as Situational Leaders," distinguishes among the concepts of administration, management, and leadership. The distinction between successful and unsuccessful and effective and ineffective leadership is explained. To enhance future effective union leadership, situational leadership is presented as a workable design for successful leadership behavior. And since leadership acts can and do lead to some conflict, methods of conflict management are presented.

Chapter 2, "Situational Leaders as Power Managers," extends the leadership model presented in Chapter 1 by focusing on the little discussed power aspect of leadership. The power management model presented in this chapter seeks to enhance leadership behavior by having the leader, or potential leader, analyze the power elements present in a leadership situation and understand the personality(s) of those involved. Together the situational leadership model and the power management model provide union leaders with a comprehensive framework for making some successful and effective leadership decisions.

Chapter 3, "Managing Unions," provides a plan for local union management that includes the leadership models of the first two chapters. This chapter puts forth six important functions of management and how these functions, if practiced by union officials, will strengthen a local. The functions discussed are managerial roles, planning, organizing, leading, control, and managing for change.

Chapter 4, "Labor's Message through the Media," is concerned with a major leadership challenge faced by local union leaders. With union membership declining and its image tarnished, it is imperative that union leaders quit ignoring or arguing with the media and start using them as a means of getting labor's message to the general population. This chapter gives a thumbnail sketch of how a local leader can start turning this negative into a plus.

Chapter 5, "Strengthening Your Local through Education," points to local union education as a primary agent in the renewal effort unions must undertake. Traditional on-the-job-only training by an "old boys" network is not effective. The dictum of a local president or business agent of keeping the troops ignorant is no longer operational. Local member concerns and needs, as well as talents and abilities, must be understood and utilized by those in leadership positions. Likewise, the effects of political and economic decisions (one and the same?) on the union as an organization and its members as individuals must be known and understood. A local's education committee can serve as the hub of this understanding process. Working in concert with other committees such as political action, organizing, safety and health, and bargaining, the education committee can educate both the members and their leaders. The local can better adapt as conditions change. Or, in a novel stroke, unions might even be able to anticipate change. This chapter outlines how this important *leadership committee* can be set in motion.

Chapter 6, "Computerizing the Local," poses the question of whether or not local unions need computers. The authors' answer is a qualified yes. To aid in local union administration and to supply information that can aid both in managerial and administrative leadership, some level of computerization is necessary. Whether or not the local buys its own system, networks with its parent union's system, or time shares on some other basis comes closest to the real question. Utilization, cost, and compatibility define the parameters of choice. The real question is not "if," but "when?" and "how much?" As with dealing with the media and education of membership, unions are behind the employers of its members. Employers utilize the media, educate their leaders, and computerize their operational functions. Labor is again in the "catch-up" mode. The Information Age has removed most of our decision-making time span. Hesitation is harmful. Careful deliberation, paralyzing. Refusal to deal with issues—fatal.

Chapter 7, "A Primer on Labor Law," is the first of four leadership informational or reference chapters. Labor law and protective labor legislation are environmental facts that reach into the very heart of each and every union. Yet Americans seem reluctant to understand the connection between the people they elect and the laws they pass. Our rights to organize as workers and bargain hinge not solely on the collective bargaining agreement, but on federal and state law, occasional executive orders, and decisions made in regulatory agencies. Many, if not most, management decisions made in a local are in some way constrained or elevated by labor law. It is for this reason that each local union leader must have some understanding of the form and history of labor law. Its substance is the subject of other books.

Chapter 8, "Conducting Union and Committee Meetings," is the longest chapter in this book. This is no accident. The general membership meeting and the local's standing and special committees are still one of the best means of getting member input in the goal-setting process. They are also important parts of the communication structure. These two activities are integral parts of a healthy union. It is in these same two areas that local union leaders seem to fail with alarming predictability. Learning how to plan and conduct large and small meetings will not alone improve poor attendance and a "who cares" membership attitude. Rather, better run meetings of all sorts provide a platform for member involvement—the dynamics needed to keep the organization alive. If these meetings fail, the organization, the union, slowly withers and becomes more insulated within a false vision of reality. Chapter 8 is a reference guide, a game plan, to greater and higher-quality membership participation.

Chapter 9, "Personal and Public Communication Techniques," contains hints for better oral communication. Potential union leaders and officials, plus many incumbents, often refrain from more influential activities because of a fear of speaking before various-sized groups. Additionally, they may believe that they cannot meaningfully persuade, inform, or even argue an issue on a one-to-one basis. It is too threatening. Whether or not such problems are real or perceived, locals are constantly losing talent because of these feelings and fears. The best solution is to practice, be it in front of a mirror, before family and friends, or at small gatherings. Suggestions for such practice and for the real thing are supplied in this chapter.

Chapter 10, "Effective Writing Skills," is a companion to Chapter 9. Just as one's perception of speaking inadequacy often curtails a willingness to participate, a writing deficiency can have a similar effect. A steward who fails to turn in grievances may be doing so because he feels he cannot write or spell well enough. Volunteers may not come forward to work on a newsletter because they do not want to be asked to contribute a column or report. Chapter 10 is not a definitive writing guide. But it does provide ten principles for writing, a punctuation guide, a style primer, notes on how to edit, clues to nonsexist writing, hints for better letter writing, and a list of misused words and phrases.

Chapter 11, "Leadership Case Study: The Steward System," draws together the principles laid out in the earlier chapters and illustrates how local officers can increase the efficiency and quality of their steward system by using good management principles and successful leadership behavior. It is hoped that the sample system provided in this chapter will serve as a basis for evaluation in local unions and that ultimately locals will evaluate all their committees and structures (subsystems) in the light of their goals, communication networks, and membership participation.

Chapter 12, "Coping with Stress: The Forgotten Skill," is the final chapter of our book. Union officership is a high-stress job for some, an avocation for others. Few if any local leaders are aware of stress-management techniques. For many, such a topic is vague. If it is not directly union related, it is often considered to be of little or no value. For the authors, this skill is of great value. Unions gain little from leaders who drop out after a few years from an extreme case of burnout. Nor is the union favored by the worn-out hulk of a leader who stays on too long. Unchecked stress reduces effectiveness, plain and simple. Thus, it is fitting to end this book with a chapter about stress. The authors do not want their readers to move on to new highs in leader and managerial effectiveness only to drop out from stress. Read this important chapter, even if it does not have collective bargaining or labor law in its title.

Most chapters end with a combination of discussion questions, a glossary, and a suggested reading list. Where practical, there will be exercises or suggestions for activities that the authors hope will bring the concepts presented into sharper focus.

This book may be read in any one of several ways. For the new officer or active member, the book should be read completely. If this prospect is too unnerving, then read only Units One, Three, and Four. Save Unit Two for later. The more experienced officer, perhaps feeling a bit self-assured and knowledgeable, may feel the need to read only Units One, Two, and Four. Unit Three can be saved for a quick reference. The authors contend that the entire book should be used as a reference guide, a resource, as you manage—and lead—your local union.

## IV

Some authors disdain the acknowledgment portion of a book. Others write it, but then apologize for it. The authors of *Labor Guide to Local Union Leadership* could not have completed their task without the help of family, friends, union officers and members, and co-workers. We intend to thank them at this time.

Gene Daniels wishes to thank his labor education mentors, Keith Knauss and Martin Duffy, for their personal commitment to his development as a labor educator. Thanks goes to Mark Smith (Iowa Federation of Labor, AFL–CIO) for encouraging the author's study of leadership and power and to Ron Abshire (of CLEAR, University of Kentucky) for sharing his understanding of the process of leadership. This book could not have been finished without the generosity of Ray Barnes (formerly of AFGE), Russell Gibbson (USWA), Wayne Goldsworthy (AFGE), Paul Hersey, Don McKee (AFSCME), Mary Lopes, Frank Ritzinger (ICWU), and Francine Zucker (CWA). A special thanks go to AFGE Local 1969, CWA Locals 7200 and 7102, the Central States Council of RWDSU, and the Minnesota Federation of Teachers for allowing the author to test the book's materials on their stewards and officers. Again, the patience of my wife Roberta and son Brandon still endures and I thank them. Finally, if there were a dedication to this book, I would wish to dedicate my portion to Lynn Feekin, who first hired me as a labor educator and taught me more about leadership than she will ever suspect.

Roberta Till-Retz would like to acknowledge the members of the Labor Advisory Committee of the Labor Center (University of Iowa), who gave so generously of time and resources in talking with her about the problems of grievance handling and local union education. Local union officers, stewards, and rank-and-file members who provided inspiration for this effort and a great deal of feedback over the many years of labor education in the field have contributed more to this book than they will ever know. She would also like to thank her husband and daughter for editorial and typing assistance and for the patient endurance of many evenings and weekends taken away from family activities. Their support of the labor movement has made possible her own.

Larry Casey wishes to thank John Barry (AFL–CIO), John Carney (USWA), Charlie Crown (IAM), Charles Yancey (UAW), Joyce Hegstrom and Vicki Lachelt of the Labor Education Service; and especially his children Nicole and Christopher for their patience and his wife Phyllis for her skillful word processing, superior spelling ability, and valued criticisms. He would also like to thank Dartell, E. P. Dutton, General Publishing Company of Canada, Random House, and Robert's Rules Associates.

Tony DeAngelis would like to thank his mother, Katherine, and father, Nick, for providing the opportunity for his education; Martin Duffy for educating him; and his friend and wife Carol for caring for and supporting him.

All the authors wish to thank Ted Buchholz, Shelley Gelbert, Catherine Rossbach, and Linda Zuk of Reston Publishing Company for their faith in our project and their guidance in its creation.

Gene Daniels
Roberta Till-Retz
Larry Casey
Tony DeAngelis

# UNIT ONE

## PERSONAL AND MANAGERIAL LEADERSHIP

- *Union managers as situational leaders*
- *Situational leaders as power managers*
- *Managing unions*

# CHAPTER 1

# Union Managers as Situational Leaders

As we begin our discussion of situational leadership and how unions can benefit from such leadership, some space must be given to the concepts of administration and management before one can move on to an understanding of contingency or situational leadership. Administrators and managers alike have their own behavior, which together constitute important parts of the process of managing an organization—a union.

## ADMINISTRATION

The most basic aspect of managing an organization is that of administration. Administrative practices and procedures generally change little over time, at least until there is some sort of organizational or technological adaptation to the environment or to internal pressure. These duties are often clear-cut and leave little to one's imagination or discretion. Administrative duties are the "nuts and bolts" of getting a job done. Leadership behaviors may emanate from this organizational role position, but usually not to the degree found in the management role positions.

One union administrative office that stands out among others is that of secretary or recording secretary. This person takes minutes of meetings, relays correspondence to the officers, and reads the minutes of the previous membership meeting or executive board meeting to those in attendance at the current meeting. Sometimes the secretary summarizes correspondence received or actually reads such correspondence in excruciating detail at the membership meeting.

This office, as well as that of vice-president, treasurer,[1] sergeant-at-arms, and trustee are frequently seen as positions without substance or power, as stepping stones to other more important local union offices. They may also be used as dead-end or token positions to satisfy the clamor for attention by rising leaders or pressure groups within the local.

Treasurers, however, are now finding that their administrative office may not be as routine as it once was a few years ago. There is a regularity in handling dues checkoff or collection, paying per capitas and other disbursements, filing quarterly, semiannual, and annual state and federal reporting forms, and making reports to the membership meetings. But because of a changing environment within which the union operates (political, governmental, economic), the *responsibility* for precise adherence to bookkeeping and reporting standards as dictated by the 1959 Labor–Management Reporting and Disclosure Act has increased. Old and often imprecise money-handling procedures used by largely untrained or self-trained local treasurers must now be replaced with more accurate procedures in the wake of increased federal enforcement since 1980 of the union-related portions of the Act. The treasurer is a prime example of how the most basic administrative role in an organization can be affected by external changes in the environment. It will be interesting to see if the office of treasurer, with increased position pressures and perhaps more training, emerges in the future with more leadership opportunities than now accorded to it.

## MANAGEMENT

The more complex organization role is that of management. The emphasis on management behavior falls on *directing the organization toward its goals* or *acting to maintain the organization's existence.* Managerial activities include the allocation of the people, materials, and monetary resources needed to achieve goals. Unlike administration, there can be a fair measure of impreciseness—ambiguity—as management adapts to the internal and external forces affecting the organization. More than in administrative roles, leadership behaviors are more likely to arise from this organizational role position. In the case of unions, the two offices that quickly come to mind are that of president (or shop/committee chairperson) and chief steward. For purposes of illustration throughout this book, the authors will consider the president to hold the locus of power in the local union. We are quite aware that this is not always the case.

---

[1] The authors recognize that in some cases the role of treasurer and business agent are combined, and therefore are more complex than depicted here. Also, in some locals the treasurer is the only paid full-time officer with many responsibilities. However, the treasurer is most often the keeper of the checkbook and maker of the monthly financial report—an administrative position.

## President

In the management of a local union, the president is the primary manager. (As we will see later, this designation does not mean that she is necessarily the primary or only leader.) Within the framework of the decisions made by the union's executive board and the parameters of its constitution and bylaws, the president is responsible for seeing that the local's goals and membership's interests (not always identical) are pursued.

The local president often follows seemingly time-honored if not rigid practices in the pursuit of the union's goals, the selection and operation of standing and ad hoc committees, the operation of contract negotiation and grievance-handling structures, and the like. The president manages all these functions. As the relationships change among the union, its members, the employer, and the regulating governmental agencies, the president is allowed to exercise a degree of freedom to shift with the flucuations. Such adaptations are short term. Normally, changes of a greater degree can be dealt with only within the boundaries of the executive board decisions and membership mandates. Short-term adaptations may or may not involve some leadership behavior. On the other hand, if the president is seeking to influence others in the adoption of a change, be it short or long term, then she is said to be engaging in leadership behavior. What one does not know here is whether or not the behavior has been effective. This important distinction will be studied later in the chapter.

## Chief Steward

Because a major goal of any local is to handle its bargaining unit's grievances fairly and quickly, the office of chief steward is an important union managerial position. While the president must coordinate all the substructures of the union, the chief steward's main role is to oversee—manage—the grievance committee and its network of stewards. This person has to be concerned with the recruitment of new stewards, grievance-handling education for all stewards, and the proper enforcement of the contract and protection of member's rights through the effective use of the grievance procedure.

The chief steward also can operate with a fair degree of latitude. There are numerous ways he might slow down, speed up, or even stall the grievance process. As the primary enforcer of the contract, both administrative and managerial options are at the disposal of the chief steward. To the degree that this person can ably direct stewards and process grievances in a timely fashion through the steps, we can call this chief steward a good administrator. To the degree that the chief steward not only does the above but also seeks to educate her stewards to grow as individuals, to create more favorable interpretations of language and policy, to create an active Steward's Council to serve as a support structure to the stewards, to integrate grievance results into the contract negotiations process—and more, we can call this chief steward a good manager because a wider range of activities, some of them not clearly defined, are performed in an effort to move the union closer to achieving its goals. Administrative or managerial leadership also takes place if the chief steward has influenced others to achieve his or her goals.

## LEADERSHIP

Leadership, as opposed to the concepts of administration and management, "is any attempt to influence the behavior of another individual or group."[2] But not all leadership activities are successful, nor are they effective. Figure 1-1 illustrates possible leadership outcomes.

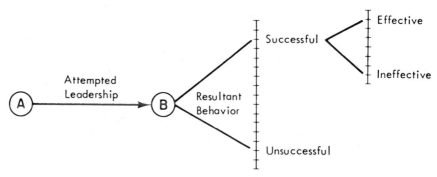

**FIGURE 1-1.** Outcomes of attempted leadership (Paul Hersey and Ken Blanchard, *Management of Organizational Behavior: Utilizing Human Resources,* 4th ed., Prentice-Hall, Inc., Englewood Cliffs, N.J., 1982, p. 110)

Take for example the case of the chief steward who is getting poorly screened and written grievances from a new steward in a particular work area. As a result, several grievances have either been lost or barely salvaged. Twice over the past six months the chief steward has briefly talked with his new steward, offering a few suggestions and telling a "war" story or two. Yet, there has not been any improvement in the steward's handling of grievances. Judging by the flow of the diagram in Figure 1-1, the authors have concluded that the chief steward's leadership behavior in both cases has been unsuccessful and ineffective. What should he do now?

### Three People Skills

The chief steward has to change his leadership behaviors if he wants the new steward to stay on the job and grow. To make a successful change, he must practice three important diagnostic and human relations skills. He must:

[2]Paul Hersey, *The Situational Leader.* Warner Books, Inc., New York, 1985, p. 14.

1. Understand people's past behavior.
2. Predict future behavior.
3. Direct, change, and control future behavior.[3]

The net result of the steward's past grievance-handling behavior is obvious, but not so obvious is why the poor quality. Can it be she does not know the grounds for a grievance? (She has been doing it now for half a year!) Are some people in her work area pressuring her to process their gripes? (Anyone could handle the people she works with!) Is she just passing the buck and blaming other officers for her failures? (If she is cutting my a __ __ , I will fix her!) The chief steward has to determine the motivation behind his steward's behavior. Next, he has to decide whether or not the steward's past behavior will continue. Given past situations and behaviors by the steward, the chief steward can reasonably assume that she will continue sending up poor grievances until something changes. This conclusion leads him to his third activity, the decision to act.

The chief steward now has to decide if he wants to alter or terminate, if possible, the poor grievance-handling behavior of his new steward. He has to decide a course of action and take responsibility for it. A third and perhaps more successful and effective set of leadership behaviors is now to be instituted in an effort to change and control her future grievance-handling activities. For the union's grievance procedure to operate more smoothly and for the steward to grow and become a more capable grievance handler, the chief steward has to influence her future actions. The problem: so far his leadership style in relation to her problem has failed. How is he going to turn this situation around?

## Leadership Style

If a certain behavior or cycle of leadership behaviors is decided to be ineffective in a situation, then the leader should shift, or flex, to another leadership style. The authors understand that the

*Leadership style* of an individual is the behavior pattern that a person exhibits when attempting to influence the activities of others as perceived by those others. This may be very different from how the leader perceives his or her own behavior . . . . A person's leadership style involves some combination of task behavior and relationship behavior.[4]

Note the two important concepts contained in this definition. The first is that one's leadership style is determined by others. The chief steward in our example, who considers himself to be a concerned and even a kind person, is probably perceived by his steward to be a cold and distant person. (He has

---

[3]Paul Hersey and Ken Blanchard, *Management of Organizational Behavior: Utilizing Human Resources,* 4th ed. Prentice-Hall, Inc., 1982, Englewood Cliffs, N.J., pp. 10–11.

[4]Hersey and Blanchard, ibid., pp. 96–97.

offered to help me only twice since I became a steward.) We usually see ourselves only in a favorable light. It is human nature.

The second important concept in the definition is that of task and relationship behavior. Each leadership behavior contains some combination of both these behaviors. Task behavior is defined as

> the extent to which the leader engages in spelling out the duties and responsibilities of an individual or group. The behaviors include telling people what to do, how to do it, when to do it, and who's to do it.[5]

Relationship behavior is defined as

> the extent to which the leader engages in two-way or multiway communication if there is more than one person. The behaviors include listening, encouraging, facilitating, providing clarification, and given socioemotional support.[6]

It would seem from these definitions that our chief steward is providing little task direction and only minimal relationship behavior. If this style has not been effective with the steward in question, what are the chief steward's other style options? Altogether, there are four situational leadership behavior styles and they are depicted in Figure 1-2.

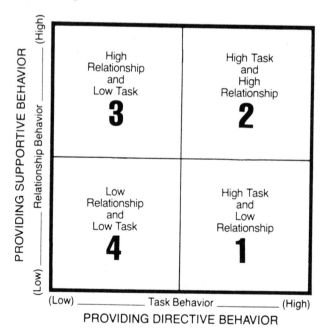

**FIGURE 1-2.** Basic leader behavior styles (Paul Hersey, *The Situational Leader,* Warner Books, Inc., New York, 1985, p. 33)

[5] Hersey, op. cit., p. 29.

[6] Hersey, Ibid., p. 30.

*Leadership style 1* (S1) does not contain relatively equal amounts of the two basic behavioral components of leadership style. Rather, it is high in directing task behavior and lower in relational two-way communication behavior. This style is a strong one-way means of influencing others toward the achievement of goals.

*Leadership style 2* (S2) contains relatively equal and high amounts of task and relationship behavior. Task-directed guidance by the leader is accompanied by explanations for the actions taken (or about to be taken) and allows for clarification. This style is less directive (task) and more personal (relationship) than style 1.

*Leadership style 3* (S3) is high in relationship behavior and low in task behavior (opposite of S2). In contrast to the first two styles, an S3 leader engages in ample amounts of listening, encouraging, facilitating, discussion, and other measures of personal support. The follower's ability to perform a given task is generally assumed.

*Leadership style 4* (S4) is low in both task and relationship behavior. The leader allows those being led to pursue their activities and goals on their own. Very little direction (or guidance) or supportive behavior is provided by the leader. In many ways, the S4 leadership style is characterized by risk. There is little leader control exercised here. Such a set of conditions may be either refreshing or frightening.

With a better understanding of the four basic leader behavior styles, which style do you feel the chief steward has been using with the steward in our example? The authors judge it to be S4. Do you agree? The authors also judge that this style has been unsuccessful because the steward's performance has not changed and the conflict, at least as the chief steward sees it, is growing. This brings us to the next aspect of situational leadership. It is one thing to know one's leadership style options; it is quite another to use them effectively. Figure 1-3 describes the effectiveness and ineffectiveness of each style as perceived by others.

The three dimensions of leadership behavior (task, relationship, and effectiveness) are brought together in Figure 1-4. Taken together, this diagram represents Hersey and Blanchard's *tri-dimensional leader effectiveness model.*

## Diagnosing the Situation

For a leader to select the most effective style in a given situation, that person must be able to diagnose the elements of a situation in light of the effects of the environment. Elements with their varying degrees of impact on a situation include the styles and expectations of the leader, the follower(s), the organization, one's superiors (bosses), one's associates, and the demands of the job. Correct analysis of each and every element is important, but the correct assessment of the *readiness* of the person(s) to be led is *critical* to leadership effectiveness.

Readiness is not a personal trait. It is the level of *ability* and *willingness* one has to accomplish an assignment—a task. Readiness often changes as the tasks change. Ability is defined as "the knowledge, experience, and skill that an indi-

| Basic Styles | Effective | Ineffective |
|---|---|---|
| High Task and Low Relationship Behavior | Seen as having well-defined methods for accomplishing goals that are helpful to the followers. | Seen as imposing methods on others; sometimes seen as unpleasant and interested only in short-run output. |
| High Task and High Relatinship Behavior | Seen as satisfying the needs of the group for setting goals and organizing work, but also providing high levels of socioemotional support. | Seen as initiating more structure than is needed by the group and often appears not to be genuine in interpersonal relationships. |
| High Relationship and Low Task Behavior | Seen as having implicit trust in people and as being primarily concerned with facilitating their goal accomplishment. | Seen as primarily interested in harmony; sometimes seen as unwilling to accomplish a task if it risks disrupting a relationship or losing "good person" image. |
| Low Relationship and Low Task Behavior | Seen as appropriately delegating to subordinates decisions about how the work should be done and providing little socioemotional support where little is needed by the group. | Seen as providing little structure or socioemotional support when needed by members of the group. |

**FIGURE 1-3.** How the basic leader behavior styles may be seen by others when they are effective or ineffective (Hersey and Blanchard, 1982, p. 99)

vidual or group brings to a particular task or activity," and willingness is defined as having the "confidence, commitment, and motivation to accomplish a specific task or activity."[7]

As with leadership style choices, there are four basic readiness levels that people (followers) may bring to any given leadership situation. Again, *it is critical that the leader correctly determine the follower's readiness level so that the most effective leadership style can be used to move everyone closer to achieving the goals of the organization and interests of the followers.*

*Readiness level 1* (R1) is marked by the follower's inability to do the activity and by either an unwillingness (through a lack of commitment and motivation) to do the task or a feeling of insecurity (lack of confidence) at the prospect of trying it.

*Readiness level 2* (R2) is marked by the follower's inability to do the activity but also by a willingness (motivation) to do the task or by a feeling of confidence at the prospect of trying it. Thus, there is inability to do the activity at both R1 and R2, but in R2 there is commitment or motivation to at least attempt the activity.

*Readiness level 3* (R3) is marked by the follower's ability to do the activity and by either an unwillingness to do the task or by a feeling of insecurity at the prospect of doing it.

[7]Hersey and Blanchard, op. cit., pp. 41–44.

*Readiness level 4* (R4) is marked by the follower's ability to do the task and by a willingness to do the activity or a feeling of confidence at the prospect of trying it. Ability is present only in levels R3 and R4. Both ability and willingness are found only in R4.

With these four readiness levels now in hand, at which level would you place the steward in our example? It is difficult for us to judge her level without more facts, just as it might be difficult for the chief steward—without the facts. The authors judge her readiness level to be either R1 or R2, with R1 being the leading choice because she is a first-time steward without education or training for the position. She reluctantly took the position when it was clear that no one else would. Regardless of which level she occupies, the chief steward's leadership style of S4 is inappropriate for both levels.

As this ongoing example indicates, assessing the situation is not as clear-cut as one might like it. The more facts and observable behaviors available to the leader, the more accurate will be the diagnosis of the follower readiness and the selection of leadership style. In our example, S4 is not the style to be used. Our

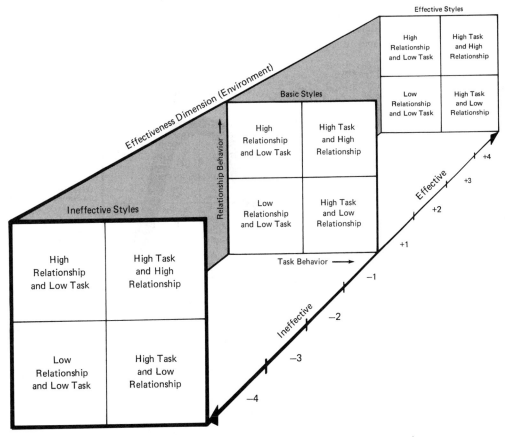

**FIGURE 1-4.** Tri-dimensional leader effectiveness model (Hersey and Blanchard, 1982, p. 98)

chief steward now has to flex his style to either an S1 or S2 set of behaviors focusing on increasing the steward's ability to screen and write grievances and a willingness to do the best she can. Our chief steward still needs more information before deciding the leadership style he will use in his third effort to influence the grievance-handling behavior of the new steward.

## THE SITUATIONAL LEADERSHIP MODEL

To lead effectively in a given situation, one has to influence others. The best way to do this is to match one of the four leadership styles with one of the four readiness levels. This particular leadership process is known as situational leadership. The authors have presented this model of Hersey and Blanchard because of its ability to be used by any union leader at any level of union management and administration. The example of the chief steward's problem is but one small example of how situational leadership can be effective in a union organizational setting. For a better overall visualization of this process and how one can make use of its, the situational leadership model is given in Figure 1-5.

The four leader behavior styles shown earlier in Figure 1-1 are now even more detailed, as we have added in Figure 1-5 the readiness concepts of the last few pages. Each leader behavior quadrant now indicates the degree and manner

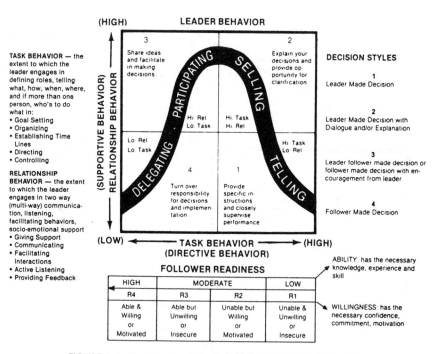

**FIGURE 1-5.** The situational leadership model (Hersey, 1985, p. 123)

of communication in the leadership process for that style, as well as the combination of task and relationship behaviors. Brief definitions of task and relationship behaviors are supplied to the left of the quadrants, and decision styles (whether leader versus follower-made) are provided to the right of the quadrants. Follower readiness levels, as well as definitions of ability and willingness, are placed below the quadrants.

The solid curved line is the new part of the model not yet discussed. In each style quadrant, this line represents the combination of task and relationship behaviors found in that style. For each quadrant there is a one-word descriptor that best describes that quadrant's communication and decision style. S1 is a *telling* style. S2 is *selling*. S3 is *participating*. S4 is *delegating*.

To determine which style to use in a situation, the leader first judges the readiness of the person or group, and then draws a perpendicular line from that R value up through the quadrants until it meets the curved line. The intersection of the two lines represents the combination of task and relationship behaviors (style) that should be the most effective in the current situation.

In the case of our chief steward, he would mentally mark a point on the R1 box just below the quadrants and draw a line upward. In this case, the line intersects the style curve somewhere in the S1 or telling leadership style. He will use a high-task, low-relationship behavior style with the steward until she exhibits a greater degree of security and confidence. He will also nurture her technical skills in the grievance-handling areas of screening and writing. (Situational leadership, to remain effective, relies on education. A purposeful local education program enhances successful local union leadership. Not all union officers adhere to this belief. See Chapter 5.) If and when the steward exhibits a greater willingness, then the steward can flex to an S2 style. Flexing is another key to situational leadership. As people change in their ability and willingness to do a task, the leader must also change styles to meet the new readiness level of the followers. Failing to flex will result in less successful and effective leadership behavior. The result: slower progress toward the organization's goals, in this case, the development of a better grievance-handling steward.

## Power as Influence Potential

Engaging in leadership behaviors means influencing people or groups of people. Power, then, is a leader's *influence potential.*[8] Power is the other side of leadership that is often ignored or misunderstood. This neglect often accounts for ineffective or failed leadership acts. In our grievance-handling example, matching leadership style with readiness is crucial; however, the appropriate matching of the chief steward's power base(s) with style and readiness is also a critical element in situational leadership. His efforts to "bring her along" could unravel at this point with the use of inappropriate influence—power.

---

[8] Paul Hersey, Kenneth H. Blanchard, and Walter E. Natemeyer, *Situational Leadership, Perception, and the Impact of Power,* Center for Leadership Studies, Escondido, Calif., 1979, p. 1.

In the situational leadership model, up to seven power bases are available. Each leader, through organizational position and/or personal acquisition, has some combination of these power bases at her disposal. They are:

*Organizational (position) bases:*

**Coercive power** is based on fear. A leader high in coercive power is seen as inducing compliance because failure to comply will lead to punishment, such as undesirable assignments, reprimands, or dismissal.

**Connection power** is based on the leader's "connections" with influential or important persons inside or outside the organization. A leader high in connection power induces compliance from others because they aim at gaining the favor or avoiding the disfavor of the powerful connection.

**Legitimate power** is based on the position held by the leader. Normally, the higher the position, the higher the legitimate power tends to be. A leader high in legitimate power induces compliance or influences others because they feel that this person has the right, by virtue of position in the organization, to expect that suggestions will be followed.

**Reward power** is based on the leader's ability to provide rewards for other people who believe that compliance will lead to positive incentives, such as pay, promotion, or recognition.

*Personal bases:*

**Expert power** is based on the leader's possession of expertise, skill, and knowledge, which through respect influences others. A leader high in expert power is seen as possessing the expertise to facilitate the work behavior of others. This respect leads to compliance with the leader's wishes.

**Information power** is based on the leader's possession of or access to information that is perceived as valuable by others. This power base influences others because they need this information or want to be in on things.

**Referent power** is based on the leader's personal traits. A leader high in referent power is generally liked and admired by others because of personality. This liking for, admiration for, and identification with the leader influences others.[9]

Effective situational leaders know the bases of power and which leadership styles and follower readiness levels they work best in. Thus, leadership effectiveness must also include the proper matching of style with power base. How is this match made? Figure 1-6 demonstrates the relationship between the readiness of the follower(s) and the power base(s) most effective for that level. (Note: Earlier work by Hersey and Blanchard refers to readiness as *maturity*, with a symbol of M. In Figure 1-6, substitute R for readiness wherever M for maturity is used.)

[9]Ibid., p. 2.

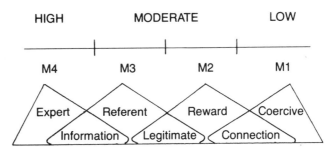

**FIGURE 1-6.** Power bases necessary to influence people's behavior at *specific levels of maturity. (Hersey and Blanchard, 1982, p. 184)*

The match between leadership style, readiness level, and power base is given in Figure 1-7. (Again, substitute R for M.)

Which power bases should our chief steward utilize in his efforts to influence a change in the steward's behavior? Which bases match with leadership style S1 and readiness level R1? According to Figure 1-7, coercion and connection. For a readiness level of R2 and style of S2, power bases of reward and legitimate should be used. If the chief Steward's leadership behaviors are effective and over time the steward's ability and willingness grow, the emphasis in power bases will move from one of *power over* to *power with.*

The use of power, or the perception of its use, is an integral part of leadership. Its use or potential use, even under the most proper conditions, can lead to conflict. Conflict can destroy an organization or reduce its ability to obtain its goals, or it can clarify and redirect the energies of the organization. Conflict, like power, is often abused or at best misunderstood. The authors believe that conflict can be healthy for an organization—for a union—if its leaders know how to manage it.

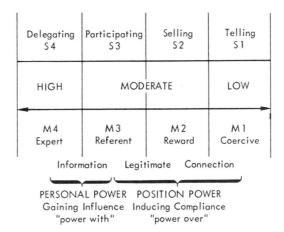

**FIGURE 1-7.** Summary of relationship between power base, maturity level, and leadership style (Hersey and Blanchard, 1982, p. 185)

## The Nature of Conflict

There is an old adage that, when paraphrased, goes something like this: "One who leads and has no enemies has in truth not led at all." The use of influence and its agent, power, will yield conflict. It cannot be avoided. It exists between individuals and between groups. The question for the situational leader is one of how best to manage conflict that one knows will arise.

In any situation where conflict arises, it can be said that it came as a result of the divergence of views or their basic incompatibility.[10] Organizational conflict seems to be generated from any of three major sources:

1. Competition for scarce resources
2. Autonomy
3. Goal divergence[11]

An example of scarce resource conflict in a local union is the constant debate on whether or not to spend general fund money. Union officials differ, union members differ, and both of these groups often differ with each other. Each leader and each group has its own ideas of how best to spend general fund money.

Protecting one's "turf" is a common example of autonomy behavior that leads to conflict in organizations. Those privy to the internal operation of a local union will often notice a high level of autonomy among the officers. Much energy is devoted to either protecting one's position and scope of activities or seeking to enlarge one's position and scope of responsibilities. Established officers often view newly or constantly active members with suspicion. Rather than seeking to utilize the talents and energies of these members, measures are taken to suppress them. By the same token, "up-and-comers" often have blinders on when it comes to their dealings with the "old boys" who actually might welcome their participation in the union. In both cases, the goals of the union suffer as its energies are diverted to the mismanagement of conflict.

We are now to the third source of organizational conflict, that of goal divergence. Unions seem to contain more than their share of this type of conflict. The demographics of unions play a special role in this case. Differentials such as age, sex, race, education, and individual economic well-being lead to differing views of what the union should be doing. Often union goals as stated by the parent union do not mesh with the local's outlook. And within the local union itself, opinions will differ. It is both a headache and a challenge to union leaders to sort out these goals. The authors suggest that union officers have not done a very good job of this sorting of late. While top union officers espouse the goals as ably put forward by the likes of Lewis, Ruether, and others, some unionists want

---

[10]Robert G. Owens, *Organizational Behavior in Education,* 2nd ed., 1981. Adapted by permission of Prentice-Hall, Inc., Englewood Cliffs, N.J.

[11]Louis R. Pondy, "Organizational Conflicts: Concepts and Models," *Administrative Science Quarterly,* 12 (Sept., 1967), pp. 296–320. A refining of these three sources of conflict yields two additional sources of conflict. See Chapter 9.

fewer taxes, private schools, and other trappings. There is a fundamental conflict of goals in unions today, and the conflict is not being adequately managed by union officers.

## Managing Conflict

Leaders within the situational leadership model manage conflict as they lead, from situation to situation, all the time recognizing that the players and the elements change. There are, however, a few prerequisites one must have before conflict can be effectively managed.

First, the leader hoping to deal positively with conflict within her organization has to be able to determine whether or not the conflict *actually* exists or if it only *appears* to exist. That is, is there genuinely a dispute or is there only a misunderstanding as to the other's actions or intentions? If it is misreading of the situation by one or more of the parties, the leader has only to deal with clearing the air. There is no real conflict.[12]

On the other hand, if the parties are truly in conflict, the leader has to adopt a problem-solving style that will effectively bring the conflict under control and create as many positive outcomes as possible, while minimizing the negative aspects of the conflict. In selecting the proper problem-solving style, the leader must first determine the *cooperativeness* and *assertiveness* of the parties to the conflict. The degree to which a party is willing to cooperate or satisfy the concerns of the other party to the conflict is cooperativeness. Assertiveness is the degree to which one hopes to satisfy one's own concerns.[13]

The extent to which people or groups in conflict are cooperative and/or assertive relies on their respective views of the conflict. There are five major orientations from which one might view a conflict.

1. *Competitive* behavior is a win–lose view in which the pursuit of one's goals at the possible expense of others is the pattern.

2. *Avoidant* (unassertive, uncooperative) behavior leaves the conflict to be dealt with later.

3. *Accommodation* (high cooperativeness, low assertiveness) behavior is typified by abandoning part or all of one's goals to appease the other party.

4. *Sharing* (moderate assertiveness, moderate cooperativeness) behavior leads to compromise, which may either be a win–win or a win–lose proposition, depending on the commitment and power levels involved.

5. *Collaborative* (high assertiveness, high cooperativeness) behavior is a win–win relationship where problem solving turns conflicts into a set of positive outcomes for the parties.[14]

[12]Owens, op. cit., p. 291.

[13]Kenneth Thomas, "Conflict and Conflict Management," Marvin D. Dunnette, ed., *Handbook of Industrial Relations,* Rand McNally & Company, Chicago, 1976, pp. 296–320.

[14]Ibid., pp. 296–320.

To sum up, managing conflict in a situational manner calls for the determination of the existence of a conflict, the degree to which the parties are cooperative and/or assertive, and the views on the nature of the conflict (how one solves it). Given this information, the leader can then select one of four conflict managing styles to fit the situation. These styles are *avoidance, bargaining, power struggle,* and *collaboration.*

### Avoidance

Two adjectives to describe this conflict management method might be withdrawal and indifference. In a short-term situation, such appeasement behavior can benefit the parties because it avoids an early and unnecessary commitment of resources. The problems genuinely may be too small to need such attention. Regardless of the degree of conflict, avoidance does not solve any of them. The potential for future and possibly greater conflict remains if this style is adopted.

### Bargaining

As a conflict resolution method, bargaining seeks to share the outcomes of the conflict among the parties. Rather than having an absolute winner and loser, those involved negotiate a compromise that is livable to all. For this method to be effective, the parties must want to negotiate and need to be willing to collaborate sometime during the process if there is to be compromise. Sometimes mediation by a third party in the organization is needed. Despite best efforts, a settlement suitable to all is not always one liked by all. Depending on how the outcomes are shared and the tactics used in the bargaining to gain these outcomes, bargaining can lay the groundwork for future conflict. Win–win bargaining can deteriorate into a win–lose power struggle.

### Power Struggle

One way to resolve a conflict is to engage in a strategy designed to completely subdue the others. Such behavior may very well put an end to the immediate conflict, but it will certainly cause new and perhaps greater conflicts. From the start, this is a destructive style.

### Collaboration

The method of conflict resolution most appealing to organizational managers is that of collaboration. This style is resource consuming, but the results are generally more favorable to all, especially in the long run. There has to be openness and trust, as well as good communication skills. It is the best method to resolve conflicts, but the most difficult to implement. The parties have to work to make this style effective.[15]

Our chief steward still has another decision to make. He has already decided to approach the steward and genuinely try to start the process of increasing her

---

[15]Owens, op. cit., pp. 292–296. Refer to Chapter 9 for some communication and problem-solving hints on managing conflict.

readiness level in terms of being a better grievance handler. But how will she view his actions? What if she misreads his motives? How will he handle the potential for conflict that will arise once he starts attempting to influence her behavior?

There is every reason to believe that the steward will greet the chief steward's newest attempts at leadership with some disdain. He has not exactly been a big help in the past six months. He has to be careful how he communicates his S1 instructions. We already have a hint of his unfavorable initial reactions to her poor grievance handling. If the chief steward wades into their meeting with those same thoughts, there certainly will be a confrontation where nothing will be solved.

But our chief steward has learned a great deal since first deciding that another attempt at correcting the steward's performance was needed. He has learned more about her situation and realizes the mistakes he made in failing to educate and support this new steward. Our chief steward is now afraid he is going to lose her!

He has made his last decision on how he is going to approach this leadership situation. If, at the start of the meeting, the steward is defensive about her past grievance-handling performance and how she perceives the meeting to be going, he will do everything he can with positive relationship behaviors to calm the situation. Our chief steward now believes that he and the steward are not in conflict over her work. There have been major misunderstandings on both sides as to what is to be done and how best to do it. He has decided to clear these clouds up and begin S1 behaviors to start the steward's journey toward becoming a willing and able steward. If any conflicts do arise at the meeting, a collaborative style will be used to solve them.

From the beginning, the chief steward's main concern was to make the grievance handling in a particular department better. This concern has not changed, but his means of dealing with the situation have altered. The knee-jerk confrontative inclinations have been replaced with a model of more effective leadership behaviors. Better management of the grievance process and steward system should result. The chief steward, as a situational leader, is a more effective leader.

## A LITTLE TOO EASY?

The authors believe that the practice of situational leadership by local union managers will result in better union management and administration. Increased positive results in critical areas demanding successful and effective leadership will better enable unions to meet their challenges and to make progress toward the attainment of their goals. Members, too, will express more satisfaction with the local and will make new commitments once they see and understand that they are the union and give it its direction and power.

But unions do not inhabit the world of "Oz" or the "Land of Green Ginger." Rather, they operate in a world of people making decisions for a host of reasons about the welfare and well-being of others. Each person has a personality and a range of power. In the example of our chief steward and steward, an early ruffled chief steward cooly applies the rational model of situational leadership to a grievance system problem. The reader has just left him about to use the appropriate leadership style to influence his steward to some level of more acceptable behavior. But too much is left unexplained. It is almost too easy.

Situational leadership focuses on the match of leadership style with follower readiness. Power and personality are not ignored, but neither are they given the treatment the authors feel they deserve. To use the most effective leadership behaviors in a situation, the authors believe more attention must be paid to the power and personalities of the people present in that situation.[16] The Power Management Leadership Model presented in the next chapter gives union leaders a vehicle with which they can better determine the role of power and personality in a leadership situation. Taken together, both models represent what the authors believe to be an extremely useful framework for local union leadership.

## DISCUSSION QUESTIONS

1. If you currently hold a union position, what is it? Explain whether it is an administrative or management position. List your duties and responsibilities. If you do not hold an office, describe one that you are considering seeking.

2. Which of the four leadership styles do you believe you use most often? Second most? Least used? How would you rate your effectiveness? Give examples.

3. What power bases do you possess? Detail how you have acquired these bases and how you have used them in past leadership situations. Provide one example for each power base.

4. When faced with a conflict, what is your approach to that situation? What conflict management method do you use? Do you use more than one? Give examples.

5. Look to the future in your local union and select something (large or small) that will require leadership on your part. Design a possible approach to the situation, outlining the environment, the readiness level of those involved, your leadership style, and possible avenues of handling potential conflict.

## GLOSSARY

**administration:** Organizational procedures and practices that are routinely done with little variation or change. Leadership behaviors may arise, but are usually limited in scope.

---

[16]The authors realize that the power and personality of a person not physically present in a leadership situation can nevertheless affect the outcome(s).

**conflict:** A divergence of incompatible views over a competition for scarce resources, or the need for autonomy, or over a difference in goals.

**leadership:** Any attempt to influence the behavior of another individual or group.

**leadership style:** Of an individual, the behavior pattern that a person exhibits when attempting to influence the activities of others as perceived by those others.

**management:** Organizational activities, including administration, that direct the organization toward the attainment of its goals. Leadership activities are more likely to arise from this organizational role.

**power:** A leader's influence potential.

**readiness (maturity):** The level of ability and willingness that one has to accomplish a task.

## ADDITIONAL RESOURCES

Blake, Robert, and Jane S. Mouton. *The Management Grid.* Houston, Tex.: Gulf Publishing Company, 1964.

Bothwell, Lin. *The Art of Leadership Skill Building Techniques That Produce Results.* Englewood Cliffs, N.J.: Prentice-Hall, Inc., 1983.

Burns, James MacGregor. *Leadership.* New York: Harper & Row, Publishers, Inc., 1978.

Chapman, Elwood N. *Put More Leadership Into Your Style.* Chicago, Ill.: Science Research Associates, Inc., 1984.

Dressel, Paul L. *Administrative Leadership.* Columbus, Ohio: Ohio State University, 1965.

Miller, Robert W., Frederick A. Zeller, and Glen W. Miller. *The Practice of Local Union Leadership.* Columbus, Ohio: Ohio State University, 1965.

Yukl, Gary A. *Leadership in Organizations,* Englewood Cliffs, N.J.: Prentice-Hall, Inc., 1981.

# CHAPTER 2

# Situational Leaders as Power Managers[1]

If the reader will recall, part of the definition of leadership adopted by the authors (see Introduction) states that "it follows that the leadership process is a function of the *leader,* the *follower,* and other *situational* variables. . . ." In Chapter 1, the leadership model as given by Hersey and Blanchard goes a long way toward providing local union leaders with an understanding of how to be more *successful* and *effective* leaders; leadership style should flex to meet follower readiness; readiness is a function of one's level of task and relationship abilities. Leadership, for Hersey and Blanchard, seems to be a function of this leader/follower, style/readiness match. The authors agree, but we also feel that more attention must be paid by leaders to other situational variables, power and personality in particular.[2]

The effective local union leader needs to know or understand as many of the variables as possible contained within a leadership situation. A practical means of gaining such understanding is the use of the power management model. This model permits the potential leader to better evaluate the personalities and

---

[1] This entire chapter has been adapted from James H. Brewer, J. Michael Ainsworth, and George E. Wynne, *Power Management: A Three-Step Program for Successful Leadership.* Prentice-Hall, Inc., Englewood Cliffs, N.J., 1984, 166 pp.

[2] Hersey and Blanchard's model does not ignore personality. It is more of a "given" in the diagnostic skills possessed by the leader. It is not "built in" their model. Power is a part of their model's process, but is also a "given" in the diagnostic process. Somewhere the leader or potential leader learns about these two variables and uses them, but not as prominent weights in the style/readiness match.

power levels operating in the situation. Officers must understand the linkage between power and leadership and leadership and management. Indeed! Union managers and administrators need to know what power is. Once these parameters are understood, attention can be given to the study of the key power components of the power management model (position power, personal power, and action power) and how to use the model to understand the power and personality variables functioning within a leadership situation.

## LEADERSHIP AND MANAGEMENT

From Hersey and Blanchard, we have learned that power is *influence potential* and leadership is the process of *influencing* others. Add to these the following guidelines: *power is the essence of leadership and leadership is the essence of management*. The union manager has to realize that leadership in the managerial role is vital. One cannot separate the two. Unions have had enough caretakers. They need leaders. There is more to leadership and management than style. As a manager, one must know what it takes to accomplish a goal or task. As a leader, one must also know the substance and perception of power. Together they are managerial leadership.

To achieve a goal or task, a union manager needs to operate with more than style. Style without a plan, resources, or motivated and/or skilled people will move the organization or its people forward only temporarily and with little net gain. In any endeavor where membership or organizational goals are being sought there has to be a clear vision of the task to be accomplished, the resources necessary and available to complete the task, and the personalities of those being asked to carry out the task.

Applying these criteria to our chief steward in Chapter 1, one can readily see his failures as a manager of the steward system (relative to one steward). The chief steward, at least in the early stages of the conflict/misunderstanding, knew nothing of the steward's personality. Few union resources were made available to her in terms of training and education, consultation, encouragement to use past grievance and arbitration files, and the like. Finally, one cannot be sure that she ever was given a picture of what it is a steward does in the workplace.

The chief steward failed in the proper use (or perception of use) of power as well. While we were not present at the first two meetings of our two grievance handlers, we can guess the levels of power present and who possessed what. All was on the side of the chief steward. Total power, whether used or not used, is not conducive to trust and openness. As we have noted, neither of these two meetings qualify as leadership acts. They were neither successful nor effective.

We noticed a change in the attitude and behavior of the chief steward after the second meeting and continued failure on the part of the steward. For simplicity's sake, we can assume that he learned (or remembered) the importance of the leadership style/follower readiness match. We will also now assume that he knows to seek out the power and personality variables present in a leadership situation. He discovered that:

1. Leadership involves power.

2. Power is more productive when it increases the power bases of both leader and follower.

3. Followers have power that can be developed.

4. There are two kinds of leadership power, personal and position.

5. Leadership models serve only as a guide to effective leadership.

6. Personality, circumstances, leader behavior, and power affect productive leadership.

7. Power is the essence of leadership.[3]

His understanding of these power axioms have now placed him in a position to utilize the power management model.

## POWER

What is power? For the last time, Hersey and Blanchard tell us that it is *influence potential*. What does this mean? It means that power is the force by which events, people, and organizations are changed.[4] Power as a positive force in union management takes place when:

1. The existence of power is recognized.

2. The concept of power is seen as having a positive side.[5]

3. One learns how to analyze and use positive power.

4. Communication, motivation, leadership, and the organization (union) are used to enhance everyone's power.

5. The developmental process is understood and used in helping everyone reach a mature use of power.[6]

Finally, a powerful union is one where its officials and members understand that:

1. Humans are interdependent on each other.

2. An *economy of power* exists in any organization.

3. The organization is a system that must respond to the demands of external and internal environments.

[3] Brewer, Ainsworth, and Wynne, op. cit., p. 37.

[4] Ibid., p. 4.

[5] Power is said to be bad when it serves the few and good when it serves the many. Ibid., p. 6.

[6] Ibid., p. 9.

4. Change creates power plays among the organization's members.

5. Members of any powerful organization must participate in the power of that organization.

6. Participation by members must be carefully planned.

7. The delegation of power to followers must be based on circumstances surrounding the task assignment.

8. Motivational tools, communication, and interpersonal relations should be studied and calculated to meet specific needs of individual members.

9. Leadership in the organization should be based on a rational, structured, and unemotional decisionmaking process.[7]

Now that you have a better framework for understanding the role of power in the organization, as well as within personal interaction, it is time to consider the three power elements of the power management model. Once this is done, the authors will demonstrate how to use the model so that the reader can complete the one–two leadership tandem (situational leadership theory/power management model), which we hope will assist you in your bid to be a more effective local leader.

## Position Power

Simply put, position power consists of all power elements found in the total organizational circumstance or situation. Furthermore, a power element is any major factor that has an effect on the performance of a task. Finally, position power elements can be used by the leader or by the followers. The major power elements in an organization, in a union, and the questions a union leader ought to ask when analyzing their impact on a situation include:

1. **Degree of uncertainty in the environment** (for a union, economy, law, etc.)

   *Questions to ask:*

   A. What are the natural characteristics of the organization?
   B. What are the inside or outside forces that are upsetting those natural characteristics?
   C. Are decisions about changing the environment based on logical assumptions or are they a reflection of the personality traits of the leader?
   D. In terms of the specific task to be accomplished, what degree of certainty or uncertainty does the follower have to endure?

2. **Complexity of the tasks to be performed** (for a union, negotiate a contract, handle an arbitration case, etc.)

[7] Ibid., p. 22.

*Questions to ask:*

    A. Is the task different from other routine tasks? Why?

    B. What is the length of time needed to accomplish that task? (May indicate complexity.)

    C. Are new skills or training needed for this task?

    D. Does the task involve new things, data, or people?

3. **Ability and training of the followers** (for a union, personal skills such as reading, writing, and public speaking, and training such as steward training or the handling of benefit claims, etc.)

*Questions to ask:*

    A. What is the specific task to accomplish?

    B. Does the follower have the specific ability, information, and training to accomplish the task?

    C. What are the performance discrepancies between what is being done and what should be done?

    D. What are the other possible causes of poor performance other than training? (Motivation, resources, time, environment, etc.)

4. **Amount of information accessible to the follower** (for a union, departmental steward never being told how second and third steps of grievances are handled, etc.)

*Questions to ask:*

    A. How much information is available about the task to be accomplished?

    B. How much information does the leader have and how much does the follower have?

    C. Is the understanding between the leader and the follower about time limits, specifications, roles, quality, and so on?

    D. Will there be wasted time on tasks because of a lack of information?

    E. What is the goal of the task assignment?

5. **Amount of resources available** (for the union, dues, a committee, past records, copying/duplicating machine, time, etc.)

*Questions to ask:*

    A. Is the task necessary to meet organizational objectives?

    B. Are there adequate specific resources to accomplish the specific task?

    C. Does the follower have access to these resources?

    D. Can the task be accomplished by the follower with limited resources?

    E. Should a go, no-go decision be made in relation to resources?

6. **Time available to complete a task** (for the union, time limits on a grievance, specific mediation and interest arbitration periods, etc.)

*Questions to ask:*

A. In this specific task, what effect does time have on accomplishing the task?
B. Is the task of such a priority that it overrides other considerations?
C. Will the follower have enough time to complete the task without having problems of quality?
D. Does the use of the follower's time move the organization toward its objectives?
E. Is the lack of time a perception problem or an actual situation?

7. **Motivation of the followers** (for the union, commitment of personal ideals, advancement, self-satisfaction, etc.)

*Questions to ask:*

A. With all other power elements at a satisfactory level, is the follower producing?
B. Are personal incentives (ones meaningful to the follower) present and associated with the successful completion of the task?
C. Does the follower seem to relate to these incentives by increasing production?

8. **Personalities of the individuals involved**[8] (this power element is the subject of the "Personal Power" portion of this chapter which immediately follows this section).

As you think about these position power elements, you discover that they are not new to you. Several of them were dealt with in Chapter 1, and the authors are sure that you do consider the others during the course of your leadership decision making. But what we are suggesting is that you are probably not very systematic in evaluating how these elements affect your union and its members. Such is one of the common faults of local union leadership—as the authors see it.

## Position Analysis

A means of organizing the position power elements in a manner that tells you something about an upcoming leadership decision is the use of the *position analysis exercise* (see Figure 2-1). The authors do not think for a moment that local union leaders will use this exercise every time a leadership situation presents itself. Rather, it is a learning device and an ordering instrument to be used when

[8]Ibid., pp. 41–49.

This exercise helps the leadership to determine the style to be used with an individual or group. The leader gains a view of the overall position by completing this analysis. In addition, the leader should find "soft spots" and be able to adjust his or her leadership accordingly.

NAME OF INDIVIDUAL/GROUP
BEING ANALYZED _____

TASK _____

|  | Environment | Task | Training | Information | Resources | Motivation | Time |
|---|---|---|---|---|---|---|---|
|  | Certainty | Simple | Trained | Well informed | Adequate | Motivated | Adequate |
| Q 4 |  |  |  |  |  |  |  |
| Q 3 |  |  |  |  |  |  |  |
| Q 2 |  |  |  |  |  |  |  |
| Q 1 |  |  |  |  |  |  |  |
|  | Uncertainty | Complex | Untrained | Limited | Limited | Unmotivated | Inadequate |

Total _____ ÷ 7 = Q _____

To find the overall position index, add the answers and divide by seven. The degree of supervision moves from High (1) to Low (4). Chart the position index on the line below.

| Degree of Supervision | High | Above Average | Below Average | Low |
|---|---|---|---|---|
| ———————————▶ | Q 1 | Q 2 | Q 3 | Q 4 |
| Leadership Styles | Directive | Developing | Co-Producing | Self-Pacing |

**FIGURE 2-1.** Position analysis exercise (Brewer, *Power Management,* p. 51)

*time* permits. Once practiced, the local union leader will perform the exercise mentally in a split second. But it must be practiced—just like learning to determine the readiness of a follower.

Using the position analysis exercise, or some form of it, yields at least two important benefits for its user. The first benefit is the overall view of one's power position for a particular situation. The second benefit is an indication to the leader as to which leadership style best matches with the power present in the situation. This process, in our opinion, is part of the leadership decision-making process needed to complement the Hersey–Blanchard model.

To use the position analysis exercise, first fill in the blank with the title of the group or the name of the person(s) being analyzed. Next, precisely outline the task to be completed by the person or group. Then rate the position of each power element by checking the appropriate box under each element's column. There are descriptors for the highest and lowest levels to assist you. Once the power elements have been rated, sum the total of numbers in each box and divide the total by 7 to determine an overall *position power index*. See Figure 2-2, where the authors have assumed the role of the chief steward and have completed the exercise. The object of the analysis is the "troublesome" steward. It comes after the second meeting. There are still problems.

There is a third benefit to the leader who carefully evaluates the position power in a situation. The results can indicate to the leader areas of high position power and those elements that need more development. Armed with such information, assignments to tasks can be made more precise. Future educational moments can be planned to increase areas of deficiency. These weak areas may be called "soft spots." Knowing who or which groups have the soft spots makes the crucial managerial job of matching task, resources, and people easier. Leadership behavior is usually more successful and more effective. Here is a tool local

NAME OF INDIVIDUAL/GROUP
BEING ANALYZED ___ Roberta Lee / Steward

TASK ___ Improve: Grievance Handling Skills

| | Environment | Task | Training | Information | Resources | Motivation | Time |
|---|---|---|---|---|---|---|---|
| | Certainty | Simple | Trained | Well informed | Adequate | Motivated | Adequate |
| Q 4 | | | | | | | |
| Q 3 | ✔ | | | | | | |
| Q 2 | | ✔ | | | | ✔ | ✔ |
| Q 1 | | | ✔ | ✔ | ✔ | | |
| | Uncertainty | Complex | Untrained | Limited | Limited | Unmotivated | Inadequate |

Total _12_ ÷ 7 = Q _1.7_

To find the overall position index, add the answers and divide by seven. The degree of supervision moves from High (1) to Low (4). Chart the position index on the line below.

| Degree of Supervision | High | Above Average | Below Average | Low |
|---|---|---|---|---|
| ⟶ | Q 1 //// | Q 2 | Q 3 | Q 4 |
| Leadership Styles | Directive | Developing | Co-Producing | Self-Pacing |

**FIGURE 2-2.** Completed position analysis exercise

union leaders can use to make selection of leadership style and analysis of follower readiness more precise.

## Personal Power

Personal power is one's ability to influence others without the use of organization, office, or position. And how we perceive ourselves has a great effect on our leadership behaviors, our ability to find a commonality in all circumstances, and a means of communicating with different personalities. Both personal and position power change with the circumstances, but changes in personal power are often more dramatic.

It is important to distinguish between leadership attitude and behavior. Attitudes are difficult to change. They are the deep-rooted feelings behind an action. Behaviors, being observable, can and do change for reasons large and small. It is difficult to keep up new long-term behaviors that contradict personal attitudes. For example, if, as a local union officer, you remain in office by curbing the flow of information, by giving orders without member input, and by playing membership interest groups off against each other, it would be difficult for you to adopt an educational program for your local, take direction from a new and more demanding executive board, or utilize the richness of personality a diverse membership can bring to the local. As a rule, unless there is a genuine change in a basic belief, newly adopted behaviors will lapse within a year or so—at the latest. Therefore, it is critical that you understand the *psychology* of your union leadership. Why do you lead the way you do?

## Four Personality Types

To engage in the most effective of leadership behaviors, the potential leader should have, must have, at least an awareness of and, better, an understanding of the personality of the follower. Just as importantly, the leader has to know something of his or her own personality. The more that is known about all the personalities involved in a leadership situation, the greater the likelihood of successful leadership. Brewer, Ainsworth, and Wynne have developed a descriptive means of identifying four types of personality. Taken together, this part of the power management model is known as BEST: *bold (B), expressive (E), sympathetic (S),* and *technical (T).* Figure 2-3 illustrates the wants and needs of each of these personality types. Refer to this figure as you read the general descriptions of each personality that follow.

### Bold (B)

Those possessing a bold personality style usually demonstrate a need to dominate the situation and those in it. Such a person is often a good short-term decisionmaker, but may be weak on long-term or strategic planning. An aura of independence and direct, one-way communication often isolates a bold personality from others. The bold-style person needs to develop a sensitivity to others, become better at planning, and develop more two-way communication skills.

**FIGURE 2-3.** Wants and needs of personalities (Brewer, *Power Management,* p. 65)

### Expressive (E)

Expressive personalities are generally likable people. They like to be around others and bubble with enthusiasm. There is a lot of energy here. It overwhelms the follower. Yet, the expressive-style person tends to overlook important details and needs a goal or task to focus on. This person tends to delegate too much and can often be accused of wearing rose-colored glasses.

### Sympathetic (S)

People who have a sympathetic personality are good listeners, patient, dependable, loyal, and hard-working. They are often the "glue" that seems to hold an organization together. A need for security and belonging can usually be found in the background. Because of this need, sympathetic-type persons often resist change. They do not want the environment to change after they have worked so long to get their niche. They might hoard information or other resources to hinder change. Those with an S personality need to be a bit more assertive, confident, and open to new ideas.

### Technical (T)

"Perfectionist" is another term for this personality type. Such people are very precise, controlled, and rule oriented. They, too, tend to be good listeners. They tend to be good thinkers as they carefully consider all the options before making a decision. Technical-type people ought to allow some confusion and conflict in their lives. Additionally, they need to develop greater self-confidence to go along with new-found ambiguity.

These four personality types do not exist in their own separate worlds. In a single follower/leadership situation, there can be at least two dominant personalities interacting—the leader's and the follower's. As each additional follower is added to the group to be influenced, the possibility of new personality interactions multiplies. While rational leadership decision making is the goal of this book, so much of what is effective leadership revolves around the interaction of personalities. Because of these dynamics, a leader should:

1. Understand each type of personality.
2. Anticipate how each will react to a task assignment.
3. Help build understanding of the four personality types with each member of the team or organization.
4. Make assignments based on the follower's personality strengths.
5. Understand his or her own personality.[9]

Returning to our steward leadership scenario, which of the four personality types fits the personality of the steward (from the chief steward's point of view as an emerging situational leader and power manager)? Do we know enough yet? Does the chief steward? Probably not. He might have to wait until the upcoming meeting to make a sound decision. But, tentatively, let us say that he judges her to be *expressive*. Finally, what is the personality of the chief steward? He could be *bold*. What do you think?

Despite one's best efforts to follow these guidelines, each leadership act is capable of creating conflict. The better one follows the role of personality in leadership and in conflict, the more likely one can appoint followers to tasks with a minimum of conflict. Conflict can be minimized by the methods outlined in both Chapters 1 and 9, as well as by the following suggestions. A leader can reduce conflict by:

1. Helping subordinates understand their own personality types.
2. Showing subordinates how other personality types behave.

---

[9] Ibid., p. 66. Task assignments also include consideration of the follower's readiness, from Chapter 1. One can now see more of the merging of the two leadership models into a single, more comprehensive plan for leadership action.

3. Teaming personality types according to the task to be accomplished.

4. Teaching followers how to communicate with different personality types.

5. Using personality analysis as one factor in evaluating organizational performance.[10]

A proper and continued use of these suggestions will increase follower performance, move the organization and its members toward their goals, and increase the personal power of the leader.

## The Leader's Personal Power

It is often stated that an organization's image is frequently a reflection of its leader's style. This statement is no less true for unions than for businesses, churches, schools, and the like. Leaders often do put their imprint on their organizations. But we often misjudge the source of the power that allows this to happen. We attribute power as coming from the leader when in reality power comes from the follower(s). Followers give and followers take back. One only has to look at the large number of union officers thrown out of elected positions following the employer's emphasis over the last five years on take-away bargaining. Local officers, caught unprepared or prepared but with no power to stop the onslaught, were removed from office by their members.

Can such power shifts be controlled or at least minimized? Some argue that these defeated officers got what they deserved because they were out of touch with their members and the environment. The authors are not prepared to second this indictment because it is too general and sweeping; however, we would like to tentatively suggest that if union leaders follow to some degree the ideas presented next, their personal power should be enhanced and they should be better prepared to handle changes in the internal/external environment. Because personality affects personal power, leaders should:

1. Be aware of their basic personality.

2. Be aware of how personality affects the performance and actions of others.

3. Learn how their own personality influences followers.

4. Be aware of how personality is affected by circumstances.[11]

By knowing how personality affects personal power, a person can work to develop important bases of personal power. Building more on the definition of personal power given at the start of this discussion, the authors now wish to refine the definition to state that personal power is any type of leader influence or power that develops in the follower a willingness to be led.

[10]Ibid., pp. 66–67.

[11]Ibid., p. 67.

Identifying the different bases of personal power has become somewhat of a problem in leadership theory because different researchers compile different lists depending on the focus of their research. The same situation is also true for position power elements. So, before the authors go on to discuss the personal power bases attributed to the power management model, we have to detour for a page or so.

In Chapter 1, you discovered that the Hersey-Blanchard model provides for four position power bases and for three personal power bases:

| POSITION | PERSONAL |
|----------|----------|
| Coercive | Expert |
| Connection | Information |
| Legitimate | Referent |
| Reward | |

In this chapter, you have found eight position power bases in the power management model, and we will now list its personal power bases:

| POSITION | PERSONAL |
|----------|----------|
| Environment | Expert |
| Task | Referent |
| Training | Persuasive |
| Information | Association |
| Resources | Comparison |
| Time | |
| Motivation | |
| Personalities | |

Is one list right and the other wrong? The authors say no. Instead, we believe that each list demonstrates the point of view of the theory to which it belongs. We also think that the lists demonstrate that position and personal power bases are not mutually exclusive. For Hersey and Blanchard, *information* is a source of personal power. For Brewer and his coauthors, it is a position base. Likewise, *association* is a personal base for Brewer, yet it (as connection) is a position power base for Hersey and Blanchard. Do not become flustered because of a difference in the lists of power bases between these two leadership models and the lists of other theories you might read. Instead, understand how they are used in each theory and decide for yourself, while in a leadership situation, which perspective is at work at that moment.

Looking back to the list of the five personal bases of power found in the power management model, the authors believe that there is no need to discuss again the expert, referent, and association (connection) bases of power. A quick glance back to Chapter 1 can refresh one's memory on these three power bases. This leaves us with two to discuss: persuasive and comparison.

## Persuasive Personal Power

While listed as a separate power base, the authors look at this personal source of power to be a "shade" of the *referent* power base. We use the term shade because persuasion in this case means the ability of a leader to convince followers to act even in the face of contradictory facts. Persuasion can be used in a negative sense. On the other hand, it can be a weighty force behind a good task or goal. It is a matter of "user beware."

## Comparison Personal Power

Comparison power, like its counterpart, persuasive power, can swing two ways. Comparison power is given to a leader when he is the survivor of some sort of evaluation or election process. If most or all of the competitors are rated highly, the survivor is accorded positive comparative personal power. On the other hand, if the field is marginal, the survivor (should we say winner?) is still given a measure of comparative power, but its level and quality are suspect. If you are involved in such a situation and win, make sure you do not over- or underestimate the personal power given to you.

## Gaining Personal Power

The personal power bases discussed in Chapter 1 and this chapter are but a part of a greater realm of personal power bases available to leaders. Regardless of the specific type of personal power, gaining such power comes from:

1. Understanding personality types.
2. Using the strengths of each type of personality.
3. Increasing personal expertise through training and reading.
4. Making every effort to communicate to followers a sense of caring and concern with increased human relations activities.
5. Communicating with followers with personality type in mind, and recognizing the followers' own personal power when they turn a minus into a plus.[12]

The positive and rational use of both personal and position power puts the leader in the position of being able to better diagnose a follower's place in her own power process. As a leader enhances the power of followers, the leader's own power is made greater. Another name for this power process is *action power,* the third power component of the power management model.

---

[12] Ibid., p. 70.

## Action Power

*Action power* is a leadership power process, rather than a single power element. However, when a leader properly and consistently uses this process, the leader's power and the follower's effectiveness are increased. Action power can, therefore, become a power base.

The two components of action power are the follower's *power cycle* and the leader's choice of *leadership behaviors*. Everyone has a power cycle that contains four levels, and our perception of where we fit in that cycle alters with each new task and situation. The four levels are identified as *basic, teaming, contributing,* and *independence*. Our perceptions of place in the power cycle change as the perception of power in a situation changes. Looking back to the bottom line of the position analysis exercise in Figure 2-2, one will find four basic sets of leadership behaviors: Q1, *directive,* Q2, *developing,* Q3, *co-producing,* and Q4, *self-pacing.*

## The Power Cycle

Figure 2-4 is an illustration of a power cycle. The cycle depicts the movement of an individual's power base in acquiring the skills and understanding for a new task. Note that one can either progress up through the cycle or regress down-

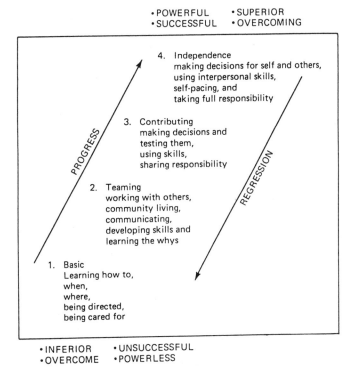

FIGURE 2-4. Power cycle (Brewer, *Power Management,* p. 75)

ward. Movement through this cycle may be as quick as a few minutes or as long as weeks or months, depending on the complexity of the task and the person's position on the cycle—the individual's power level.

The lowest level of power in the cycle comes at the *basic* level where a person learns to do only the elementary requirements of the task. Level 2 is where *teaming* takes place. Here a person learns to communicate and work with others. *Contribution* is the third level. Shared decision making with the leader and the acceptance of responsibility are the hallmarks of this level of power. Finally, the fourth level is *independence*. It is at this level that one can direct others in their power cycles. People at this level take responsibility for both their actions and the actions of others.

An understanding of the power cycle will assist the leader with the proper match of task to follower power base. Looking back at Figure 2-4, where on the cycle did the chief steward place the steward (if he had this tool) in our example? It looks like he put her at the independence level, which we know from later events was wrong. Where should he rate her now? The authors guess basic, but it could be teaming if he finds out at the upcoming meeting that she has more power than he figured. At this point, do you see any similarity between our two leadership models? While they both focus on different elements of the leadership process, a pattern of leadership behavior is emerging. And we are beginning to understand why our chief steward has undergone a leadership behavior change. Either he failed initially to use his leadership diagnostic tools or he just learned them (probably from some long-winded labor educator). Regardless of the reason, he is now engaging in more successful leadership behavior and through both models we are understanding how he is doing it. The question we cannot answer is whether or not this change in behavior is a short- or long-term alteration. The answer is crucial.

## Power and Leadership Styles

Unlike the situational leadership theory, where follower readiness is the main determinant of leadership style, power and personality are the leadership style selectors in the power management model. Personality has been discussed. Now it is power's turn.

A person at the *basic* power level should receive from the leader Q1 or *directed* leadership behaviors. It is the leader's responsibility to supervise this person's learning and performance of routine tasks. There is almost no chance of communication and new skill development.

A *developing* leadership style is used with followers who are on the second level of the power cycle, the *teaming* level. This leadership style encourages the beginnings of communication, cooperation, greater skill development, and an understanding of the purpose of the task being accomplished. People at this level begin to work beyond the basic requirements of the task.

Level 3 on the power cycle (*contributing*) calls for a *co-producing* leadership style. It is at this point that the leader and follower share in the decision-making process relative to how the task may be accomplished. There is two-way communication as the leader and follower discuss problems, procedures, and solutions. The follower takes on more responsibility.

A leader who has followers at the *independence* level of the power cycle (level 4) will use the *self-pacing* style of leadership behavior. Trust in the follower is the important element as the follower takes charge of the situation.

There are several critical points or matches in the successful use of leadership behavior. Matching leadership style with follower readiness as seen in Chapter 1 is one example. A second is the proper match between leadership style and the follower's position on her power cycle. As a leader analyzes a follower's position and personality power, these questions should be answered:

1. What is the overall power position related to this specific task?

2. What power elements indicate some weakness in the power position?

3. What type of leadership behavior should be used as a result of the position analysis?

4. What are the personalities involved and how will they react to the assignment?

5. Will there be any possibility of negative power discrepancies as this assignment is made?

6. Will the leader/follower interaction result in more power for both parties?[13]

## POWER MANAGEMENT MODEL

The authors cannot put it off any longer. You are now ready to see the power management model. Having studied its different personality and power dimensions, it is now time to see how you, as a local union leader, can use it as a tool for more successful and effective managerial leadership.

The power management model (see Figure 2-5) has three components: position, leadership behavior, and personality. For the first component, the *current* position power or circumstance in a situation determines the quadrant number or power position. This power position factor is determined by using the position analysis exercise from Figure 2-1. Leadership behavior, which is a mix of task-directed and human-relations behavior, is the second component. The proper style is also determined by using the position analysis exercise. Personality is the final dimension or component of the power management model. An understanding of the B.E.S.T. personality framework provides the leader with this final part of the model.

---

[13]Ibid., p. 81.

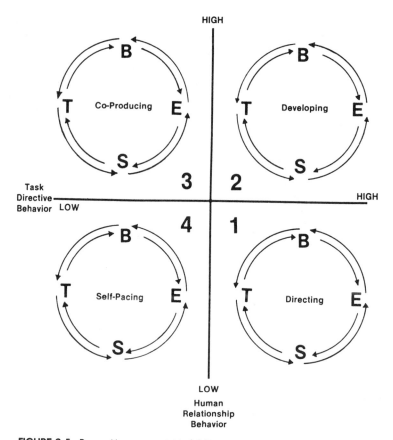

**FIGURE 2-5.** Power Management Model (Brewer, *Power Management,* p. 85)

The three steps in the decision-making process using the model are:

1. Use the position analysis of all power elements to determine the overall power position. This will indicate the degree of supervision needed under the circumstances.

2. Identify the leadership behavior that is under the circumstances in a given quadrant in the model (directing, developing, co-producing, and self-pacing).[14]

3. Determine the type of personality of the follower and what effect that will have on the leadership approach.[15]

---

[14] The mix of leadership behaviors by quadrant are: Q1 = high task and low relationship, Q2 = high task and high relationship, Q3 = low task and high relationship, and Q4 = low task and low relationship. Look familiar?

[15] Ibid., p. 87.

To make the use of the model easier, one can place the essentials of the process on a single page—the leadership action plan. See Figure 2-6. When the power cycle is added for a better understanding of where the follower's position is in terms of his or her power base, the power management model is complete.

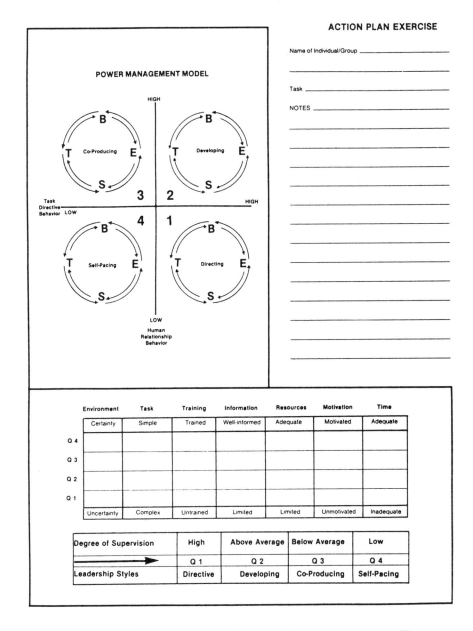

**FIGURE 2-6.** Leadership action plan (Brewer, *Power Management,* p. 97)

## THE WHY OF IT ALL

No single leadership theory puts it all together. The concept is just too complex and is constantly being refined. Yet the authors consider the combination of situational leadership theory and power management—the joining together of these two contingency leadership models—to be a positive step in the direction of finding a practical plan for increasing the practice of effective leadership. In the case of this book, the authors hope these models can be used to better the practice of managerial and administrative leadership in local unions.

These models do not carry excess baggage. That is, the essentials of both models can be reduced to one page of paper, front and back. They can fit into a pocket, a purse, or a notebook for a quick reminder. While these models rest on research going back 50 years, there is no bulk in these models as tools for the potential leader. The authors have been able to provide only the surface of each of these decision-making processes. More reading and practice are a must.

The authors feel local union managers and administrators need to become situational leaders and power managers. The times demand this. Unions do not need any more caretakers. This belief goes to the root of the *real* intent of this book. We believe unions need leaders who can manage *change*. To manage change, one needs a plan of action and people to carry it out. There cannot be one without the other. Leadership is needed to influence such change. Unions must change.

Chapter 3 is about management—management of an organization. Management and leadership are different; yet they are a part of each other. It does no good to learn the principles of the next chapter if you do not know how to lead your local toward these changes. The authors had to provide you with a device for the larger plan—leadership for the management of change. Chapters 4 to 6 are about three of many challenges a union situational leader will face. They represent three different but related areas of need. Unions need external public relations, which will in turn affect the unions' internal and external environment. Education is the cornerstone of understanding change. Information computerization is the technical advance needed to span time and barriers. Other change will be more difficult if these challenges are not met and won over. Chapters 7 to 10 provide personal skills that should enhance various aspects of one's leadership. They add to one's power base. Chapter 11 is a meager attempt to pull this book together, while Chapter 12 is about selfishness. This last chapter is about stress management. A situational leader certainly needs it. We want you to have it. You will have failed, we will have failed, if you burn out and thereby become ineffective. Such is the lot of the local union leader/manager.

## DISCUSSION QUESTIONS

1. Compare and contrast the power management model and the situational leadership theory. Give particular attention to leadership styles, position power bases, personal power bases, and personality.

2. Using position analysis, analyze the position elements in a leadership situation in your own local. What leadership style does your analysis call for?

3. Next, analyze the personality(s) of the follower(s) and yourself. How would you describe them?

4. What leadership behaviors will you use in this situation?

5. Analyze this same situation using the situational leadership theory. How do the two compare in terms of style and behaviors to be used? Do you favor one model over the other or do you see them as working together to provide a more complete picture of the leadership situation? Explain.

## GLOSSARY

**personal power:** One's ability to influence others without the use of organization, office, or position.

**position power:** Consists of all power elements found in the total organizational circumstance or situation.

**power cycle:** Depicts the movement of an individual's power base in acquiring the skills and understanding for a new task.

**power element:** Any major factor that has an effect on the performance of a task.

**soft spots:** Weak areas in one's position power element.

## ADDITIONAL RESOURCES

Bacharach, Samuel B., and Edward J. Lawler. *Bargaining: Power, Tactics, and Outcomes.* San Francisco: Jossey-Bass, Inc., 1981.

_____. *Power and Politics in Organizations.* San Francisco: Jossey-Bass, Inc., 1980.

Pfeffer, Jeffrey. *Power in Organizations.* Boston: Pitman Books Ltd., 1981.

# CHAPTER 3

# Managing Unions

The basic assumptions underpinning this book are that many union officials are ill prepared to lead, to manage, and that the effectiveness of unions in achieving their objectives and goals is less than it used to be. The authors are not suggesting that there are no effective union managers and leaders. What we are saying is that there are simply not enough of the good ones around and that not all the good ones hold office. Nor are the authors seeking to lay blame and find a scapegoat. What we do wish to emphasize is that what we often do as college and university labor educators and as union staff people is to perpetuate the old myths and structures about how unions should operate.

## THE UNION AS AN ORGANIZATION

One of the main ways current and potential union officials are socialized into outdated managerial ways is the use of the one-page union structure chart. They should all be burned or at the least replaced with a series of diagrams that reflect more accurately the structure of unions in the light of their internal and external environments. Figure 3-1 is a structure chart of the AFL–CIO, and Figure 3-2 is a structure chart of the American national union. After taking a moment to glance at them, answer the following questions based on information provided by the charts.

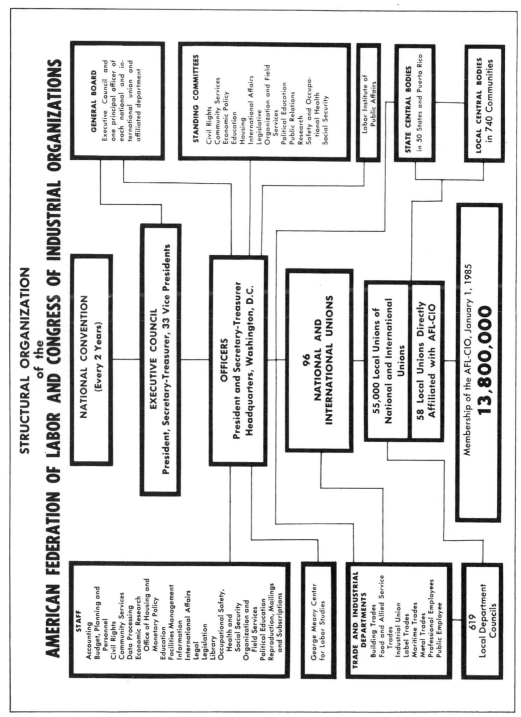

## STRUCTURAL ORGANIZATION
### of the
## AMERICAN FEDERATION OF LABOR AND CONGRESS OF INDUSTRIAL ORGANIZATIONS

**GENERAL BOARD**
Executive Council and one principal officer of each national and international union and affiliated department

**STANDING COMMITTEES**
Civil Rights
Community Services
Economic Policy
Education
Housing
International Affairs
Legislative
Organization and Field Services
Political Education
Public Relations
Research
Safety and Occupational Health
Social Security

Labor Institute of Public Affairs

**STATE CENTRAL BODIES**
in 50 States and Puerto Rico

**LOCAL CENTRAL BODIES**
in 740 Communities

**NATIONAL CONVENTION**
(Every 2 Years)

**EXECUTIVE COUNCIL**
President, Secretary-Treasurer, 33 Vice Presidents

**OFFICERS**
President and Secretary-Treasurer
Headquarters, Washington, D.C.

**96 NATIONAL AND INTERNATIONAL UNIONS**

55,000 Local Unions of National and International Unions

58 Local Unions Directly Affiliated with AFL-CIO

Membership of the AFL-CIO, January 1, 1985
**13,800,000**

**STAFF**
Accounting
Budget, Planning and Personnel
Civil Rights
Community Services
Data Processing
Economic Research
Office of Housing and Monetary Policy
Education
Facilities Management
Information
International Affairs
Legal
Legislation
Library
Occupational Safety, Health and Social Security
Organization and Field Services
Political Education
Reproduction, Mailings and Subscriptions

George Meany Center for Labor Studies

**TRADE AND INDUSTRIAL DEPARTMENTS**
Building Trades
Food and Allied Service Trades
Industrial Union
Label Trades
Maritime Trades
Metal Trades
Professional Employees
Public Employee

**619 Local Department Councils**

**FIGURE 3-1.** Structure chart of the AFL–CIO

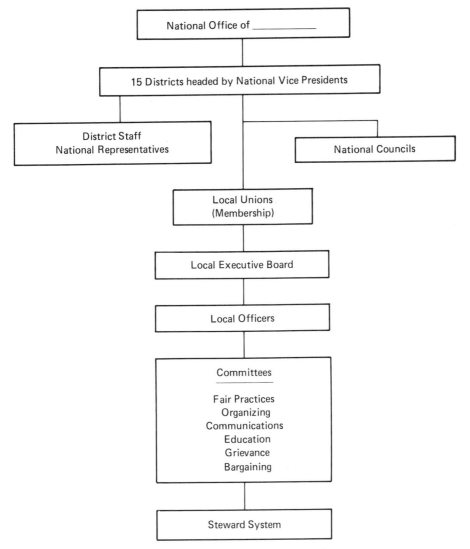

**FIGURE 3-2.** Structure chart for a national union

1. Is there a connection between the two labor organizations in the two exhibits?

2. Is there a connection between these labor organizations and other labor organizations? Or organizations other than labor?

3. How do internal environments such as relationships and resources affect each organization, if at all? Does a change in one organization's internal environment affect the other organization in any way?

4. How do external environments such as politics, law, and the economy affect each organization, if at all? Does a change in one organization's external environment affect the other organization in any way?

More questions could be asked, but these few get the point across. The point is that organizational charts such as these reveal little that is true about the units being described. Unionists schooled with these charts often leave with the idea that unions are structures that stand alone in society and, being as stalwart as they are, are rarely subject to change. Nothing could be farther from the truth and more damaging to the perceptions of local union leaders. Unions that stand alone eventually die a solitary death. Secondly, unions are in constant change, at least informally. The problem is that most union managers and administrators have their heads in the sand waiting for someone to magically *lead* the glorious countercharge. These officials fail to see the power that is within. The members rant and rave or emotionally resign in disgust as their officials appear dazed. Events in the 1980s just are not working out according to the charts!

Labor officials are conditioned to think of their union in terms of hierarchy and bureaucracy. Structure charts reflect the top-to-bottom order of belonging and function and hint at the maze of bureaucratic controls built in at each level. Each chart reflects the contradictions the members know to be true.

Contradiction 1. The union is only as strong as its membership; yet members are at the bottom of the organizational structure—and they know it.

Contradiction 2. The local steward is the backbone of local union management; yet American stewards are often reduced to poorly trained complaint takers with no commitment to the job.

Contradiction 3. Union officials are responsible to their members. Since when?

The list can and does go on.

Unions are actually *open natural systems,* not the closed hierarchy of boxes the charts indicate. Local union managers and members alike need to *know* and *understand* the relationships their union has with other organizations and the political, economic, and legal climate that affects the local's ability to achieve its goals. These same people need to *know* and *understand* the needs of the membership. No union official *owns* her position. Be it by election or appointment, the position is given. One of the constant problems has been, however, the notion that once in office, that office is owned. In a natural system, there is a constant flow of change as members come and go and needs change. Nowhere in the charts does a potential manager or leader learn of the change and conflict that is inherent in that organization. As a consequence, most of these people either fail or serve less effectively than they could otherwise. Our education of union leaders is deficient.

## WHAT IS TAUGHT AND WHAT IS NOT

Leadership behavior is power behavior. Yet few if any of the educational materials prepared for use in teaching what is known as "union leadership" mention power. Second, again with few exceptions, the process of leadership is poorly discussed. Leadership traits and skills are often passed off as being leadership. Participants leave conferences armed with better speaking skills and such, while still not fully appreciating that all the skills in the world will not hold up when you are powerless in a given situation. We teach them our brand of leadership and then wonder why they do not lead successfully and effectively once they are on their own. Why is this done?

One reason why the concept of leadership as a process and the impact of power have been largely omitted from labor education may be because it is often hard to personally relate or write precisely how one leads. One just does it. Either you do it or you don't. It is hard to break into steps how one "sizes up" someone else.

A second reason for the leaving out of these concepts may arise from the fact that not all unions have a full-time education department, let alone a full-time education director. Even when a parent union has such a person or department, they often get involved with bargaining and arbitration research and other important projects. While some good leadership material has originated from education department staffs, much of it is like that found in university and college labor education staffs. It is borrowed, copied, and passed out often without a genuine understanding of the content.

Third, who really knows how the leadership process works? And what is power and how does it work? More importantly, can anyone teach leadership and power? These are good questions. There are conflicting theories of leadership and power. This book provides the union official and member with one perspective—contingency theory focusing on behavior. Others focus on leadership attitudes. What to do! Can it all be taught? The authors believe it can be, but others do not. This lack of preciseness may have led those who put together early leadership materials for unionists to focus on the skills, hoping that the individual could then somehow put it all together.

The last reason for omitting important concepts in the teaching of leadership is a sinister one. Formal education is, among other things, a socializing process. The participants learn what the instructor wants and receive that person's value judgments about the content. If one is taught that the union is structured a certain way and that all things have a certain route, then it follows that those paths are to be followed. As long as one is taught personal and technical skills, that person remains a good administrator or manager, but without leadership capability. The main union path to higher office is still through the ranks, barring a major upheaval in the organization. One only exercises leadership when sanctioned by those in higher office. Union tradition and education tend to suppress leadership and innovation. Is this statement true? If it is, then is it by accident reinforced by tradition—or is it by design supported by calculated strategy?

The final result is that we have done a poor job thus far of providing good local union leadership and management education to current and potential union officials. Regardless of why or how we have failed, it is time to put into practice better principles of management at the local level. The balance of this chapter attempts to outline a model of contingency or situational management for union leaders.

At the start of Chapter 1, the authors briefly distinguished between administration, management, and leadership, noting that leadership behaviors *may* be a part of both administrative and managerial roles. It is now time to take the distinction further. The authors hope that local union administrators do exhibit leadership when the time calls for it; however, these people should not fool themselves into thinking that by being good administrators they *manage* the local. Administrators and their processes are managed along with the members of the organization—the union. It takes wider vision and greater acceptance of responsibility to manage an organization. But even this is not enough. One can learn how to manage just as one learns how to administrate. Managers who seek to move their organization closer to a goal must also lead. Managerial leadership is what is needed for an organization to succeed. Managerial leadership is what seems to be lacking in many local unions.

## LEADERS AND MANAGERS

Leaders and managers have differing views about an organization and how it is to be operated. Zaleznik has noted at least four contrasts.[1] The authors have put them in the context of union organization.

### Attitudes and Goals

Managers are not necessarily committed to goals. They see the need to meet goals only as a function of the organization. They often are not personally committed to the goal in question. On the other hand, leaders take goals personally and this attitude shows in their management style. A chief steward who asks only for the routine handling of grievances will get just that. Compare this to the chief steward who educates his stewards to police the contract. There is a difference in spirit by the followers. They get it from their leader/manager.

---

[1] Abraham Zaleznik, "Managers and Leaders: Are They Different," Eliza G.C. Collins, ed., *Executive Success: Making It in Management,* Harvard Business Review Executive Book Series, John Wiley & Sons, Inc., New York, 1983, pp. 126–134.

## Conceptions of Work

Managers match resources (including people), skills, ideas, and tactics to enable the organization to function. The manager may display an admirable range of tactics and understanding, something an administrator cannot or will not do. Thus, the work that a manager does is the "enabling process" that permits the organization to function. Leaders work in just the opposite fashion. Managers use their techniques to narrow the choices of action down to one. Leaders seek new approaches to old problems and solutions to new issues. Leaders seek to exploit risk; managers seek to control it.

## Relation with Others

Managers like to work with people. People for the manager serve as the means to get the job done. Managers relate to people within the organization according to their role in the organization and the degree to which they are important to the decision-making process. (Power!) When described by subordinates, the manager is often made out to be a manipulator. This less than flattering feeling for the manager is contrasted by how people feel about a leader in their organization. A leader evokes emotion: like–dislike, love–hate, admire–detest. Regardless of the extreme, leaders bring emotion to the surface in their followers. Such emotion can move a union to incredible actions.

## Sense of Self

Managers often perceive themselves as "keepers of the flame." Their function is to keep the organization functioning as it has been. A manager's goal is often to leave the organization as she found it. These people are limited, whereas leaders seem unlimited. Leaders want to change things. Human, economic, and political relationships are constantly being altered as a leader moves to keep the organization and its members on the edge of change. Union leaders are often the "keepers of the flame"—of the status quo. Unions do not need such people. Unions need leaders who can manage their organizations in times of internal and external change. Such is the *future* leader who is needed *now!*.

## SITUATIONAL MANAGEMENT

Union leaders who manage locals effectively these days are those who can live with change and the uncertainty and risk change brings. They are situational leaders and they manage the same way. That is, they permit, if not insist on, the union's structure and the roles of its officials and members flexing to meet new demands brought on by new events and issues. As goals are added, discarded, or modified, members and officers are shifted to different positions to meet new objectives. Existing roles are enlarged or constricted, sometimes eliminated, in the face of organizational transition. What seems chaos to the transitional manager is more realistically seen by the situational manager as a simple shifting of the organization and its members to meet a new task, a new challenge. Thus, union situational management can be defined as:

> The approach that takes into account the local's goals and objectives, its organizational structure and roles, the skills, abilities, and talents of its members and officials, its environments, and the available pool of managerial skills as management decisions about planning, organizing, leading, and controlling are made.

The new elements in this definition for you, the reader, are planning, organizing, leading, and controlling.[2] These are the four main categories of managerial functions, each containing additional separate and distinct subfunctions. Add to these categories the span of roles a manager might fill in a situation and the all-important job of managing organizational change and one will total six central functions of management. The successful union situational manager will have the prerequisites for these functions in place within the local and will know how to properly utilize them.

## The Manager's Job (Role)

In Chapter 1, several distinctions were made about the roles certain union offices tend to hold for those persons occupying them. (Roles are behaviors that can be attributed to an organizational position, such as local union president.) The roles cited varied in terms of goals to be achieved and the methods used for their achievement. Some union roles require technical skill or knowledge, while others need more of a human-relations (personal) touch. Power and leadership fluctuate from role to role. There is no inconsistency here. Rather, the variance reveals the fact that at any time when a manager is doing her job, the manager may be using one or more of 10 possible roles spread over three categories. There are interpersonal roles, informational roles, and decisional roles.[3] Let's see what they mean for union managers.

### Interpersonal Roles

A manager has three possible interpersonal roles: figurehead, leadership, and liaison. As a figurehead, a union president may be looked up to by the membership as someone who cares and listens. He might also be admired for being a "mover and a shaker" when it comes to dealing with the employer. Leadership is the manager's interpersonal role the authors are most interested in. Since leadership must involve people and the process of influencing them, leadership is a

---

[2]These are the four universally understood parts of the process. To these four parts the authors have added the managerial roles found in an organization and organizational development (OD). All have been put in the context of local union management.

[3]Henry Mintzberg, "Managerial Work: Analyses from Observation," *Management Science*, October 1971, pp. 97–110; and Henry Mintzberg, "The Manager's Job: Folklore and Fact," *Harvard Business Review*, July–August 1975, pp. 49–61.

critical managerial role. Finally, there is the role of liaison where the manager acts as the hub of information and activity networks. The chief steward is a fine example of such a role.

### Informational Roles

One who fills an informational role is an information processor. As such, she might be considered a nerve center, a disseminator, and/or a spokesperson. When a chief steward assimilates grievance and arbitration data from stewards, supervisors, the parent union, and published sources, that person is acting as a nerve center. When she processes it and distributes the information to the steward system, that person is filling the managerial role of disseminator. Then, to the extent that the chief steward goes on official record relative to a grievance issue or policy, the chief steward is acting as a spokesperson.

### Decisional Roles

When it comes to making a decision, the manager may choose from four decision-making roles: entrepreneur, disturbance handler, resource allocator, and negotiator. At any given moment, the union manager might decide to implement or participate in some sort of organizational change or activity (some risk here), be forced to settle a dispute, allocate local union resources (money or people) to a project, or negotiate a compromise between any number of individuals or groups. When all 10 roles are put in perspective, it is clear that during any single managerial behavior a role from all three categories might be present.

## The Planning Process

Nobody seems to want to plan. "It takes too much time" is the frequent justification for managing without planning. By the time a plan is made, so the story goes, it has become outdated. Thus, what little is done in the way of planning by local union officials tends to be very short term. It is more like crisis management than management planning. The old maxim that claims that our nation's educational system is always 20 years behind applies equally to union management techniques. One means of closing the gap is better and more managerial leadership. In this chapter, the authors are talking about more organizational planning.

## GOALS

The starting point for meaningful planning is goal setting. For the purposes of this book, we are talking about union organizational goals. Historically, union goals have been stated in terms of the *end result* of collective union action: better education, equal opportunity, care of the needy, better wages and benefits, safer working conditions, and so on. These goals represent the *aspirations* of top union officials on behalf of their members. However, it cannot be said that all union members share a commitment to these same goals. Herein lies the rub. Personal membership and local union goals are often at odds with well-worn higher goals as preached by a parent union. One of the main criticisms of union officials is that they are out of step with the needs and wants (two different things) of their members. Goal divergence is not unusual in the union setting. More effort must be made to adopt goals that the whole organization can relate to.

First, goals serve as a reflection of the philosophy held by the union. As such, they serve as a benchmark for the efforts of officers and members. Second, the union's plans, the way it is structured, and its activities should point toward achievement of its goals. If the local's goals are to keep the status quo, its structure will be quite different than if it were seeking more members and other units. Third, goals are motivators. The rewards that come with goal achievement or intensive activity in the pursuit of a worthwhile goal move members and officials alike. Fourth, union managers can measure progress against the goal as a tool for evaluation and control. Such a comparison will tell them where there has been progress, where improvements might be needed, and where some controls might have to be instituted.

For goals to serve a local union in any of the above four ways, they must meet certain standards. Goals must be stated clearly and precisely. A time frame must be established for the achievement of the goal. The goal must be consistent with the organization's environments. Finally, the goal's degree of difficulty (or achievement) must be understood by all. How do your local's goals measure against these criteria? How about those of your parent union?

## Goal Level

Goals may be stated in *official, operative,* and *operational* terms. Generally, official goals are those that are formally written down somewhere, like in the union's constitution and bylaws. These goals are usually inspirations, but vague. Or they are clear but without a time frame.

Operative goals are the local's statement of what part of the official goals the union is seeking. The best example of this is probably the pursuit of contracts that should bring benefits to its members within a certain time period.

Operational goals are those that build in a means of evaluating the level of goal achievement. That is, the official goal of better wages can be stated operatively in terms of seeking to negotiate a new contract with good wage increases in each of two years. Operationally, this goal would be stated as "We intend to start negotiations on our two-year contract on June 1, 1986. We expect 5½% the first year and 6½% the second." It is the author's belief that unions have an abundance of official goals, some operative goals, and few operational goals. Most union operative and operational goals tend to be both informal and vague. The result is wasted resources and minimal goal achievement. When local officers espouse official goals to their members who want to know operationally what that means for them, the local officers are often at a loss. This has to stop.

## Goal Focus

Goals can be further classified by their focus. *Maintenance* goals are ones that tend to exist over time. For example, a local organizing committee goal might be to have one active campaign on the books at all times. *Improvement* goals indicate a specific change. A political action committee might seek to have 80% of its membership registered to vote instead of the current 55%. Finally, *developmental* goals, which are similar to improvement goals, seek to achieve some level of growth or advancement. The treasurer might decide to implement a training program for trustees whereby they will better learn their duties and responsibilities come audit time.

## Long- and Short-term Goals

Time frames have a lot to do with goal setting and their achievement. For simplicity's sake, the terms long term and short term are often used. (We use them in Chapter 8.) Usually, long-term goals are those that last longer than five years. Anything less is a short-term goal. But none of this is all that precise. Each category of goals can be either lengthened or shortened depending on the changes in the internal and external environments.

## Making Goals Work

There are at least six guidelines a union situational manager might follow if progress is to be made toward goal achievement:

1. Get membership acceptance and commitment to the goal.
2. Utilize all communication and feedback networks, both formal and informal.
3. Do not allow goals to conflict with each other.
4. The connection between achieved goals and their rewards should be clear.
5. Diffuse competition among officers and members who are seeking the goals.
6. Do not let personal survival become a substitute for goal achievement.

Do any of these conditions for successful goal achievement look familiar to you? Within your local, are its members committed to the local's goals? How well do they really know what is going on? Do *you* know what is really going on? Is there conflict among the members and/or officers over some of the goals? Is there any genuine reward for good work—a job well done? Finally, have any of your local's officials substituted personal survival for goal achievement? (You do not have to answer this one.) To improve on your local's management, get the goals straight and then plan around them.

## ORGANIZATIONAL PLANNING

The policies, procedures, and methods used by union managers to achieve goals can be referred to as that local's *organizational planning process.* As such, any organizational plan is made up of any number of subplans. And organizational planning does not deal with future decisions; rather, it is concerned with the future impact of current decisions. Finally, planning is not inflexible forecasting done only by a few. At least it should not be.

Planning for unions or any other organization is multifaceted. It can be broken down into seven parts, one of which we have already discussed.

1. Goal setting
2. Goal achievement strategy
3. Top-level planning
4. Medium-level planning
5. Base-level planning
6. Goal implementation
7. Goal evaluation and control

### Goal Achievement Strategy

In any effort to achieve goals, a local union manager may adopt any one of five strategies:

1. Stability
2. Service development
3. Organizing development
4. Merger
5. Retreat

A union management planning strategy seeking stability is usually found where a local is satisfied with things as they are. Goals and behaviors designed to either minimize the effects of change or to channel change in other directions so as not to affect their situation are adopted. Some people claim that was the overall strategy of the American labor movement (we use the term loosely) during the 1950s, 1960s and much of the 1970s. There are, however, notable exceptions to this sweeping generalization.

The second union management planning strategy can be termed as service development. Once a union believes that it has achieved reasonable success with its basic goals, it often turns to providing other services to help its membership and help enhance the image of the local. Credit unions, child care, legal advice on matters such as will and divorce, unemployment and worker compensation hearing services, and the like are part and parcel of a union actively seeking a service development strategy. (United Way labor counseling is yet another example.)

Organizing is a third management goal-achieving strategy a local might pursue. Locals seeking to enlarge their membership, either internally or through new units, seek to organize more people. Often additional outside organizing is a form of protection. You organize those who might have an impact on where you work. The authors, however, have seen comparatively little local organizing. Many locals have passed the organizing mantle over to the parent union. A lot of potential talent and resources go unused as a result.

The merger strategy has been used a lot lately by parent unions. As a result of several environmental factors, unions are merging. One union becomes larger while a smaller one retains some vestige of its former identity. The smaller unions can no longer meet their goals on their own. The larger ones may also be having trouble, and the infusion of additional members and contracts will help. Mergers on the local level, while not unheard of, are happening at a slow pace. The desire to keep one's separate local identity sometimes is voiced as being preferable to a merger with a sister local. Sometimes the healthier local does not want the burden of the troubled one. Because of organization roles held by officers and problems with assets, local and national union mergers are difficult.

The fifth and final goal attainment strategy for local union officers is that of retreat. A well-planned retreat during hard times may be necessary to allow the local to continue pursuing its other goals. One common example of retreat is the taking of a paid, full-time officer and putting that person back in the workplace. A second is the selling of the union hall. A third is disaffiliation with local and state central labor councils. Retreats are not popular, but the alternatives are often even less so. It boils down to which goals are more important. There is never an easy answer.

## TOP-, MEDIUM-, AND BASE-LEVEL PLANNING

Because top-level planning by a union's officers and executive board is based on that organization's goals and strategies, such planning is often referred to as *strategic* planning and sometimes, although not always, as long-range planning. Planning at this level is distinct from other levels of planning because all other medium- and base-level plans are supposed to derive from strategic planning. Thus, when an executive board announces that the local is establishing a child-care system for its members, all other planning starts from this point. The decision has been made and the union is ordered into action.

With a goal firm in mind, middle-level planning managers work to determine the scope of their activities, which will move them closer to goal achievement. In the case of the child-care goal, committee chairs will convene their members in order to develop the *tactics* necessary to carry out the mandate of the executive board. Key committees concerned with benefits, public relations, women's issues (although child care is not just a woman's issue), contract negotiations, and the like all work to discover what it will take to have union-sponsored child care.

Finally, base-level planning takes place when the chief steward and his stewards work out the departmental implementation of the plans from above. While knowing the overall goal, they will be more concerned with achieving the daily, weekly, or monthly objectives that will make the overall goal reality. The scope of planning is more precise, more accountable.

## Time Frame

When discussing a plan, one must at some point specify the plan's time frame or horizon. *Long term* and *short term* are the descriptors most often used. Here the authors wish to add a third: intermediate-range planning. When dealing with long-range planning (more than five years), it is important that the local's managers make sure that the strategies of the plan are consistent with the goals, that any impact the plans might have on the operations or functions of the local are clearly stated, and that somewhere in all this planning there is a place for evaluation and revision. The important points about long-range planning are:

1. It can be shorter than five years in length.
2. The longer the plan, the less detailed it will be.
3. As environmental changes take place, have flexible alternative plans (situational management).
4. All long-range plans of the local and their strategies should be integrated.

Whereas long-range plans can be in most cases anything over five years, intermediate planning generally covers two to five years, and short-term planning is most often anything less than one year. Intermediate plans tend to have more detail than their longer counterparts, with short-range plans being even more specific. Where intermediate planning for a child-care program might call in general terms for a range of resource allocation from the local, short-term planning will translate such parameters into specific budget and personnel allocations. Remember that the longer the time frame, the more general its details are likely to be.

## Situational Planning

Earlier the authors mentioned that, while one should establish workable plans for union action, she or he should not be wed to them. Situational planning calls for flexibility built into the organizational planning process. For our purposes, situational planning is the *advanced preparation of a plan of action to meet a situation that is unexpected, but that, if it does occur, will have a major impact on the union.*

Situational planning applies to all levels of planning, although it seems to take place most in the intermediate to base levels of planning (medium and short range). At all levels of management, union officers must be able to pinpoint the cause of the change, where in the current plan the alternative plan should be inserted, and what this new plan will be expected to accomplish (and how). A situational planning checklist is given next.

1. Have the people who originated the existing plan develop the alternative or contingency plans.

2. Contingency plans may never be implemented; so their contents should not be a source of general knowledge because some of the alternatives might cause some emotional distress if known in advance.

3. Do not plan just for negative changes in the environment. Plan for some positive changes as well.

4. Situational planning should be a part of the local's regular organizational planning process.

5. Without adequate warning systems, undetected change will demolish the best-laid contingency plan.

Such is the scope of union organizational planning. It is based on goals and strategies. All three components are interwoven. The management system will lose its effectiveness if any one part of the process is left out. Likewise, how a union is organized should be a reflection of its goals, strategies, and plans. As these parts of the process change, so should the organization. The authors submit that for the most part unions have not changed the way they do "business" since the turbulence of the 1930s. Is it time for a change? Is it too late? What do we mean by union organization?

## The Organizational Dimension

Local union structure has hardly changed, if at all, in decades while the world about it changes and the members within change. The reluctance of unions to change structurally—organizationally—has meant that they have often been out of position to react to a major change or implement change on their own. If goal setting and plan development can be considered as the *formulation* part of a union manager's job, then the means of *implementing* the plans start with the coordinated organizing of the local's tasks, authority, people, and communication networks.

## UNIONS AS BUREAUCRACIES

As we moved from the nineteenth to the twentieth century, many ideas about how organizations should best be organized were being talked about. One theory that carried a lot of weight with those in business was put forth by Max Weber, a

German sociologist. For Weber, the best organizational design is the one that concentrates on efficiency in achieving goals. While there are many key components to his theory, there are three that unions have taken to quite strongly. Unions have adopted the notion of a division of labor, rules and procedures, and authority. The authors believe that unions adopted these tenets to the extreme.

Unions have a precise division of labor. Each official has a prescribed set of duties to perform and tasks to accomplish. Most of these duties and tasks are administrative, at least for the stewards, the vice-president, the trustees, the recording secretary, and the sergeant-at-arms. Managerial duties are generally left to the president, chief steward, the executive board (to some degree), and the treasurer (where the treasurer functions as the business manager or full-time officer for the local). Each knows the limits of her office and therefore the point at which another official takes over on a task that might be more complex than her office calls for. If there is one thing local union education programs do well it is to define the duties of their officials.

Union officers are bounded by endless rules and regulations from a variety of sources. Each local usually has both a constitution and bylaws to govern its activities. The parent union also has prescribed rules and regulations it imposes on local officers. The contract with the employer often has some terms and conditions regarding union activity. Local, state, and federal law also affects how a local union official operates. Finally, there is the unwritten law of the organization. Each and every local has its own unofficial way of doing things. It is understood. It is learned. It is obeyed. "Knowing the ropes" has been an important tradition in local union leadership training. It is not enough to know how to complete a task within the letter of the law. One must also know the local's way of doing business. (The powerful hold of unwritten local "law" has been dealt a devastating blow to unions in traditional occupations. Job loss due to technology, runaway employers, planned recessions, and the like have wreaked havoc with what was once an orderly progression to office and the knowing of one's boundaries within the union.)

If there is one thing unions know well it is authority. Every union office comes with a certain amount of authority. This authority varies widely from union to union, from office to office. As individual jobs, the offices of president and chief steward carry a great deal of authority. The treasurer is another office that might also carry much weight. A few years ago, the head of the local safety committee was a person with authority. The authority held by this position is now in question. As groups of people, the executive board carries more authority than trustees, although trustees could have more if the point were pushed. Everyone in the local knows what formal authority each official has. They also know where one's position authority ends and personal influence takes over.

Weber's model of organization brings with it some troublesome points that local unions seem to manifest all too clearly. These excesses are *too many rules, inflexibility, too much authority,* and *position permanence.* These problem areas can best be illustrated by a series of questions you might ask about your local.

1. Is it too difficult to participate in your general meeting?

2. What does it take to qualify to run for union office?

3. Do your officers continually refer all issues to the same committees for the same kinds of deliberation?

4. When was the last time your local established an ad hoc (temporary) committee to deal with an issue or problem?

5. Do your officers share their authority with others or do they horde it?

6. Are there any individual or group "empires" in your local?

7. Do any of your officials believe they have a "right" to their union jobs?

If some of these questions hit too close to home, then one can safely assume that your local is suffering from a too strict adherence to the tenets of Weber's ideal and efficient organization. A more flexible structure is needed to cope with change. Unions need to become contingency organizations.

## A PLAN FOR CHANGE

Just as there is no single best union leadership style, neither is there a single best way to structure (organize) a union. Yet, on the whole, unions seem to be organized along the traditional Weber model and have acquired its excesses. In taking the bureaucratic organizational model as their own, unions implemented a functional strategy of attempting to provide local members with workplace dignity and personal economic well-being. This strategy and organizational design served union leaders and managers until the years just following the end of World War II. Since the days of victory in 1945, this same union strategy and organization has acted more like a hindrance than a help in achieving goals. Labor has not been able to blunt legal and employer attacks on the rights of workers to organize and take collective action. Unions have not been able to organize the newest members of the work force. American trade union strategy has been outdated for the past 40 years and so has its mode of organizational structure.

Union strategy and structure is finally showing signs of change. During August 1983, the AFL–CIO's Committee on the Evolution of Work issued a report entitled *The Future of Work*. This initial report was followed by a second in February 1985. In *The Changing Situation of Workers and Their Unions*, the committee states:

> Unions are, first and foremost, organizations seeking to improve the lives of those they represent . . . . The labor movement has also sought to improve the conditions of life for its members by improving the conditions for all in our democratic society through political action and legislative efforts. Organized labor seeks, in sum, through collective bargaining, political participation and legislative activity to bring about a broader sharing of the riches of the nation.

It is against the background of these basic and unchanging principles that we review the numerous and complex factors which have created the current situation confronting workers and their unions. The United States—indeed, every industrialized nation—is undergoing a scientific, technological, economic revolution . . . . There is now a world economy . . . . Technological advances have eliminated jobs . . . .

We are confident that the labor movement has the capacity to continue the never-ending process of renewal and regeneration that has enabled and will enable unions to remain the authentic voice of workers and their chosen vehicle for expressing their will . . . .

In sum, a period of resurgence—of sustained growth—is within our grasp.[4]

Here we have the seeds for a new managing process in America's unions. There are goals and strategy for a "renewal" and "regeneration." Some long-range-plan specifics from the report include:

1. New methods of advancing the interests of workers

2. Increasing members' participation in their union

3. Improving the labor movement's communication

4. Improving organizing activity

5. Structural changes to enhance the labor movement's overall effectiveness[5]

*The Changing Situation of Workers and Their Unions* is a strategic statement about the future of unions. It is a starting place for all local union managers and leaders. We have provided the text of this document in Appendix 3A of this chapter and a discussion guide in Appendix 3B. As the authors bring this organization aspect of union management to a close, we ask you to take the time to read the report before you go on to the next managerial function—leadership. To manage in the future, local union officials must have goals, strategies, plans, and an organization that will permit them to do their jobs. For you to implement change at the local level, you have to influence those around you—above and below. The process of redefining how your local operates and making it work takes leadership. Leadership style and power were the subjects of the first two chapters. How leadership fits into the management process is the subject of the next few paragraphs.

## Managerial Leadership

At the start of both this chapter and Chapter 1, the authors pointed out that, although related, leadership and management are not the same. Leadership is a people-influencing, goal-achieving process. Management is an organizational

---

[4] *The Changing Situation of Workers and Their Unions,* A Report by the AFL–CIO Committee on the Evolution of Work, February 1985, pp. 5-7.

[5] Ibid., p. 4. There is already debate as to whether or not this report represents a change in direction. See Steve Early, "Viewpoint: AFL–CIO's Solutions Are Part of the Problem," *Labor Notes,* no. 74, April 1985, pp. 11–12 and David Moberg, "New AFL–CIO report outlines labor revival," *In These Times,* March 13-19, 1985, pp. 5 and 11.

goal-achieving process where the people of the organization are but one of several "managerial" resources. One can lead with a poor managerial plan but success and effectiveness will be limited. Likewise, one can manage an organization without leadership, but goal achievement will be less than it could be with good leadership. In the case of unions, it appears that many leaders lead without the benefit of any real plan and just as many, if not more, manage without leadership. The result has been stagnation and, in some cases, demise.

This book has now provided you with most of the essentials needed to become a managerial leader: a two-pronged model for successful leadership and a six-part road map to the science (art?) of management (although we still have two parts to go). To assist you in implementing these new-found sets of behavior, Unit 3 contains personal skills and power base education in verbal and written communication, problem solving, and more on conflict management. What remains for you, the reader and union leader (please notice that we have avoided using *union* and *leader* together) is to practice situational leadership, power management, and situational management. Then and only then will the real managerial leadership education take place. Let's now finish this already long chapter with the fourth and final management function and the fifth part of our union management process.

## A Different Kind of Control

By control, the authors do not mean the veiled fist of authority some local union officials tend to exhibit. Rather, we mean control as that managerial function which is a set of behaviors instituted to make sure that the local's activities conform to its goals and plans. Is the local on the right track or is it off course? And, if it is off course, what should be done to get back on?

## THE CONTROL PROCESS

A union's control process can and should be relatively simple in design. When your local's plans are made, include a means of checking the features of the plan and their progress. Usually, such a process needs only four parts:

1. Performance standards
2. Performance measurement
3. Comparison of performance to standard
4. Corrective action

Formal performance standards appear for the most part to be nonexistent in local unions. What they do have in abundance are informal standards that change with officers. The reader has only to recall our example of the chief steward. Union managers need to establish formal standards for their officials to work by. Informal personal and technical standards need to be evaluated and then established as uniform and understood performance standards.

Once standards are set, the methods by which performance is measured should be established. Quantitatively, a steward might be measured by the number of grievances filed. Qualitatively, the more important measure might be how many grievances were filed that had merit or how many were won. Additionally, consideration must be given to how often the performance measurement should be taken. Once a year? Once a term?

Once standards and criteria for measurement are set, then one's performance can be compared. If the two match, the management process continues on as before. If, on the other hand, there is a mismatch, corrective action needs to take place.

Corrective action may mean one of two things: the performance was *more* or *less* favorable than the standard. Where the performance is better than the standard, perhaps the standard needs to be revised. Where the behavior is less favorable, action to ensure standard compliance should be taken. However, any corrective action or standard change should be considered carefully in light of the entire situation. In fact, there are six basic guidelines one should follow when managing an organization's control process.

1. Keep the control process simple, accurate, and timely.

2. Use the process to anticipate problems, as well as to measure past activities.

3. When analyzing information gathered from a control process, look at it in light of the whole situation.

4. A good management control process will clue the manager to possible corrective actions.

5. Conclusions drawn from the control process need to be straightforward and clear, not ambiguous.

6. The control process, like the rest of the management process, ought to be adaptable to change.

## Managing Organizational Change

Situational management is about managing organizational change as one successfully pursues the integrated organizational and membership goals. To the extent one management style allows for a review of goals, permits strategy revision and the scrapping of outdated plans, situational leadership, organizational flexibility, and the evaluation of performance, then it can be said that one has been managing change. This chapter has been about nothing else.

Most local unions react to change, they do not manage it. Parent unions are not doing much better, but they are showing signs of adaptation. One can look to AFSCME, CWA, GCIU, and UFCW as a few prime examples over the past few years. Some unions are managing a growth situation, be it through organizing or merger, while others are learning how to manage a *reduced* organization. Regardless of the direction of change, most are doing it on their own.

## Organizational Development

When a trained and experienced member of an organization or an outside *change agent* (an individual or group) is used to make an organization become more effective, it is said to be engaged in *organizational development* (OD). To the extent that *The Changing Situation of Workers* seeks planned, long-range strategies and plans for making unions more effective, it is an OD document.

Organizational development can be used to facilitate change in an organization that already has a situational management system in place (but needs additional assistance), or it can be used to set the current management system on the road to a new, more effective management system. It is our opinion that most unions need some sort of organizational development to put them back on the road to organizational effectiveness. There are six major stages to the successful implementation of an OD plan.[6]

1. Entry
2. Diagnosis
3. Planned change
4. Stabilization
5. Program evaluation
6. Follow-up

For example, if it is decided that, in principle, the AFL–CIO's report is correct and that certain changes should be made, how are we (a local union) to do it? How do we make over our bureaucratic dinosaur into a nimble road runner? One uses the preceding six steps.

### Stage 1: Entry

Logically, the first step in a union OD program is *entry*. During this stage the local's management team realizes the need for organizational change and either uses the services of a trained local official from within the union or contracts with an outside person to start the process. It is not unusual for two change agents to work together, one from inside the organization and one from the outside.

As soon as the change agent identifies the union's needs, she prepares and submits a proposal for action, normally only five to ten pages in length. It is best if the proposal is the result of collaboration between the change agent and the local's management. The proposal should contain the following elements:[7]

---

[6] Don Warrick, "Managing Organization Change and Development," James E. Rosenzweig and Fremont E. Kast, eds., *Modules in Management Series,* Science Research Associates, Inc., Chicago, p. 16.

[7] Ibid., p. 14.

1. Statement of purpose

2. OD program objectives

3. Program design and time line

4. Program cost and resource needs

5. Background information on the qualifications of the change agents

The sixth and final element of this first stage is one that carries on through the remaining stages—*commitment building.* All the local's officials need to know what is going on. Members ought to know that some aspects of the local are about to change in order to make the union more effective in achieving its goals—and their goals. Organizational change cannot be successful if there is resistance from these two groups.

### Stage 2: Diagnosis

The second stage in an OD program, *diagnosis,* provides the planners of change with a schematic of the local's strengths, weaknesses, and more precise information about its needs. Issues and problems are formally recognized and interest is generated as everyone senses something new is about to take place. To complete this information-gathering process, some combination of the following techniques may be used.[8]

1. Questionnaires to a sample or all members and officials.

2. Personal interviews with a representative group of members and officials.

3. Evaluate existing information on membership change (personal demographics such as age, sex, etc.), resources (such as money in the general fund, number of volunteer activists), services provided to members over the years, turnover in officials, and the like.

4. If possible, conduct group interviews (a committee, a stewards group, a department).

5. Report the findings of steps 1 to 4 back to the members and officers.

### Stage 3: Planned Change

The heart and soul of any OD program is its strategies for *planned change.* A great many things can happen here as members and officials try to implement and then cope with the changes they are trying to bring about. Listed next is a set of activities one might find in the third stage of a local union OD plan.[9]

1. *Program design reevaluation:* The proposal presented in stage 1 is compared with the data gathered in stage 2 for possible plan adjustments.

2. *Problem solving:* The results of the second stage are used by both members and officials as the basis for team and group problem solving. The local's

---

[8]Ibid., p. 14. These techniques have been placed in the union setting by the authors.
[9]Ibid., pp. 14–15.

executive board discusses issues affecting the entire local. Various permanent committees convene and the chief steward calls his stewards together. Ultimately, each steward will meet with the members she represents. All these meetings are aimed at group discussion and input solving personal and technical problems related to the change process.

3. *Training:* Programs on such skills as communication, decision making, conflict management, group dynamics, stress management, and the like, are provided to encourage all members and officials to participate in the meetings and other aspects of the OD process.

4. *Intragroup team building:* The various groups within the local (executive officers, executive board, chief steward and stewards, committees, etc.) are educated as to how they can make their group work more efficiently and more effectively. Classes in climate building, process and structure evaluation, problem solving, planning, goal setting, and such might be offered.

5. *Intergroup team building:* The same groups mentioned in the previous activity also need some perspective as to how the other groups function within the local and how they contribute to its effectiveness. Joint group-problem-solving exercises are practiced.

6. *Strategic planning:* During the time of planned change, it is important that the local's management team clearly establish the goals and plans for the organization. Make sure that the local is organized properly to handle the new change. If it is not, perhaps some structural changes will be necessary.

### Stage 4: Stabilization

Once the planned changes are well on their way, it is time to make sure that they continue to progress. Effort must be given to the provision of emotional support for all those taking part in the changes. As values are challenged and possibly new skills and procedures have to be learned, a sense of stability amid rapid change is needed to reassure the members and officials. Without such stability, the changes might be too much for some people and they might turn to resistance.

### Stage 5: Evaluation

Once stabilization is in place, time is given to the local's officers and the change agent to evaluate what has taken place: what has gone right and what has gone wrong. There are always surprises. Things do not always turn out as planned. The evaluation process will yield information on where the trouble spots remain and where the planned change is working.

### Stage 6: Follow-up

Do not omit this stage from the OD plan. Many do and pay a price later. The idea is that a major OD intervention should not be needed again. The best way to assure this is to make follow-up plans that will keep the local alerted to change and able to flex with it. This way, there will be small OD adjustments in the local as time goes on, but the major overhauls need not take place again unless there is some unusual change that renders the current plans and union organization ineffective. Following an OD plan is a lot like taking medicine. The cure is incomplete if all the medicine is not taken. So it is with organizational development.

## THE FOUNDATION HAS BEEN LAID

One cannot manage change and therefore lead without first knowing the principles of organizational management and the process of leadership. Traditionally, administration and leadership skills are passed off as management and leadership in union and university education of local union officials. All these elements need to be given to these people if they are going to manage the change that now confronts them.

Unit 2 consists of three chapters containing areas of change important to local unions. To be sure, there are more. But these chapters represent challenges that need to be managed now. Unions must deal with the media more effectively. The technology of the computer is changing the everyday operation of locals and how well they make progress toward their goals. And our officers and members need more education on a variety of topics. If you can handle these changes in a positive way, it is our belief that your local will be much healthier and a part of labor's resurgence. This unit has been an effort at providing you with the technical skills to direct this regeneration. We only hope we have not befuddled you with new-fangled ideas. Instead, we hope we have given new highs in personal power. It is time to put them to work.

## DISCUSSION QUESTIONS

1. Locate a diagram of your national or international union's organization chart and one that depicts how a local union is to be organized. Redraw each one and/or combine them in one or more charts to illustrate the impact of various internal and external factors.

2. What are the formal duties of your local's officials and what role do they play in the management of the local? What authority does each have? How effectively do they use this authority?

3. What are the goals of your local—the membership? Have they changed over the past years? What caused any changes?

4. Does your local follow a plan of action? If yes, what are its parts? If no, what governs what the local is doing?

5. If you could reorganize the structure of your local, how would you do it—and why?

6. Is your local capable of its own planned change through OD? Does it need such a change? How would you go about implementing OD in your local?

# GLOSSARY

**control:** The managerial function of ensuring that an organization's activities conform to its goals and plans.

**OD:** Planned, long-range strategies for making an organization more effective.

**official goals:** Formally written or adopted statement of purpose, usually of top management.

**operational goals:** Formal or informal goals that provide a means of evaluating the degree to which a goal has been achieved. Operational goals appear at the most basic level of management.

**operative goals:** Formal or informal goals that state more precisely the goals of an organization at the medium level of management.

**planning:** The policies, procedures, and methods used to achieve goals.

**role:** The behaviors that can be attributed to an organizational position.

**situational management:** The management approach that takes into account external and internal environmental factors in its managerial decision making.

**situational planning:** The advanced preparation of a plan designed to manage the unexpected as well as one can.

# ADDITIONAL RESOURCES

Fritz, Roger. *Rate Yourself as a Manager.* Englewood Cliffs, N.J.: Prentice-Hall, Inc., 1985.

Hunsaker, Phillip L., and Anthony J. Alessandra. *The Art of Managing People.* Englewood Cliffs, N.J.: Prentice-Hall, Inc., 1980.

Kuhn, Alfred, and Robert D. Beam. *The Logic of Organization.* San Francisco, Calif.: Jossey-Bass, Inc., 1982.

Mink, Oscar, James M. Shultz, and Barbara P. Mink. *Developing and Managing Open Organizations.* San Diego, Calif.: University Associates, 1979.

Plunkett, Lorne C., and Guy A. Hale. *The Proactive Management: The Complete Book on Problem Solving and Decision Making.* New York: John Wiley & Sons, Inc., 1982.

Scott, W. Richard. *Organizations: Rational, Natural, and Open Systems.* Englewood Cliffs, N.J.: Prentice-Hall, Inc., 1981.

**APPENDIX 3A**

# The Changing Situation Of Workers and Their Unions

A Report by the
AFL-CIO Committee on
the Evolution of Work

February 1985

# The Committee on the Evolution of Work

The AFL-CIO Executive Council in August 1982 established the Committee on the Evolution of Work to review and evaluate changes that are taking place in America in the labor force, occupations, industries and technology.

The members of the Committee are:

Kenneth T. Blaylock, president, American Federation of Government Employees;

Kenneth J. Brown, president, Graphic Communications International Union;

William H. Bywater, president, International Union of Electronic, Electrical, Technical, Salaried and Machine Workers;

Patrick J. Campbell, president, United Brotherhood of Carpenters and Joiners of America;

Frank Drozak, president, Seafarers International Union of North America;

Murray H. Finley, president, Amalgamated Clothing and Textile Workers Union;

Barbara Hutchinson, vice president, American Federation of Government Employees;

John T. Joyce, president, International Union of Bricklayers and Allied Craftsmen;

Richard I. Kilroy, president, Brotherhood of Railway, Airline and Steamship Clerks, Freight Handlers, Express and Station Employees;

Gerald W. McEntee, president, American Federation of State, County and Municipal Employees;

Charles H. Pillard, president, International Brotherhood of Electrical Workers;

Albert Shanker, president, American Federation of Teachers;

John J. Sweeney, president, Service Employees International Union;

J.C. Turner, president, International Union of Operating Engineers;

Glenn E. Watts, president, Communications Workers of America;

Lynn R. Williams, president, United Steelworkers of America;

William W. Winpisinger, president, International Association of Machinists and Aerospace Workers;

William H. Wynn, president, United Food and Commercial Workers International Union;

Paul J. Burnsky, president, Metal Trades Department;

Robert A. Georgine, president, Building and Construction Trades Department;

Jack Golodner, director, Department for Professional Employees;

Robert F. Harbrant, president, Food and Allied Service Trades Department;

Jean F. Ingrao, executive secretary-treasurer, Maritime Trades Department;

John F. Leyden, executive director, Public Employee Department;

John E. Mara, secretary-treasurer, Union Label and Service Trades Department;

Howard D. Samuel, president, Industrial Union Department.

The chairman of the Committee is AFL-CIO Secretary-Treasurer Thomas R. Donahue.

The Committee met regularly during the past 2½ years and received reports from a number of experts, including Professor Richard B. Freeman of Harvard University and the National Bureau of Economic Research; Louis Harris of Louis Harris and Associates; Peter Hart of Hart and Associates; Professor Thomas A. Kochan of Massachusetts Institute of Technology; Professor Sar Levitan, director of the Center for Social Policy Studies at George Washington University; Professor James Medoff of Harvard University and the National Bureau of Economic Research; Professor Steven M. Miller of Carnegie-Mellon University; Jerome M. Rosow, president of Work in America Institute; Paul A. Strassman, vice president of Xerox Corporation; and Professor Paul Weiler of Harvard University Law School.

This is the Committee's second report; its initial report, **The Future of Work,** was issued in August 1983.

# Table of Contents

# The Changing Situation Of Workers and Their Unions

The nature of work, the organization of the workplace, and the size, location, composition and background of the workforce have been changing at an especially rapid rate in recent years and that process of change is continuing unabated.

Given the magnitude and velocity of these destabilizing changes, the labor movement has demonstrated a notable resiliency. Unions represent over 20,000,000 working men and women in the United States. Organized labor remains a vital force for progress in this nation; no serious observer denies that unions have played and continue to play a civilizing, humanizing and democratizing role in American life.

But despite their accomplishments, unions find themselves behind the pace of change. During the 1960s and 1970s, the American workforce grew in an unprecedented way — adding 1.3 million new workers per year in the 1960s and 2.1 million new workers per year in the 1970s — whereas the labor movement's membership remained static as gains made in organizing were offset due to job losses in basic industries. In the 1980s, union membership has shown a decline in absolute numbers as well as in percentage terms. The proportion of workers who are eligible to join a union and who in fact belong to a union has fallen from close to 45 percent to under 28 percent since 1954; using the measure of percentage of the entire workforce, the decline has been from 35 percent to under 19 percent.

The AFL-CIO Executive Council created the Committee on the Evolution of Work as part of its efforts to assess the significance of the changes in the work environment for the Federation and its affiliates. To do so, it is first necessary to review the labor movement's premises.

Unions are, first and foremost, organizations seeking to improve the lives of those they represent by improving their conditions of work and by insuring respect for their dignity as workers. Organized labor believes that each worker is entitled to a fair day's pay for a fair day's work. That pay should include a share in the profits the worker helps to create and, thus, unions seek a larger share of those profits than "market forces" might dictate. And we recognize that those profits can only be created in a well-managed enterprise, where both capital and labor contribute to the result.

Since its earliest days, the labor movement has sought to improve the quality of worklife, create workplace democracy and participate in joint employer-employee decision-making — long before these approaches became fashionable.

We understand that confrontation and conflict are wasteful and that a cooperative approach to solving shared present and future problems is desirable. (The problem always is finding those who wish to cooperate in a system of true equality — and until the time our desire for cooperation is fully reciprocated, unions must maintain the ability to meet employer confrontation.)

The labor movement also has sought to improve the conditions of life of its members by improving the conditions of life for all in our democratic society through political action and legislative efforts.

Organized labor seeks, in sum, through collective bargaining, political participation and legislative activity to bring about a broader sharing in the riches of the nation.

It is against the background of these basic and unchanging principles that we review the numerous and complex factors which have created the current situation confronting workers and their unions. The United States — indeed, every industrialized nation — is undergoing a scientific, technological, economic revolution every bit as significant as the industrial revolution of the nineteenth century. There is now a world economy in which workers in underdeveloped nations, working at subsistence wages, are producing the most sophisticated goods, and even services, for more developed nations. Technological advances have eliminated scores of jobs, altered the requirements of an equal number, and created entirely new jobs. The success of the labor movement in improving wages and working conditions has had its effect on what workers see as their right, on what workers seek in further improvement, and on what employers recognize as the minimum conditions they must offer.

All of those developments are affecting labor unions throughout the industrialized world; none warrants prophecies of doom and despair regarding the future of the labor movement. Such prophecies were ventured 50 years ago, after American unions in the 1920s and 1930s had suffered serious setbacks and the number of unionized workers had declined dramatically; some predicted the demise of the labor movement at that time. In fact the reverse occurred: trade unionists of that era developed approaches attuned to their situation which caught the allegiance of a generation of workers and organized labor experienced a period of remarkable growth.

We are confident that the labor movement has the capacity to continue the never-ending process of renewal and regeneration that has enabled and will enable unions to remain the authentic voice of workers and their chosen vehicle for expressing their will. It is the purpose of this report to offer recommendations along that line — capable of accomplishment and consistent with the labor movement's tested ideals. As the predicate for those recommendations, we begin by setting forth as clearly as we can the realities we now face and will face in the coming years and our grounds for believing that the labor movement can thrive amidst these changing conditions.

# Changes In
# The Workforce

The workforce has grown with enormous rapidity and will continue to grow at a rapid, albeit reduced pace, in the 1980s and 1990s; some 17 million people will join the workforce by 1995. Three aspects of this growth have had a particular effect on the labor movement.

First, the growth of the workforce has occurred, and will continue to occur, principally in those sectors of the economy that have not traditionally been highly organized. Manufacturing and construction, for example, currently account for 50 percent of the AFL-CIO's membership, but these sectors have declined relative to others and currently employ only 22 percent of the civilian workforce. In contrast, the service sector of the economy has had, and will continue to have, the largest growth. During the 1970s, about 90 percent of all new jobs were added in service organizations. By 1990, service industries will employ almost three-quarters of the labor force. Yet, less than 10 percent of the service sector is organized, and only 20 percent of the AFL-CIO membership is in unions representing workers primarily in the service industries.

Second, the growth in the workforce has been and will be concentrated in relatively unorganized geographic areas. Since 1970, population in the "Sun Belt" has grown six times as fast as in the Great Lakes and New England regions, and the states with the greatest increase in the number of jobs were California, Texas and Florida. In the latter two states, only 12 percent of the workers are organized — third and fourth lowest in the nation; in contrast, in New York, Michigan, Pennsylvania and West Virginia, between 35-40 percent of the workers are organized.

Third, the growth of the workforce is creating new patterns in which working people are less likely than in the past to be long-term, full-time employees. Increasingly, workers are members of two-earner families and even three-earner families in which one or more individual works part-time; indeed, approximately 20 percent of the workforce holds a part-time job. At the same time, more workers are employed in unstable operations whose life span is a few years, rather than several decades, and are classified as "independent contractors" or "managers" or "supervisors" rather than as "employees." These interrelated developments dilute the incentive to run the risks currently associated with engaging in organizing activity; indeed, working people not classified as "employees" in the labor laws are subject to open reprisal for seeking to join a union and have no legal right of recourse.

# The Failure
# of the Law

In 1935, Congress enacted the Wagner Act which declared that "Employees shall have the right to self-organization, to form, join or assist labor organizations, to bargain collectively through representatives of their own choosing, and to engage in other concerted activities for the purpose of collective bargaining or other mutual aid or protection." By the 1950s and 1960s, this principle had gained at least some measure of acceptance, and to a large extent employers did not choose to interfere with their employees' exercise of the right of self-organization; to some extent, employers resisted unionization by improving their employees' wages and working conditions. And if workers chose a union, employers by and large complied with their legal duty to bargain with that union in an honest effort to reach a contract.

In recent years, this trend has been reversed. The norm is that unions now face employers who are bent on avoiding unionization at all costs and who are left largely free to do so by a law that has proven to be impotent and a Labor Board that is inert.

It is difficult to quantify this change in employer attitudes and actions, but we all know it is there. A study of organizing campaigns in the private sector shows that 95 percent of employers actively resist unionization, and 75 percent of all employers hire so-called "labor-management consultants" to guide their efforts to avoid unionization at an estimated cost of over $100,000,000 annually. Many employers — how many thousands each year cannot be determined — discharge union activists. In 1957, the NLRB secured reinstatement for 922 workers who had been fired for union activity. By 1980, that figure had reached 10,000. Professor Paul Weiler of Harvard Law School has concluded that in 1980 there were at least 1.5 discriminatory discharges for every representation election conducted.

Even when workers opt for unionization, unions often face massive resistance in securing a contract; the rate of employer refusal to bargain has been rising twice as fast as even the rate of unlawful discharges. Consequently, after a bargaining unit organizes, the employees are not able to obtain a collective bargaining agreement approximately 35 percent of the time — a substantial increase since the

1960s. And the law's remedy — when it comes — is most often too late to matter.

Nor are anti-union actions confined to not-yet-organized or just-organized employers. Employers with longstanding collective bargaining relationships are closing unionized plants and diverting work to their established non-union plants or to new plants established in non-union areas in the United States and elsewhere. The owners of unionized companies are creating new, paper corporations to do the same work as the organized corporations and are transferring all or most of the work done to these new entities. And unionized employers are engaging in intransigent, bad-faith bargaining in order to provoke a strike so that the employer can replace his employees and oust their bargaining representative.

Two principal factors have combined to make it possible for employers to engage in such hostile actions against employees who wish to bargain collectively. First, as the Committee explained in its first report, **The Future of Work,** the United States has become a society with persistently high levels of unemployment. Unless current policies are changed, this will continue; under even relatively optimistic projections, there will be a structural shortage of at least 4,000,000 jobs throughout the 1980s.

Second, the federal government has done its part to encourage hostile employer actions by providing less and less protection to workers who exercise their right to organize and by setting an example for the most virulently anti-union employers. The Reagan Administration's handling of the air traffic controllers provided a signal to, and the model for, anti-union employers. Thereafter, the Administration turned over the labor law to an NLRB Chairman who has publicly declared that "collective bargaining frequently means . . . the destruction of individual freedom and the destruction of the marketplace," and that "the price we have paid is the loss of entire industries and the crippling of others." Not surprisingly, the Board he chairs has, at every turn, cut back on the extent of protection the law provides to workers who desire to unionize.

Because of these developments, the costs associated with organizing are increasing while the resources available are declining. The experience in this country is that a catalyst is usually needed for a group of individuals to shake the habits of a lifetime and to assert themselves by taking advantage of the opportunities provided by collective action; that is especially true when those individuals are subject to economic reprisal. Union members have always accepted it as their responsibility to start the process of organization. But in recent years, as the size of the workforce has expanded rapidly, the number of union members has declined and the needs of the already-organized have increased, it has become increasingly difficult for union members to meet that responsibility.

# The Desires and Perceptions of Workers

The Committee, with the assistance of Professor James Medoff of Harvard University, Louis Harris and Associates, and Professor Thomas Kochan of MIT, reviewed all published surveys on the public attitude toward unions conducted during the past 25 years and supplemented that material with additional surveys. Four aspects of that data are of special relevance to the labor movement.

1. **Attitudes Toward Work** — Americans by and large see themselves as independent, self-confident, self-reliant and skeptical of claims of authority. In line with that perception, workers, particularly better-educated workers, are becoming more insistent on securing more freedom in the workplace. It is increasingly true that the measure of a good job is high discretion as much as high pay. And despite claims to the contrary, the "work ethic" — the personal need to do one's best on the job — is stronger in the United States than in other western democracies. The striking new factor is a shift in which Americans are less likely to see work as a straight economic transaction providing a means of survival and more likely to see it as a means of self-expression and self-development.

2. **Job Satisfaction** — Fifty-one percent of non-union workers report that they are "very satisfied" with their jobs. But when probed for specifics, only 40 percent or less say they are very satisfied with their fringe benefits or their opportunity to participate in decisions affecting their jobs, and only 28 percent say they are very satisfied with their pay or their opportunity for job advancement. There is, moreover, some indication that the degree of job satisfaction is **decreasing.** In 1973, 57 percent of all workers — figures limited to non-union workers are not available — reported that they were "very satisfied" with their jobs, whereas in 1984 the comparable figure was 51 percent.

3. **Attitudes Toward Unions and Employers** — American workers, and especially non-union workers, are ambivalent in their attitudes toward unions. Over 75 percent of all workers — and over 75 percent of non-union workers — state that they agree that unions in general improve the wages and working conditions of workers. Over 80 per-

cent of all workers agree that unions are needed so that the legitimate complaints of workers can be heard. Yet when asked to assess the effect of organization on their present employer, 53 percent of non-union workers state that wages and fringe benefits would not improve and 74 percent state that job security would not improve.

This same discontinuity is reflected in survey data concerning attitudes toward employers. Almost 60 percent of employees believe that most companies make enough profit so that they can afford to raise wages without raising prices. Yet over 50 percent of workers believe that their own employer provides all the pay and benefits he can afford — and that is true both of unionized workers (54 percent feel that way) and non-union workers (57 percent).

4. **The Policies of Unions** — One fact emerges from the survey data quite clearly: non-union workers do not perceive unions as pursuing an institutional agenda drawn from the needs and desires of their members. Sixty-five percent of such workers express agreement with the statement that "unions force members to go along with decisions they don't like." Sixty-three percent state that they believe that union leaders — as distinguished from union members — decide whether to go on strike. Fifty-four percent believe that "unions increase the risk that companies will go out of business;" 57 percent believe that "unions stifle individual initiative;" and 52 percent believe that unions fight change. And, among the population as a whole — there are no data limited to non-union workers — 50 percent state that they believe that most union leaders no longer represent the workers in their unions. Significantly, workers who are in unions express very different — and far more positive — views of their union.

*    *    *

It is apparent from the foregoing that the labor movement must demonstrate that union representation is the best available means for working people to express their individuality on the job and their desire to control their own working lives, and that unions are democratic institutions controlled by their members and that we have not been sufficiently successful on either score.

# The Seeds
# of a Resurgence

All of the foregoing provide grounds for the most serious concern. But the data we have studied, as well as our own common sense, provide grounds for hope as well and, indeed, suggest the seeds for a resurgence of the labor movement.

To begin with, it is important to recognize that the decline in union membership that occurred in recent years has **not** been the result of dissatisfaction of union members with their unions but was, instead, a function of the economic recession which hit with particular force in those sectors of the economy that are heavily unionized. (Union decertification, while on the rise because of increased employer stimulation, remains statistically insignificant — one-tenth of one percent.)

Second, despite all the changes that have occurred and are occurring in the workforce, the value of organization for workers remains as great today as when unions began. Our own experience shows that to be true and the data confirm it; unionized workers earn on average 33 percent more than their non-union counterparts. The higher pay of unionized workers generally prevails among all age groups, occupations, and industries.

Third, workers who already are organized appreciate the benefits of unionization. Over 90 percent of organized workers believe that unions improve the wages and working conditions of members; 67 percent reject the proposition that unions are unnecessary to assure fair treatment; and over 60 percent of unionized workers believe that if their own employer were not unionized, wages and fringe benefits would be lower. Furthermore, almost 75 percent of unionized workers state that they are very satisfied or somewhat satisfied with their union.

Fourth, unions are increasingly successful in enrolling the types of workers who are forming an increasingly large share of the workforce. Labor union members are better educated than the general population, with a higher proportion of both high school and college graduates. Only 16 percent of union members (vs. 28 percent of the general population) have not graduated from high school. Forty-four

percent are high school graduates (vs. 39 percent of the total population), and a total of 39 percent have either had some college or completed a college degree (vs. 33 percent). Twenty-one percent of union
members (vs. 16 percent) actually completed their college degrees.
Economically, union households are typically middle class, with 65
percent earning incomes between $20,000 and $50,000 (vs. 53 percent
of the general population). This is in large part because union members are much more likely (58 percent) than the general population
(34 percent) to see their work as "a career, not just a job." By occupational category, 41 percent of members (vs. 33 percent) are in
white-collar jobs. Another 20 percent are craftsmen or foremen (vs. 7
percent). And the public understands this: only 24 percent of non-
union workers express the belief that unions are only for blue-collar
workers; 69 percent disagree.

Fifth, the opinion survey data show that non-union workers accept
the fundamental premise on which the trade union movement has
been and is based: that workers are more effective in insuring democracy in the workplace and in obtaining redress for their grievances
when they act in concert than when they act alone. Forty-seven percent of non-union workers endorse that proposition (as compared to
only 42 percent who disagree). And among unorganized service workers, unskilled workers and professionals — groups that will expand in
size in the coming years — support for the usefulness of concerted
activity is even stronger; over 60 percent agree that a group approach is more effective than an individual approach.

Sixth, and finally — and, in our view, most important of all — experience demonstrates that the current generation of workers, when
given a fair chance to form a union at their workplace, elects to do so
in large numbers.

The Canadian experience is especially instructive. Canada has
roughly the same type of economy, many similar employers, and has
undergone the same changes that we previously have described with
respect to the United States. But in Canada, unlike in the United
States, the government has not defaulted in its obligation to protect
the right of self-organization; rather, Canada's law carefully safeguards that right. And in Canada, the percentage of the civilian labor
force that is organized increased in the period 1963-1983 from roughly
30 percent to 40 percent, at the same time that the percentage of
organized workers declined in the United States from 30 percent to
20 percent.

Developments in the public sector in the United States have been
similar to those in Canada. From 1971 to 1983, AFL-CIO public sector membership grew by over 1,000,000 workers (while membership
in the private sector declined by 2,000,000). Today, approximately 50

percent of full-time state and local government employees are organized. Public sector employees are not a breed apart from their private sector counterparts. But in the public sector, while strong anti-union pressure is not uncommon, most workers are free to join a union, either because of effective state laws or because public employers do not deprive workers of that right to the same extent as in the private sector.

In sum, a period of resurgence — of sustained growth — is within our grasp. The recommendations that follow are designed to spur such a resurgence.

# Recommendations

Our recommendations are based upon the fundamental premises stated at the start of the report: that the labor movement exists to advance the interests of workers as workers see their interests, and that to continue to perform their role, unions must come to grips with the current and changed realities workers face. Our aims — achieving decent wages and conditions, democracy in the workplace, a full voice for working people in the society, and the more equitable sharing of the wealth of the nation — remain unchanged. The means of securing those aims, while grounded in experience, must meet today's needs and anticipate tomorrow's aspirations.

There are, we believe, steps that can be taken to improve the efficacy of our traditional programs, and we will discuss those steps below. But from what has been said already, it is apparent that it is not enough merely to search for more effective ways of doing what we always have done; we must expand our notions of what it is workers can do through their unions. Accordingly, we begin with recommendations for new approaches that we believe worthy of examination.

# New Methods of Advancing the Interests of Workers

**1.1. Unions should experiment with new approaches to represent workers and should address new issues of concern to workers.** The diversity of approaches different unions have developed to meet the myriad of interests and desires of a diverse workforce in workplaces scattered throughout this country is an essential part of the genius of the American labor movement. The opinion data indicate that many workers, while supporting of the concept of organization, wish to forward their interests in ways other than what they view as the traditional form of union representation — in their view, an adversarial collective bargaining relationship; the data also suggest that there are issues of concern to these workers that have not been at the center of the traditional collective bargaining agenda. A two-fold response by unions is then required.

First, unions must develop and put into effect multiple models for representing workers tailored to the needs and concerns of different groups. For example, in some bargaining units workers may not desire to establish a comprehensive set of hard and fast terms and conditions of employment, but may nonetheless desire a representative to negotiate minimum guarantees that will serve as a floor for individual bargaining, to provide advocacy for individuals, or to seek redress for particular difficulties as they arise. In other units, a bargaining approach based on solving problems through arbitration or mediation rather than through ultimate recourse to economic weapons may be most effective.

Second, and equally important, unions must continually seek out and address new issues of concern to workers. For example, the issue of pay inequity has become a proper concern of women workers; collective action provides the surest way of redressing such inequities. There is a strong concern among workers about health and safety issues and a high degree of impatience with the inadequacy of government programs in this area. Again, collective action through labor unions can develop constructive steps to meet these concerns.

In this regard, the survey data suggest, and our experience indicates, that there is a particular insistence voiced by workers, union and non-union alike, to have a say in the "how, why and wherefore" of their work. These needs and desires are being met in some cases by union-management programs affording greater worker participation in the decision-making process at the workplace. Several major unions have developed such programs and report a positive membership response. The labor movement should seek to accelerate this development. Quality of worklife programs can only serve their humanizing purpose when they are based on the concepts of worker dignity and equality and grounded in collective bargaining. The reality is that some employers have used quality of worklife programs as "union avoidance" measures or as simple "speed-up" efforts without any commensurate commitment to increasing worker involvement and improving worklife. Programs of this latter type can only engender disappointment and discontent.

It is not our purpose here to detail the full range of options for meeting workers' needs through variations on the basic collective bargaining system; a new orthodoxy is the precise opposite of the proper approach. Collective bargaining is not, and should not be, confined by any rigid and narrow formula; the bargaining process is shaped by the times, the circumstances and the interplay between particular employers and employees. It is the special responsibility of the individual unions that make up the labor movement to make creative use of the collective bargaining concept and to adapt bargaining to these times and to the present circumstances.

**1.2  Consideration should be given to establishing new categories of membership for workers not employed in an organized bargaining unit.** The polling data indicate that approximately 28 percent of all non-union employees — 27,000,000 workers in all — are former union members; most of those individuals left their union only because they left their unionized jobs. There are hundreds of thousands more non-union workers who voted for a union in an unsuccessful organizing campaign or who are supporting or have supported efforts to establish a union in their workplace. These individuals might well be willing to affiliate with a union with which they have had contact or with which they have some logical relationship provided that the cost were not prohibitive; this would be especially true to the extent unions offered services or benefits outside of the collective bargaining context of the kind described below. New categories of membership should be created by individual unions or on a Federation-wide basis to accommodate individuals who are not part of organized bargaining units, and affiliates should consider dropping any existing barriers to an individual's retaining his membership after leaving an organized unit.

**1.3 The AFL-CIO should undertake a study of providing direct services and benefits to workers outside of a collective bargaining structure.** The survey data indicate that a large number of non-union workers desire a number of employment-related services (such as job training) and fringe benefits (such as supplemental medical insurance) that are not normally available to them. Indeed, 61 percent of non-union workers say that they would be very interested or fairly interested in joining an organization that provides information about job training and job opportunities, and 47 percent of non-union members state that they definitely or probably would join an organization in order to receive certain specified benefits.

The labor movement provides a logical vehicle for meeting these employee desires, and doing so could introduce some non-union workers to the benefits provided by union representation. Such services could also be made available to current members through their own unions, thereby increasing the benefits of unionization, and could be made available to persons in the new category of membership described above. A feasibility study should therefore be done to determine what services can be provided on a cost-effective basis, what vehicles would be most effective in providing such services, and to whom the services should be made available.

**1.4 Unions should expand their use of the electronic media.** The survey data show that despite the labor movement's efforts, we have failed to overcome the misconceptions about what unions do and have failed to make the public aware of the contributions of unions in the workplace and in society at large. This country is, moreover, in the midst of an information revolution that has greatly increased the choices available to American media consumers and created a much more fragmented communications industry through which we must have an integrated program to attempt to communicate our message. It is therefore imperative that, within the limits of our resources, we mount and sustain a coordinated and long-range communications program, employing every technique and medium available.

The AFL-CIO, through the work of the Labor Institute of Public Affairs, and its affiliates have begun to lay the groundwork for labor's transition into the electronic era. We recognize that the labor movement cannot apply better communications techniques as an afterthought but must communicate the substance of its activities as they occur. We are committed to reversing the near invisibility of American trade unions and their members in TV and radio programming and to introducing new technologies — such as teleconferencing, spot advertising, videocassettes, cable TV programming, and full-length broadcast programs — to help make unions more effective.

**1.5 Coordinated-comprehensive corporate campaigns and the pressure of public opinion should be used to secure the neutrality of employers whose employees seek to organize a union and to assure good faith bargaining.** In the past, organizing has often proceeded on the assumption that the law could be relied upon both to assure employees a fair and free choice on whether to form a union and also to require the employer to bargain with a union chosen by a majority of the employees. Members of the general public assume that such a law is in place and is scrupulously observed by employers. This assumption is fanciful; an employer bent upon opposing unionization is not even inconvenienced by the present law in carrying out his anti-union activities. Accordingly, neutralizing employer opposition and compelling good faith bargaining should be considered an essential part of organizing.

In some circumstances, a neutrality agreement can be obtained from an employer voluntarily (for example, in collective bargaining with an already-organized employer who operates non-union facilities). Where this is not the case, other steps must be taken to convince the recalcitrant employer not to interfere with the employees' right of self-organization (and to bargain in good faith where a union has been chosen). The use of non-workplace pressure, including all forms of publicity — generally referred to as a "corporate" campaign or "coordinated" or "comprehensive" campaign — has proven to be an effective means toward that end. Although the corporate campaigns that have attracted the most attention were large-scale campaigns at the national level, such as the J.P. Stevens and Beverly Enterprises campaigns, non-workplace pressure can be exerted on a smaller scale as well.

Unions should develop the research and other capabilities needed to mount an effective corporate campaign, and organizers should be trained in the various types of corporate campaign tactics. The AFL-CIO and its departments should gather together the already substantial body of experience unions have garnered in corporate campaigns and develop the necessary expertise to provide instruction and information concerning coordinated corporate or comprehensive campaign techniques.

**1.6 The AFL-CIO should establish a pilot project of experimental organizing committees.** The experience gained in earlier periods of union growth suggests the potential usefulness of organizing committees. That experience suggests that an entity single-mindedly devoted to the task of assisting unorganized workers in forming unions may be more successful than an ongoing entity whose first priority must be to provide service to its present members. To test this theory, a carefully designed AFL-CIO program should be developed under which one or more organizing committees, bringing together interested unions, would be established for a defined period of time and charged with the task of organizing the unorganized in a given area, industry or company.

\*    \*    \*

While the new approaches described above are promising and worthy of trial, the heart and soul of the labor movement will continue to be the representation of workers through the medium of traditional collective bargaining and traditional organizing campaigns. The recommendations that follow are designed to enhance the efficacy of our efforts in these regards. They are divided into three categories: increasing membership participation in their unions; developing better communications with the public; and improving organizing techniques.

# Increasing Members' Participation In Their Union

Unions are their members. A union resurgence requires that the individual union member have the fullest possible opportunity to participate in his or her organization and receive the highest quality representation from the union.

**2.1 Unions need to provide additional opportunities for members to participate in union affairs in ways quite different from traditional attendance at meetings.** In a world filled with available diversions, attendance at monthly meetings — important as those meetings are to maintaining the democratic nature of our movement — cannot be the principal form for membership participation. A broad range of activities to attract membership participation, improved community services and community-related activities, and an expanded committee structure to provide membership advice and guidance to the leadership are all ways of involving more members in the affairs of their local union. Moreover, the union can increase its communication with members, as well as the general public, by reaching directly into the home with radio, television and cable TV programming that can heighten the sense of community and earn an enlarged legitimacy for unions and their issues.

**2.2 Unions should increase the opportunities for members and national leaders to interact with each other.** A strong labor movement requires that its members understand that the union is theirs and that the union leadership remain attuned to the desires of the members. Elections, regular membership meetings and conventions all provide members the right to participate in, and to control, the fundamental decisions of the organization. But more must be done to enhance the members involvement in the union. For example, periodic regional, divisional or state conferences at which national or regional leaders speak, and listen, to members can be useful in these regards. Local, regional and national events in which members participate, such as Solidarity Day, Labor Day celebrations and Union Label, legislative, political or other "issue" conferences are likewise important. So, too, are opinion surveys which provide the membership yet another opportunity to express their views.

**2.3  Unions should make special efforts to provide an orientation program for new members.** Each year up to a million employees join existing bargaining units. These workers and all new members should be provided an orientation explaining how the union functions, what it has accomplished, what its goals are, and how the individual can become involved in the union. Orientation should also be provided concerning the labor movement generally and its accomplishments and goals. Older members should be involved in these programs to help give new members a sense of the history of the organization and to provide another opportunity for membership participation.

**2.4  Unions should devote greater resources to training officers, stewards and rank-and-file members.** In a vastly more complicated world, there is an increased need to provide training opportunities for local leadership and potential leaders. Training must encompass the skills local leaders need to function effectively and the information local leaders need to confront the issues of the day. Each affiliate should establish an education function of this type, and the George Meany Center for Labor Studies and the Education Department should explore new ways of serving affiliates by developing education materials and model curricula and by expanding the number of members reached by the Center. In addition, alternative sources for funding such training through collectively bargained programs or through additional funding of public education facilities should be fully explored.

# Improving the Labor Movement's Communications

**3.1 Efforts should be made to better publicize organized labor's accomplishments.** Too often, only "bad" news about organized labor gets publicized; successes are ignored, and efforts made by unions to further the interests of workers and the general public go unnoticed. Unions should be far more aggressive in publicizing their successes and their work for causes that provide benefits far beyond our membership rolls. Programs to provide information about unions, and about the trade union movement and its contributions to workers and to American society, in the schools, must be enlarged. Current curricula in elementary and secondary schools pay scant attention to these matters. Each central body and state federation should develop, in cooperation with the Education Department, a "Labor in the Schools" program. These programs can draw on local union members, leaders and retirees, and can provide another opportunity for the involvement of members in the affairs of their union.

**3.2 Union spokespersons need training in media techniques.** Union spokespersons must be skilled in securing the public ear and eye and in communicating effectively when attention is attracted. The Labor Institute of Public Affairs, the George Meany Center for Labor Studies, and the AFL-CIO Department of Information have begun media technique programs; these need to be continued and expanded.

**3.3 Efforts must be made at every level to better inform reporters about unions and trade unionism.** Most non-union workers obtain their information about unions from the media. Too often, reporters are uninformed about unions and have contacts with unions only in crisis situations. Attention must be given to communications with reporters on a regular basis in a non-crisis atmosphere about what we do and how we function. Union leaders at all levels should expand their efforts to meet with reporters on a periodic basis for such discussions and should devote greater efforts to providing a trade union perspective on political, economic and social events.

**3.4 The AFL-CIO should develop a pilot project for a targeted area to test the usefulness of advertising to improve the public's understanding of labor.** Several unions have devoted considerable resources to advertisements designed to improve the public under-standing of the union and/or its members with considerable effect. A detailed feasibility study should be made of a targeted Federation-wide program of this kind.

**3.5 Interferences with the right of workers to form a union should be forcefully brought to the attention of the general public to de-velop public support for labor law reform.** The survey data indicate that over 80 percent of the American public agree with the proposi-tion that workers should have the right to join unions. But the Amer-ican public does not realize that under existing labor law that right exists only in theory and not in practice — that employers can, in fact, intimidate and coerce their employees and that the law's reme-dies are too little and too late. The public needs to be informed of these facts, through exposes of particular cases, in order to develop a constituency for real labor law reform in private employment and for the passing of legislation legalizing collective bargaining for public employees at the state and local levels.

# Improving Organizing Activity

There must be a renewed emphasis on organizing. The large increase in the workforce and in the extent of employer opposition requires an equal increase in the emphasis placed on, and the resources devoted to, organizing. All of the destabilizing changes we have detailed above have had the effect of decreasing the time and effort put into organizing. This trend must be reversed if any of the recommendations made below are to have any effect.

**4.1 Organizers should be carefully chosen and trained.** Organizing is a skill; it is not something that everyone can do and is not something that can be taught in a one-week training session. There should be broad recruitment efforts within and outside the labor movement for organizers, and organizers should be extensively trained. Moreover, organizers should be matched to the particular target to be organized since the most effective organizer for a particular workforce is ordinarily one whose education and background is similar to the people the organizer works with and who is familiar with the type of work those individuals perform.

**4.2 Organizers should make greater use of modern technology.** Modern communications technology enables workers at an unorganized plant to see first-hand what unionization is about and what it can accomplish and to communicate with workers at other plants who have formed a union. The persuasive impact of this technology cannot be doubted; indeed, anti-union employers often use it effectively. It is as important for organizers to master the use of video in small groups, of electronic conferencing for the press, of strategic advertising campaigns, and other media skills, as it is for them to devise effective messages aimed at potential members in an organizing drive.

**4.3 Union leaders and rank-and-file members should be more involved in organizing efforts.** In organizing, personal contacts both with union leaders and with rank-and-file members who have formed a union can be of critical importance. Union leaders at all levels must continue to be directly involved in organizing and must place renewed emphasis on bringing the benefits of trade unionism to the unorganized as a prime function of every labor organization. Greater use also should be made of rank-and-file members in campaigns because they are the best witnesses of trade union effectiveness. (Additionally, this activity provides another opportunity for membership participation in the affairs of the union.)

**4.4 Organizing targets should be carefully chosen to maximize the chance for success.** From the national polling data, it is possible to identify particular types of employers or employment conditions which are conducive both to organizing and, of equal importance, to obtaining a first contract, and it is also possible to identify particular groups which are more likely to want union representation; for example, former union members and younger workers tend to be more favorably inclined to unionization than are older workers who have never been in a union. Before a union expends significant resources on an organizing campaign, objective analysis should be done of the likelihood of successfully securing majority support and negotiating a first contract. Where feasible, polling of the workers should be conducted before the organizing begins, and polling should continue during any large scale organizing campaign.

**4.5 Small units should not be overlooked as organizing targets.** Thirty-five percent of the national workforce is employed in companies with less than 25 employees. Labor conditions in smaller companies tend to be inferior to conditions in larger companies, and employers in these companies are less likely to resist their employees' desire to form a union; not surprisingly, therefore, unions have been more successful in representation elections in small bargaining units than in elections in larger bargaining units. However, servicing these units effectively can be difficult. Accordingly, special attention should be given to developing techniques for organizing and representing workers in small units.

**4.6 Unions should experiment with new organizing techniques.** Traditionally, organizers have focused their efforts on obtaining authorization cards and securing recognition in order to negotiate a collective bargaining agreement. In the climate we now face, this may be too large a first step to attempt, at least in certain situations. Experimental efforts to organize workers around particular issues, rather than around the principle of collective bargaining, are worth exploring; an organizer might be more effective in achieving the ultimate end of majority support for collective bargaining if the organizer has first demonstrated the potential of concerted activity by achieving results on a particular issue of concern to the workers in the unit.

**4.7 When a unit is organized, unions representing other units of the same employer should coordinate assistance to the new unit to obtain a first contract.** Coordinated bargaining and, where necessary, coordinated pressure maximizes labor's strength. Such strength is especially important in attempting to obtain a first contract in a newly-organized unit. Accordingly, all unions representing employees of such an employer — at all of the employer's worksites — should work together to help obtain a collective bargaining agreement for the newly-organized unit, as such an agreement will benefit all the employees of the employer. The AFL-CIO and the trade and industrial departments should facilitate such coordination.

**4.8 Unions should make special efforts to attract those who belong to organized bargaining units but have not joined their union.** By most estimates, 2,000,000 of the employees who are covered by AFL-CIO union contracts are not union members. These workers are known by the local leadership and are a natural audience for the union's message, and every effort should be made to turn them from free riders to full and enthusiastic members. These "internal organizing" campaigns can produce a far more closely-knit work group and can add to the union's effectiveness in the workplace.

# Structural Changes to Enhance the Labor Movement's Overall Effectiveness

There are a number of structural changes within the labor movement that would enhance our overall effectiveness.

**5.1 The AFL-CIO Executive Council should adopt guidelines for use by affiliates contemplating mergers.** Roughly 50 of the AFL-CIO affiliates have under 50,000 members and another 30 have under 100,000 members. These unions have, by and large, been hardest hit by membership loss and have the least ability to grow to offset the loss. Some of the unions enjoy a strong position in their industries or crafts and are well able to serve their members. Many of the others are suffering a reduced capacity to serve their members and have begun to examine the efficacy of merger with other unions. But mergers are difficult to effectuate and, if poorly conceived, can cause a union to lose that identity which helps bind the members and the organization.

Accordingly, both active AFL-CIO encouragement of mergers and guidelines as to appropriate and inappropriate mergers deserve a high priority. For example, mergers are more likely to be effective if the partners share a community of interest either because of a substantial overlap in the industries in which their members work, or because a substantial portion of their members work in industries that are vertically integrated, or because a substantial portion of their members work for a common, conglomerate employer. Similarly, mergers are more likely to be effective where there is potential for growth either because of projected increases in employment in the principal industry of one or both unions or because of the possibility of substantial organizing gains. The Committee has considered appropriate criteria and recommends the adoption by the Executive Council of the "Merger Guidelines" set forth in the Appendix.

**5.2 The AFL-CIO officers and staff should provide assistance to affiliates in effecting successful mergers.** The AFL-CIO officers and staff can aid in assessing whether a proposed merger is viable and, if not, they can suggest alternatives. They can also assist in resolving some of the complex issues that arise in the merger process. Such assistance should be readily available to affiliates and should be proferred where it seems appropriate. The ad hoc Committee on Mergers should continue to work as an additional resource for unions considering merger and should report periodically to the Executive Council.

**5.3 The AFL-CIO should establish a mechanism for resolving organizing disputes among unions.** All too often, precious organizing dollars have been expended on competition among different affiliates to organize the same bargaining unit. This competition is wasteful and may result in a weakened union. Following the pattern of Article XX of the AFL-CIO Constitution, which has been successful in resolving raiding disputes, the Federation should establish machinery, including a mechanism for mediation, to resolve these actual and anticipated organizing conflicts and to resolve competition for the affiliation of independent unions as well. The operating principle should be a preference for the union with the highest degree of support in the bargaining unit, taking into account the extent of organization that has taken place and the relative connection of the competing unions to the bargaining unit and employer in question.

**5.4 Unions must adapt modern budgeting, program analysis and planning techniques to union structure and finances.** As resources become more restricted and demands on them increase, the need for the use of the most modern financial management methods becomes more manifest. While unions have particular difficulties in applying budgeting techniques — given the unpredictable nature of organizing and collective bargaining activities — it is clear that some of the management, budget and planning techniques so highly developed in American business circles can be successfully adapted to union needs. A number of unions are currently engaged in both long- and short-term planning and in adjusting their financial allocations to the goals thus developed as instances warrant. A few unions are experimenting with long-range strategic planning and with other management techniques. These tools need to be developed further by the AFL-CIO and its affiliates.

**5.5 A new method of funding state and local central bodies should be developed.** It is essential in the current climate that labor's voice be effectively heard at the state and local levels as well as at the national level; this is the role of the state federations and the city central bodies. At present, the state federations benefit all unions but are funded by only some unions; the average level of affiliation with the state federations in recent years has been 55 percent. This means that certain affiliates carry a disproportionate share of the responsibility for sustaining the state federations and that those federations are not as strong as they could and should be. A similar pattern prevails at the local level. Accordingly, the Committee recommends that the Executive Council Committee on State and Local Central Bodies be instructed to develop a solution to this problem of inadequate and inequitable financing of these important bodies, such as a system under which, in lieu of the optional payments to the various state and local central bodies by AFL-CIO affiliates or their subordinate bodies, each affiliate should be required to make a per capita payment to the AFL-CIO for the state federations and local central bodies, which payments would then be distributed to these organizations based on the size of the population they represent. The Committee on State and Local Central Bodies should examine whether it is feasible to phase in, over a four- or five-year period, such a system, or any alternative that Committee may develop which would address the problem of the inadequate and inequitable financing of these important bodies.

*    *    *

The preceding recommendations result from a searching self-examination and honest appraisal of our strengths and weaknesses and encompass a wide range of proposed actions to strengthen our unions and our movement and to enhance our ability to serve present and future members. This process of examination and appraisal must be continued within the Federation and within every affiliate as the basis for planning realistically for the future.

As the final note of this report, two quotes from our predecessors provide both a call to action and a reassurance:

> "... the labor movement cannot be content with defending the status quo, or reliving past glories. We must constantly look to the future, develop new leadership, adapt policies to changing conditions and new technologies, but — always, always — with unswerving loyalty to the mission of the trade union movement as the instrument for improving and enhancing the working and living conditions of those who work for wages."

**— President George Meany at the 1979 Convention.**

> "Ten thousand times has the labor movement stumbled and bruised itself. We have been enjoined by the courts, assaulted by thugs, charged by the militia, traduced by the press, frowned upon in public opinion, and deceived by politicians.

> "But notwithstanding all this and all these, labor is today the most vital and potential power this planet has ever known, and its historic mission is as certain of ultimate realization as is the setting of the sun."

**— Eugene V. Debs after the Pullman strike in 1894.**

# Appendix

## Merger Guidelines

Since the merger of the AFL and the CIO in 1955, the number of AFL-CIO affiliates has declined from 135 to 96, primarily through the process of merger. A review of the membership trends and structure of the remaining affiliates, together with an analysis of structural changes in the workforce, demonstrates that more and more unions are considering mergers as a means to increased collective bargaining power and heightened organizing ability.

While most of the mergers that have taken place to date have proved to be mutually beneficial to the organizations and membership involved, it is important that future mergers provide the optimum combination to confront the problems of a rapidly changing economy. As the emphasis on mergers increases and the number of unions declines, care must be taken to insure that future mergers represent the optimum, beneficial combination.

To help both the AFL-CIO and its affiliates achieve these goals, comprehensive, specific guidelines should be adopted. Guidelines dealing with mergers cannot adequately incorporate all of the factors that might make a merger rational and appropriate, and it is essential that the guidelines not retard the affiliates' interest in consolidation.

After careful review, the Committee feels that mergers should take place among unions whose members share a community of interest based on their employment sector. However, since many affiliates' members work in several industrial occupational sectors, the community of interest concept must be defined broadly enough to include a substantial number of unions in each category.

Where two or more unions enjoying substantial community of interest merge, the Executive Council should approve such mergers without hesitation. A merger meeting the criterion of vertical integration should be similarly approved. Where no community of interest or vertical integration is apparent, serious examination of all relevant considerations should be given by the Executive Council before approval of the merger is granted.

To be considered as having a presumptive community of interest with the other unions in an industrial grouping, based on federal government classifications, an affiliate either should have at least 20 percent of its members employed in that industrial category or its members in that category should constitute at least 20 percent of the total AFL-CIO members therein. A union meeting one of these two criteria would satisfy the community of interest objective. But other unions which do not meet either criteria could still have an opportunity to demonstrate a sufficient community of interest with certain unions or even all unions within the grouping to make a merger both rational and appropriate.

# APPENDIX 3B

## DISCUSSION GUIDE for Local Unions

## THE CHANGING SITUATION OF WORKERS AND THEIR UNIONS

**AFL–CIO**

**Department of Education**

# INTRODUCTION

This discussion guide has been prepared to assist local union officers in educating their membership on the new AFL-CIO report on **The Changing Situation of Workers and Their Unions.** The report was issued by the Committee on the Evolution of Work. The Committee was established by the AFL-CIO Executive Council to review and evaluate changes that are taking place in America's labor force, occupations, industries and technology. It is clearly recognized that this report will only have value to the labor movement if it drives the discussion which will make change possible. To that end we have prepared this guide for use at the local level.

Each local union will want to select those points for discussion which are most relevant to its particular situation. Certain sections of the report apply directly to national officers and union staff and they are not highlighted in this guide. Several points have been selected from each section for the focus of the discussion. The questions are designed to elicit discussion among the group and to bring them to an understanding of the problems and the necessity to be open and supportive of new strategies and methods. At the same time, the discussion leader should reinforce the premise that the recommendations are consistent with the labor movement's ideals and capable of accomplishment.

## Suggested Pre-Discussion Assignment

1.    Make copies of the report available to all members, with notification of where and when the discussion of its contents will take place.

2.    Ask members to read the report beforehand and to come to the discussion

meeting with any questions they may have. These may or may not be used, depending on how the discussion will cover the issues involved, but the purpose of having a prepared group for a more meaningful discussion will have been served.

### Changing Situation of Workers and Their Unions  pp 5-7

Discussion leader should open the session by summarizing this section with the following five points:

*   labor movement has been successful and will retain its basic mission -- to improve conditions of workers

*   has not kept up with massive workforce growth and changes; steady decline in percent organized

*   major technological changes have affected employers and workers

*   labor has suffered setbacks in the past -- it has proven flexible

*   this report provides the wherewithal to adjust

### Changes in the Workforce  pp 8-9

Discussion points:

*   major changes in geographic and industrial makeup of workforce as well as growth in part-time, short-term and small firm employment

*   most of these trends are counter to traditional union membership base

**Questions:**

-   How has your industry and area been affected?

-   Give examples of new patterns of employment as opposed to the traditional single earner family.

-   How many part-time workers do you know? How long do people hold a job? Does your contract cover part-time employees?

### The Failure of the Law  pp 10-11

Discussion points:

* recognize change in employer attitudes and how that affects enforcement of the law

* employers can get away with illegal conduct and thus thwart organizing and collective bargaining for two reasons:

    (1) high unemployment limiting the workers' strength

    (2) federal government hostility to collective bargaining and its refusal to enforce laws for protecting workers' rights

**Questions:**

- How has your employer changed?

- Have you ever felt the frustration of dealing with the NLRB?

- How has the unemployment rate affected your job and bargaining strength?

### The Desires and Perceptions of Workers  pp 12-13

Discussion points:

Polls show:

* American worker is independent, self reliant, skeptical of authority and desiring workplace freedom

* job satisfaction has declined somewhat

* workers view unions as a positive force for improvement in working conditions generally but are skeptical that they can improve their particular working conditions

* important union actions are dictated by leaders and public holds a number of other negative perceptions of unions

**Questions:**

- Define the work ethic. Do you believe American workers retain this traditional value?

- Do you believe your union is run democratically? Do you have and exercise a voice in policy decisions? Cite examples. Do you have suggestions for change?

- In what ways does your union or central labor council relate to the community the way that your union functions? Can you suggest ways to publicize the democratic process of unions for your community?


## The Seeds of a Resurgence pp 14-16  --   The Good News

Discussion points:

* membership decline not due to dissatisfaction, but economy

* union workers appreciate the benefits of organization

* unions are successful in enrolling workers in growth areas

* non-union workers accept the fundamental premise of the labor movement: workers are more effective when acting together than when acting alone

* public sector and Canadian growth in union membership prove that when employers give or are forced to give workers a change, they will join unions in vast numbers

**Questions:**

- Are you better off with a union?

- Do most of your non-union friends agree with you?

- Do you think union workers earn more? are better educated? are almost all blue collar?

# RECOMMENDATIONS

## New Methods of Advancing the Interests of Workers  pp 18-22

Discussion points:

* to develop and test new ways to represent workers -- expanded flexibility in bargaining goals

* to be aware of and to address new issues of concern to workers -- pay equity for women, participation in work process decisions

* to establish new categories of membership for those not employed in organized bargaining units -- cite numbers of former members and great numbers of supporters who don't belong

* to have the AFL-CIO provide services and benefits to non-union workers which currently are not available to them

* to expand the use of electronic media to tell labor's message. Use LIPA as resource.

**Questions:**

- Can you cite different examples of collective bargaining relationships?

- What are some concerns in your workplace that haven't been addressed by your union?

- How does your union maintain contact with retirees?  Former members? Those who move on to other jobs?  What is your local's relationship to a group of workers who lost an election in your town?  What advantages are there to unions in maintaining a relationship with former members?  What problems does it create?  Can you keep them attracted to union?  What is needed?  What about union eligibility for those who can't get majority support?  Perhaps at lower dues?  Would you resent it?

- Give suggestions for local use of cable, radio.

**Discussion Leader Note:**    You should encourage consideration and support for the new approaches, but point out the work of the movement also needs new commitment to proven effective means and they are covered in this next section.

## Increasing Members' Participation in Their Union   pp 23-24

Discussion points:

Unions should --

* provide additional opportunities for members to participate in the work of the local

* plan activities that allow members to interact with the local, regional or district and international leadership

* recognize the importance of making special efforts to welcome and provide orientation for new members

* plan for increased recources for education and training of leadership and membership, and particularly stewards

**Questions:**

- How many rank-and-file members of your local have attended union rallies or meetings outside your local during the past year?  How many local members have met regional or international officers?

- Were you given an orientation program when you first joined the union? Did a member accompany you to your first meeting?  If not, how might this have affected your attitude toward the union?

- Do stewards in your local have a planned training program?   Is it coordinated by the local union?  Do you have an Education Committee?

- Have your local officers attended training programs sponsored by the international or a labor studies center?   Does your contract have a provision for educational leave or other coverage?

- Give a recommended action agenda for your local to improve participation and education.

## Improving the Labor Movement's Communications pp 25-26

Discussion points:

* to be more aggressive in publicizing success and work in the community at large
* to train union spokespersons in dealing with the media
* to enchance and establish regular communication with reporters for better communication about trade unions and their perspective
* to publicize unfair employer labor practices which interfere with the rights of workers to organize

**Questions:**

- How often does your union local have speakers in schools? Articles in the newspapers about your community work?
- Do you know your local (labor) reporters or those who are usually assigned to cover your strikes or stories? and school work? What impact on public attitudes about unions can such programs have?
- Where can a local union find assistance to improve communitations (international union, Labor Institute for Public Affairs, George Meany Center courses, labor center at a university)?

## Improving Organizing Activity pp 27-29

Discussion Points:

Unions should --

* give new emphasis to organizing efforts -- time, money, resources

\* broaden recruitment of organizers and improve and intensify training: ensure proper matchup with work group to be organized

\* utilize the persuasive impact of the electronic media

\* involve as broad a base as possible of union leadership and membership to help in organizing

\* carefully analyze potential organizing targets, both large and small units

\* explore new techniques, experiment with phases of campaign tactics in authorizations and elections

\* coordinate bargaining efforts with other unions to help gain the first contract -- over two million free riders -- special attention needed

**Questions:**

- How does your union select organizers? Are special training sessions conducted for organizers at the local level?

- Does your local and its members help during a campaign? In what way? Are they asked systematically? Would you help? Have you ever? What would you be willing to do? What do you think would be the most helpful things you could do?

- Do you and most of your membership know cost of a carefully planned campaign?

- Has your local assisted in the organization of another union of your employer? Was it effective?

- Do you have an internal organizing program in your local? Is it active and effective? If not, what suggestions would you offer to the membership for establishing such a program?

## Structual Changes to Enhance the Labor Movement's Overall Effectiveness  pp 30-32

Discussion points:

* unions must adapt modern budgeting and planning techniques to union structure and finances

* a new method of funding state and local central bodies should be developed

**Questions:**

- Does your union have a planning session to outline its program for the year, and the cost of the program?

- Is there a special budget committee that sets priorities for expenses? Are rank-and-file members participating in the process?

- Is there a membership report annually that reviews the programs and costs?

- Are you affiliated to the local central body or the state federation?

- How is your membership represented by these bodies even if you are not affiliated? Does your union work with the state and local central bodies on legislation of importance to all workers? In political campaigns?


**Discussion Leader**

### CALL TO ACTION

Seeds of resurgence must be sown at the local level -- the health and vitality of the labor movement rests with its local unions.

Appropriate conclusion for meeting is to select union's priorities from the recommendations and develop a program of action.

Concluding quotes in report from George Meany and Eugene Debs provide encouraging historic conclusion.

# UNIT TWO

## CRITICAL CHALLENGES
## FOR LOCAL UNION LEADERS

- *Labor's message through the media*
- *Strengthening your local through education*
- *Computerizing the local*

# CHAPTER 4

# Labor's Message
# through the Media

Labor's message through the media has been, in the eyes of most unionists, distorted. A social movement improving the lives of millions of Americans has been turned into a selfish, special-interest group. Organized (BIG) labor is depicted by editorial cartoonists as an overweight, white, middle-aged male with a cigar stuck between his teeth. No wonder that the relationship between labor and the mass media has been marked by suspicion and distrust. For years unionists have spoken out against what they feel has been unfair treatment by the corporate media. "The journalistic trespasses committed against the labor movement are both sins of omission and sins of commission. They are both flagrant and unwitting."[1] So said Lane Kirkland, the president of the AFL–CIO to a convention of the International Labor Press Association. "'It's almost assumed there will be hostility toward unions and they will be poorly covered,' says Sam Pizzigatti, associate director of the National Education Association's communications department."[2] Gordon Cole of the Machinists Union claims: "No institution in the country is the victim of such biased treatment as American labor receives in the media."[3] Are these fears and allegations true? Does labor get

[1]Lane Kirkland, "Labor and the Press." AFL–CIO *Federationist,* AFL–CIO, Washington, D.C., 1975.

[2]As quoted in Michael Hoyt, "Is the Press Anti-Labor . . . Or Just Out of Touch?" *Columbia Journalism Review,* March/April 1984, p. 40.

[3]Gordon H. Cole, "The Big Bad Lie: How the Media Shapes the News on Labor." *The IUE News,* February 1977.

a raw deal from the media? Most unionists think so. In a study done at Harvard University, researchers found that 50% of the coverage of unions by *Time* and *Newsweek* in the 1970s was "unfavorable." This figure was a dramatic rise from the 34% unfavorable coverage of the 1950s.[4] Is it deliberate? Again, some unionists think so. " 'I take it as a given that a newspaper is a business, and a business is going to protect its own interests,' says Anthony Mazzochi '. . . I don't buy the notion of a free press.' "[5]

If newspapers and the other media are businesses, it should follow that their coverage of "business" would be more positive. "It strikes me that management is just as angry with the media as most labor people I know,"[6] says Walter Davis, director of the Department of Information of the United Food and Commercial Workers International Union. Many of the same criticisms of the media that organized labor has offered are echoed by the business community. Bernard O'Keefe of the National Association of Manufacturers claims that business people on television are "either crooks or greedy . . . ."[7] Indeed, even the education community has criticized network news's coverage of education issues. Increasingly the media has become the scapegoat for many groups and individuals, with charges of unfair coverage or no coverage at all. It is important to note that despite the criticisms of the media, "65 percent of the American public relies on television . . ."[8]for news, and union members are part of that American public.

If it is true that the mass media distort the image of organized labor, and if it is true that most people use the mass media as their main source of information, then how can unions get their *true* image across to the public and their members, and not the image that is currently being reflected?

In this chapter, the authors will outline the existing relationship between organized labor and the media, along with some suggestions designed to improve that relationship. We will also discuss the different types of media available and how local unions can use them to their benefit.

We are in the midst of a communication and information revolution. Some are comparing it to the industrial and corporate revolution of the late nineteenth century. That revolution changed the structure and composition of the American labor movement. This one is doing the same thing. Rather than resist inevitable change—like the dinosaurs some people compare the labor movement to— unions must participate in and help lead this revolution. Use of new communications technologies is one way of achieving some part of this goal and is therefore one of the major challenges facing local union leaders.

---

[4]Richard L. Freeman and James Medoff, as cited in Hoyt, op. cit.

[5]Anthony Mazzochi, former vice president of the Oil, Chemical and Atomic Workers Union. Ibid.

[6]Excerpt from a speech made at the George Meany Labor Studies Center, University of Colorado, and several other places.

[7]Eric Pace, "The Businessman as Villian: On TV and in Novels, the Bad Guy Sells." *New York Times,* April 15, 1984.

[8]Michael J. Robinson, "How the Networks Cover Education." *American Educator,* Spring 1984, p. 20.

# THE MEDIA

For the purposes of this chapter, the authors define the media as:

Electronic media
    Television
    Radio
    Movies
Print media
    Newspapers
    Magazines

We can further define the media by dividing it into two categories: the news media and the entertainment media. *News media* reports information on workers, unions, and union/worker issues. *Entertainment media* depicts workers and unions in fiction, nonfiction, and "docudrama." (Docudrama is a mix of fact and fiction, i.e., a story based on a factual historical event, with a little "fiction" to spice it up.)

There are many communications "voices" in this country. There are approximately:

900 television stations

9000 radio stations

7 major movie studios

1700 daily newspapers

1000 magazines

Fifty corporations own most of these voices. Most of them are media corporations and most of them are interlocked with other nonmedia corporations. Many others are subsidiaries of nonmedia corporations. Three television networks attract 98% of the audience and 20 newspaper chains sell over half of all the daily newspapers.[9] There are a lot of voices, but they are concentrated in a few corporations. Criticism of this concentration comes from the left and the right. Liberals argue that "big business" controls the information system, while conservatives say that the "mediacracy" is controlled by the liberals. However, the controlling factor in any company is profit. Newspapers, magazines, television, and radio are businesses. What news and how they report it and what shows they air *are* affected by circulation and ratings. The media are sellers of a product: *you.* The buyers are the advertisers. How well you are "sold" to the advertisers

---

[9] Ben H. Bagdikian, *The Media Monopoly.* Beacon Press, Boston, 1980, pp. xv, 9, and 14.

determines their financial support of a particular newspaper, network, or station. The functions of the media may be to inform and entertain, but certainly not at a loss.

## LABOR'S RELATIONSHIP WITH THE NEWS MEDIA

**Reprinted from *Labor's Joke Book*, Paul Buhle, editor.**

How well does the news media cover union and worker issues? Most union officials and reports say, *not as good a job as they should or could be doing.*

What are some of the specific criticisms that organized labor has of news coverage? The United Steelworkers of America called them the "Seven Ordinary Sins of Labor Reporting" at the 1979 Convention of the International Labor Press Association. Lane Kirkland has said that they are sins of both commission and omission.

The most common criticism is that of coverage of strikes. Strikes are equated with violence (by workers, not police). "A picket line was set up today, and fortunately there was no violence" is often the message on the evening news. This is the sin of commission. The sin of omission is "ignoring the settlement." Over 95% of all labor negotiations are settled *without* a strike. Why do the media pay so much attention to strikes and so little attention to settlements without strikes?

> "To attract the maximum audience, the press emphasizes the exceptional rather than the representative; the sensational rather than the significant . . . .
>
> Sensationalism and an emphasis on controversy are unfortunately typical of media coverage: crime, riots, strikes, and quarrels are the consumer product that a profit-oriented media must sell to its audience."[10]

[10] Robert Coulson, president of the American Arbitration Association (also quoting Robert M. Hutchins), "The Media's Love Affair with the Strike," Linda Miller, ed., *Impact of the Media on Collective Bargaining.* American Arbitration Association, New York, 1980, p. 1.

"Labor Bosses" and "Big Labor" are labels that the media use to identify *elected* union officers and international and local unions. The sin of commission is implying that a "czar of labor" can wave his hand and a general strike by millions of unionists will paralyze the nation. The sin of omission is that, although we often read of "Big Business," how often do we see corporate executives referred to as "Management Bosses"? Is Big Labor really that big? Some of the public thinks so. In a poll taken by Research & Forecasts, Inc., for the Hearst Corporation, 40% of the people surveyed believed that half of the nation's work force was unionized.

Unions are corrupt. The headline read: "Organized Crime: How Big a Role in Unions? Criminals hold sway in hundreds of locals, Congress is told."[11] The story then explained that crime was a problem in only a small minority of the thousands of union locals in America. One study compared those same government reports to studies done by *Fortune* magazine and the American Management Association. It found that unions and their leaders were affected much less by corruption than their business counterparts.

Unions are greedy. Samuel Gompers, first president of the AFL made the mistake of saying that labor wanted "More . . . ." Of course he said more schools, more books, more learning, more work, more leisure (and less greed), more justice, and more opportunities "to cultivate our better natures . . . ." Today that quote is constantly translated by news commentators into "More money."

Why does labor "demand" and management "offer?" Who is buying whose labor? When reporters write about economics, are they "objective" about our economic system, or do they assume its premise and view unions as an intrusion into the model? Labor leaders (and business leaders) question reporters' understanding of basic economics.

Unions are out of date. "There was a need for them back in the 1920s and 1930s, but not today. Management is different today." Unions were just as popular with the news media back then. "There is an uncanny similarity to the late 1920s, when respected journalists were saying that we don't need unions anymore," replies Lance Compa, an attorney for the United Electrical Workers Union. Union struggles of the 1930s were also seldom depicted favorably by the media.

Union leaders are out of touch with their members. They do not vote the way they are "told to" by union leaders, either in political elections or in contract ratifications. Unfortunately, democracy and the "tyranny of the majority" don't sell news.

Why don't they print the good news? As Robert Hutchins said, "crime, riots, strikes, and quarrels sell." The media does report some good news. And unions can get their good news reported. The section on "Using the Media to Tell Your Story" will show how.

---

[11] *U.S. News & World Report,* May 8, 1978, Russ Gibbons, Director of Public Relations, as reprinted in "Seven Sins of Labor Reporting." United Steelworkers of America, Pittsburgh, Pa., 1979.

## LABOR AND THE ENTERTAINMENT MEDIA

### Television

Critics of the entertainment media have argued that television does not offer a realistic view of the world. Both business and labor claim that their true images are being distorted. Studies support their allegations. A University of Pennsylvania study found that one out of three business people on prime-time network TV is a "bad guy."[12] Other analysts found that businessmen were portrayed as "evil and selfish, social parasites," who "come down squarely on the side of the bad guys."[13]

If the business community of America—the economic lifeblood of our nation—is treated this way by the entertainment media, then how is the labor movement depicted? Eric Pace argues that vis-a-vis the capitalist, the working class hero is "lionized."[14] There are many people, however, who do not share this opinion. In fact, rather than lionizing American workers, the media (especially television) generally maligns them and in many cases, ignores them.[15] Union leaders have often criticized the depiction of workers on television as distorted. The International Association of Machinists monitored television entertainment and news shows to see how unions, workers, and labor issues were portrayed. Some of their conclusions were:

1. Television depicts unions as violent, degrading, and obstructive.

2. Occupational prevalence on television is grossly disproportionate to reality.

3. Television portrays workers in unionized occupations as clumsy, uneducated fools who drink, smoke, and have no leadership ability.

4. The majority of workers in unionized occupations may as well be robots. They are nameless, personalityless people who take orders, do their jobs, and disappear.

5. Unions are almost invisible on television.[16]

---

[12] Pace, op. cit.

[13] Linda S. Lichter, S. Robert Lichter, and Stanley Rothman in an article in *Public Opinion,* as quoted by Pace, ibid.

[14] Ibid.

[15] Ralph Arthur Johnson, "World without Workers: Prime Time's Presentation of Labor." *Labor Studies Journal,* vol. 5, no. 3, Winter 1981, pp. 199–206.

[16] "IAM Television Entertainment Report Part II: Conclusions and National Summary of Occupational Frequency in Network Primetime Entertainment for February 1980." *Machinist,* June 12, 1980.

Mil Lieberthal of the University of Wisconsin found that "Workers frequently are portrayed as ignorant, prejudiced, and incompetent."[17] Ralph Johnson maintains that what is *not* shown is as bad as what *is* shown. He says that network television shows ignore workers, and that most television characters' occupations do not correspond with the real-life distribution of occupations. He also says that most programs "ignore economic need; (and) collective bargaining, collective action, and serious problems associated with work are virtually ignored or are presented from an upper-middle-class perspective."[18]

Are there positive images of workers and unions on TV? One show that has been cited is "Skag." This was a short-lived series about the life of a steelworker. Although it showed workers in a more favorable light, it was criticized by the Steelworkers' Union for being unrealistic in its portrayal of Skag's job in the mill and how the union leadership responded to problems at the workplace.

Does the unrealistic portrayal of workers have an effect on viewers' perceptions of reality? In the words of one unionist, "I watch TV to escape. I don't want to watch somebody working; I work all day long." Is it an escape from reality?

The average household watches around 50 hours of television per week, with cable subscribers watching even more. Most of this viewing comes during prime-time hours. "Watching television is an act of citizenship, participation in culture. The networks entertain the viewer; in return, the viewer entertains thousands of notions on what to buy (that is, how to live)."[19] Television does have an impact on its viewers, but to what extent has not been fully measured. It is more likely that the impact comes from day-to-day exposure to entertainment series than special events.[20] "Beliefs, attitudes and values are more palatable and credible to an audience when they are molded and reinforced by characters and program plots than when they are preached by a newscaster or speaker for a particular cause."[21] People who watch television for entertainment are affected by what they see and hear. They are also affected by what they do not see and hear, again the sin of omission. Or, in one expert's opinion, "the message gets across in inverse proportion to its being made conscious . . . . The unspoken assumptions are what mold the audience."[22]

[17] Mil Lieberthal, "TV and Movie Images of Workers—Reinforcing the Stereotypes." *Labor Studies Journal, vol. 1, no. 2, Fall 1976, p. 168.*

[18] Johnson, op. cit., p. 205.

[19] David Marc, "Understanding Television." *Atlantic Monthly,* August 1984, p. 42.

[20] Ibid., p. 34.

[21] Johnson, op. cit., p. 200.

[22] Alan Alda in Robert S. Alley, *Television Ethics for Hire.* Abingdon Press, Nashville, Tenn., 1977, p. 33; as cited in Johnson, op. cit.

## Movies

Have movies done a better job of portraying workers and unions? Nonfiction documentaries by independent film makers have offered a candid view of organized labor. Unfortunately, Hollywood movies have not done the same. Ken Margolies of the Communications Workers of America has traced the history of Hollywood's treatment of workers and unions.[23] His findings reveal some of the stereotypes unionists have come to expect from the media. Early films (pre-World War I) showed unions as "ineffectual, un-American and inspired by unscrupulous or misguided agitators." Individual workers were able to achieve their gains without joining unions. Movies of the 1920s portrayed organizers as "outside agitators" and unions as "evil." Unions in films of the 1930s were accepted as a "necessary evil" and were associated with labor unrest. One exception to this view was **Grapes of Wrath,** which realistically depicted the plight of the farmworkers in California. By the 1950s unions were established as a part of society. Hollywood first turned to the theme of violent corruption in *On the Waterfront* in 1954 and has continued it through recent films. Along with corruption, "Big Labor versus the Individual Worker" was added by two films of the 1970s: *FIST* and *Blue Collar*. In the first, the working class hero fights his way up through the ranks and becomes president of his national union, the Federation of Interstate Truckers (FIST). He makes an unholy alliance with organized crime, crushing democracy in his union, and subsequently is crushed by his partners in crime. In *Blue Collar* the union is portrayed similarly. The union's logo is a "circle of interlocking swastikas."[24] "The shop steward in the film is an unresponsive glad-hander trying to hang onto his so he does not have to return to the assembly line. The union president is a kindly looking white-haired man who is prepared to use bribes or murder to cover up the union's illegal activites."[25] Great entertainment, but not reality. Like the *Grapes of Wrath,* the film *Norma Rae* was an exception. But even this film showed the international union representatives (in a brief appearance) to be callous and indifferent to the individual worker, Norma Rae. *Norma Rae* proved that honest stories about workers and their unions can sell tickets. Unfortunately, it was an exception to Hollywood's rule.

The theme of Hollywood movies about workers has repeated itself: the individual worker trying to improve his or her situation is viewed positively (the American way). Unions have been shown as incompetent, violent, corrupt, powerful, bureaucratic, and obstructionist. As representatives of unions, its leaders have been portrayed in the harshest light.

[23] Ken Margolies, "Silver Screen Tarnishes Unions." *Screen Actor,* Summer 1981, p. 44.

[24] Richard Corliss, "Schrader's Nightmare of Normality." *New Times,* February 6, 1978.

[25] Margolies, op. cit., p. 52.

## CONCLUSIONS

This section has outlined a problem: the distorted picture of workers and unions presented by the print and electronic media in America. Can the labor movement change the image? Yes, but its efforts should be directed toward the most effective methods. One restriction is money. Unions cannot hope to compete with network television and Hollywood. Where unions can have an effect is at the local level. Most polls have shown that people's negative feelings are directed at "Big Labor" and "Labor Bosses": international unions and their leaders. Working at the local level to change the public's perception has an advantage: the people can see you in the community and not just in the media. Give them the opportunity to see "real" unions instead of the Hollywood ones and then you can work on their perception of your international unions. Organized labor's beginnings can be traced back to local movements. It is here that your union's media program, with effective managerial leadership, must begin.

## USING THE MEDIA TO TELL YOUR UNION'S STORY

You can get your message across to the public through a number of different media. People can read about it in newspapers and magazines; they can hear about you on radio and see you on television. This section concentrates on the media that local unions can use. Despite what you may think, there are many ways your union can gain exposure through the media. The three main media tools available to a public-relations committee are:

1. Written words: news releases, feature articles, news stories, letters to the editor.

2. Spoken words: face-to-face meetings, news conferences, radio spots (free and paid), telephone calls, speeches, individual interviews with reporters on radio.

3. Visual images: photographs, slides, film, videotape, the union logo, rallies and demonstrations, TV spots (free and paid), public-access cable TV.[26]

The selection of media tool(s) is based on who is to be reached, how available the media tools are, and the resources available to use the tools.

---

[26] *CWA Local PR Handbook: A Guide for Telling and Selling Our Union's Story.* Communication Workers of America, Washington, D.C., p. 13.

## Planning

Any media effort will require planning. If the local is going to conduct an external public-relations campaign, it should be coordinated with internal public relations (PR). If the community is being told what a great union one has, its members should know that such a campaign is on and give their support. Some questions one should ask before starting a media campaign include:

1. Does the local have a PR committee? Is it alive and well? What does it do?

2. Should a separate PR (media) committee for external public relations be established? Who will staff it?

3. How much money does the local have to support a media effort?

Once the local has considered the preliminary questions, the next step is to carefully analyze the situation.

1. What is the local's image in the community? Do people know it exists? What do they think about the union? Do they know what unions do?

2. What is the local's image with its own membership.? Will membership perceptions have to be dealt with first?

3. What is the message to be sent to the public?

4. Who will see or hear the message?

5. What do you want them to do? What is the purpose of the union's message?

6. What media tool(s) will be used?

A good external PR effort will take a lot of time, especially during the early stages. All committee members should be willing to spend time learning and working on the campaign. The chairperson should serve as the coordinator and spokesperson for the committee with media representatives. Responsibilities should be spread around. Conducting a media campaign is a team effort.

There are two basic types of publicity: free and paid. Free media include: news reports and features, public service (public-service announcements, talk shows, documentaries), and editorial contacts. Paid advertising can be used on radio or television, newspapers and magazines. Free media will obviously cost less, but there is less control over content. If the union wants control, it will have to pay for it. Money plays a large part in the decision process, even for free media coverage. Set up a budget. No salaries are involved, but other considerations are:

Stationery and other supplies

Equipment (typewriters, photocopying, printing)

Photography, audio- and videotapes

Mailing and possible long-distance phone costs

Special-event costs (rallies, news conferences, etc.)

An example of a media budget is given in Appendix 4A.

## Carrying Out the Local's Program

Establish the goals of the PR program and develop a strategy to make them happen. Do not wait for something to happen and then react to it. Commit members and resources to an ongoing program of external public relations. Act and anticipate events. Lay the groundwork for communication with media contacts by developing a constant working relationship with these people. Find out what media outlets are available and take advantage of them. They will not make your case for you based on a last-minute call from a stranger. It is just good management (Chapter 3).

Finally, the PR program should be evaluated periodically. Is the local accomplishing what it set out to do? Is the union's image more positive than before? How are the members reacting to the public campaign? Are there any changes that should be incorporated in other current campaigns noted for the future? Discover what worked—and *why*. Discover what did not work—and why.

Monitor the union's media coverage. Have committee members and other local volunteers document any coverage of the local. Clip news articles, editorials, letters to the editor, and feature pieces. Keep a scrapbook of them. Also record air time you may have received (literally and figuratively). Use the technology (audio and video) to tape news stories and public-service announcements. Analyze your message. Document air time in your scrapbook. Even if coverage has been little or nonexistent, through your efforts the media will at least be aware of your presence. This alone can change *how* they report about issues of concern to you.

One can survey the membership to find out whether they have seen, heard, or read positive things about the union. This is helpful to track publicity in community newspapers. Use the survey to find out what media your members watch, listen to, and read.

Give the program time to succeed. Developing a working relationship with the media requires time. A poor first evaluation does not necessarily mean the end of your program, although some changes might be necessary to make it more successful. What are its strong points and weak points? Implement the suggestions and continue the program with continuing periodic evaluations. Learn and lead.

# STRUCTURE AND FUNCTION
# OF THE NEWS MEDIA

Just what is "news?" Some people claim that news is "whatever the editor says it is." Others say that to become news the story should be "newsworthy." How does the media determine what is newsworthy? One authority defines newsworthy as "The story that offers the most information with the most urgency to the most people . . . ."[27] He measures newsworthiness by "the interest and attention of the majority of the audience, which may arise from any combination of information, urgency, significance, relevance, and uniqueness."[28] All the media compete for the public's attention. This is true not just for the entertainment media but for news as well.

Whether your story gets printed or aired depends on other factors. The news media operate on deadlines: by a certain time of each day stories must be ready for print or broadcast. Deadlines are different for newspapers, radio, and television; miss one and your story will not be used. Whether the story is newsworthy may depend on what the media perceive the public wants to hear or what they think the public should hear (based on audience surveys and polls). The availability of reporters to cover your story will often determine whether you get heard. Radio has the fewest reporters available, newspapers the most. Finally, the editorial style of each particular media outlet will have an impact. Do they sensationalize? Do they use electronic gimmicks? Do they concentrate on hard news and ignore features? What types of news stories do they feature? Crime? Disaster? Economics? Politics? Human interest? All these factors help determine if and when the media will tell your local's story.

## The Print Media

### Newspapers

Although television has become the major source of news for most people, newspapers can still be valuable communicators for your union. Within a newspaper (and magazine) there are three departments one should be concerned with:

1. Editorial department (where the news is)
2. Advertising department (where you put your paid ads)
3. Circulation department (who reads the paper helps to determine whether or not your news is printed)

You will deal most often with the editorial department. This department covers hard news stories, feature stories, editorial columns, letters to the editor, and in some cases community bulletin boards. In this department there are key people one should know: editors (chief and department) and beat reporters.

The chief editor is usually in charge of what editorials are published and decides, along with the department editors, what news stories are published. Most newspapers (except small ones) usually have a number of department editors, each in charge of a specific section of the paper. You should get to know the editors of the *business/economics, feature, editorial page,* and *op-ed* (opposing editorial) sections. Each department editor usually has a staff of reporters, photographers, illustrators, and copywriters assigned to him or her.

[27] Martin B. Winston, *Getting Publicity*. John Wiley & Sons, Inc., New York, 1982, p. 78.
[28] Ibid.

If the newspaper has assignment editors in each department, they will probably be your contacts in those departments. They send the reporters out to cover stories.

You will probably get to know the beat reporters the best. They are the people assigned to cover stories. Most newspapers do not have labor reporters anymore. Reporters who may cover you include political, environmental, economic, business, and feature story reporters. Over a period of time, you should develop a working relationship with one or more of them.

How does a newspaper function? How does the local's story get into print? Newspapers are run on a *space budget*. A total number of pages are printed; most of the space is reserved for advertising, and the remainder is for news. The editors meet daily to allocate that remaining space among the departments.

Newspaper deadlines for hard news are on a daily basis; the time depends on whether the paper is a morning or evening edition. The deadline for a feature story may be a week or longer.

The main source of news for editors is hard news, that is, coverage of events. The department editors (or assignment editors) will assign a reporter to cover a "breaking story." How does an editor know that a story is breaking? You can help. Send in a news release announcing one. Reporters also can initiate their own stories; the good ones do this often, using their contacts (you) in the field. The wire services (AP and UPI) also provide leads for editors to follow up. Finally, television and radio may also break a story that the newspaper will investigate more deeply.

After a reporter files the story or your news release is received, the department editor (and others) decides whether to use it based on its newsworthiness and the space available. The story may be edited and printed or discarded. This process is repeated every day. Your union's story competes with hundreds of others for space in today's paper. By tomorrow or the next day, your news will be old, out of date and, therefore, not very newsworthy.

How does one get the paper to print a story? There are certain procedures and techniques you can use. We will look at some of them later. The best way, regardless of the strategy, is to outwork your competition.

One can also have a story told through human interest features. These are nontimely, in-depth stories about people: union members and workers included. The feature may be in the *Sunday* magazine or part of the *Workplace* or some similar section.

You can write a guest column for the editorial or op-ed section. You can also send—and encourage your members to send—letters to the editor. These can protest unfair coverage, lack of coverage, or unfriendly editorials.

One can also use the *community events calendar* of the newspaper to announce union meetings or special events.

The disadvantage of using newspapers to communicate is that most people get their news primarily from television. Despite this drawback, newspapers do have certain advantages for you.

1. They are more likely to carry your story than TV or radio.

2. They will cover your story in greater depth: they explain the issues better than TV or radio.

3. They are adaptable: readers can read on their own daily schedule.

4. They have "staying power": the printed word can be read and reread, clipped, and used later.

5. They are influential: they are read by TV and radio media people.

6. *You* can help the reporter develop the story.[29]

### Magazines

Magazines are similar to newspapers in both structure and function. Many of the advantages are the same. But there are differences. Magazines may be of either a general or special news interest. Which magazine you may want to use will depend on the audience to be reached.

The advantages of magazine features include:

1. Longer lead times for stories (one week to many months).

2. More in-depth analysis of issues.

3. Longer "coffee-table life"; longer exposure than newspapers.

4. Articles are tailored to audience interest.

5. Like newspapers, they are read by media people.

What about the disadvantages? It's *very* difficult to get a local interest story printed in the national publications like *Time* and *Newsweek*. Because of a magazine's longer life, it might be put aside and read later when the union's news is old, too late for the desired impact.

The best bet for coverage is in local and regional magazines. These usually concentrate on human-interest stories. They can be used to your advantage if their circulation is wide among your projected audience.

Do not be afraid to use special-interest magazines. Write articles and submit stories to alternative "left" and "right" magazines. Both audiences can stand to learn more about unions.

### The Wire Services: AP and UPI

Associate Press and United Press International are the "media's media." They have offices in state capitals and large cities. Their stories are supplied by their own reporters or by free-lance writers (stringers) in smaller cities and towns. Many newspapers and radio and TV stations pick up their stories. They identify ("flag") stories for the media. In some cases, smaller papers and stations run the wire service story without change and without doing any follow-up investigation.

---

[29]Some of these examples are from *CWA Local PR Handbook*, op. cit. pp. 72–73.

One should be familiar with the regional and state wire services. When a national news story breaks, you can give them a local angle, focusing the story. You can also provide free-lance writers with local stories to be sent out over the wires to a larger audience. And you can submit news releases directly to the wire services.

## The Electronic Media

### Television

As we wrote earlier, television is the primary news source for almost two-thirds of Americans. Almost everybody owns televisions and they watch them on an average of seven hours per day. News on television is different than the other media: it is "visual." Television *shows* the viewer what happened or what is happening right now. News can be in the form of newscasts, documentaries, or magazine shows.

Television operates on a *time budget.* Newscasts are run two or three times during the day, with periodic updates. Each news program is usually no more than one half-hour. Within that time might be 6 minutes of hard news, 4 minutes of special reports, 4 minutes of weather, 5 minutes of sports, 3 minutes of special features, 1 minute of opening and closing themes, and 7 minutes of commercials and station identification announcements. The average news report on TV is 20 to 25 seconds. Special reports get more time.[30]

It is difficult to get a story on TV. Hard news such as crimes, accidents, political, and judicial actions are preferred,[31] as are stories with a visual impact. A story that can be condensed into 30 seconds with a few "quotable quotes" has a definite advantage over one that needs in-depth analysis. Television news is "urgent." Deadlines can be fatal to a story. If it breaks too late, too bad; it is not shown. What is a scoop today is history tomorrow.

People that you should know in the TV newsroom include:

1. News director: runs the overall news operation; may have the final say over what is aired.

2. News producer: puts together each newscast.

3. Assignment editor: sends reporters and technical people to cover stories; in effect, decides what stories get covered; a very important person for you to know.

4. Copy editor: edits the reporter's story before it goes on the air.

5. Reporter: covers stories in the field and has an impact on what goes into the story by asking questions and editing.

[30]Winston, op. cit., p. 21.

[31]Ibid., p. 22.

The obvious advantage of television is that it reaches a wide audience. It also *shows* your union and its logo to the community. That can have a lasting impact.

One disadvantage is that a 30-second story does very little to explain issues to the viewer. Its brevity can also lead to having your comments taken out of context or distorted. In addition, if the viewer is out of the room for a minute, they may miss the story.

### Radio

Some people call this the "underrated medium." Everybody listens to it, at home and away from home: at work, at play, and in between in their cars. In some areas, radio is the *only* local electronic media. It is a "hot" medium: words let the listener conjure up images and build emotions.

Radio newscasts also operate on a time budget. They are run for only 3 to 5 minutes per hour. Only the headlines are covered. The exception is during the evening "drive time" when a half-hour news show may air. Since radio news is broadcast every hour, they can offer a lot of different news. Therefore, radio newscasts are very accessible. In addition, most stations (other than all-news stations) have a small news staff and cannot cover breaking stories. You can supply them with such news.

The key person in the radio station is the news director. He or she decides what news the disk jockey will read every hour. Some stations have a small staff of reporters. They are usually overworked and appreciate news stories from outside sources.

The advantage of a wide audience is even greater in radio than in television. And it is much more accessible than TV. The disadvantages include a lack of in-depth analysis, a lack of pictures, and a short exposure time.

## WORKING WITH THE MEDIA: DEVELOPING A RELATIONSHIP

Before you begin flooding the news media with releases, stories, and invitations to news conferences, get to know the people involved.

Begin by developing a media file. It should include all media outlets in your area: TV and radio stations, newspapers (dailies, weeklies, and community papers), magazines, and wire services. The file can be elaborate, including coded mailing labels and a programming guide, or a simple card file (see Appendix 4B for an example). You can locate addresses and phone numbers in the yellow pages; for names, call the station or newspaper and ask for the ones you want.

Write letters of introduction to the contact people: news directors and editors. Use union stationery if possible. Include a union information sheet with the letter. It should be simple, one page, and typed. If the union has an informational brochure, attach it. The fact sheet should outline:

1. Name and number of your local union.

2. Name of your international union.

3. Local's address and phone number (if any).

4. Names of officers (who is the official spokesperson).

5. Who you represent: number of members, workplaces, occupations.

6. Background of the union: short history, contracts, etc.

7. Affiliation with the AFL–CIO (nationally/locally), if applicable.

Follow up the letter with a phone call. Ask if you can set up a visit along with your local union spokesperson. The visit will give you a chance to see their operations and meet face to face. You can find out about their deadlines, their procedures for filing stories and news releases, their editorial policy, and their format for public-service announcements. This visit may also give an opportunity to meet reporters who might be covering your stories. If you cannot arrange a meeting, let the contacts know that you are *always* available as a news contact.

Follow up the meeting or phone call. Send them notices of union meetings; invite them to attend. File news releases and give them story ideas. Keep them informed of what is going on in your local; do not wait for the crisis; make sure they know that you are alive.

## Relationships with Reporters

These are the people you will have the most contact with. Remember, they are workers and many are also union members. Also, understand that they do not have the final say as to what is printed or aired. Keep that in mind when your favorite story never sees the light of day. Their job is to get a story; you can help them to get it and at the same time develop a good working relationship. How they report the story can depend on how they were treated by you.

If the local newspaper or station has a labor reporter, contact that person in the same way you would the editors. If not, find out who covers labor stories. Meet with them, break down the social barriers. Invite them to union meetings to meet the members and officers. Give them a "feel" for what the union is all about. They do not know. Provide them with as much background information as possible. They want facts. If you provide them with facts, their stories will be more accurate and they will rely on you in the future as a source of information.

Be timely with your news. Learn their deadlines. Do not blame the reporter if you miss the deadline. Be fast, factual, frank, fair, and friendly.[32]

If you do not like a story that has been written or aired, let the reporter know first. If he or she will not correct it and you do not like the explanation, then you should complain to the editor or news director.

[32]"Involving the Media," *Citizens in Action.* League of Women Voters of Minnesota, 1982, p. 17.

If a story is not printed or aired, keep in mind that you are competing for space or time with other stories. You can call the reporter and ask why; but do not get angry. Keep the relationship going and maybe next time the local will get its coverage.

Finally, when reporters do good work, tell them; they will appreciate it. (See Appendix 4C for more suggestions for unions and reporters to improve news coverage.)

## News Releases

A news release is a good way to keep the media informed about union activities and its positions on issues. Send them out regularly. It can be the most important means of communications with the media. Send the same information to all media in the area, at the same time, and to the right person. Do not, however, expect many releases to be printed or broadcast. Editors reject six for every one they use. The local's release is competing with other events, reporters' stories, and wire services. Depending on circulation size or viewing or listening area, the media rejection rate may be even higher.

News releases can state a position (informational), announce an event (upcoming or past), or prepare the media for news.[33] If the release states a position on an issue, make sure it is timely. If you wait too long, the issue and the release will be old news, and therefore not newsworthy. One may want to call (after the editor should have received it) and ask if he or she needs any further information. If the release announces an event such as a news conference or rally, your contact person should receive it three to five days before the event. Follow up the mailing with a phone call to confirm its reception, to remind them of the event, and to fill in the details, preferably the night before or the morning of the event. See Appendix 4D for an example of a news release.

News releases should all have the same basic format. Radio and TV releases may be slightly different, as they may be read on the air. If there is special stationery with the union letterhead, use it. Otherwise, type the local name, number, and address on the top of an 8 by 11 sheet of paper. Under the letterhead in the *upper left*, type the date you are mailing it. Beneath it, put NEWS RELEASE, or FOR IMMEDIATE RELEASE, or FOR RELEASE ON OR AFTER (the date and time). In the *upper right*, type the name and phone number(s) of the union contact person(s). The contact person should be available to provide information at any time; so you may want to have two contact people. (One can reverse the format: Release on the right and contact person on the left. Just be consistent.)

Use a headline that catches the eye, or ear for radio. It should announce something.

The best format for the body of the release is the "inverted pyramid" or "collapsible copy" format. One should introduce the lead paragraph with a dateline: *where* and *when* your story is being released. Put the news (*who, what,*

---

[33] *The Media Book: Making the Media Work for Your Grassroots Group.* Committee to Defend Reproductive Rights of the Coalition for the Medical Rights of Women, San Francisco, Calif., 1981, p. 35.

*where, when, why,* and sometimes *how*) in the lead paragraph(s).[34] Supplement these facts with important details, and finish the body with a paragraph of miscellaneous information and a "for additional information" line. Often only the first paragraph is read, so that is where you want to put the news. In addition, if the editor is pressed for space or time, the last paragraphs will often be tossed out.

Follow these guidelines for writing news releases.

1. Single space your headings; double space the body. (Triple space for radio; it is easier to read on the air.)

2. Indent all paragraphs five spaces.

3. Keep your margins equal and wide (1½ inches for editing).

4. Leave space between your headings and the headline for editor's marks.

5. Center the headline above the body.

6. Do not hyphenate words at the end of a line; it makes it harder to read on the air.

7. Type on only one side of the paper.

8. Try to use only one page (two is the limit). If you use more than one:
   a. Never end a page in the middle of a sentence or paragraph.
   b. Put a "Slug line" (a description of release topic) in the upper left corner of the second page.
   c. Attach a "Fact Sheet" with additional information.

9. Indicate any enclosures
   a. Photographs may help get your story printed.
   b. Use slides with television news releases.
   c. Enclose a short printed or taped statement by the local president or other officer for radio.

10. End the release with ### or –30–.

See Appendix 4E for additional writing tips.

## Media Events: News Conferences and Other News Makers

*Suppose They Gave a War and Nobody Came?* is the title of a comic movie released in the 1960s. It is also the nightmare of a local union that plans a media event of some sort. The point: do not overuse media events; they can quickly become nonevents. Media events can, if properly planned, be successful in drawing the kind of attention you want to the local union or the issues your local wants addressed.

Before you plan the event, decide whether you should have it all. Is what you are going to announce newsworthy? Is it something new or has the media

---

[34]CWA Local PR Handbook, op. cit., pp. 59–60.

heard it before? Do not waste their time; they will not show up the next time. What may be newsworthy for a news release may not be a good reason to send reporters, cameras, and technicians. If you can communicate as effectively with a news release, there is no need to stage a news conference; save it for later. If the local is planning a rally, can you be sure of turning out a crowd? You cannot hide your lonely executive board from the TV camera. If the station is kind, it will not air the story at all. Media events are made for television. Your local can make the news.

A news conference gives a union the opportunity to make a statement and have many media hear it at the same time. It also gives the media the opportunity to have questions answered. Announce your news conference with a release to your contacts in the media. Let them know when and where the conference will be held and what it will be about. Give them enough information about the topic to pique their curiosity. Follow the instructions outlined in the previous section on news releases for format and follow-up phone calls. Time the conference so that it gets maximum media coverage. Monday and Friday are slow news days. If you want it to make the evening news on Channel 2, hold it between 10:00 a.m. and 12 noon so that the TV people can make their deadlines. If television is not your union's concern, anytime before 3 P.M. is okay. Hold the conference at the local union hall if possible. If the local does not have a hall or if the hall is not properly equipped for the conference, try holding it in a government building or in a centrally located hotel.

Prepare a media kit for reporters. It should contain details of the topic, names and biographies of the speakers, a copy of the original news release, and other general information about your union.

The union spokesperson should make a brief prepared statement to the assembled media. Allow about half an hour for group questions. Thank the media and show them out. Some may want to conduct individual interviews with the spokesperson; provide for them.

After the conference send post-event releases and kits to media who were not in attendance. Call them and let them know what they missed and offer to fill in the details. Next time they might show up. Appendix 4F has more guidelines on how to put together a news conference.

If you are planning an event other than a news conference and want media coverage, there are a number of things to keep in mind. Obviously, you want to let the media know in advance with a release. Remember what the different media need to make your event more interesting to them: TV wants visuals with action and people; radio wants sound, people speaking and crowd noise; and print media need photos and an angle for their stories. High-profile activities like rallies, fund-raisers, and debates draw the media. In addition, low-profile events like scholarship awards, testimonials, and retirement dinners can provide a human-interest angle. Appendix 4G is a partial list of events you might think of setting up, regardless of media coverage.

## Interviews

One can get good publicity with an interview. A reporter may call to ask for your union's response to an issue or incident (for example, passage or defeat of a piece of legislation affecting workers). Many union leaders pass up this opportunity to speak for fear that the media will distort their words. In some cases, their fears are well founded. Because of these experiences, unionists sometimes refuse to say *anything;* and the media reports one side of a story, with a side note: "Union officials were not available for comment."

You can use a media interview to get across a positive message. But there are some things you need to keep in mind.

1. Clear any *official* positions with the union. The local spokesperson may want to be the person who is interviewed.

2. Reporters want "inside" stories; avoid off-the-record comments.

3. Reporters are often skeptical; they will check the other side.

4. You do not have to answer a reporter's questions. Explain why you cannot; "no comment" can be damaging. But a lie is worse than "no comment."

## Bad Coverage

The union has a right to fair, honest, and accurate reporting. What can you do about what you think has been poor coverage or shabby treatment by the media? There are a number of actions you can take. Before you do, ask whether your response will help or only generate more bad publicity. Any action requires that you monitor the media to make sure that your assumption is correct.

As we outlined in Relationships with Reporters, if the local feels that a reporter wrote an incorrect or misleading story, let him or her know first. You can then carry your complaint further if you get no satisfaction from the newspaper or station. Some states have a News Council that meets periodically to hear complaints from individuals and groups about alleged poor news reporting. The council is usually a peer review group without any formal enforcement powers. But censure by this body can embarrass some reporters and media into doing a fairer, more accurate job in the future. Check to see if a council exists in your state.

## Letters to the Editor

One can send letters to the editor to respond to unfair coverage. If possible, have individual members write letters. They can identify themselves as union members or just as "concerned citizens." A newspaper may be more likely to print a letter from an individual than one from an official of a special-interest group. Readers can also identify better with the "little person" rather than a "union boss." Newspapers are also more likely to print a letter written in response to a previous article or letter than a letter stating an opinion. The purpose of the section is for rebuttal. The Letters to the Editor section is the most widely read section in most newspapers. Use it.

## Op-Ed Columns

Most newspapers have opposing editorial sections. They usually have resident and syndicated columnists and also guest columnists. If you want to speak out on or bring attention to a particular issue, submit a column. It may be printed if it is well written, brief, to the point, free from personal attacks, and factual.

## Paid Ads

You can also pay for advertising in the newspaper as a "public statement of protest." Paying for it may just "prove" to the public, however, that unions *do* have a lot of money.

## The Federal Communications Commission

The Federal Communications Commission (FCC) was established by the Communications Act of 1934. Its main purpose is to regulate the radio and television industry. Radio and TV, unlike print media, are granted exclusive licenses by the FCC to operate on certain air wave frequencies. They have exclusive jurisdiction over those frequencies. In return for granting the licenses to operate, the FCC required that stations broadcast in the "public interest." It set up three guidelines: the fairness doctrine, the personal attack rule, and the equal opportunities rule. The first two are of primary concern to unions.[35] The fairness doctrine originally said that licensees had a two-part obligation in their programming:

1. To broadcast controversial issues of public importance
2. To give time to different viewpoints on these issues.

The personal attack rule provides for rebuttal by persons whose characters are impugned by someone during the airing of a "controversial issue." In addition, stations were required to keep logs on all their public affairs programs. These rules ensured that stations remained responsive to the community in which they operated.

In 1984 the FCC "abolished its guidelines that required television stations to present a minimum amount of news and public affairs programs . . . (and) eliminated rules that required television stations to keep public records of the shows they air and to determine the programming needs of the communities in which they operate."[36] The FCC ruling wiped out the first half of the fairness doctrine requiring stations to offer public-affairs programs as a condition for

---

[35] The equal opportunities rule applies to "equal time" for political candidates.

[36] "FCC Abolishes TV-content Guidelines." *Minneapolis Star-Tribune,* June 28, 1984.

license renewal. It kept the second half intact: if stations *do* air public-affairs programs, they have to allow time for both sides of an issue. Despite the recent FCC ruling, TV stations claim that they will continue to offer public-affairs programs. Without public files, however, unions and individuals have no way to monitor a station's programs, other than videotaping all its shows.

Even without the FCC rules, if you feel that important issues are not being aired or only one side of an issue has been presented (in an editorial or on a public-affairs show), you can contact the public-affairs director or the station manager.[37] Call first, then send a letter. For the time being at least, stations will probably be responsive to an appeal.

---

## PUBLICITY: FREE AND PAID

## Public-affairs Programs

Most radio and television stations continue to offer public-affairs programming, even in the absence of FCC rules requiring them to. Station managers claim that they do so because public-affairs programs are "necessary to succeed in the marketplace . . ., a way you can demonstrate that you care about the community in which you are operating."[38] Regardless of the station's motives for airing public affairs programs, take advantage of them.

These programs include the following: talk shows, panels, round-table discussions, interviews, documentaries, short segments, or editorial comments (free speech messages). All of them are an opportunity for the union to speak out.

Write, then call the public-affairs directors of the local radio and television stations. Meet with them to find out what programs they have to offer. Bring along media kits for the public-affairs director and the producers and hosts of the shows. Give them ideas or issues that they can use for programs. Offer to have someone from the union appear on panels or in discussion groups or be interviewed on specific topics. Follow up the meeting. Try to arrange appearances on future shows with the producers of those programs. Be persistent: keep the union in their minds. Public-affairs issues are workers' issues: education, taxes, civil rights, and other community issues. These programs are an excellent chance to inform the public about where your union stands on the issues (see Appendix 4H).

### Public Television

Local public television (and radio) stations often broadcast public-affairs programs. Do not ignore them when you are looking for shows to appear on. In

---

[37] *Gaining Access to Radio and TV Time: A Union Member's Guide to the Broadcast Media.* American Federation of State, County & Municipal Employees, 1625 L Street NW, Washington, D.C. 20036, 1980, p. 12.

[38] Ron Handberg, general manager of WCCO-TV, Minneapolis–St. Paul, quoted in *Minneapolis Star-Tribune,* op. cit.

addition, since public TV and radio get part of their operating budgets from tax dollars, they are responsive to community groups. Check to see if there are any labor representatives on the advisory board of the local public television and radio stations.

## Public-service Announcements

A public-service announcement (PSA) is a short, free message aired by radio and television stations. They are noncontroversial: your union's appeal for strike support will not be aired as a PSA. But if the union is involved in any community projects, such as working with unemployed teen-agers or helping senior citizens, one can get a union's name over the airwaves or your union's logo in front of the camera.

You can produce your own PSAs (radio stations will accept cassette tapes; TV stations want broadcast-quality video tapes), or the station may help you produce programs at their facilities. Check out the possibilities. Some stations will accept a written PSA—similar to a press release, except in a conversational style—to be read over the air by an announcer or disk jockey. PSAs are run in 10-, 30-, and 60-second time slots. You should have one of each length for your message. Some PSAs run 10 seconds (25 words); some, 30 seconds (75 words); and some, 60 seconds (150 words). Television PSAs, using visuals (usually slides), run 10 seconds (12 words), 30 seconds (55 words), and 60 seconds (120 words).[39] Appendix 4I gives examples of both types.

## Paid Advertising

Paid advertising lets you control the content of your message—for a price. Prime-time network television slots are beyond the budget of a local union. International unions have used them for promotion. The International Ladies Garment Workers Union (ILGWU) sponsored a series of TV ads in the mid-1970s urging viewers to "Look for the Union Label." The United Auto Workers (UAW) and the Communications Workers of America (CWA) more recently ran a series of ads encouraging consumers to buy union-made products and union services. The American Federation of State, County and Municipal Employees (AFSCME) ran ads defending public services against government budget cuts in the early 1980s. These unions have also used paid advertisements in local television and radio to assist local organizing drives.

*Your* audience is local; use the media available to you. If you have extra money in your treasury, you might want to use television ads. Remember, however, not only will it cost to run the ad; it will cost to have someone produce it. One alternative is to produce them yourself, although quality may suffer. Another is to use ads produced by Labor's Institute of Public Affairs (LIPA). This nonprofit media arm of the AFL–CIO has produced a series of general

---

[39]CWA Local PR Handbook, op. cit., p. 92

pro-union ads that local unions and councils can add their name to and run on local television stations. Most locals, when they decide to use paid advertising, choose print or radio.

### Print

With this type of advertising, as with news, the message is in front of your audience for a longer period of time. One can also deal with more complicated issues in print. Major newspaper and magazine advertising may be too expensive to run full-page ads. Weekly community newspapers and other union newspapers offer space for ads also. Remember, your ads will have to compete with professionally made ones.

Before you begin developing an advertisement, call all the print media and ask for their rate cards. You will probably find one or more that fit your budget or message.

### Radio

Radio ads are much more affordable than television. You can also save costs by producing your own spots. Ask the radio station if they will help you produce your ad for a small fee or possibly for free. Radio spots are immediate; they reach large audiences at one time. If the projected audience is not listening at that time, however, your money will not be well spent. Try to have the station run your spot(s) when a maximum number of people will hear it (i.e., during drive time in the morning and evening). It may cost a little more, but you will get more for your money. Appendix 4J is an example of a radio spot.

Before you choose *any* type of paid advertising and spend the members' money, decide who you want to reach and for what purpose. Do you want people to buy locally made union goods? Do you want to organize workers at a certain plant? Do you want public support for your union's position for or against an issue? Do you want to begin an extensive media campaign with a high-profile kickoff? Is the goal important enough to merit the spending of union funds?

---

## PRODUCING YOUR OWN MEDIA

### The National Experience

In response to a poor public image, declining membership, and the availability of new technologies, international unions are beginning to produce their own media. Some of the same unions who have run paid advertising in the media are also leading the way in labor-produced media.

The UAW and AFSCME have their own television production facilities; AFSCME offers a Labor News Network to television stations around the country. The CWA produces a public TV and radio program, "Rewiring Your World," dealing with issues of the information age. The American Federation of

Teachers (AFT) has put together "Inside Your Schools," a combination of nationally and locally produced segments dealing with education issues that is broadcast over learning channels and public-access cable television. The Machinists' Union (IAM), the Steelworkers' Union (USWA), and the National Education Association (NEA) have used satellites and teleconferencing to talk with their rank and file membership from conventions and conferences.

The AFL-CIO funded Labor's Institute of Public Affairs (LIPA) to "get labor's viewpoint on emerging video technologies."[40] LIPA has produced a series entitled "American Works." Each show deals with a specific issue of interest to workers and the public; they are shown on local public television and cable stations. LIPA also issues bimonthly video bulletins for union members. Copies of these issues-oriented bulletins are distributed through state AFL–CIO offices and are available to affiliates for their own use or to be shown over public-access cable TV. LIPA also has test marketed a labor network called "Cableline" through cable systems in selected areas of the country.

## The Local Opportunity: Cable Television

Many of these recent developments have come with the spread of cable television. Cable is the newest medium, and it is estimated that by 1990, 62% of all TV-viewing households will receive it.[41] Cable television gives local unions additional opportunities for media coverage. In fact, *public access* gives local unions their best chance for positive local television coverage.

What is cable television and how is it different from broadcast television? Broadcast TV stations send their signal through the air and your antenna catches it. Cable sends its signal through coaxial cable to subscriber households. Only those households paying a monthly fee receive the signal.

Cable can send over 50 channels through one cable, and newer systems have the capacity for over 100. Only seven VHF broadcast channel frequencies can fit into the airwaves of a local area. Some cable systems have capacity for two-way communication: the subscriber can "talk back."[42]

The most crucial aspect of cable for local unions is community or public access. When private companies bid for local franchise, part of their agreement with the municipality *can* be to provide for local programming options. One of these options is public access. Public access generally gives individuals and community groups the opportunity to use the cable system's studio facilities and equipment to produce their own television programs. The finished products are then shown on the public-access channel(s) of the cable system to the cable subscriber households. Your union members can produce and broadcast their

---

[40] Pat Aufderheide, "Videofile: Look for the Union Label." *American Films,* October 1983, p. 76.

[41] CWA Local PR Handbook, op. cit., p. 80.

[42] Jennifer Stearns, *A Short Course in Cable.* United Autoworkers Union, 1982, Detroit, Mich., p. 9.

own programs. You provide the volunteers, the cable system provides training, and your volunteers are then "certified" to run the system's equipment.

Public-access programs vary in quality, depending on the skill, creativity, and perseverance of the producers. A number of local unions are currently producing their own public-access shows. In Pittsburgh, "Our Own Show" is put together by a steelworker. In New York City, members of several local unions broadcast a labor news show. In Fridley, Minnesota, Local 683 of the UAW offers "Focus on Labor," a look at workers and the issues affecting them. Some of these programs give the viewers the chance to call in, ask questions, and give opinions. All are produced by workers who volunteer their services.

Producing public-access programming demands an ongoing volunteer commitment by a core group of activists. Keep that in mind if you are thinking of beginning a public-access media program in your local union. One might want to involve more than one local of the union or invite other unions to participate in a joint effort. This way one can pool both volunteer effort and financial resources. Public access does not demand a lot of money if the cable system provides studio *and* portable equipment for on-location shooting. Some locals have spent money to purchase their own portapack equipment rather than relying on the availability of the cable system's equipment. This gives the local the flexibility of being able to shoot on location when incidents or events occur on the spur of the moment. The other major expense is lost time for one or more members who may have to cover an event during work time.

The use of public-access cable gives the union the chance to control the message that goes out to the audience. Obviously, the audience is smaller than that of broadcast television. But you can get on more often, and it will not cost you as much.

If you are interested in public-access programming, you should investigate the opportunity as soon as you can, if your community has a cable system and that system offers community-access programming. Many cable systems will argue for the reduction or elimination of public access if it is not being used by the community. Use it now if the community has it. If it does not, lobby your community in negotiating it into the next franchise contract. If the community is in the process of accepting bids for a cable franchise from various cable systems, join with other community groups to urge that public-access programming be a part of any franchise awarded. Appendix 4K is a checklist for cable television.

## ONE CHALLENGE LEADS TO OTHERS

The distortion of labor's image by the media reaches both local union members and the public environment of the union. If locals are to do better in the future in the areas of organizing the unorganized, internal organizing, and lobbying for prolabor legislation, the external public-relations battle has to be waged—and won. Union officers cannot wait for someone else to meet this challenge for them (i.e., the parent union) because the resources and power are at the local level. Local union leaders must thrust their committees into the world of television and radio in an effort to change community opinion until such time as central bodies, state federations, and the national federation and/or coalitions can adopt and implement a ground-up media policy.

This challenge, then, must be followed by a second one: local union education committees must be activated to back up the true image of labor with meaningful programs. Membership goals and those of the union should be the focus of these programs. Favorable impressions must be followed by concrete facts and skills, all the while allowing each member to bring his or her own special talents and creativity to these experiences. Chapter 5 is about this challenge.

## DISCUSSION QUESTIONS

1. Do you think that the media treat organized labor in an objective way? Give *specific* examples of local or national media coverage to support your answer.

2. Your local union has decided that its public image is a poor one. The executive board has authorized the Public Relations (Media) Committee to begin a program to improve that image. Put together an outline for such a program:

   What your goal is.

   What image you want to present.

   Who you want to reach.

   What local media you might use.

   How much it will cost.

   Be specific

3. The state legislature is considering a right-to-work bill, H.F. 123. Your local union opposes the legislation. Write up a news release that reflects your union's position on right-to-work and why. Use the format you learned in this chapter.

4. Your local newspaper recently printed an editorial criticizing unions. It said that:

   Unions strike too much.

   Union leaders are out of touch with the rank-and-file membership.

   Many unions are corrupt.

   Unions cause inflation.

   Unions are no longer necessary, as management is more enlightened today than in the past.

   Write either a *letter to the editor* or an *opposing editorial* rebutting the newspaper's position.

5. What type of community program(s) is your local union involved in? Choose one and, using the model format for a public service announcement, put together two PSAs, one for radio and one for television. You can choose time lengths of 10, 30, or 60 seconds to highlight your union's involvement in community activities.

6. Your local has authorized the Media Committee to begin production of a labor-oriented public-access cable television show. The cable system is offering you the time slot of 7:30 to 8:00 P.M., Monday, Thursday, and Saturday (the same weekly show is broadcast three times a week). You will be committed to producing weekly shows. Knowing who your audience is, come up with as many programming ideas as possible. Remember, you have access to equipment and volunteers, but you do not have a lot of money to spend.

## GLOSSARY

**angle:** An approach or way of looking at something; every story has one or more angles.

**assignment editor:** The person in the newsroom who decides what stories reporters will cover during the day.

**budget:** (1) **Time budget:** the budget that TV and radio work on; (2) **space budget:** the budget that a newspaper works on; (3) **financial budget:** the budget that your media committee works on.

**cable television:** A television system that sends its signals through cables instead of over the airwaves.

**editorial department:** The department of the newspaper that covers *both* hard news and editorials.

**fairness doctrine:** The FCC rule that provided for (1) programs in the public interest and (2) time for different viewpoints.

**feature story:** A news story that may have a different angle, or more angles than a hard news story; it also may get more time or space (e.g., a feature story on the hardships of the striking miners).

**media:** The voices of mass communication: (1) *electronic media* are television, radio, and movies; (2) *print media* are newspapers, magazines, and books. Media may also be classified as *entertainment* or *news*.

**media file:** A file (a card or more elaborate) kept on the local media: Who is the contact person at each, who is the audience, and how reliable is coverage? It can help you to see if your stories are being covered and by whom.

**news director:** The person in a radio or TV station who runs the news operation. In radio, he or she may function as an assignment editor.

**news release:** A printed paper issued to the news media that can state a position on an issue, announce a conference or event, or prepare the media for news.

**op-ed column:** A column in the editorial section of a newspaper or magazine that gives the reader an opportunity to respond to an editorial that has already been printed.

**public access:** Programming on a local cable system that is produced and controlled by the community.

**public-affairs programs:** A program aired by a TV or radio station dealing with issues in the "public interest." It can be a talk show, a documentary, a round-table discussion, etc.

**public-service announcement:** A free message aired by TV and radio announcing events or programs (e.g., a community calendar or charitable or civic programs).

**reporter:** The person from a newspaper, magazine, or television or radio station that covers events and news stories. The beat reporter from a TV station may or may not write his or her own stories.

## ADDITIONAL RESOURCES

*American Labor,* "Lights, Camera, Action: A Guide to Labor-related Slide-shows, Films, and Videotapes," no. 25/26.

*American Labor,* "A Local Union Guide to Using the Media," no. 22.

Benjamin M. Compaine, ed., *Who Owns the Media?* New York: Harmony Books, 1979.

Donna W. Cross, *Media Speaks: How Television Makes Up Your Mind.* New York: New American Library, 1983.

John Downing, *The Media Machine.* London: Pluto Press Ltd., 1980.

Robert D. Kahn, "Cable Programming: More Messages from the Medium," *Technology Review,* January 1983, pp. 22–26.

*Local Union Tool Box: Building Community Support for Union Organizing and Political Action.* Portland, Ore.: International Woodworkers of America, January 1982.

Public Media Center, *Strategies for Access to Public Service Advertising,* Public Media Center, 25 Scotland Ave., San Francisco, Calif. 94113.

## APPENDIX 4A
## SAMPLE MEDIA PROGRAM BUDGET

*BUDGET FOR NEWS COVERAGE*

| | |
|---|---|
| Media kits, general | $ _____ |
| Special event packet | $ _____ |
| Production of news release | $ _____ |
| Envelopes | $ _____ |
| Postage | $ _____ |
| Phone calls | $ _____ |
| Optional photoreproduction | $ _____ |
| News conference | $ _____ |
| Coffee and doughnuts | $ _____ |
| Room rental | $ _____ |
| Total | $ _____ |

*Reproduced with permission from the Committee to Defend Reproductive Rights, 1981, pp. 9, 29, and 39.*

## APPENDIX 4B
## MEDIA CARD FILE

```
_____              _____
(Station/Press)              (Phone)

_____              _____
(Address)                    (Contact Person)

                             _____
                             (Audience/Readers)

_____
(Broadcast/Deadline Schedule)

Comments: _____

_____
```

## APPENDIX 4C
### SUGGESTIONS FOR REPORTERS AND UNIONS

Reporters can:

Learn more about unions and the system of collective bargaining and its relationship with the economy

Avoid the "strike syndrome": most contracts are settled without them.

Treat the labor beat as importantly as business, city hall, courts, or crime.

Spend more time on stories, give stories more time on a broadcast, go beyond the "scoop."

Try to be objective; at least be balanced: get the other side, get facts from additional outside sources.

Realize that negotiations is a closed system, and balance that with the public right to know.

Be accurate.

Remember that union officers are elected and contracts are ratified by the members.

Avoid cliches like union "demands" and company "offers," "Big Labor," "Union Bosses," etc.

*Do not* report initial proposals as if they were final offers.

*Do* report stories on workers and their unions.

Unions can:

Accept the fact that the media have an obligation to cover contract negotiations in the public interest.

Accept the fact that the press will report a story even if union *or* management refuses to talk.

Have someone available to answer and give out information to the media during contract negotiations.

Let the reporters and editors know what the issues are in contract negotiations.

Avoid "using" the media to bring pressure on the other side too often; avoid negotiating in the media.

Understand the "nature of the beast": deadlines, scoops, television's visual impact and two-minute stories, the difference between reporters and editorialists.

Understand what is interesting to the public; do not overestimate the importance of your negotiations to the public; put yourself in the reporter's shoes.

Do not expect the media to help you resolve your problems.

Understand that the media is a business: ratings/circulation and advertisements keep it afloat.

Recognize that unions have *never* been popular.

Put out good news, too, not just announcements of strikes and rallies.

Explain the union's functions to news reporters.

Understand that reporters generally do not have a conscious bias.

Provide stories or angles for stories to reporters.

## APPENDIX 4D

## SAMPLE NEWS RELEASE

NEWS RELEASE

Clear Identification

INTERNATIONAL CHEMICAL WORKERS UNION, AFL-CIO, LOCAL UNION 000

1234 SOUTH MAIN STREET, KENT, OHIO 44240          216-678-4657

Time & Date — FEBRUARY 7, 1982          CONTACT: RALPH DARROW — Contacts
FOR IMMEDIATE RELEASE          MURVIN PERRY

(Headline)

The News! — Local 000 of the International Chemical Workers Union, which holds collective bargaining rights with the XYZ Chemical Co. plant in Kent, will award two $500 scholarships to graduates of Kent Roosevelt High School this year, the union announced today.

When Where By Whom — The scholarship plan worked out between the local's Executive Board and the Kent School System, was unanimously approved by the local's members during a meeting last Thursday at the Kent Labor Temple.

How — Murvin Perry, president of Local 000, said all Kent Roosevelt High School seniors who are in need of financial aid to further their educations are eligible for consideration for the awards. Winners will be chosen by writing an essay entitled, "How Labor Unions Benefit Our Community," Perry said. Judges for the awards will be three members of the local union and two members of the high school faculty.

Why (And a Good Way to Work in a Plug) — "Our ICWU local union is deeply concerned over the failure of the Reagan Administration to keep federal scholarship funds in its budget," Perry said, "so the members of Local 000 contributed their own money to make it possible for two students to attend college in the fall.

"In addition, the members of Local 000 who live and work in this

# # #

Add Another Page If Needed

Reproduced with permission from Frank Ritzinger, Director of Public Relations, International Chemical Workers Union, AFL-CIO, Ohio, "Sample News Release" originally published in *The Image: A Guide For ICWU Local Union Reporters.*

## APPENDIX 4E
### WRITING TIPS FOR NEWS RELEASES

Use the guidelines outlined in Chapter 10. Your release should be readable and understandable.

Be concise.

Use short sentences and paragraphs.

Avoid technical jargon.

Avoid "weasel" words; use positive, action words.

Avoid acronyms; if you use them, explain them.

Avoid using "our" or "we" unless you are stating your union's official position.

Use quotes; "quotable quotes" for radio and television.

For television and radio:

Write in a conversational style; it makes for easier reading and listening.

Spell people's names phonetically so announcers will pronounce them correctly.

Make sure your spelling is correct.

Proofread for typographical errors.

## APPENDIX 4F
### GUIDELINES FOR NEWS CONFERENCES

**Physical Setting**

Make sure the room is large enough to accommodate the anticipated number of media people, but not too large: the room will look better crowded than empty on TV.

Set up a table with a lectern in the front of the room.

Put your union logo on the front of the lectern or prominently in back of the table.

Make sure there is room for news microphones on the lectern.

Make legible name cards for the people who will be sitting at the table.

Set up charts, graphs, and other visual aids off to one side of the table. They can be effective, if seen.

Set up enough chairs facing the table for the media.

Set up a media table with press kits.

Have coffee and rolls available: you do not have to offer lunch.

Equipment

Make sure the room is well lit, or provide additional lights.

Make sure there are phones readily available.

Have a copy machine nearby.

Check the sound; will you need a microphone?

Bring your own tape recorder to tape the conference.

## Format

Greet the media people as they come in; give them their name tags and media kits.

Start the news conference by introducing yourself and by giving a background statement.

Introduce the union spokesperson, who will make an official statement. Others at the head table may be available to answer reporters' questions.

Run a controlled question-and-answer period.

When this period begins to slow down, ask for one or two more questions; do not let it drag on.

Thank the media and usher them out.

Provide for individual interviews with the union spokesperson for interested media.

## APPENDIX 4G
## IDEAS FOR NEWS CONFERENCES
## AND MEDIA EVENTS

Negotiations impasse/strike votes

Major political endorsements/political activities

Statements on major legislative issues

Demonstrations or rallies or protests

Announce the results of a poll or survey

Announce establishment of special project or program

Announce an organizing drive or an organizing success

Announce a major arbitration award

Localize a national news story

Take a position on an environmental or safety and health issue

Hold a workshop, conference, forum, debate, or mock hearing

Plan an activity as part of a local or national celebration or event (e.g., Martin Luther King's Birthday)

Hold a contest, a race, a free concert, or other public event

Give a scholarship, an award, a testimonial, a retirement dinner

Promote officer elections, state conventions

Participate or run a community program, fund raiser, or charity

Dedicate new union headquarters

Give a labor history tour

Bring in a nationally known speaker

## APPENDIX 4H
PUBLIC-AFFAIRS PROGRAMS

### Getting Ready

Find out who your audience is; ask the producer.

What point do you want to get across to the audience?

Anticipate questions you might be asked.

Be prepared to use the questions to get to your point.

Anticipate trap questions.

Role play or rehearse the show.

Keep your facts straight.

Know your topic.

### On the Program

You are speaking to an audience in addition to the interviewer and the other guests.

Keep cool unless anger is appropriate; control it.

Deflect hostile questions.

Do not worry if you stammer or stumble, you are not a professional; take your time.

Do not answer with a plain *yes* or *no;* it confuses the interviewer and causes a dead silence.

On the other hand, do not ramble on with your answer; be short and to the point.

Make sure the questions bring out your main point; if not, you take the lead.

Enunciate your words and do not slouch.

Dress conservatively and neatly: wear blue not red; avoid jewelry and short socks.

## APPENDIX 4I
## PUBLIC SERVICE ANNOUNCEMENTS

### *Sample PSA for Radio*

From:                                          Loon River Central Labor Union

Wendy Miller                          For use Sunday, March 11 through
Chairperson, Media Committee              Saturday, March 17, 1986

447 MacArthur Ave.
Loon River, ME 09000
(207) 222-4444

### *When Is Retirement Not Retirement?*

Time:     30 seconds

Words:    85

ANNCR:   Over 100,000 residents of our state over age 55 live below the poverty line. This figure includes many who receive Social Security benefits. For those retirees who are able to work, the Loon River Central Labor Union can help. Under a federal program administered by the Central Labor Union, retirees can earn $200 to $300 a month working with a public service or nonprofit agency for 20 hours a week. To find out if you qualify, call the Loon River Central Labor Union at 222-4444.

### *Sample PSA for Television*

From:                                          Loon River Central Labor Union

Wendy Miller                          For use Sunday, March 11 through
Chairperson, Media Committee              Saturday, March 17, 1986

447 MacArthur Ave.
Loon River, ME 09000
(207) 222-4444

## When Is Retirement Not Retirement?

Time:    30 seconds

Words:    85

| Video | Audio |
|-------|-------|
| Slide 1 (Elderly standing in cheese line) | Over 100,000 residents of our state over age 55 live below the poverty line. This figure includes many who receive Social Security benefits. |
| Slide 2 (Retirees working in office) | For those retirees who are able to work, the Loon River Central Labor Union can help. Under a federal program administered by the Central Labor Union, retirees can earn $200 to $300 a month working with a public service or nonprofit agency for 20 hours a week. |
| Slide 3 (Union logo with phone number) | To find out if you qualify, call the Loon River Central Labor union at 222–4444. |

# APPENDIX 4J
## SAMPLE PAID RADIO SPOT

### Script For 60-Second Radio Spot

| | |
|-------|-------|
| Announcer: | Next year, state workers will have a chance to negotiate a new contract with the state. When that time comes, we want a union representing us that won't settle for less. |
| CWA Supporter: | I'm proud of being a state worker. But no one is proud to work for less. |
| CWA Supporter: | When I go to the supermarket or to the gas station, I don't get a discount because I'm a state worker. With CWA, I'll be able to get the kind of cost-of-living increase that I need to support myself and my family. |
| CWA Supporter: | I want a strong union that will make the state respect us. CWA bargains with Bell Telephone, the largest corporation in the world. If it can bargain with them, it can bargain with the state. |
| CWA Supporter: | CWA has won decent wages and cost-of-living pay for city and county workers. And I think it can do the same for us, too. |
| Announcer: | If you're a state worker, sign up now for CWA and a PERC election this fall. With CWA, we'll get a good |

contract next year. That's CWA. The Communications Workers of America. We won't settle for less.

*Reproduced with permission from* CWA Local PR Handbook: A Guide for Telling and Selling Our Union's Story, *Public Affairs Department, Communications Workers of America, AFL–CIO, p. 99.*

## APPENDIX 4K
## CABLE CHECKLIST[43]

1. Is there a cable system in your community?  _____ yes  _____ no
   If so, what is the status of cable?
   _____ franchising
   _____ operating
   _____ refranchising

2. Is there more than one cable system?  _____ yes  _____ no
   (If so, each system should be evaluated.)

3. What franchising stage is it in?  _____

4. What companies are seeking the franchise?  _____

5. Has labor been approached by companies? the local government?
   _____ yes  _____ no

6. Which local authority does the system operate under?  _____

7. Does the company have other systems in the area?  _____ yes  _____ no

8. Who is the system manager?  _____

9. How many employees does the system have?  _____

10. How many years does the franchise cover?  _____

11. Who regulates cable?  Local government _____
    Nonprofit corporation _____  Other _____

12. How many channels are there?  _____

13. Are there access channels and if so how many?  _____

14. Who manages the access channels?  _____

15. Are there access studios for the community?  _____ yes  _____ no

[43] *Labor Communications Resource Service,* "Cable Television: A Guide for Labor," p. 75. Reprinted with permission of Labor Institute of Public Affairs.

16. Is there cable equipment for the community? Is training available?

    _____ yes    _____ no

17. Has labor been asked to participate in the cable system?

    _____ yes    _____ no
    _____ On a governing board
    _____ Given air time
    _____ Other

18. Is labor included in the definition of access programs?

    _____ yes    _____ no

19. Are there free hook-ups for the community? For the local labor halls or the central federation?    _____ yes    _____ no

20. Have problems with the local cable system been in the papers?

    _____ yes    _____ no

If you have any additional questions about unions and cable television, you can write:

Labor Institute of Public Affairs
815 Sixteenth Street NW
Suite 206
Washington, D.C. 20006

or

National Federation of Local Cable
    Programmers (NFLCP)
906 Pennsylvania Avenue SE
Washington, D.C. 20003

# CHAPTER 5

# Strengthening Your Local through Education

American unions have a long history of worker and labor education—a history filled with successes, failures, controversies, and high hopes. Labor education has been decried as subversive of the established order, heralded as the tool for ending corruption within unions, lauded as the means of achieving harmony between labor and management, and accused of fostering union elitism. With a tradition running the spectrum from vocational education to liberal arts, from grievance writing to CPR classes, from the study of economics to remedial reading, local unions have a vast field of topics from which to choose, resources on which to call, and experience both good and bad to draw on in fashioning an education program suited to their own needs.[1]

There are, however, many barriers to the development of active local education programs. A chief barrier is the belief in the efficacy of "hand-me-down" or on-the-job learning of union skills. There is a great deal to be said in favor of passing on union skills from one generation of officers to the next. That is how local union traditions and culture are created and preserved. But the local can suffer from an exclusive reliance on tradition and inherited knowledge. Every new leader may want and indeed need the advice and assistance of experienced old-timers to help with the crises as well as the day-to-day running of the union, but in today's hostile political and economic environment very few locals can

---

[1] See Richard E. Dwyer, *Labor Education in the United States: An Annotated Bibliography.* Metuchen, N.J., Scarecrow Press, 1977. This bibliography has an introductory essay on the development and structure of both union and university/college labor education.

afford a long learning or break-in period for new leaders. Locals are also ill served by a closed office cadre which handpicks a successor and concentrates on educating a single successor for office. Far-seeing locals provide broad education for active members to begin developing a new generation of potential leaders long before they may be called on to take union office.

Local unions today need to call on the enthusiasm and intelligence of active members armed with up-to-date information from formal labor education classes covering the range of both union and personal skills vital to the effective functioning of the local union. Economic conditions, labor law, protective legislation, government and agency regulations, and management styles are changing too rapidly to allow exclusive reliance on the old ways of doing things. An active education program can keep officers and members alike abreast of these changes.

A second barrier to local union education lies in the difficulties of drawing members away from the electronic entertainment media. As if old-style television were not enough, an education program must now compete with home video players and the 24-hour sports and movies of cable television. Union leaders should not underestimate this competition just because they themselves may watch very little television. Many of the target audiences of union education programs watch television several hours a week. An anti-television-watching campaign by a local union might assist members in breaking a habit that can injure their personal and family lives as well as their civic and union involvement.[2] The local union newsletter could publish articles and tips on the dangers of too much television and the ways to liberate oneself from it.

For all the sophistication and allure of the electronic screen, it cannot (yet) offer one thing labor education can offer: the chance to participate oneself—to talk back, to get involved, to be heard, to have a voice, to make a difference. This aspect of labor education is vital not only in attracting participants but in strengthening the lives of local unions and in building members' skills for broader participation in community and national politics.

Labor education in its broadest sense, then, serves not only the local union but the cause of democracy in our nation. It is one way to reach adults who may have been educationally underprivileged and to provide them with alternative sources of information and new perspectives on industrial relations, economics, politics, and culture.

Labor education has a bright future. It can, if skillfully planned, tie in to the popularity that adult learning programs of many stripes have attained in recent years. Community colleges, night and weekend programs at universities, "elder hostel" summer learning programs, public library classes—their growth testifies

---

[2]For a step-by-step guide, see Joan A. Wilkins, *Breaking the TV Habit.* New York: Charles Scribner's Sons, 1982.

to the desire of adults to continue their learning lifelong. Local unions can and must tap that interest.

This chapter discusses the connections between effective local union leadership and education, outlines the steps in developing an education program for a local union, and considers some of the problems and issues that can arise for locals as they develop and maintain their education program.

## LABOR EDUCATION AND UNION LEADERSHIP

As our chapters on leadership theory and power management pointed out, two aspects of leadership are expert and information power. How can local unionists, who will ordinarily not have degrees or formal training in law, economics, or industrial relations, acquire the information and expertise they need to serve their organizations? Although unions, community colleges, and universities have long offered officer leadership schools, it is probable that the great majority of union leaders at the local level continue to rely on a combination of on-the-job training and "hand-me-down" learning to gain the basic skills they need to carry out their functions in office. When special needs arise, they rely on outsiders for assistance—particularly on lawyers. International union services, ranging from excellent to nonexistent, are frequently inadequate or not called on because of distance and assumed inaccessibility. The trust or at least familiarity that comes from personal acquaintance can lead local union leaders to prefer the local lawyer to the far more expert and sympathetic help available from a distant international union headquarters—or even a not-so-distant union representative. The high degree of local autonomy which distinguishes American unions from their European counterparts, while encouraging democracy and participation at the local level, works against great reliance on international/national union assistance.

In the smaller cities where industrial development is occurring, reliance on local "experts" for advice can be detrimental to local unions. To rely on "crisis" learning—a hodgepodge combination of asking old-timers and/or local "experts" plus on-the-job experience—to guide the local through bargaining, strikes, arbitration hearings, and contract administration is a sign of a poorly managed local union. A well-run local should have a long-term plan to educate its leaders, develop contacts and information sharing with carefully selected local and state-wide resources, and to use international union services. Such a plan can bring to the local a rich store of expertise to replace crisis learning with systematic continuous education for the daily life of the local union—as well as its crises. Union power is enhanced. Union and personal goals become more obtainable. The local, as an *open natural system,* can better meet its challenges.

## GOALS OF AN EDUCATION PROGRAM

Each local union has its own educational goals; however, these may not always be articulated clearly. Frequently stated goals cite labor education as important to:

Prepare local officials for contract bargaining and contract administration.

Increase member identification with the union.

Educate members on union history, goals, and policies.

Strengthen and broaden the power base of leadership.

Make possible a greater delegation of tasks from top officers to committees or other officers.

Inform members and officers on current labor issues, including politics and economic developments.

Encourage and prepare members for more active participation in the life of their communities.

Allow members to see their dues money spent for a service they can benefit from.

## DEVELOPING A LOCAL EDUCATION PROGRAM

### The Education Committee

Every local should have a special committee to coordinate the education program of the union. This committee has as its main duty to ascertain the educational needs and wishes of the local union and to plan and carry out programs.

Membership on the committee should represent a cross section of local members or interest groups. The prime criteria for membership, however, are interest and willingness to commit time and energy to the work of the committee. The local union president or some other top officer should sit on the committee *ex officio*, as should a member from other key union committees, such as the political action or grievance committee. This can keep the education committee's activities focused on the ongoing needs of the local.

The education committee must keep its finger on the pulse of the local, determining needs before they become crisis areas. This requires close coordination with the executive board and officers of the local. As problems arise, it falls to the education committee to ask: Can education help here? How? Some committees have taken surveys of particular target groups (stewards, rank and file, women, members nearing retirement) to determine their educational needs and wishes. The committee may also use the prebargaining member questionnaire to pinpoint areas where the membership or stewards may be helped by education.

The education committee should develop a file of resource and contact people who can provide education or assistance for the membership. Individual committee members can serve as "talent scouts" for the local—identifying speakers, films, or agencies that can be considered for educational events. An active committee, which advertises its programs and existence, will soon begin receiving member requests and ideas for programs.

The authors are aware that locals which lack education committees can, and often do, have frequent classes and speakers, arranged by the president, business agent, chief steward, or other primary leader. But it is rare that such locals have an ongoing systematic education *program*. Planning for education requires more time and concentration than a busy union leader can often find. The designation of even one or two other members with a special education assignment is vital to the maintenance of an ongoing program and can greatly increase the local's effectiveness in educating its members.

## Resources for Educational Programs

Some local unions have regular budgets for educational purposes—sometimes running to 20% or even 50% of their total annual budget (depending on the extent to which union conferences are labeled as "education"). Much can be done with generous funding, but lack of an education budget should not deter programming, for resources that cost the local nothing are available.

The major and first educational resource of any local union should be the national or international union with which it is affiliated. Even the smaller internationals have resource people, films, and contacts with other groups or agencies that can be used by the locals. Of the larger internationals, nearly 40 have education departments. These may have entire education programs mapped out for local unions, and may provide the materials and even teaching staff.

A second resource lies in the broader labor movement. The national AFL–CIO education department and the special trades departments of the confederation have a tremendous array of educational possibilities. The state AFL–CIO bodies, the city central bodies, and even local labor alliances or councils supported by unions not affiliated to the AFL–CIO also often have education programs. Each of these should be explored for their activities, educational materials, film libraries, speakers' bureaus, and so forth. On a local level, two or more unions occasionally link up to share the costs and benefits of a particular program.

A third resource for local unions interested in developing an education program lies in the community college or university labor education programs. The international or the state federation of labor can provide union contacts and advice on when and how to best utilize these outside labor education services. They may be great sources of expertise and may have considerable sympathy and commitment to labor movement goals. Most of them will have labor advisory committees. Talk to these committee members as well as the staff of the labor program to get a sense of the areas of expertise and the philosophical direction of the program.

Some of the programs award academic degrees for workers in labor studies programs offered through evening or weekend courses. Most provide noncredit classes or conferences on campuses and/or in communities with open enrollment or by contract with a single union. These centers would be happy to add your local to their mailing list.

These centers can be important sources of help and advice for local unions in planning an education program. They can provide teachers and materials, but can also assist education committees in planning their own programs, which local officers then teach. Most of the centers will have to charge a fee to put on a program for the local, but consultation will probably be free. If a local is affiliated to a city central body, that organization may invite the labor education center in to put on a program, and the costs can be shared by all affiliated locals. University and college centers have contacts with other resources on campus that may be of assistance to the local's educational activities.

## Designing Programs

Careful planning of union programs is vital to their success, and the education committee can become a local repository of information on program planning. Interest in education may dwindle away if programs are hastily thrown together, boring, perceived as irrelevant, or so poorly publicized and promoted that attendance is scant. It is far better for the local to have only two or three high-quality programs per year than poorly planned monthly programs that give the education effort a bad name. Good planning includes good timing of topics: Have positions been newly filled or created? Then offer a school for the office-holders. Is bargaining four or five months away? Perhaps a school on bargaining skills or particular bargaining issues would be appropriate. Tie economical- and political-issue schools to political campaigns. Communication skills classes may be interesting prior to local union elections. Parliamentary procedure classes could be offered in preparation for union or political conventions.

An exciting program can be put on by anyone who plans the session with an eye to building in participation by the members. If a film is used, be sure to plan a discussion period afterward where people can react and share insights they have gained. The key to an interesting program is to avoid the passive "audience" to an "event." Remember that the active participation and involvement of all attendees is the best attraction your program can offer to lure members away from the noninvolvement of their television sets.

Integrating such considerations into program design is the heart of planning. A systematic approach to planning starts with identifying a program's intended audience.

## Target Groups

In deciding on topics and types of programming, the local must first establish the target group(s) of the program. Can the local afford a specialized curriculum appealing to the interests of various local subgroups? (If not, can it cooperate with another labor group to do so?) What topics and formats would work for those groups? Some of the groups with special education interests might be:

New members

Women

Rank-and-file members

Stewards

Officers

Single parents

Non-English-language speakers

Workers nearing retirement

Retirees

How does one target one of these groups? First, the program should be open to all members, regardless of the group targeted; the targeting comes rather in adjusting the topic, format, and publicity to the special needs of the group for which the program is intended. New members (as well as old!) will benefit from information on the structure and history of the union *and* of the local, on the contract, the steward system, and other basics. But they may be harder to get out to the union hall than longer-term members, and it might be a good idea to approach them with a one-on-one "let's go together" recruitment and publicity effort. With the target group clearly in mind, the rest of the planning falls more easily into place.

## Topics

Choice of topic depends on the perceived needs and priorities of the local union, on the local's views on the role and importance of service activities for members, and on the union treasury. A small local with a limited treasury may feel that it can only afford an occasional steward training class; a local with a huge geographic area may have such rare or poorly attended union meetings that it may opt for correspondence courses.

Often one feels that the choice of a program topic is limited by the people available to teach it. For example, there may not be available any speakers on retirement planning who seem suitable for a labor group. Yet there are excellent materials available (see for example the pamphlets put out by the IAM&AW),[3]

[3]As an example of the kind of help international unions can provide local union education committees, see the two booklets on retirement planning published by the IAM&AW, "Guide for Older Workers and Retired Members Programs" and "Guide to Pre-retirement Programs," for program planners. The latter includes tips for discussion leaders, questionnaires to hand out to participants, and an evaluation form to solicit participant reactions to the program.

and perhaps someone from the local would be able to develop enough expertise to lead a basic course on retirement planning without calling on outside experts. There may not be access to a speaker on labor history; but there are several films, including the classic *Inheritance,* available through the AFL–CIO film library, many international offices, and at most labor education centers, which can form the basis for an interesting evening's entertainment and discussion. With the wide variety of materials, films, and videotapes currently available, no topic can be considered completely inaccessible.

Topic areas for courses may be broken down into the following broad categories:

1. *Union skills:* collective bargaining issues and skills, steward training and grievance handling, arbitration preparation and presentation, safety and health hazard recognition and monitoring, labor law, union administration (e.g., financial officer training), union management, and union leadership.

2. *Political/economic education:* political skills/issues, basic economic theory, and state and national government economic policy.

3. *Special practical skills or arts:* do-it-yourself classes (e.g., auto mechanics, CPR).

4. *Remedial basic education:* reading and writing improvement, basic arithmetic.

5. *Liberal arts:* history, literature, and so on.

6. *Vocational training or retraining.*

Lest some of these topics sound farfetched for a local union education program, it should be pointed out that European unions (and some American unions) have long been involved in making vocational training available to their members and have for years taken a broad cultural view of their education activities, both in making so-called "high culture" more accessible to workers and in developing channels of cultural expression open to workers themselves as creators/performers.[4]

This list of topics prompts a couple of comments. Union skills are usually regarded as most essential to a local's effectiveness and will doubtless have the highest priority in program planning. Courses or speakers on politics and economics are common, if mainly in the form of a union speaker or political officeholder, but not commonly regarded as part of the whole education package

[4]One of our authors once heard a magnificent concert performance of Beethoven's Seventh Symphony courtesy of the Austrian metal- and mine-workers union, which had purchased a batch of tickets for its members. And she sat in on a planning session of a Swedish metalworkers local union discussing a workplace photo exhibit of workers' impressions of their jobs.

of the local. We suggest that they are and should be a part of the entire educational program, with strong involvement by the education committee, which can assist in planning the event. Practical skills of the do-it-yourself variety are offered in response to member interest or demand. These may be peripheral to the more serious business of local union education, but they share with the last three topics on the list a conception of the local union attempting to meet broader social and cultural interests and needs of members. For locals that want to play more active social roles in the lives of members and their families, such educational programming should be of special interest.

### Format of Program

The length, time, requirements, and place of any particular course are what we call its format. Here the range is wide and if broadly conceived reveals the nearly limitless possibilities for local union education. A partial list of varying formats of labor education programs includes:

1. Films shown at rank-and-file or stewards meetings or at the workplace at lunch or break.

2. Guest speakers at any function.

3. Discussions in a structured setting, sparked by a speaker, film, or pre-assigned reading.

4. Correspondence courses lasting several weeks or even months, arranged through a college or university.

5. Study circles promoted by the education committee, involving small groups of members meeting for a specified number of weeks to read and discuss materials on subjects mutually agreed on. (In Sweden, the local could get a government grant to pay for an expert discussion leader and course materials.)

6. Evening classes of two hours, held in the union hall, lasting for several weeks.

7. All-day Saturday classes lasting six hours with lunch provided by the local.

8. Residential courses lasting one to several weeks at a university or a union school such as the UAW Black Lake center or the IAM&AW's Placid Harbor facility.

9. Short noncredit courses of one to five days at a university labor education service sponsored by the university or by a district or regional union body.

10. Credit programs at a college or university with night or day-time classes lasting 12 to 16 weeks.

With regard to requirements, "education" does not necessarily mean tests or grading (although it probably will in the credit programs). It does mean reading, commitment of time and energy, and a willingness to discuss new ideas and to be challenged in the old ones. Publicity efforts for courses must reassure members that school-connected anxieties will not be reborn in these educational activities.

### Teaching Methods and Teachers

Whether the local uses outside instructors or its own officers and members to teach classes, it is important that their teaching methods be suited to a sophisticated adult audience that brings to the "classroom" a large body of information, experience, and (let's face it) prejudice and misinformation. It is the duty of the education committee to assure that teachers address this audience in a manner that respects its intelligence and experience.

Labor education should introduce new ideas or information in an open, stimulating manner so as to encourage discussion and dissent and channel it into informed debate and genuine learning. Formal labor education as conducted by international or national union education departments or by university labor education services generally uses this method, as does almost the entire array of European trade union education. The Swedish study circle theory most clearly embodies this approach, in the very design of the circle rather than the podium-audience format, in its assignment of a discussion leader rather than "teacher" to the circle, and in its belief that learning is a shared and collective experience in which the leader learns with, and from, the other members of the group.

*Dialogue pedogogy* is based on give and take among all members of the group and rejects the barrier between teacher and pupil, which a podium and the lecture style of teaching can so easily create. It has been used with great success with educationally deprived adults in Third World countries. Its adaptation to adult education in Europe and America has helped us answer the questions: How does one "teach" mature, intelligent adults who bring so much with them to the learning experience? And how can their experience of the world be mobilized and used to help them incorporate new information and develop new perspectives?

Instructors brought in or developed by the local should be encouraged to approach their teaching with this perspective. Teaching techniques should be elicitive rather than straight lecture, and students should be involved in what is being discussed; they should be encouraged to analyze their own assumptions and statements and justify them in terms of their own experience as workers and citizens.

Labor education centers or international unions offer (or can be asked to conduct) "train-the-trainer" programs where union members can be instructed in these teaching techniques and can learn more about resources for discussion leaders and how to get students involved in the learning process.[5] Every local union has potential discussion leaders; the education committee should seek these people out and assist them in adding to the internal resources of the local.

---

[5] As an example of how an international union can assist locals in building their own educational resources, see the UAW "Local Union Discussion Leader" program whereby local unionists are trained in discussion techniques.

### Building in Participant Involvement

Do not expect participant involvement simply to happen without careful planning. Someone on the education committee should work out the program schedule with the speakers, insisting that their presentations include room for appropriate participant activities. Exhibits 5-1 and 5-2 are two brief sample program schedules suggesting ways of turning formal presentations into more varied programs with built-in participation.

---

### EXHIBIT 5-1
### Political Action Program: Developing Participation in the Local
### (A Two-Hour Evening Program: 30 People)

| | |
|---|---|
| 7:00–7:15 | Introduction of all participants/speakers, including an outline of what will be covered and when the program will end. |
| 7:15–8:00 | "Political Issues for Labor" panel and discussion: local union political education committee chair; state representative; professor of economics from local community college. Each speaks 7 to 10 minutes on one topic. Then open to questions *from audience.* |
| 8:00–8:05 | Break for coffee. |
| 8:05–8:30 | "Bringing the Issues into the Workplace: How to Talk Politics at Work." Presentation. Small group work. Ten-minute presentation on how to start and how to guide political discussions at work. Then group breaks into threes; two discussants and one observer. Fifteen minutes discussing the issues presented earlier. |
| 8:30–8:50 | Whole group meets together: small groups report briefly on strategies that worked best in raising and discussing the issues. Convenor summarizes; stresses importance of carrying issues back to workplace and using techniques that worked tonight. |
| 8:50–9:00 | Participants fill out evaluation forms. |

---

EXHIBIT 5-2
**Steward's Class: Focus on Writing and Documenting the Grievance;
Stewards' Roles Dealing with Members
(Four Hours: 150 People)**

8:00–8:15        Introduction of speakers, departments represented, and day's schedule.

8:15–9:15        How to write the grievance.

15 minutes:  purpose and elements of a written grievance (situation; contention; remedy, using handout with sample grievance written up).

10 minutes:  whole group critique, led by instructor, of actual grievances which have been written up by stewards (handouts, with identities of parties *concealed*).

25 minutes:  writing up a mock grievance. Participants read facts of mock case, write up a grievance on a blank form. Break into groups of five and circulate grievances for comments and helpful criticism.

10 minutes:  recapitulation by instructor. Review of three elements; reminder of purpose of the written grievance.

9:15–10:30       Collecting facts for grievance investigation.

10 minutes:  presentation on importance of collecting facts and of using fact sheet/investigation form of the local. Why that skill must be improved in the local.

20 minutes:  presentation on rights under law and the contract of stewards to collect documents and interview witnesses. Questions and answers.

10 minutes:  how to request documents under the contract and/or practice of the workplace. (Review of any special forms, etc., used.)

20 minutes:  how to interview witnesses. In groups of two, participants interview each other on mock incident presented in handout and fill out fact sheet during interviews.

15 minutes:  group reconvenes as a whole; instructor goes over main facts of case: did they dig them out? What witnesses or documents are still needed to complete the fact file on this case?

10:30–10:45      Coffee break.

10:45–12:00      The steward's role in dealing with the member.

10 minutes: presentation on problems that have arisen; failure to explain representational role of steward to member; failure to screen out "gripes" and say "sorry, no grievance"; failure to suggest other avenues of assistance local can provide; failure to maintain contact through all steps of grievance procedure.

30 minutes: individual casework on handout. Participants read a one-page transcript of a worker's statement with description of worker's physical appearance and attitude. Then participants make notes on:

> Worker's state of mind.
> Was worker concealing anything?
> Does worker understand contractual provisions that apply here?
> What are three questions you would ask worker; in what order?
> *Note:* This part of the program can be made accessible to those with literacy problems by having the leader read the descriptions and transcript and then have people work in groups to answer the questions.

20 minutes: developing your interpersonal and communication skills as a steward. Instructor and participants work through handout together, which outlines pointers on communication skills, including how to read body language, how to phrase questions, how to take notes while listening; how to explain to a grievant that the case is being dropped.

10 minutes: wrap-up presentation, stressing central importance of steward's role in grievance process and entire union structure; review of union expectations of stewards and of resources available to help them carry out duties.

5 minutes: fill out evaluation forms.

---

Participation techniques and exercises that can be used with most topic areas are suggested in Exhibits 5-1 and 5-2. They include:

1. *Casework:* instructor presents facts of a case (verbally, in handout, in role play or videotape). Participants respond, applying principles outlined in

earlier presentation, either individually on paper, in small groups, or as a whole group.

2. *Buzz groups:* participants discuss question or issue in groups of about five people. Come up with opinions, present back to whole group.

3. *Role plays:* two or three volunteers act out a situation in front of the whole group. Group discussion and critique of issues raised.

4. *Individual work sessions:* each participant works on problem, question-naire, writing assignment, etc., that illustrates previously presented material. Report back to whole group or small group for critique and evaluation.

Outside speakers, as valuable as their expert knowledge and their possibly more polished teaching skills may be, can be overused. They can be expensive and can make the local so dependent on their services that it fails to develop its own internal resources. Unionists in this country have a peculiarly ambivalent feeling about outside, and especially academic, expertise—on the one hand over-valuing it to the point of uncritical worship, on the other, viewing it with hostility and suspicion. Realistically, there are limits to local union do-it-yourself legal skills, economic analysis, and arbitration expertise. Unions have become dependent on experts for many services in today's complex industrial-relations world. We may look back with regret and nostalgia to an imagined time of local union self-sufficiency and the self-taught local leader, but the need for outside expertise is here to stay.

Suspicion of outsiders, which can be a barrier to tapping the sometimes vital expertise of professionals, may be justified in many cases, but it could be turned to the advantage of the education program. Do members of your local question the sincerity, credentials, or "pro-unionism" of the experts you want to use in your program? Then let them interview the experts! Most professionals inter-ested in helping the labor movement would (or should) be willing and even anxious to have their biases and professional credentials carefully examined by a local before they are hired. A healthy scepticism and insistence on excellence of outsiders can enhance the screening process of guest speakers or labor education centers.

Outside experts, carefully selected, can be used in such a way as to assist the growth of knowledge within the local union and even become part of the educa-tion program. Many locals use their lawyer or economist as a teacher as well as legal counsel or researcher. Often these people will welcome the opportunity to get to know members of the local union personally and to become familiar with the local's overall structure and its leading issues. Occasionally a local will make a package deal with a lawyer to handle arbitration cases and also to teach an occasional class on grievance handling or labor law.

University or college labor educators can also be called on to help the local develop its own expertise. Many locals simply contact a labor education center and ask for a class—any class—to fill a blank spot on a union calendar or to spice up a dull program. Others will sit down with university staff, outline the local's needs, and then brainstorm *together* to come up with a program or series of programs. In every such use of outsiders for a program, the local should consider reserving a teaching slot for one or more of its own members. That in-house teacher can collaborate with the invited teacher on topic, materials, and teaching approaches, and gain confidence and expertise to bring back to the local. It is important after such classes to have a debriefing session among the local leaders, education committee, and perhaps even the invited teacher(s) to discuss the session frankly. This can be helped by the use of participant evaluations.

There is a fine line between using education to build support for the union and using it to propagandize for current leaders and their policies. Even the most well-intentioned union leaders can inadvertently slip into a style of education that members perceive as self-serving. If members begin to suspect that leaders are using classes as personal forums for propaganda and the development of personality cults, the entire program may be put in jeopardy. When local leaders are teaching or helping teach the classes, there will inevitably be some talk about this. Such suspicion can be reduced by building a response-and-reaction time into every presentation, by the use of the anonymous evaluation form, by keeping the education committee open to volunteer members, and by the occasional use of outsiders. When members realize that the choice of topics and speakers springs ultimately from *their* wishes and needs, these suspicions lessen.

### Publicity and Recruitment

Advertising the class is vital, regardless of the group targeted. Even a class for officers should be made known to the members; for publicizing that the local is actively attempting to improve the quality of its service to members can pay off in terms of showing members that they are getting something for their dues. Use the local newsletter, the bulletin boards, handbills when appropriate, and word-of-mouth recruitment by stewards in the workplace. Attractive fliers, using graphics and boldface headlines, can be quickly and cheaply prepared.[6] They should stress the usefulness of the class ("What's in it for me?") and make it sound interesting. It is also important to mention a contact person on every flier for those wanting more information.

### Evaluating the Program

A systematic evaluation of each program after its conclusion is a must if the education committee wants to develop and improve its overall programming. There are two phases to this process of evaluation, immediate and long range.

***Phase 1. Participant evaluations and summary sheets.*** Participant evaluations need not be complex: they can be typed and handed out, but it might be enough simply to write the questions about the course on a chalkboard and ask people to

---

[6] Nancy Brigham, *How to Do Leaflets, Newsletters, and Newspapers.* PEP Publishers, P.O. Box 289, Essex Station, Boston, Massachusetts 02112 (1982).

jot down their thoughts in the last five minutes of the session. Evaluations can be most helpful if participants are given a chance to respond anonymously and in their own words. Evaluation forms with numerical responses are far less helpful to a planning committee.

1. Which sections of the class were most helpful? Why?

2. Which were least helpful? Why?

3. Do you have any suggestions on how we might improve it if we ran it again?

Answers to these questions will be a very valuable aid to the education committee in planning future programs. A fourth question can also be of assistance to the committee: What other topics would you like to see addressed in upcoming programs?

Soon after the session is over (no longer than a day) while impressions are still fresh, the committee members should sit down with the participants' evaluations and read them over together, commenting and adding their own reactions to the program. A reaction summary sheet for each program can help the committee when planning a similar program in the future. It might look like Exhibit 5-3—and include other summary information:

---

### EXHIBIT 5-3
### Program Summary Sheet

Name of program  _____

Date  _____     Place held  _____

Speakers  _____

Cost to local  _____

Participant evaluations summarized (see originals attached)  _____

_____

_____

Committee reactions  _____

_____

Objectives of program  _____

_____

---

***Phase 2. long-range program impact.***    Attempting to ascertain the longer-range effectiveness of a given program can be very difficult, as the gains of education may be broad and incremental and appear in areas where one is not looking. A stewards school may not result in much change in how grievances are handled, but it may get more stewards out to meetings, or it may get them talking more "union" with the members in their departments. Education nearly always has some of these intangible benefits; the education committee should try to be sensitive to and on the lookout for such changes in attitude and morale.

But the committee should also be actively looking for tangible, even quantifiable, changes in union activity levels that can be credited to the education program. Committee members must keep in touch with the officers and stewards committee to see if there are changes in stewards' use of fact sheets and improvement in grievance documentation, for example; improvement in attendance at meetings; improvement in the quality of the newsletter; more skills and confidence among bargaining committee members, to list but a few areas where classes might have targeted skills or members' interests.

### Planning a Program: Worksheet for the Education Committee

Careful planning cannot assure the success of a program, but it can help your committee avoid some small disasters and do a great deal to promote the comfort of speakers and participants (see Exhibit -54). Many locals have great turnover in their committees and lose the accumulated wisdom of the members who leave. That wisdom can be distilled into and preserved on a checklist.

---

EXHIBIT 5-4

OVERALL ADVANCE PLANNING

1. Target group _____

2. Why a class is relevant now _____

3. Overall topic of class _____

4. Has a similar class been offered before? _____
   When? _____    Number of participants _____
   Cost to local _____
   Benefits to local _____

5. Consultation with local officers? _____

6. Estimated total cost of program _____

WORKING OUT THE DETAILED AGENDA (once the program has been approved)

7. Possible speakers/areas of expertise _____
   Cost of speaker(s) _____
   Person responsible _____

8. Time of class _____

  Lost time for target group _____

  Estimated cost _____

9. Location of class _____

  Rent _____

10. Chalkboard _____    AV needs _____    AV cost _____

11. Coffee breaks _____    Person responsible _____

  Cost _____

12. Meal _____    Person responsible _____    Cost _____

13. Child care _____    Person responsible _____

  Cost _____

14. Handouts for session _____

  Will speakers provide their own? _____

  Person responsible _____    Cost _____

15. Program agenda. Does it include:

  Time for introduction of all participants? _____

  Time for coffee breaks after about every two hours? _____

  A balance between presentation of information and individual or group activities? _____

  Time at the end for evaluation by participants? _____

16. Have speakers been consulted regarding:

  a. Content of their session _____

  b. Teaching method _____

  c. Time and place of session _____

  d. Reimbursement for expenses/fee _____

  e. Handouts for participants _____

  f. Equipment needs _____

  Person responsible _____

17. Have special needs of target group been addressed?

  Child Care? _____

  Accessible? _____

  Smoke-free areas? _____

  Sugar-free drinks? _____

PUBLICITY/RECRUITMENT

18. Verbal notification _____    Person responsible _____

  Fliers _____    Person responsible _____

  Steward's telling members _____    Person responsible _____

  Newsletter _____    Person responsible _____

  Media _____    Person responsible _____

  Other _____    Person responsible _____

CLOSING OUT THE PROGRAM

19. Committee meeting to evaluate session  ————————————————

20. Discussion of participant evaluations  ————————————————

21. Report to union executive board  ————————————————

22. Actual dollar cost to local  ————————————————

23. Anticipated benefits to local:
    Additional library resources  ————————————————
    Local members' teaching experience  ————————————————

## Making Education Accessible to All

Our country's work force is, as it has always been, a heterogeneous group. Over the last half-century, however, changes in our economy, demographic structure, and laws protecting certain categories of workers from discrimination have increased the diversity of union membership in every type of service or industry. Labor education must be designed to appeal to and be accessible to this varied constituency from which the local union can draw so much energy and ability.

The education committee should keep the needs, interests, and possible difficulties of special constituency groups in mind every time a new program is planned. Some of these considerations might include:

Is the location of the program wheelchair-accessible?

Is there provision for hearing augmentation?

Are there materials for non-English-speaking participants?

Is child care available?

Is the teaching method designed to invite and encourage participation from those with poor reading and writing skills?

Is the location of the class inviting and/or familiar?

Can the classroom be made smoke-free in whole or in part?

Do coffee breaks include sugar-free alternatives to soft drinks and caffeine-free hot drinks?

Are nonalcoholic beverages available whenever alcohol is served?

Can a car pool or buddy system be worked out to facilitate travel to and from the class?

Can the class be repeated at a different time of day for shift workers?

Most of these arrangements can become routine once they are systematically and seriously addressed by the education committee. The committee might select one or two members, possibly representatives from one of the constituencies in question, who can take on the job of seeing to these arrangements.

### Education for the Disabled Worker or Worker with a Health Problem

Thanks in large part to union efforts in the legislative arena, as well as through collective bargaining and cooperative programs with the employer, many workers who once would have been forced out or kept out of the work force are now able to continue work and play productive roles in our economy. Just as our public facilities and workplaces have been made accessible, so must our union halls and places of union education. If the hall is not wheelchair-accessible, it can often be made so with relatively little capital investment. When building a union hall, be sure that easy access is part of the original design. If an education program is being held in a rented facility, check to make sure it is accessible for all.

When planning meals or coffee breaks, keep the situations of the diabetic or alcoholic member in mind and be sure that alcohol-free and caffeine-free as well as sugar-free beverages are available. Increasing numbers of members are choosing low-fat or vegetarian diets; keep them in mind when catering meals, and offer cheese or bean-based dishes along with the ham and beef.

If deaf or hearing-impaired members may be among your target group, check on the feasibility of hiring someone to provide sign language interpretation of the presentations or of acquiring hearing augmentation devices or simply an amplification system for the hall.

Increasing numbers of union members, many of them former smokers, find it difficult to breathe in smoke-filled rooms and are speaking up about their rights to clean air in their union halls. Solutions here might range from outright smoking prohibitions (with more frequent breaks) to division of the room into smoking and nonsmoking sections or to purchase of one of the new powerful room air cleaners. If the latter route is chosen, be sure to get a quiet model that does not drown out your speakers.

### Education for Parents of Young Children

Parents with young children, particularly single parents, will need some special thought with regard to child-care arrangements and the time of the class. Try to avoid conflicts with dinner preparation and early bedtimes for children. One local scheduled a time-management class for these target groups from 5:30 to 7:30 and started it off with a meal prepared (not a potluck!) by the auxiliary and featuring a children's activities center in an adjacent room.

Child-care arrangements need not be elaborate or expensive, but they are absolutely necessary for a local that wants to attrack women members and enable them to play active roles in union activities. A small number of men are also single parents and can be active only if thought is given to providing assistance to child-care. Child care can range in sophistication from the teen-age daughter of a member playing with children in an unused conference room of the union hall to reimbursement of baby-sitting costs by the local. How do you know if your local needs child care for union functions? A questionnaire may give some answers, but an easier test is to look at the child-rearing status of women activists. "All our active women are either childless or have grown-up kids," said one union business agent, defending the lack of child care in her local—which had 60% women in its membership! One can rest assured that child care *was* a problem in that union.

### Education for Those with Literacy Difficulties

A great barrier to labor education is one of the growing social problems of our country: the declining literacy among all Americans. It is a problem that people tend to conceal, but one that can and should be addressed by the education committee. There are two approaches to this situation: promote literacy classes and make other classes more accessible to those who lack literacy.

The education committee can contact the local or state education agencies or the state federation of labor to ascertain what courses in basic English are available locally. At the least, these can be publicized by the local union for its members; some unions may wish to undertake an "Improve Your Reading Skills" campaign and run classes in the union hall.

Classes that involve reading and writing skills—stewards' training classes, for example—should be structured so as to enable those with reading and writing difficulties to participate.

With the growth of non-English-speaking members of our work force, many unions are making sure they have basic union education materials available in the languages of their major non-English groups. Contact your international or national union to see what is available there. A stewards' class might well be divided into language groups for instruction where this seems feasible and appropriate.

### Education for Shift Workers

With shift work spreading to new sectors of the economy, unions once unfamiliar with this phenomenon are starting to adjust union rank-and-file meetings to coincide with shift ends or beginnings. The same adjustments can be made to education programs. Even outside speakers can often be persuaded to offer their class two or three times in one day to different groups of workers.

### Education for the New or Previously Inactive Member

Members who are unfamiliar with the union and its programs may be intimidated by the thought of coming out for the first time. The education committee might take on the job of arranging car pools or the buddy system for such members to make that first trip to the union hall a little easier. Some long-time union activists may be intimidated by the thought of going to class at a university or college campus location. The buddy system might work here as well. Or the classes might be moved to the more familiar setting of the union hall. Some workers will be more willing to come there than to a campus. Attendance at a union-university course series improved markedly in southeastern Iowa when it was moved from the spacious, free-of-cost community college classrooms to the cramped and smoky but comfortably familiar atmosphere of a Teamsters hall. Holding classes in the union hall serves to make the hall and the union a center of activity and interest for members. A member who attends a CPR class at the union hall may be more inclined to begin attending rank-and-file meetings!

## A STARTER LIBRARY FOR THE LOCAL UNION

One way to spread learning throughout the membership and to build broad support for the education program is through a local union library. The education committee can begin to catalogue the books and pamphlets the local has on hand, centralize their physical location, publicize their availability, and add to the local union collection.

Even small local unions often wish to have a collection of basic books and periodicals on labor issues. Listed in Appendix 5A are some starter books for your library and some of the major union periodicals. There are many other good books as well.

## A TEST FOR THE 1980s

A local education program is in many ways at the heart of the union's ability to cope with its environmental pressures and internal membership demands. The "new unionism" that will characterize the labor movement of the 1990s and beyond will of necessity stress the development of the local union as a vital part of members' personal and social lives. Unions will reach out to the families of their members, they will touch the hopes for continuing personal growth of members, forging a sense of this individual growth through and with the collective membership of the local. They will reach out to groups within the local that have been shut out and give them voice and influence. In striving for these goals, local unions will lean heavily on the education committee for ideas and programs to carry them out. A test of local union leadership in the next decade will be the extent to which leaders have created education programs able to meet these challenges. The health of the union, its existence, is at stake.

## DISCUSSION QUESTIONS

1. How can a year-round education plan assist local union officers and actually make their jobs easier?

2. Draw up a year's education program for your local union.

3. Identify possible speakers in your geographical area for a program on industrial policy. Outline a three-hour program for 150 people, focusing on

developing recruitment among area unions, community groups, and the public.

4. Plan a Saturday morning program for local union retirees, balancing social, political, and age-group components.

5. What distinguishes university labor education from union-based education programs? How can the two programs cooperate?

## GLOSSARY

**buzz groups:** Small groups broken out of a large class to discuss a particular issue or problem, often with "report-back" to the larger group.

**dialogue pedagogy:** Nonauthoritarian learning through sharing of experience and practical knowledge among all participants in a class.

**labor education:** Usually refers to noncredit education aimed at union members and officers stressing skill building in, for example, collective bargaining, grievance handling, labor law, safety, and health.

**labor studies:** Credit programs at some colleges and universities offer degrees ranging from Associate (2 year) to Masters in Labor Studies. Course work will often include economics, labor history, collective bargaining, etc.

**study circle:** Informal group started by workers who want to read and discuss issues together. Most highly developed in Sweden.

**workers' education:** Noncredit education for workers usually with a strong political/economic component.

## ADDITIONAL RESOURCES

*American Federationist.* Washington, D.C.: AFL–CIO. (No longer published except in reduced scope in AFL–CIO *News.* See back issues.)

Flagler, John J. *Building the Local Union Education Program.* State University of Iowa, Bureau of Labor and Management Information Series, No. 4, 1961.

*How to Improve Workers' Education.* Geneva, Switzerland: International Labor Office, 1976

Long, Huey B. *Adult and Continuing Education: Responding to Change.* New York: Teachers College Press, 1983.

Smith, Robert M. *Learning How to Learn: Applied Theory for Adults.* Chicago: Follet Publishing Company, 1982.

Wertheimer, Barbara M., ed. *Labor Education for Women Workers.* Philadelphia: Temple University Press, 1981.

*Workers' Education and Techniques.* Geneva, Switzerland: International Labor Office, 1976.

## APPENDIX 5A

### A STARTER LIBRARY FOR LOCAL UNIONS

1. *Theory and practice of Unionism*

   *American Unions: Structure, Government and Politics.* Jack Barbash. Random House, 1967. 183 pp.

   *Basic Communication Skills: A Handbook for Unions.* Austin Perlow. Bureau of National Affairs, Inc., Washington, D.C., 1981. 333 pp.

   *Essentials of Labor Relations.* David H. Rosenbloom and Jay M. Shafritz. Reston Publishing Co., Reston, Va., 1985. 272 pp.

   *Labor and the American Community.* Derek C. Bok and John T. Dunlop. Simon and Schuster, New York, 1970. 542 pp.

   *Story of a Steward.* Terrence F. Connors. UAW Education Department, 8000 E. Jefferson Ave., Detroit, MI 48214, 1980. 265 pp.

   *Survey of Labor Relations.* Lee Balliet. Bureau of National Affairs, Inc., Washington, D.C. 198 pp.

   *Talks with Stewards.* Terrence F. Connors. UAW Education Department, 8000 E. Jefferson Ave., Detroit, MI 48214, 1966. 117 pp.

   *Union Government and Organization.* Jim Wallihan. Bureau of National Affairs, Inc., Washington, D.C. 1985. 250 pp.

   *What Have You Done for Me Lately?* Austin Perlow. Rutledge Books, New York, 1979, 289 pp.

2. *Labor History*

   *Labor in the U.S.A.: A History.* Ronald A. Filapelli. Knopf. New York. 1984. 315 pp.

   *Labor's Untold Story.* Richard O. Boyer and Herbert Morais. United Electrical Radio and Machine Workers of America, 11 E. 51st St., New York, NY 10022. 402 pp.

   *Out to Work: A History of Wage-Earning Women in the United States.* Alice Kessler-Harris. Oxford University Press, New York. 400 pp.

   *A Pictorial History of American Labor.* William Cahn. Crown Publishers, New York, 1972. 241 pp.

   *Toil and Trouble: A History of American Labor.* Thomas R. Brooks. Delacourte Press, New York, 1971. 402 pp.

   *U.S. Department of Labor Bicentennial History of the American Workers.* Richard B. Morris, ed. Superintendent of Documents, U.S. Government Printing Office, Washington, D.C. 327 pp.

*We Were There: The Story of Working Women in America.* Barbara M. Wertheimer. Pantheon Books, New York, 1977. 427 pp.

*Working: People Talk about What They Do All Day and How They Feel About What They Do.* Studs Terkel. Pantheon, New York, 1974. 589 pp.

3. **Economics, Technology, Safety and Health**

*America in Ruins: Beyond the Public Works Pork Barrel.* Pat Choate and Susan Walter. Council of State Planning Agencies, Hall of the States, 400 North Capitol Street, Washington, D.C. 20001, 1981. 97 pp.

*Corporate Flight: The Causes and Consequences of Economic Dislocation.* Barry Bluestone, Bennett Harrison, and Lawrence Baker. Progressive Alliance, 1757 N. Street NW, Washington, D.C. 20036, 1981. 94 pp.

*Don't Let Your Job Kill You.* Frank Wallick. Progressive Press, Washington, D.C., 1984. 288 pp.

*Fear at Work, Job Blackmail, Labor and the Environment.* Richard Kazis and Richard L. Grossman. Pilgrim Press, New York, 1982. 206 pp.

*Global Reach: The Power of the Multinational Corporations.* Richard J. Barnet and Ronald E. Muller. Simon and Schuster, New York, 1974. 508 pp.

*Labor and Reindustrialization: Workers and Corporate Change.* Donald Kennedy, ed. Department of Labor Studies, Pennsylvania State University, University Park, Pa., 1984. 190 pp.

*Labor and Technology: Union Response to Changing Environments.* Donald Kennedy, Charles Craypo, and Mary Lehman, eds. Department of Labor Studies, Pennsylvania State University, University Park, Pa., 1982. 206 pp.

*Let's Rebuild America.* IAM&AW, 1300 Connecticut Avenue NW, Washington, D.C. 20036 (no date). 263 pp.

*Micro-Electronics at Work: Productivity and Jobs in the World Economy.* Colin Norman. Worldwatch Paper 39, October, 1980. Worldwatch Institute, 1776 Massachusetts Ave. NW, Washington, D.C. 20036. 508 pp.

*The North Will Rise Again: Pensions, Politics and Power in the 1980s.* Randy Barber and Jeremy Rifkin. Beacon Press, Boston, 1980. 508 pp.

*Office Automation: Jekyll or Hyde?* Daniel Marschall and Judith Gregory, eds. Working Women Education Fund, 1224 Huron Road, Cleveland, Ohio 44115, 1983. 229 pp.

*OSHA Standards,* U.S. Department of Labor, Washington, D.C.

*Work Is Dangerous to Your Health: A Handbook of Health Hazards in the Workplace and What You Can Do about Them.* Jeanne Stellman and Susan Daum. Random House, New York, 1973. 448 pp.

*Workplace Health and Safety: A Guide to Collective Bargaining.* Paul Chown. Labor Occupational Health Program, Institute of Industrial Relations, University of California at Berkeley, 1980. 68 pp.

### 4. Collective Bargaining

*Basic Patterns in Union Contracts,* 10th ed. Bureau of National Affairs, Washington, D.C., 1983. 118 pp.

*Inside the Circle: A Union Guide to QWL.* Mike Parker. South End Press, Boston, Massachusetts, 1985. 156 pp.

*Labor Guide to Negotiating Wages and Benefits.* Gene Daniels and Ken Gagala. Reston Publishing Co., Reston, Va., 1985. 256 pp.

*Organizing and the Law,* 3rd ed. Stephen I. Schlossberg, and Judith A. Scott. Bureau of National Affairs, Inc., Washington, D.C., 1983. 431 pp.

*The Practice of Collective Bargaining,* 4th ed. Edwin F. Beal, ed. Richard D. Irwin, Homewood, Ill., 1972. 792 pp.

*Problems in Local Union Collective Bargaining.* Terrence F. Connors. UAW Education Department, 8000 E. Jefferson Ave., Detroit, MI 48214. 233 pp.

*Public Sector Bargaining.* Benjamin Aaron, ed. Bureau of National Affairs, Inc., Washington, D.C., 1979. 327 pp.

*Union Organizing and Staying Organized.* Ken Gagala. Reston Publishing Co., Reston, Va., 1983. 307 pp.

*The Use of Economic Data in Collective Bargaining.* U.S. Department of Labor, Labor Management Services. Superintendent of Documents, U.S. Government Printing Office, Washington, D.C., 1978. 76 pp.

### 5. Labor Law

*Labor Guide to Labor Law.* Bruce Feldacker. Reston Publishing Co., Reston, Va., 1983. 527 pp.

*Labor Law for the Rank and Filer,* rev. ed. Staughton Lynd. Singlejack Books, Box 1906X, San Pedro, CA 90733. 72 pp.

*Labor Relations Law,* 4th ed. Benjamin J. Taylor and Fred Witney. Prentice-Hall, Englewood Cliffs, N.J., 1983. 914 pp.

*Unions, Workers, and the Law.* Betty W. Justice. Bureau of National Affairs, Inc., Washington, D.C., 1983. 291 pp.

6. *Grievance Handling and Arbitration*

*Contract Administration.* Bob Repas. Bureau of National Affairs, Inc., Washington, D.C., 1984. 247 pp.

*Discipline and Discharge.* Duane Beeler. Union Representative, Chicago, IL, 1978. 225 pp.

*Evidence in Arbitration.* Marvin Hill and Anthony Sinicropi. Bureau of National Affairs, Inc., Washington, D.C., 1980. 201 pp.

*The Grievance Guide,* 6th ed. Bureau of National Affairs, Inc., Washington, D.C., 1982. 375 pp.

*How Arbitration Works,* Frank Elkouri and Edna Elkouri. 4th ed. Bureau of National Affairs, Inc., Washington, D.C., 1985. 898 pp.

*Remedies in Arbitration.* Marvin Hill and Anthony Sinicropi. Bureau of National Affairs, Inc., Washington, D.C., 1981. 355 pp.

7. *Selected Periodicals of the AFL–CIO*

(815 Sixteenth Street NW, Washington, D.C. 20006)

| Title | Frequency | Cost | Publisher |
|---|---|---|---|
| *AFL*–CIO News | Weekly | $10/year | AFL–CIO |
| Labelletter | Bimonthly | Free | Union Label and Service Trades Department |
| Memo from Cope and AFL–CIO Legislative Alert (also every 2 weeks as part of *AFL*–CIO News) | Biweekly in session; not printed in recess | $5/year | Committee on Political Education and Legislative Department |
| Ourself: Women and Unions | Monthly | Free | Food and Beverage Trades Department |
| S.T.I.R. *(Statistical and Tactical Information Report)* | Quarterly | Free | Department of Organization and Field Services |

8. *Other Periodicals with Economic and Political Information*

*Dollars and Sense.* Monthly publication offering interpretations of current economic events from progressive perspective. 38 Union Square, Room 14, Somerville, MA 02143. $16/year.

*Economic Notes.* Monthly labor economics bulletin from a labor/progressive perspective. Labor Research Association, Inc., 80 East 11th Street, New York NY 10003. $10/year.

*In These Times.* Weekly. 1300 W. Belmont, Chicago, IL 60657. $29.50/year.

*Mother Jones.* Monthly. 1663 Mission Street, San Francisco, CA 94103. $20/year.

*The Nation.* Weekly. Subscription Services, P.O. Box 1953, Marion, OH 43305. $30/year.

*UAW Ammo.* Monthly. UAW, 8000 E. Jefferson Ave., Detroit, MI 48214. $1.50/year.

*UAW Washington Report.* Weekly. 1757 N. Street NW, Washington, D.C. 20036. Free.

# CHAPTER 6

# Computerizing the Local

With the passing of each year, it becomes more difficult to manage and administer the business of a local union. The effects of legal, economic, and membership environments on the local make it difficult to operate the local's finances out of two shoe boxes (receipts and disbursements), track grievance histories, and keep up with a changing membership. The traditional methods of running a union office are literally being tossed out the window.

The usual way of conducting local union business has often involved the use of a full-time officer, one half-time clerical person, one typewriter (not always electric), one or two four-drawer file cabinets, and a local treasurer who will not let the executive board buy anything (often this same treasurer is the full-time officer). Only now are copiers and electric typewriters, let alone electronic memory-writers, making their way into union offices. And, remember, many locals still do not even have what one could call an office, let alone people to staff one.

The lightning speed with which the Information Age is now hurrying data across the heavens makes the outdatedness of local union office administration and management nearly fatal. Most employers have access to or own their own automated office systems. This development is evidenced by their ability to track arbitration results and arbitrators from coast to coast instantly with a computer and telephone-modem link. Management collective bargaining counterproposals are returned to union negotiators the next day—already word processed into a complete new version of the proposed contract. Production decisions made in

New York on a daily basis control the output of a new facility in Arkansas. Information, a base of power in leadership and essential to basic administrative and management needs, moves rapidly everywhere. Everywhere, it seems, except in unions.

A leadership decision of major magnitude faces union managers concerning their ability to access and interpret information in a timely fashion. The decision to automate the union office must be faced. The authors feel that a "no" to this challenge will only leave those unions further behind the strides of their employers. Our answer to the challenge is a qualified yes. Unions need to computerize their offices. It needs to be done as soon as possible. Computer policy needs to be established. This chapter attempts to provide some information useful in formulating such a policy.[1]

## A QUALIFIED YES

The authors' answer stems from what we see to be confusion over who should lead the move to union computerization, the parent union or its locals or districts, and just how far said computerization should go. This confusion comes as a result of little or no policy making on the use of computers. Some parent unions and some locals have identified several uses for a computer and/or word processor. Their concerns are not mutually exclusive. However, there is a difference in priority between the levels of union organization as to how a computer system can best be used. Unions seem to be bringing computers on line for at least the following administrative and managerial reasons.

1. Local/international union finances

2. Membership data

3. Union payroll

4. Political action

5. Contracts

6. Arbitration/grievance handling

## UNION USES FOR THE COMPUTER

### Union Finances

Local unions, depending on their size, may or may not need a computer to keep track of dues, per capita payments, political action checkoffs, receipts, disbursements, and the like. Smaller locals tend to use a combination of employer-

---

[1] Parts of this chapter are from Gene Daniels and Kenneth Gagala, *Labor Guide to Negotiating Wages and Benefits,* 1985. Reprinted by permission of Reston Publishing Company, 11480 Sunset Hills Road, Reston, VA 22090.

provided computer information and the local's treasurer, who often does the job as she was trained to do it 15 years ago. Larger locals are starting to acquire computers to handle these details. Parent unions are also finding it almost impossible to function financially without the use of computers. Funds need to be deposited or transferred more rapidly and accurately these days. Staff reductions are causing delays and errors. Finally, the impact of legal developments and finances has caused more unions to act "businesslike" in the sense that monies need to earn as much as possible to augment declining membership. The handling of union funds must be done properly—administratively to satisfy legal requirements and managerially to keep the union's assets liquid.

## Membership Data

The heart and soul of any local is its membership. Currently, union membership is in a tremendous flux for several reasons, some of which are:

1. Aging of the American work force.
2. Layoffs caused by massive changes in communications, automation, and high technology.
3. Corporate flight from the United States.
4. Unemployment as a political choice to curb inflation.
5. Continuing efforts by women and minorities to gain equality in the workplace.
6. Deregulation in industries such as trucking and airlines.
7. Tactics, legal and illegal, of consultants and employers to create a union-free environment.

As a result of these and other factors, trying to keep up with pertinent data, which include addresses, phone numbers, social security numbers, job classifications, transfers, pay rates, layoffs, and such, is a nightmare, regardless of the size of the local. Attempting to keep the membership informed and active, as well as being able to verify dues and per capita payments, is no longer a routine administrative task that can be done in one's spare time.

## Union Payroll

Hand in hand with union finances and membership data is the need to properly handle the union payroll. The wages and benefits for officers, clerical support, stewards, and union hall maintenance people have to be paid, along with deductions for federal and state taxes. Lost-time payments for union business and expenses for union-related activities also must be paid. For the smaller local, this aspect of managing one's payroll is not a large one; however, larger locals and parent unions have vast amounts of payroll data to record. Finally, quarterly and year-end federal and state tax reports vary in difficulty with the size of the union.

its payroll, and its expenses. The use of a computer in generating the totals for these reports is a definite administrative plus.

## Political Action

Everything a union can or cannot do, as well as what an employee can or cannot do, is governed to some degree by federal or state law. Therefore, unions and their members have a vested interest in what happens in the legislatures, courts, governors' mansions, and the Capitol. As a result, unions lobby, solicit funds for political activity, and educate their memberships. But they are still doing it largely the way they did it 30 years ago (at the local level). Slowly, computers and word processors are changing the method of local union political activity. Computerized mailing lists based on membership data and computerized voting tallies from state and federal agencies are enabling unions to do a better job of voter identification and registration, voter/member education, and fund raising. Parent unions are giving computers high marks in this area of political-action administration. Computers can, therefore, assist in the more effective management of a political-action campaign.

## Contracts

One national union vice-president related to one of the authors that, every time a local he assisted with negotiations proposed new or revised contract language, the employer would come back to the table the next day with a newly word processed copy of the contract containing their counters to the union's proposals. It is hard to fight this kind of power without having equal word processing or computer capacity. The same goes for contract costing and financial analysis by the employer. Projections can be made more easily. Many times costing for the local is done by the representative from the parent union or it is done by the research department. There is no doubt that parent unions need to have the capability to computerize contract costing. But locals also need to have access to this same capability, because more local officers are having to carry the brunt of negotiations while their parent union is faced with staff cutbacks and overwork. When it comes time at the table for final best offers, compromises, and counters, accurate and fast economic and cost data are essential.

## Arbitration/Grievance Handling

Whereas suing may seem to be the national pastime, going to arbitration seems to be the thing to do in grievance handling. Whether the cases going up are a result of grievances based on legitimate disputes or stem from employer efforts to stall the grievance machinery and the steward system, the frequency and cost of arbitration are on the rise. Union managers at all levels are feeling this pressure and are turning to computers to create grievance-handling data systems suitable for aiding them in the resolution of grievances at the local level or for use in selecting arbitrators and case research.

Computers can save hours of work, phone calls and bills, correspondence, and clerical support time. Additionally, a computer-enhanced grievance system helps fight off frivolous duty of fair representation suits by providing proof of reasonable effort. Employers are certainly making the best use of computers in preparing their cases, especially in arbitration. Unions should do the same. The computer provides an excellent means for a chief steward or grievance committee chair to administer the various levels of grievances as they wind their way through the system, all the while watching for time limits and such. Grievance histories can be routinely produced and checklists for case evidence can be worked through. Such assistance leaves time for steward development, policy study, and all those things needed to manage the steward system.

With the cooperation of AFSCME/IOWA Council 61, the authors have provided in Appendix 6A a portion of that council's computerized grievance and arbitration system. The exhibits begin with an overview of the grievance start-up procedure and extend through notification and request letters, ending with a withdrawal from arbitration—all keyed to a computer program.

If your local is considering the purchase of a computer or a word processor, you will want to make sure your union finds the right system, has access to professional assistance, properly considers what information/data are to be stored, and determines what functions the computer will perform. This comes back to the authors' "qualified yes." If you do not do these things, you have no business purchasing or leasing a computer or word processor.

## BEFORE PURCHASING A COMPUTER SYSTEM

A computer may be physically the size of a Christmas catalog, the size of a two by three box, or a floor unit weighing hundreds of pounds. Many union officers are being lured by computers costing as little as $200. Not yet knowing what they want the computer or word processor to do, how fast it must work, and where their budget stands for a purchase such as this, many local unions are plunging into personal computer systems that they soon find out cannot deliver. The result is either to reinvest in a larger, more costly system or to give up in disgust and pronounce computers to be a waste of time.

**Rule 1:** Before your union decides to purchase a computer or word-processor system, decide the following:

1. What data-processing needs will the system serve?
2. How fast do we need the output?
3. How much of a budget do we have?
   a. Initial costs
   b. Continuing costs

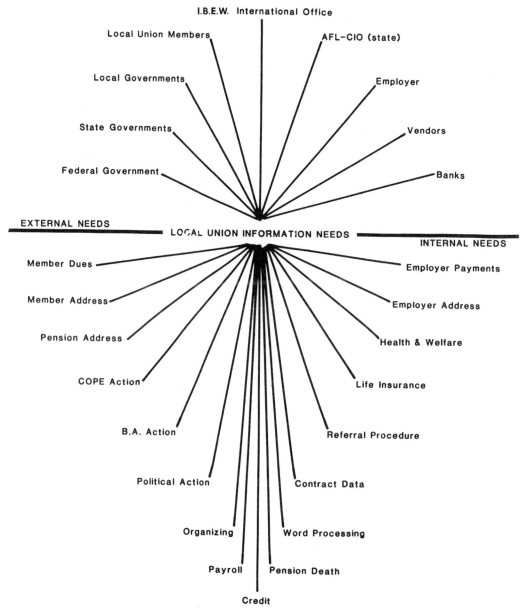

**FIGURE 6-1.** Local union's internal and external data-processing needs.
*(Source: IBEW Computer Information Guide)*

To help clarify the magnitude of this rule for you, consider Figure 6-1, a chart of one international's internal and external data-processing needs.

**Rule 2:** Find out if your national or international has or is setting up a system and network whereby your local will be supplied a monitor, keyboard, printer, and a modem, all hooked up to the mainframe system at headquarters.

**Rule 3:** Find out whether or not your union can time share (rent computer time) with another union, central labor body, or state federation/CAP councils.

## Questions to Consider before Purchase

Rules 1 through 3 only highlight the many questions a union must ask itself. The following specific questions are but a few of the many found in the *General Membership Information Network* manual of the International Association of Bridge, Structural and Ornamental Iron Workers, AFL–CIO:

### Hardware

1. Can the system be locked?
2. How much disk storage will the union need?
3. Will there be a separate physical device for printing on various forms or can the union use the same paper for all printing needs?

### Policy and Procedure

1. Will members still have membership cards and will the local union still have office copies of the same? (This question needs to be asked when the local is interfacing with a computer at either regional or national headquarters.)
2. Will there by an ID number for each person using the system?
3. Are additions to local union staff necessary?
4. Can the local modify programs supplied by the international?
5. Can the local develop and use its own programs?

### Functional Capabilities

1. Who will design the computer system?
2. Will there be printed copies of all displays?
3. Can the local union transmit general information letters to the international?
4. Will there be dues posting on both the computer and member's printout?
5. Can the local union duplicate receipts?
6. Will each member's telephone number be listed?
7. Will the local union be able to recall activities for a particular day? How far back?
8. Can the local union recall activities during the same day?
9. Can the local union maintain a record on layoffs?
10. Can the local maintain a record of checks returned for nonsufficient funds?
11. Will the local union have the information on persons who have previously been members or are members of another local union?

12. Can the local union provide a member's history printout?

13. Can the local union have the contractor or employer name and number included on the member's history display?

14. Will the computer keep the date of information changes (e.g., address)?

15. Will suspended members or those who withdraw from the union have a record in the system?

16. Will there be a memory bank in the system containing former members showing last paid, last worked, and address?

17. Will the members be listed alphabetically?

18. Can the local union use the system for other things: savings accounts, accounts payable?

19. Would all be lost if a program was running and the operator decided to work with another program?

20. If a local has more than one terminal, can only one terminal be operated at a time?

21. Can the local union categorize members by zip code for election purposes?

22. Will the computer prepare a monthly statement?

23. Will the local union have sort capabilities?

24. Is it possible to produce a set of address labels?

Consider also these questions from *Computer Information Guide* provided by the International Brotherhood of Electrical Workers, AFL–CIO:

### Questions for the Manufacturer

1. Is it union made (hardware and software)?

2. How long has the manufacturer been in business? Are they making a good profit?

3. Does the manufacturer make a complete system? Or only one part? If they make only the CPU, where do they get the rest of the system? Is this a problem or an opportunity?

4. What kind of training and support documentation does the vendor offer? Is this an extra cost?

5. Does the manufacturer support the equipment with service or must you go to someone else? Is there a company outlet near the local union that will provide the service?

6. Is systems and application software available from the manufacturer?

7. Who installs the machine?

8. What are the warranty items?

9. Who is responsible for seeing that the entire system operates as it is supposed to do?

10. What are the "hidden" costs?

11. Are computer sales and service the main business of the supplier?

12. Will the vendor commit costs and delivery schedule to writing?

## Maintenance

1. Contract or time and materials?

2. How much documentation is provided?

3. Is the language either BASIC or COBOL? If not, why?

4. Does the system include the CP/M operating system? If not, why?

5. Is the language interactive in nature?

6. What error messages and routines are included?

7. Does the software require any minimum hardware configuration?

8. Does the software have a warranty period?

## Hardware Checklist

### CPU

1. How much memory does the CPU hold?

2. Can more memory be added? Is this important to your needs?

3. What type of electrical power does the CPU require?

### Mass Storage Devices

1. Does the system support floppies? Hard disks? Do you need both?

2. How many diskettes may be used at once?

3. How many million bytes does the hard disk hold?

4. What is the maximum system storage?

5. Can storage units be added after installation? At what price?

### Work Station

1. Do you need more than one work station? Does the system support more than one work station?

2. Can work stations be added after installation?

3. How many characters can be displayed on the screen at a time (24 by 80 is standard)?

4. Does the work station require special furniture?

5. Is the ten-key numeric keypad standard or optional?

### Printer

1. Do you need more than one printer? If so, will the system support more than one?

2. How fast is the printer?

3. What operator features are available?

4. Is the printer letter quality? Dot matrix? Band printer?

5. Can the printer print multipart forms?

6. Can the printer be added or changed after installation?

7. Can the printer and work station operate simultaneously?

8. Can the printer provide hard copy of the information on the CRT screen?

### Hidden Costs

1. Insurance

2. Installation: physical changes, new room, antistatic rugs, line analyzer, etc.

3. Energy consumption

4. Supplies, including backup diskettes, file folders, etc.

5. Training time, personnel additions (possibly)

6. Interest on borrowed money

7. Future changes in systems or additions

## Problem Areas

The need for adequate advanced planning cannot be overstressed; yet there will always be problems arising regardless of how well one plans. The IBEW has identified at least seven problem areas for its locals:

1. Hidden costs

2. Oversell

3. Manager participation

4. Dues reporting responsibilities

5. Transition period

6. Quality control and validation

7. Staffing

### Hidden Costs

Potential union purchasers of computer systems tend to overlook the need for a total system, adequate physical environment, development of a data base, program software development, and training and staffing. Additionally, union officers often anticipate only a few of the many uses of a system and initially fail to provide adequately for efficient overall computer operations.

## Oversell

Just as we have suggested that computers and word processors can greatly simplify union administrative tasks in at least six broad categories, computer salespersons oversell the versatility of computers while neglecting to point out the whole new set of operational and administrative changes that the union as an organization will face and must overcome. It seems, to the consumer at the very least, that all one has to do is plug in the parts, push a button or two, and all the drudgery and thinking is done. Not so.

## Manager Participation

It is not unusual for union officials to hope or believe that their role and responsibilities to the union will be less burdensome because the computer system will do a lot of the office work and carry the responsibility (take the blame) for these details. Again, not so. The union's management must be involved with all activities relating to the purchase, installation, and implementation of the system. Training seminars will have to be attended. Those who operate the system must report to the leaders, and the leaders in turn need to monitor the system to see that it is providing the output expected. The union leader's role and responsibilities actually enlarge with the purchase of a computer system.

## Dues Reporting Responsibilities

Per capita transactions have to be prompt and precise. Initial changes to a computer system will cause some confusion as errors are made and programs corrected. Until a parent union deems a local's system and operators to be working properly, it is not unusual for a local to have to continue sending per capita reports to the parent union in the old form as well as in the electronic form.

## Transition Period

It is not unusual for a period of three to six months to elapse before a union's new system is declared operational and running "normal." There can be a lot of stress and strain on many people as all the quirks and costs come to the surface. The parent union will expect the local to create a correct data base and buy or develop proper programs. The local leadership and operators of the new system will be mumbling to themselves about long hours and bugs in the programs. And the membership will be wondering if they just purchased a lead balloon.

## Quality Control and Validation

This problem area follows closely on the heels of the transition-period problem. Data have to be correct, programs functional, and staff well trained. Furthermore, programs should contain input-data checks with the expressed purpose of limiting the amount of error. Such programs cost more to develop or buy, but their ability to check data files for validity assures better transactions.

### Staffing

The key to quality in a computer or word-processing system is the operator. Very careful consideration must be given to the selection and training of those who will operate the system. In some cases, a new person will have to be hired expressly to handle computer transactions. She or he must be capable, cooperative, and highly motivated. Adequate initial training is a must, and continuous update training is desirable.

## Costs of Going Computer

Just about all the questions a union asks itself as it contemplates purchasing a computer system have a direct or indirect cost attached to them. At least five general cost areas can be identified.

1. *Hardware costs.* This cost area includes initial costs and installation costs. The initial costs include the purchase or rental (usually rental) of the system's hardware components. Installation costs include the preparation of system space with acoustical flooring, antistatic rugs, air conditioning, and fire protection.

2. *Software costs.* Software costs can include the purchase of existing programs, the creation of your own, the modification of other programs, the implementation of the programs, and the occasional installation of "releases" provided by the vendor for system updates.

3. *Data-base costs.* It will take countless hours of officer, operator, and maybe even programmer time to input data, validate data, create files, and test programs. Union officers often underestimate this cost area.

4. *Possible personnel costs.* Depending on the size of the union and the range of functions the system is to run, it is not out of the question that the union might have to hire at least one person, perhaps two.

5. *Maintenance and continuing costs.* Maintenance costs will include regular contracted maintenance for the hardware, data update, program revisions, backup copies of programs, and data stored elsewhere in case of fire or other loss, and there will be higher utility bills. This is a second cost area that is frequently underestimated by unions.

An initial investment of $12,000 to $15,000 just for hardware, software, and installation is not at all unreasonable.

## WHAT IS A COMPUTER SYSTEM?

Up to this point, the emphasis of this chapter has been on the need for adequate planning prior to the purchase of a computer or word-processing system. We have yet to consider the computer itself. What is a computer? What makes up a computer system? What is software?

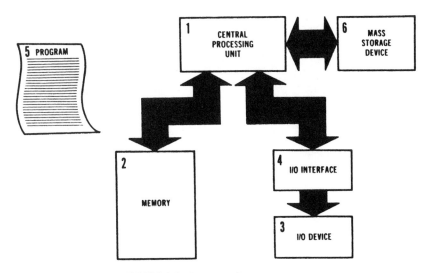

**FIGURE 6-2.** Six parts of a computer.

## The Computer

The computer, in its most basic sense, is an information-processing machine. That is, it can remember, rearrange, sort, and combine information or numbers under the direction of instructions stored in its memory. Today a union can buy or rent a microcomputer for simple tasks, a minicomputer for much more extensive tasks (*more memory*), or a mainframe computer with the capacity to do the most lengthy and complex jobs. There are five main component areas to a computer, six if one adds additional magnetic memory storage to the central processing unit (CPU) (see Figure 6-2).

1. *Central processing unit (CPU)* (hardware). The "brain" of the computer. This is where the actual computing is done. The CPU usually controls all the operations of the computer.

2. *Memory* (hardware). An electronic storage medium used to hold the program that instructs the CPU and other components of the computer.

3. *Input/output devices (I/O)* (hardware). These are the links between the computer and the person. They vary in types and complexity according to the processing requirements. Input/output devices include keyboards, teletypewriters, punch cards, line printer, and video displays.

4. *Input/output interfaces* (hardware). These are the connectors between the CPU and the I/O device. They provide actual hard-wired control of the I/O device, according to the commands that are issued by the CPU.

5. *Program* (software). Without a program, a computer is no more than a collection of parts that sits there and draws current. The program coordinates the operations of the computer in order to perform some desired process.

6. *Mass storage* (hardware). In micro- and minicomputers, the amount of main memory storage is small when compared to mainframe computers. Memory capacity is one of the big cost items in a computer. To add onto the main memory, additional mass storage is obtained by adding a secondary memory, usually in the form of a magnetic disk storage device. It utilizes what is known as a *floppy disk*.

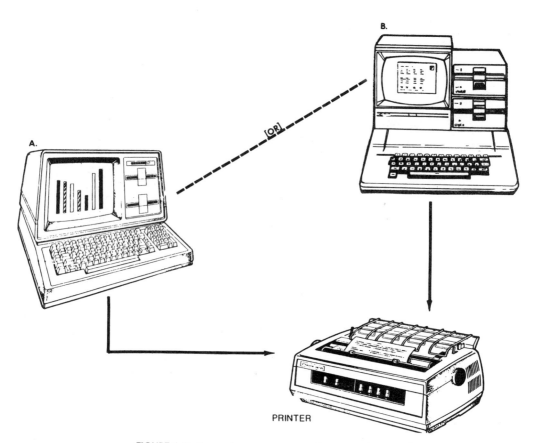

PRINTER

**FIGURE 6-3.** Personal computer system. Two examples (A and B) of all-in-one microcomputers hooked up to an optional printer. A modem can also be added.

The distinctions between micro- and minicomputer are becoming less clear as microcomputers now have approached memory capacity once available only with larger minicomputers. Now, all-in-one or multiple-component microcomputers can do some of the work of minicomputers. Figures 6-3 and 6-4 are examples of personal microcomputers (all-in-one and components) and a mainframe computer system.

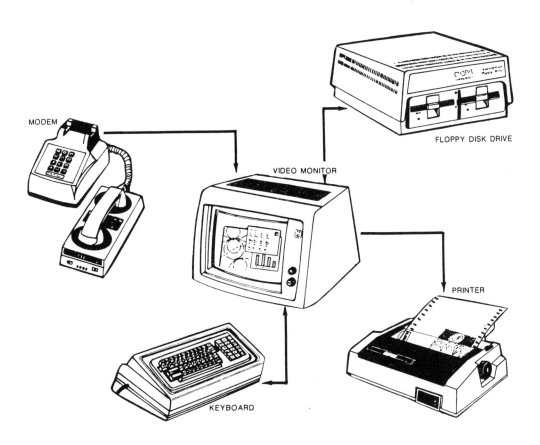

**FIGURE 6-3.** (continued).

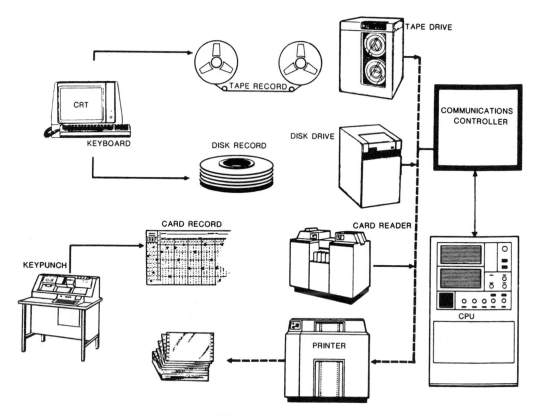

**FIGURE 6-4.** Mainframe computer system.

## Software

If a computer is in the broadest sense an information-processing machine, and hardware such as video displays and printers produce our output, then software is that part of the computer system that makes it "hum." A piece of software, in simple terms, is a set of electrical instructions that tell the computer what operations it is to perform. These instructions can be stored on magnetic tapes or floppy and hard disks. The complete set or package of software used by a computer is said to be the computer's operating system. We usually think of software in terms of programs. As a local union decides what tasks it wants a computer to perform, it buys complete or modifies existing programs. Some international unions are developing their own programs for use by their locals, especially in the area of membership data. Another source for programs or data networks for unions includes the use of Shared Union Systems, Incorporated (a unionized computer support service company). Software for union use can range from basic membership data, to benefit reporting, to financial analysis programs aimed at assisting contract negotiations. All the programs used by the union can be utilized at contract time to best determine current and future contract costs, employer ability to pay and industry performance, past arbitration decisions, meaningful grievance cases, and so on.

There are two basic types of software: systems and applications. Systems software consists of those programs used to control the execution of the computer's basic functions, such as assembling and compiling programs, debugging, and such. Systems software usually is supplied by the company supplying the computer. Application software, on the other hand, is designed to handle specific information in specific ways. Such programs for the union would include those mentioned previously, as well as union payroll, per capita payments, and many more. Operating a computer system, then, is like being a part of a circle. One needs the hardware, but the hardware cannot operate without systems software, and both these parts of the system have no purpose without applications software. The only element of the system we still have not talked about but that is vital to the system is the data needed by the computer so that it can perform its task. We need to talk about the computer's data bank.

## Data Bank

The computer must have data in order to give us the output we desire. So, all one should have to do is simply type in names, addresses, other numbers, dollars and costs, and the like. Right? Wrong! All input data have to be coded per the program's needs for proper running. There is a specific system need for each program and for data in general. Generally, all data are organized in files for easy topic or reference pickup. Each file is assembled for a particular purpose, such as membership data. Any file can be subdivided into records, which are usually similar in form and content. Finally, within a record there may be several fields that further classify data. Once all needed data are supplied, coded, and placed, the computer is ready to go, given that it has all the programs and such.

Setting up a data bank is time consuming. Software and data base costs will quickly equal your local's hardware expenses and keep on rising. Once your core memory is filled, floppy disks and maybe additional drives might be added. In any case, all input has to be properly entered, debugged, and tested through the program. Someone has to be trained to do this, and union officers should oversee this whole process. We are back to that circle again. Each element relies on the others in order for the system to work. Any missing or incorrectly operating part neutralizes the advantages of the computer or word processor. And standing right in the middle of this circle is the operator and the union officer(s). They have to throw the switch, hit the keyboard, and pay the bills.

## COMPUTERS AND UNION LEADERSHIP

Computers and word processors should be a part of the local union manager's tool kit. This book is about developing successful leadership behaviors and managerial talents and skills. *Leaders lead people, not machines.* Computers can *assist* the modern union manager with his or her administrative duties or managerial responsibilities by ordering and reordering data, but the computer cannot—*must* not—be expected to become the decision maker in the local. Properly utilized, the computer adds to the power bases of the union as an organization and of its leaders. Ignored or improperly used, this technology can be a frightful enemy.

Such is the internal automation question facing local union managers. Unions have to be brought fully into the Information Age. Like the challenge of taking the union's message to the people via broadcast media and doing a better job of educating its own members, union leaders must move their locals into automated office technology. None of the challenges presented in this unit carry the baggage of options and time for extra deliberation. Union leaders must act now on these issues, for we are already tardy in coming to grips with these and other important problems. The authors believe that an effort to meet these three challenges will go a long way toward filling the union's prescription for better health.

## DISCUSSION QUESTIONS

1. Does your parent union have a policy regarding a local's use or purchase of a micro- or minicomputer? If yes, what are its general guidelines? If no, why not?

2. What tasks could a computer system do to assist your local's management team? Make a list and then estimate the hardware and software requirements. Estimate the cost (include hidden costs, etc.).

3. Given the computer system you outlined in Question 2, who would create the data base and who would have access to the system? What information would be in the data base?

4. How long will it take to get this computer system on line with a complete data base, working programs, and trained operators?

5. Is your system worth the time and resources you would have to allocate to it? Would the decision to buy and maintain such a system be a managerial decision or an administrative one? Is leadership behavior involved?

## ADDITIONAL RESOURCES

Computer "how-to's" are on the book shelves by the thousands. They range from the simple to the complex, from cartoon presentations to schematics. The authors recommend that the reader ask for advice from a local book store or computer salesperson. Second, most public school districts, community colleges, and extension divisions of colleges and universities offer introductory noncredit courses in computers at fairly low prices. Finally, labor education/studies programs and some unions are providing education in this area. The George Meany Center for Labor Studies conducts such a course on a regular basis. See the article by Neill De Clerq, Alec Meiklejohn, and Ken Mericle, "The Use of Microcomputers in Local Union Administration," *Labor Studies Journal,* vol. 10, no. 1, Spring 1985, pp. 3–24.

# APPENDIX 6A
## SAMPLE PARTS OF A COMPUTERIZED
## GRIEVANCE AND ARBITRATION SYSTEM

# AFSCME/IOWA COUNCIL 61

**2525 E. Euclid, Suite 205 — Des Moines, Iowa 50317-6064**

**515/266-2622**
**1-800/372-6054**

Don McKee
*President*

Don Winter
*Executive Vice President*

Dick Palmer
*Secretary-Treasurer*

*District Vice Presidents*

*District 1*
Wendy Burgess
*Des Moines*

Dale Pradovich
*Des Moines*

*District 2*
Sue Snapp
*Glenwood*

Rod Klein
*Council Bluffs*

*District 3*
Louise Kruithoff
*Sioux City*

Larry Beyer
*Belmond*

*District 4*
Rick Brinkema
*Waterloo*

Emory Wunn
*Marshalltown*

*District 5*
Jan Grim
*Mt. Pleasant*

Mike Oster
*Center Junction*

July 5, 1984

**(STEW FIRST NAME) (STEW LAST NAME)**
**(STEW STREET ADDRESS)**
**(STEW CITY), (STEW STATE)   (STEW ZIP)**

Dear **(STEW FIRST NAME):**

This is to inform you that the following grievance was received on **(DATE GRIEV RECD C61)** by the Council 61 office in Des Moines.  The Steward assigned to this grievance is **(STEW FIRST NAME) (STEW LAST NAME):**

**(GRIEV FIRST NAME) (GRIEV LAST NAME)**
Local **(LOCAL)**
Grievance number **(GRIEVANCE NO)**
Filed on **(DATE FILED)**
Contract **(CONTRACT)**
Type **(TYPE)**
Article(s) **(ARTICLE VIOLATION)**    Section(s) **(SECTION VIOLATION)**
Contract Violation **(CONTRACT VIOLATION)**
Adjustment Requested: **(ADJUSTMENT REQUIRED)**
Agency **(AGENCY)**
Work Location **(WORK LOCATION)**
Staff Rep assigned **(STAFF REP NAME)**

First step hearing date **(STEP 1 DATE RECD)**

First step disposition **(STEP 1 DISPOSITION)**

Second step hearing date **(STEP 2 DATE RECD)**

Second step disposition **(STEP 2 DISPOSITION)**

Third Step hearing date **(STEP 3 DATE RECD)**

Third step disposition **(STEP 3 DISPOSITION)**

DMcK:sk
cc:   File

cs-1 06/83

Sincerely,

Don McKee
President
AFSCME/Iowa Council 61

# AFSCME/IOWA COUNCIL 61

2525 E. Euclid, Suite 205 — Des Moines, Iowa 50317-6064

515/266-2622
1-800/372-6054

Don McKee
*President*

Don Winter
*Executive Vice President*

Dick Palmer
*Secretary-Treasurer*

*District Vice Presidents*

*District 1*

Wendy Burgess
*Des Moines*

Dale Pradovich
*Des Moines*

*District 2*

Sue Snapp
*Glenwood*

Rod Klein
*Council Bluffs*

*District 3*

Louise Kruithoff
*Sioux City*

Larry Beyer
*Belmond*

*District 4*

Rick Brinkema
*Waterloo*

Emory Wunn
*Marshalltown*

*District 5*

Jan Grim
*Mt. Pleasant*

Mike Oster
*Center Junction*

July 5, 1984

Loren Schutt
2404 Bartelo Rd.
Iowa City, Iowa  52240

Dear Loren:

This is to inform you that the following grievance was received on  by the
Council 61 office in Des Moines.  The Steward assigned to this grievance is
Loren Schutt:

Laurence Mooney
Local **12**
Grievance number **5472**
Filed on
Contract BC
Type CONTRACT
Article(s) XII    Section(s) 1, 3, 4
Contract Violation No protective footwear for cleaning showers.
Adjustment Requested: That management provide protective footwear for all
housekeeping personnel and that grievantbe made whole in all matters.
Agency UofI
Work Location Hillcrest Dorm U of I
Staff Rep assigned Steger

First step hearing date _____

First step disposition _____

Second step hearing date _____

Second step disposition _____

Third Step hearing date _____

Third step disposition _____

Sincerely,

Don McKee
President
AFSCME/Iowa Council 61

DMcK:sk
cc:   File

cs-1 06/83

# AFSCME/IOWA COUNCIL 61

**2525 E. Euclid, Suite 205 — Des Moines, Iowa 50317-6064**

515/266-2622
1-800/372-6054

Don McKee
*President*

Don Winter
*Executive Vice President*

Dick Palmer
*Secretary-Treasurer*

*District Vice Presidents*

*District 1*

Wendy Burgess
*Des Moines*

Dale Pradovich
*Des Moines*

*District 2*

Sue Snapp
*Glenwood*

Rod Klein
*Council Bluffs*

*District 3*

Louise Kruithoff
*Sioux City*

Larry Beyer
*Belmond*

*District 4*

Rick Brinkema
*Waterloo*

Emory Wunn
*Marshalltown*

*District 5*

Jan Grim
*Mt. Pleasant*

Mike Oster
*Center Junction*

July 5, 1984

Loren Schutt
2404 Bartelo Rd.
Iowa City, Iowa  52240

Dear Loren:

Enclosed is the Settlement Agreement for grievance number 5472 listed as active. Your responsibility as the steward representing this grievance is to fill out this form if any settlement or offer is accepted prior to Council 61 involvement and return it to AFSCME/Council 61.

The reason we are asking you to do this is that we are tracking all of our grievances with our computers so that when we go to the Bargaining Table we can pull out the grievances and have a settlement that will be helpful to the negotiating. Thanking you in advance for you cooperation.

Sincerely,

Don McKee
President
Council 61

DM:sk

## SETTLEMENT AGREEMENT

Laurence Mooney
3 Westgate Circle
Iowa City, Iowa  52240
319/338-0386

Grievance number **5472**
Date Filed
Article(s)  XII
Section(s)  1, 3, 4
Local **12**   Contract BC

I, **Laurence Mooney,** hereby accept the following resolution of the above cited grievance.  The settlement agreed to is as follows:

**SETTLEMENT:**(TYPE, PRINT OR ATTACH COPY OF SETTLEMENT)


| | |
|---|---|
| Laurence Mooney<br>(OPTIONAL) | Steger |
| Date signed | Date Signed |
| Loren Schutt-Steward | Management |
| Date Signed | Date Signed |

cc:   Laurence Mooney

Steger  (2)

Management

Chief  Steward  (2)

File


s-1  06/83

# AFSCME/IOWA COUNCIL 61

2525 E. Euclid, Suite 205 — Des Moines, Iowa 50317-6064

515/266-2622
1-800/372-6054

Don McKee
*President*
Don Winter
*Executive Vice President*
Dick Palmer
*Secretary-Treasurer*

*District Vice Presidents*

*District 1*
Wendy Burgess
*Des Moines*
Dale Pradovich
*Des Moines*

*District 2*
Sue Snapp
*Glenwood*
Rod Klein
*Council Bluffs*

*District 3*
Louise Kruithoff
*Sioux City*
Larry Beyer
*Belmond*

*District 4*
Rick Brinkema
*Waterloo*
Emory Wunn
*Marshalltown*

*District 5*
Jan Grim
*Mt. Pleasant*
Mike Oster
*Center Junction*

### MUTUAL AGREEMENT TO
### EXTEND TIME LIMITS

It is hereby agreed to extend the time limits for the _____ step for the grievance of Laurence Mooney, AFSCME Grievance number **5472**, filed on ,
concerning BC Contract violation:

Article(s) XII

Section(s) 1, 3, 4

until _____ .

_____          _____
Steger
Staff Representative                          Management
AFSCME/Iowa Council 61


_____          _____
Date                                                    Date

cc:     Steger

        Management

        Local 12 Steward

        File

e-1 06/83

**AFSCME**
*in the public service*

# AFSCME/IOWA COUNCIL 61

2525 E. Euclid, Suite 205 — Des Moines, Iowa 50317-6064

515/266-2622
1-800/372-6054

Don McKee
*President*

Don Winter
*Executive Vice President*

Dick Palmer
*Secretary-Treasurer*

*District Vice Presidents*

*District 1*

Wendy Burgess
*Des Moines*

Dale Pradovich
*Des Moines*

*District 2*

Sue Snapp
*Glenwood*

Rod Klein
*Council Bluffs*

*District 3*

Louise Kruithoff
*Sioux City*

Larry Beyer
*Belmond*

*District 4*

Rick Brinkema
*Waterloo*

Emory Wunn
*Marshalltown*

*District 5*

Jan Grim
*Mt. Pleasant*

Mike Oster
*Center Junction*

TO:    Mike Hansen

FROM: _____

RE:    Grievance number _____          Local _____

        Grievant's Name _____          Date filed _____

After reviewing this grievance, I am not able to make a clear recommendation to withdraw this grievance or appeal it to arbitration.

I am requesting the arbitration team, which will consist of you and myself, to meet for a review of this grievance to decide which action should be taken. I am requesting that this review to take place on or before the following date _____ .    Please contact me as soon as possible so that we may set a time for this review.

at-1 06/83

# AFSCME/IOWA COUNCIL 61

2525 E. Euclid, Suite 205 — Des Moines, Iowa 50317-6064

515/266-2622
1-800/372-6054

Don McKee
*President*

Don Winter
*Executive Vice President*

Dick Palmer
*Secretary-Treasurer*

*District Vice Presidents*

*District 1*

Wendy Burgess
*Des Moines*

Dale Pradovich
*Des Moines*

*District 2*

Sue Snapp
*Glenwood*

Rod Klein
*Council Bluffs*

*District 3*

Louise Kruithoff
*Sioux City*

Larry Beyer
*Belmond*

*District 4*

Rick Brinkema
*Waterloo*

Emory Wunn
*Marshalltown*

*District 5*

Jan Grim
*Mt. Pleasant*

Mike Oster
*Center Junction*

DATE_____

Mr. Bill Snyder
Employment Relations
State Capitol
Des Moines, Iowa   50319

Dear Mr. Snyder:

In accordance with the BC Unit Agreement between the State of Iowa and
Iowa Public Employees, AFSCME/Iowa Council 61, AFL–CIO, Article IV
(Grievance Procedure), notice is hereby given that Council 61 and its affiliated
Local 12 **appeal** the grievance of Laurence Mooney AFSCME Grievance
Number **5472** to arbitration.

The grievance was filed on  and alleges a violation of Article(s) XII, Section(s)
1, 3, 4, of the BC Unit Agreement.

Sincerely,


Steger
Union Representative
AFSCME/Iowa Council 61


cc:    Bill Snyder
       To be returned as received.

       Steger

       Local 12 President

       File


a-1 06/83

 12

# AFSCME/IOWA COUNCIL 61

### 2525 E. Euclid, Suite 205 — Des Moines, Iowa 50317-6064

**515/266-2622**
**1-800/372-6054**

Don McKee
*President*

Don Winter
*Executive Vice President*

Dick Palmer
*Secretary-Treasurer*

*District Vice Presidents*

*District 1*
Wendy Burgess
*Des Moines*
Dale Pradovich
*Des Moines*

*District 2*
Sue Snapp
*Glenwood*
Rod Klein
*Council Bluffs*

*District 3*
Louise Kruithoff
*Sioux City*
Larry Beyer
*Belmond*

*District 4*
Rick Brinkema
*Waterloo*
Emory Wunn
*Marshalltown*

*District 5*
Jan Grim
*Mt. Pleasant*
Mike Oster
*Center Junction*

DATE _____

James A. McClimon, Manager
Fact-Finding and Arbitration Services
Public Employment Relations Board
507 10th
Des Moines, Iowa  50309

Dear Mr. McClimon:

RE:  Laurence Mooney, Grievance No. 5472

AFSCME/Iowa Council 61 hereby requests a list of five arbiters to strike names from in the arbitration proceedings of Laurence Mooney, AFSCME Grievance Number 5472.

The other party is the State of Iowa represented by Mr. Bill Snyder.

Sincerely,


Steger
Union Representative
AFSCME/Iowa Council 61

cc:   Bill Snyder
      Employment Relations
      State Capitol
      Des Moines, Iowa  50319

      Local 12 President

      Steger

      File


a-2 06/83

# AFSCME/IOWA COUNCIL 61

2525 E. Euclid, Suite 205 — Des Moines, Iowa 50317-6064

515/266-2622
1-800/372-6054

Don McKee
*President*

Don Winter
*Executive Vice President*

Dick Palmer
*Secretary-Treasurer*

*District Vice Presidents*
*District 1*

Wendy Burgess
*Des Moines*

Dale Pradovich
*Des Moines*

*District 2*

Sue Snapp
*Glenwood*

Rod Klein
*Council Bluffs*

*District 3*

Louise Kruithoff
*Sioux City*

Larry Beyer
*Belmond*

*District 4*

Rick Brinkema
*Waterloo*

Emory Wunn
*Marshalltown*

*District 5*

Jan Grim
*Mt. Pleasant*

Mike Oster
*Center Junction*

## ARBITRATOR EVALUATION SHEET

**Prepared by** _____

DATE _____

**ARBITRATOR** -

ADDRESS -

CITY -

STATE -

ZIP -

PHONE -

**RATED: SUPERIOR    GOOD    FAIR    POOR    DO NOT RECOMMEND**
(Circle One)

CASE NAME AND NUMBER: _____

Grievance Number _____    Local _____

Grievant's Name _____

**SUMMARY OF AWARD:**

**REMARKS:**

ae-1  06/83

# AFSCME/IOWA COUNCIL 61

2525 E. Euclid, Suite 205 — Des Moines, Iowa 50317-6064

515/266-2622
1-800/372-6054

Don McKee
*President*

Don Winter
*Executive Vice President*

Dick Palmer
*Secretary-Treasurer*

*District Vice Presidents*
*District 1*

Wendy Burgess
*Des Moines*

Dale Pradovich
*Des Moines*

*District 2*

Sue Snapp
*Glenwood*

Rod Klein
*Council Bluffs*

*District 3*

Louise Kruithoff
*Sioux City*

Larry Beyer
*Belmond*

*District 4*

Rick Brinkema
*Waterloo*

Emory Wunn
*Marshalltown*

*District 5*

Jan Grim
*Mt. Pleasant*

Mike Oster
*Center Junction*

July 9, 1984

Laurence Mooney
3 Westgate Circle
Iowa City, Iowa    52240

Dear Laurence:

This letter is to advise you that Council 61 is withdrawing from arbitration your grievance, Grievance Number 5472, on the recommendation of Staff Representative Steger and Local 12.

If you disagree with the recommendation to withdraw your grievance, please contact me in writting within fourteen (14) calendar days (of the postmark on the envelope) at the Council 61 office in Des Moines. If I do not hear from you within 14 calendar days, your grievance will be withdrawn and no further action can be taken.

Sincerely,

Don McKee
President
AFSCME/Iowa Council 61

cc:  Steger

     Don Winter
     Local 12 President
     2809 Wayne Ave.
     Iowa City, Iowa    52240

     File

CRR #_____

wd-1 06/83

**AFSCME**
*in the public service*

# AFSCME/IOWA COUNCIL 61

2525 E. Euclid, Suite 205 — Des Moines, Iowa 50317-6064

515/266-2622
1-800/372-6054

Don McKee
*President*

Don Winter
*Executive Vice President*

Dick Palmer
*Secretary-Treasurer*

*District Vice Presidents*
*District 1*

Wendy Burgess
*Des Moines*

Dale Pradovich
*Des Moines*

*District 2*

Sue Snapp
*Glenwood*

Rod Klein
*Council Bluffs*

*District 3*

Louise Kruithoff
*Sioux City*

Larry Beyer
*Belmond*

*District 4*

Rick Brinkema
*Waterloo*

Emory Wunn
*Marshalltown*

*District 5*

Jan Grim
*Mt. Pleasant*

Mike Oster
*Center Junction*

July 10, 1984

Laurence Mooney
3 Westgate Circle
Iowa City, Iowa   52240

Dear Laurence:

RE:  Grievance number 5472

Your appeal to the Council 61 President, Don McKee, has been accepted. Within 5 days of the date of this letter you will need to call the Council 61 office in Des Moines at 515/266-2622 to set up an appointment for a meeting in the Des Moines office with myself to discuss your grievance.

Sincerely,

Don McKee
President
AFSCME/Iowa Council 61

DMcK:sk

cc:  Corderman

Don Winter
AFSCME Local 12 President
2809 Wayne Ave.
Iowa City, Iowa   52240

File

wd-1aa 06/83

**AFSCME**
*in the public service*

# AFSCME/IOWA COUNCIL 61

### 2525 E. Euclid, Suite 205 — Des Moines, Iowa 50317-6064

**515/266-2622**
**1-800/372-6054**

Don McKee
*President*

Don Winter
*Executive Vice President*

Dick Palmer
*Secretary-Treasurer*

*District Vice Presidents*

*District 1*

Wendy Burgess
*Des Moines*

Dale Pradovich
*Des Moines*

*District 2*

Sue Snapp
*Glenwood*

Rod Klein
*Council Bluffs*

*District 3*

Louise Kruithoff
*Sioux City*

Larry Beyer
*Belmond*

*District 4*

Rick Brinkema
*Waterloo*

Emory Wunn
*Marshalltown*

*District 5*

Jan Grim
*Mt. Pleasant*

Mike Oster
*Center Junction*

July 10, 1984

Mr. Bill Snyder
Employment Relations
State Capitol
Des Moines, Iowa  50319

Dear Mr. Snyder:

The Union, AFSCME Council 61 and its affiliated Local 12, hereby **withdraws** from appeal to arbitration the grievance of Laurence Mooney, AFSCME Grievance Number **5472**; filed on ; concerning BC contract violation:  Article(s) XII, Section(s) 1, 3, 4.

It is understood by the parties that the withdrawal of this grievance will not constitute a precedent for any subsequent grievance.

Sincerely,

Don McKee
President
AFSCME/Iowa Council 61

DMcK:sk

cc:   Steger

Don Winter
Local 12 President
2809 Wayne Ave.
Iowa City, Iowa  52240

File

wd-2 06/83

## APPENDIX 6B
## COMPUTER ACRONYMS
## AND VOCABULARY

### Computer Acronyms

Hundreds of acronyms are in use by computer users. The list grows each year with new advances. Generally, computing acronyms can be categorized in at least one of three areas: computer abbreviations, computer programs, and communications. Listed here are 53 of the most common computer acronyms.

| | | | |
|---|---|---|---|
| EPROM | Alternating current | LPM | Lines per minute |
| ACC | Accumulator | LSB | Least significant bit |
| A/D | Analog to digital | LSI | Large-scale integration |
| BCD | Binary-coded decimal | MPU | Microprocessor unit |
| BPS | Bits per second | MSB | Most significant bit |
| CPS | Characters per second | MSI | Medium-scale |
| CPU | Central processing unit | | integration |
| CR | Carriage return | MUX | Multiplexer |
| CRT | Cathode-ray tube | PC | Program counter or |
| D/A | Digital to analog | | personal computer |
| DC | Direct current | PLA | Programmable logic |
| DIP | Dual in-line package | | array |
| DMA | Direct-memory access | POS | Point of scale |
| ECL | Emitter-coupled logic | PROM | Programmable ROM |
| EOR | Exclusive OR | PSW | Program status word |
| EPROM | Electrically program- | Q | Positive logic output of |
| | mable ROM | | a flip-flop |
| FET | Field-effect transistor | $\overline{Q}$ | Negative output logic |
| GIGO | Garbage in, garbage out | | of a flip-flop |
| GP | General purpose | RAM | Random-access memory |
| HEX | Hexadecimal | ROM | Read-only memory |
| IC | Integrated circuit | RTC | Real-time clock |
| INT | Interrupt | R/W | Read/write |
| I/O | Input/output | SR | Shift register |
| $I^2L$ | Integration injection | SSI | Small-scale integration |
| | logic | SUB | Subroutine |
| K | 1024 | TSS | Time-sharing system |
| LED | Light-emitting diode | TTY | Teletypewriter |
| LIFO | Last in first out | X | Index |
| LP | Line printer | XOR | Exclusive OR |

## Computer Vocabulary

There are literally hundreds of terms pertaining to computers and their operation. Listed here are over 80 of the most common and useful.

**acronym.** A word derived by combining the first or first few letters of many words. Countless computer terms are acronyms.

**algorithms.** A sequence of steps followed to define and solve a specific computation or problem.

**alphanumeric.** The set of human-readable symbols containing the letters A–Z and the numbers 0–9, as well as special characters.

**array.** A set of related items grouped under a single name.

**ASCII.** American Standard Code for Information Interchange (pronounced askee): a method of encoding alphanumerics.

**assignment statement.** The statement in a programming language that involves the transfer of a value to a variable.

**BASIC.** Beginner's All-Purpose Symbolic Instruction Code: a widely used high-level program language.

**bit.** BInary DigiT: a 0 or a 1; the smallest unit of computer information.

**bug.** An error that causes a computer program to malfunction.

**bus.** The pattern of power, informational, and memory connectors and conductors in a computer system.

**byte.** A sequence of bits, normally 8 in number (although 4, 12, and 16 are used). Depending on computer design, a half-word is 2 bytes and a full word is 4 bytes (32 bits).

**chip.** Also known as an *integrated circuit*. A chip is a silicon wafer containing thousands of semiconductors.

**COBOL.** COmmon Business-Oriented Language: a high-level programming language geared toward business and commercial applications.

**code.** A specific way for representing data and symbols.

**coding.** The writing of a program in a specific programming language, such as BASIC or COBOL.

**collating sequence.** The order in which a list of items is sorted. When collating, it is the comparing or merging of two lists or files into one.

**compiler.** A special computer program designed to translate high-level programming language into machine language.

**computer.** A system minimally consisting of a CPU, memory, I/O units, and a power supply.

**console.** The console is used by the programmer/operator to communicate with the system. It usually contains the keyboard and an on/off switch.

**core.** Doughnutlike ferrite material strung on wires to store bits. Core memory is also referred to as principal, main, or primary memory.

**CP/M.** Programs that utilize a mass storage device, which in turn facilitates the use of floppy disks, are called CP/Ms. Data files can be created, manipulated, and erased from disk to disk, or transferred from disk to disk.

**CPU.** Central processing unit: also called the central processor or mainframe. This is the part of the computer that executes the program.

**CRT display.** Cathode-ray tube display: the part of the computer terminal that provides the video, or televisionlike, display.

**cursor.** An underscore marking the portion at which the next character is to be entered on a CRT screen.

**data.** Coded information.

**data base.** The complete set of data that can be recalled to make decisions, calculations, and tabulations.

**data processing.** The use of computers and other devices or machines to handle the acquisition, storage, and manipulation of information.

**debug.** To eliminate errors in a computer program.

**disk.** A mass storage technique that stores information on magnetically sensitive surfaces; it resembles a hi-fi record.

**diskette.** Floppy disk: a thin, circular object that is usually stored in a square envelope, sleeve, or storage book. It is used as a low-cost storage medium for smaller computer systems.

**EDP.** Electronic data processing: the performance of data processing using an electronic digital computer.

**EPROM.** Electronically programmable read-only memory: a memory type that can hold data forever.

**execute.** To run a program.

**file.** A collection or sequence of related records or data sets.

**floppy disk.** See *diskette.*

**flow chart.** A drawing depicting the steps, logic, and reasoning behind a program. It is used to make the program more understandable.

**FORTRAN.** FORmula TRANslation: a program almost as easy as BASIC, but more mathematical. It is a high-level programming language used in engineering and science.

**graphics system.** Hardware and software that enable the computer to translate data into drawings, graphs, and pictures.

**IC.** Integrated circuit; see *chip*.

**ID.** Identification.

**input.** Data entered into a computer via a terminal.

**interface.** That point at which any two computer system components (hardware and software) join together.

**interpreter.** A computer program that *immediately* translates high-level programming language into machine language. BASIC is an interpreter language.

**I/O.** Input/output.

**K.** May be used to mean a factor of about 1000. This figure is derived from the numerical expression of $1024 = 2^{10}$. A 16K memory is ordinarily 16 bytes = 16,384 bytes of memory.

**keyboard.** The part of the terminal that contains keys. They resemble closely keyboards on electric typewriters.

**keyword.** A reserved word in a programming language.

**LCD.** Liquid-crystal display.

**LED.** Light-emitting diode: used to display characters by glowing light in the readout area on screen.

**line printer.** A high-speed peripheral device that can print an entire line (usually up to 144 characters) at one time. This varies with the cost of the printer. Electronic typewriters, when hooked to a word processor, usually print between 24 and 32 characters per second. Line printers utilize either a daisy-wheel or ink-dot method of printing, with the daisy wheel usually the most favored.

**list.** A sequence of data items.

**machine language.** Also called binary code: the lowest level of computer programming language.

**mainframe.** See *CPU*.

**memory.** The primary or secondary memory of a computer system. It stores data and/or instructions. In a system, the primary memory may also be called the main, core, or principal. In the same system, the secondary system may also be called auxilliary or peripheral.

**menu.** The list of instructions or commands of a program displayed on a CRT screen. The operator, by use of a cursor or a "mouse," selects the function desired from this listing.

**microcomputer.** A small computer built around a microprocessor.

**microprocessor.** Computer electronics usually placed on a single chip in an integrated circuit with multiple leads.

**minicomputer.** A computer, smaller than a mainframe computer, but larger than a microcomputer.

**modem.** Modulator–demodulator: usually connects a computer to telephone lines and then converts computer signals to audio tones, and vice versa.

**MPU.** Microprocessor unit: another way to say microprocessor.

**network.** A set of devices that connects computers, terminals, or telephones.

**OCR.** Optical character reader: a hardware input machine using light-sensitive devices.

**off line.** Refers to computer equipment not at the time directly connected to the computer: a method of data processing without being under direct control or in direct communication with the CPU.

**on line.** Refers to computer equipment directly connected to the computer: a method of data processing while being under direct control or in direct communication with the CPU.

**output.** Data transmitted to a peripheral device, such as a terminal or a line printer: the result of processing.

**overflow.** Usually applies when the limits of computer, especially the memory, are exceeded.

**pascal.** A higher-level programming language devised to use the best features of BASIC, FORTRAN, and COBOL. It is used especially to *teach* computer science and programming.

**peripheral.** Any device, especially one used for communication, that can be connected to the computer (same as I/O devices).

**program.** A set of instructions, written in the program language in use, and noting the type of computer and its capabilities, which will permit the computer to carry out the prescribed tasks.

**PROM.** Programmable read-only memory.

**RAM.** Random-access memory: floppy disks are RAMs.

**ROM.** Read-only memory.

**run.** The execution of a program.

**software.** Term given to the computer programs, since they lack "hardware" such as electronic circuits and such.

**storage.** Memory.

**system.** The sum total of devices, people, data and information, methods, and anything else needed to accomplish an objective.

**table.** The arrangement of data into rows (horizontal) and columns (vertical).

**terminal.** An I/O device through which one communicates with a computer.

**value.** A constant or quantity stored in a variable.

**variable.** A location in the memory that stores a particular value.

**video display terminal.** A televisionlike device with a keyboard that presents data on the screen.

**wafer.** A silicon medium that has integrated circuits built on it.

**word.** A logical group of bits. A word usually consists of at least 4 bytes (32 bits).

**WP.** Word processing: a computer system designed for typing, editing, and output of written material, such as letters, reports, and notices.

# UNIT THREE

## INFORMATIONAL AND PERSONAL LEADERSHIP SKILLS

- *A primer on labor law*
- *Conducting union and committee meetings*
- *Personal and public communication techniques*
- *Effective writing skills*

# CHAPTER 7

# A Primer on Labor Law

As an environmental agent affecting the purpose and structure of unions, labor law is almost unequaled. The right of workers to band together and form a union for the purpose of bargaining collectively is based in statute law. Federal and state laws alike influence, if not dictate, the ways unions do business. The laws, as they are interpreted, and agency rules, as they are applied, change over time as elected officials and administrative officers change. Unions necessarily change as well.

A local union manager cannot properly conduct the business of the local union without a basic understanding of labor law. Such information serves to enhance information and expert power bases supporting one's leadership style. Knowledge of current laws is required if legal reporting requirements (an administrative task) are to be done properly and in a timely matter. Often good management is required to bring the data together in order to complete forms LM-2, LM-3, 990, and the like. Finally, organizing, bargaining an agreement, and the operation of the grievance system cannot function properly without knowledge of the law.

This chapter is not intended to make lawyers of union leaders. Rather, its intention is to give a dash of labor law in hopes of defining the legal parameters within which unions must operate, and to demonstrate the environmental impact of labor law on unions. Unions have changed and will continue to alter their activities in the light of new law or new legal interpretation.

## FROM THE FACTORY SYSTEM
## TO THE NEW DEAL

Before the rise of the modern factory system, there was little need for collective bargaining in the United States. When America was young and agricultural, most citizens provided for their food, housing, and shelter through the use of their own tools and hands. Those who worked in the small handicraft shops of the eighteenth and nineteenth centuries were also very self-sufficient. The need for collective bargaining was not yet necessary and came about only when a worker sold her labor to another.

For a variety of reasons, the American worker has never developed a working-class attitude. Historically, the American worker has been a person seeking to achieve more than his or her parents. As the nation expanded westward, many workers chased the dreams of a better tomorrow by looking elsewhere for jobs, land, and opportunity.

The opportunities for wealth, along with the basic freedoms of property ownership, helped shape America's early approach to workers who tried to form trade unions. The resistance that employers put forth was unmatched in its fury. Workers not only had their employers with their ideas about free enterprise to combat, but also the courts and the judges who framed American law. Given these conditions, it was difficult for workers to organize and remain organized prior to 1935. Employer antiunion practices were regularly accepted and advanced by the courts. These tactics included regular use of strikebreakers, yellow dog contracts, labor spies, firings, and blacklistings of union activists.

### Evolution of Labor Law

During the early 1800s, the employer solicited help from the courts to deal with almost any labor dispute. Early organizations that represented shoemakers were considered "conspiracies in restraint of trade."[1] In those days, conspirators could be indicted and found guilty without committing any definite act. To be a jurist at the shoemaker trials, one had to meet certain property requirements. Therefore, the juries generally consisted of the merchant class with whom the strikers had a dispute. This feature undoubtedly influenced the outcome of the trials, which are commonly referred to as the Cordwainers Conspiracy Cases.[2]

This attitude in law, that labor unions were conspiracies and therefore unlawful organizations, prevailed until 1842 in the *Commonwealth* v. *Hunt* case. In this case, Chief Justice Shaw of the Supreme Court of Massachusetts declared unions to be lawful.[3] The employers shrugged this decision off and moved on to another tactic to halt trade unionism—the labor injunction.

---

[1] Joseph A. Rayback, *A History of American Labor.* The Free Press, New York, 1966, p. 56.

[2] Ibid.

[3] Ibid., pp. 91–92.

An injunction is a court action directing a person or organization to refrain from pursuing a course of action. The judges who ruled on whether or not to grant the injunction were no doubt influenced by the prevailing attitude of defending private property. The *injunction* or the *temporary restraining order* was used to protect businesses from "irreparable damage" due to a work stoppage. If workers ignored these court actions, they were jailed and viewed as lawbreakers by the public.

Another employer tactic used to discourage union organization was the *yellow dog contract*. As a condition of employment, a worker had to sign a contract stating that he was not a member of a labor organization and, while employed at that workplace, would not join a union. The Supreme Court upheld the legality of yellow dog contracts. The Court considered the contract legal and binding between the employer and employee, one that was a voluntary transaction between both parties.

The legislative branch of the government was slowly trying to respond to the rise of the factory system following the Civil War and to the new industrial relations climate. By the 1890s, some 15 states had tried to curtail the effects of injunctions, restraining orders, and yellow dog contracts. Various legislators had to be responsive to their electorate while courts still lagged behind. The judges kept their traditional philosophies, identified with employers and property owners, and consistently ruled in their favor. These men were not under the direct control of the electorate and could not be voted out by those seeking collective bargaining rights. The judges identified with corporate America rather than working-class America. Time and again the Supreme Court ruled unconstitutional any attempts to challenge yellow dog contracts, child labor laws, and minimum wage rates. The courts consistently found that workers voluntarily agreed to sell their labor and to rule in their behalf would violate the Fifth Amendment to the U.S. Constitution.[4] To the judicial branch, once the worker sold her labor she became the company's private property, which was to be "protected" by interstate commerce law.

Except for a brief period of time during World War I, the government consistently sided with employers during organization attempts. If the war was to be won, uninterrupted productivity would be necessary. The War Labor Board maintained that collective bargaining was permissible through labor representatives. The effects of yellow dog contracts were cancelled, permitting the number of organized workers to grow by 33%.[5]

The phenomenal union growth rate during World War I pointed to the important role government had in helping workers organize. When the government is on the workers' side, mountains can be moved. But after the war, the Labor Board was dissolved and union organizing declined. Employers went on a

[4] Benjamin J. Taylor and Fred Witney, *Labor Relations Law.* 2nd ed. Prentice-Hall, Inc., Englewood Cliffs, N.J., 1975, p. 138.

[5] Ibid., pp. 141–142.

rampage during the 1920s with an open-shop campaign and American Plan, which seemingly declared it unpatriotic to join a trade union.

## Railway Labor Act

The railroads were a very important part of our country's early economic development. They controlled and moved most interstate commerce. Railway industrial peace was a necessity and the government knew it. Westward expansion meant that continuous transportation of goods was essential and work stoppages could not be tolerated. The company unions that the railroads were expected to support only brought potential time bombs to the industry.

In 1926, Congress passed the Railway Labor Act in order to avoid a potential national problem on the railroads. It was believed that if workers were permitted to bargain with representatives of their own choosing there could be true industrial peace. Workplace democracy would be in place and a dialogue could be established with the captains of the industry and the workers.

Naturally, the employers ran to their friends, the courts, to test the validity of the act. However, the Supreme Court ruled in favor of the worker and held that "promotion of the collective bargaining process was of the 'highest public interest,' for such a procedure prevents 'the interruption of interstate commerce by labor disputes and strikes.'"[6] The Court, in an unprecedented decision, had ruled that collective bargaining *promotes* commerce among the states rather than hinders. Collective bargaining became a means for industrial peace.

This Supreme Court ruling was also significant because it reversed precedent from all its previous decisions whereby unions were viewed as a hindrance to commerce. In reality, the Court said that it was time for a change and reversed the decades of established precedent. This is no small task for a group of men who usually pride themselves on precedent, some of which they have helped establish. However, as the political climate shifted and the socioeconomic picture changed, the Chief Justices addressed the commonsense side of the issue rather than precedent. The nation was changing and the attitudes of the courts had to change before more serious problems developed.

Despite both congressional and judiciary efforts to bring collective bargaining into the twentieth century (see Table 7-1), the worker still had another obstacle to overcome—the employer. Employers used any loophole they could find to circumvent the law. At other times, they just broke the law and took their chances. To get around the laws, the employer used all his tricks and guile, including the establishment of *company unions*. The law was very slow in evolving and it took until 1935 with the passage of the Wagner Act to tighten everything else up.

[6]Ibid., p. 145.

**TABLE 7-1.**   Notable Labor Laws[7]

| ACT | YEAR | INTENT |
|---|---|---|
| Erdman Act | 1888 | Outlaw yellow dog contracts by railroads |
| Newlands Act | 1912 | Dispute resolution on railroads |
| Clayton Act | 1914 | Limit the use of labor injunctions and legalize trade unions |
| Adamson Act | 1916 | Establish 8-hour day on railroads |
| Railway Labor Act | 1926 | Establish right to bargain collectively with representatives of own choosing on railroads |
| Norris–La–Guardia Act | 1932 | Outlaw yellow dog contracts and further limit use of labor injunction |

## THE NEW DEAL

The Great Depression brought on a wave of despair for the American worker. Franklin Roosevelt and his New Deal was swept into office in 1932, and the administration began to do what it could to get the economy moving again. The Roosevelt administration decided to help the worker and not the corporations, as had been the case in previous administrations. To help workers, the proper legal climate had to be established. Collective bargaining and organizing were to flourish under favorable legal conditions.

Prior to the Wagner Act, the New Deal sought and passed the National Industrial Recovery Act (NIRA) in 1933. Section 7(a) of the act provided legal protection for the right of workers to collective bargaining. It was believed that this would bring an end to industrial tensions and warfare.

Section 7(a) contained two major principles: (1) that employees had the right to organize and bargain collectively through representatives of their own choosing and shall be free from employer interference in electing these representatives; and (2) that no employee or one seeking employment shall be required to join a company-sponsored union as a condition of employment or to refrain from joining a union of his or her own choosing.[8]

The major flaw in the NIRA was that the law provided no means of enforcement. It did not take long for employers to exploit the loopholes by firing union activists, sponsoring company unions, and refusing to bargain. There was also a challenge made regarding the validity of such a law. In 1935, the NIRA was ruled unconstitutional.

[7]Rayback, op. cit., pp. 269–319.

[8]Taylor and Witney, op. cit., p. 148.

## The Wagner Act

Modern industrialism meant the end of individual bargaining. It was foolhardy to imagine a sole employee working in a United States Steel mill going to the president and asking for a raise. This technique might have worked in a cottage industry, but it is useless in a mass-production industry with hundreds or thousands of workers.

Congress recognized that the modern relationship between employee and employer needed a law so that the worker was more in balance with the corporation. This struggle had its roots in 1806 with the conspiracy doctrines and continued into the 1930s with enormous employer resistance to worker input and organization. To bring about balance and extend democracy into the workplace, Congress passed the National Labor Relations Act of 1935. This act is more commonly referred to as the Wagner Act because it was sponsored by Senator Robert Wagner of New York, and it was built on the good foundation of the NIRA.

The Wagner Act was economic in nature because it sought to redistribute the money generated by the worker back to her or him. The act sought to improve the overall operation of the economy by putting greater purchasing power in the hands of the worker. After all, how many cars, refrigerators, and radios could the president of U.S. Steel buy? If he had less and the worker more, the economy would pick up. So the logic seemed.

Additionally, the worker was provided with a means of self-determination in the workplace. The law would establish a bilateral relationship at work as opposed to the employer-preferred unilateral arrangement. Dialogue between labor and management was now sanctioned by the government.

The employers did not exactly accept Wagner with open arms. Again there was huge employer resistance, with the National Lawyer's Committee waging a national campaign against the law.[9] Injunctions were still issued because many local judges did not understand Wagner and were probably looking for it to be declared unconstitutional like the NIRA. The new law was also ridiculed in the press, and workers began losing confidence in what the Wagner Act promised.

The Wagner Act went through a stormy two-year period, but was declared constitutional on April 12, 1937. The Supreme Court could have invalidated Wagner, but it was no doubt influenced by a very popular president who was soundly re-elected in 1936 and had also threatened to "pack" the court with men who looked favorably on the law. These events, along with continued industrial warfare over union organizing, helped the Court validate Wagner.

## Major Provisions of the Wagner Act

Sections 7 and 8 of the Wagner Act were its heart and soul and where most of the early controversy came from. Section 7 of the statute declared:

[9] Ibid., p. 160.

Employees shall have the right to self-organization, to form, join or assist labor organizations, to bargain collectively through representatives of their own choosing, and to engage in concerted activities, for the purposes of collective bargaining or other mutual aid protection.

Section 8 of the new law spelled out the unfair labor practices and set the tone for the entire act. Part of this section states that it shall be an unfair labor practice for an employer:

1. To interfere with, restrain, or coerce employees in the exercise of their rights guaranteed in section 7.
2. To dominate or interefere with the formation or administration of any labor organization or contribute financial support or other support to it. . . .
3. By discrimination in regard to hire or tenure of employment or any term or condition of employment to encourage or discourage membership in any labor organization . . . .
4. To discharge or otherwise discriminate against an employee because he has filed charges or given testimony under this Act.
5. To refuse to bargain collectively with representatives of his employees . . . .

The Wagner Act accomplished what it set out to do, with collective bargaining being protected by the government. Organized workers grew at an unprecedented rate. In 1935 fewer than 4 million workers were organized, but by 1948 those numbers had swelled to about 16 million. Organizational strikes were reduced and the trade union movement expanded. The law had sought to and did indeed balance the scales of strength between employer and employee. Worker input and majority rule were now acceptable forms of industrial relations and industrial democracy.

## TAFT–HARTLEY: THE BALANCE CHANGES

If the Wagner Act was largely responsible for the growth of organizing, the Taft–Hartley Act was just as responsible for halting that pace of growth. The Labor–Management Relations Act (Taft–Hartley) of 1947 is actually an amendment to the Wagner Act. It is also very controversial and has done much to change the course of industrial relations. The law helped spur the growth of industrial relations as a discipline of higher education and became a full-employment bill for labor lawyers.

The Wagner Act was certainly never popular with the business community. Each session in Congress brought attempts to repeal the law.[10] Also, the Wagner

[10] Ibid., p. 203.

Act was not very popular with the media and consequently the general public's image of the act was also low. The Wagner Act was perceived as anti-American because it discouraged individualism and promoted collective action.

A number of misconceptions followed the passage of the Wagner Act. Perhaps the biggest misconception was that, once passed, there would be less strike activity. As previously mentioned, the Wagner Act was intended to lessen organizational strikes and never addressed other types of strikes. So when any strike occurred the Wagner Act was blamed. The act also did not stop workers from being discharged, force a contract between labor and management, or establish terms and conditions of employment.[11] In short, there was a huge perception that the Wagner Act was both powerful and abusive.

The supporters of Taft–Hartley had momentum going into 1947, especially after the wartime work stoppage of the coal miners and the wave of post-World War II strikes. The amount of worker-days lost to production increased by 300% between 1945 and 1946. Although almost two-thirds of these strikes were over wages, hours, and working conditions, something that the Wagner Act does not address, the 1935 law was blamed.[12] With inflation running at about 30% and reduced working hours as the nation switched to a peace economy, it is not hard to understand the economic aggressiveness of the post-World War II worker.

The proponents of the Taft–Hartley Act now claimed the scales would be balanced. For 12 years they said that the Wagner Act was pro-labor, that the law went too far in its attempt at worker protection. If passed, labor would no longer be a monopoly and the public would be protected against strikes and union bosses. They also said that the Taft–Hartley Act would protect and foster individual rights.

Several states enacted their own anti-Wagner laws between 1935 and 1947. These laws limited the rights of employees to boycott, strike, picket, and organize. These attacks on the state level paved the way for Taft–Hartley and much of the national statute was adapted from the various state restrictions. While labor unions did criticize these state laws, there was no real effort to prevent the national presures for change.[13]

Those who opposed the bill claimed that union expansion would be threatened and that organizing would be more difficult; they entitled Taft–Hartley the "slave labor law."[14] The leadership of the CIO and the AFL took strong positions against the bill during Senate hearings just prior to enactment. However, on June 23, 1947, Congress overrode a veto by President Truman and enacted Taft–Hartley. The president stated, rather strongly, that the law would "plague this nation for years to come" and reverse the basic direction of America's labor policy by being in conflict with basic democratic principles.[15]

[11] Ibid., p. 205.

[12] Ibid., p. 211.

[13] Ibid., p. 204.

[14] Ibid., p. 202.

[15] Ibid., p. 212.

## Major Taft–Hartley Provisions

The Labor–Management Relations Act (Taft–Hartley) amended but did not displace Wagner. The most significant changes were:

Unions could now be charged with unfair labor practices.

The closed shop was outlawed.

Union shop arrangements were greatly reduced.

Individual rights were stressed.

Section 8(a) of the Wagner was left virtually intact under Taft–Hartley, but an entire section, 8(b), added unfair labor practices of labor organizations. This was the balance that the employer associations had sought since 1935.

Perhaps the portion of Taft–Hartley that labor most dislikes is section 14(b), which states:

Nothing in this Act shall be construed as authorizing the execution or application of agreements requiring membership in a labor organization as a condition of employment in any State or Territory in which such execution or application is prohibited by State or Territorial law.

This simply means that individual states have the right to outlaw union and agency shops. Organized labor maintains that this is an open invitation to engage in union busting and have it sanctioned by the government.[16] The proponents of the law sought to protect individuals *against* labor organizations. Under 14(b), workers do not have to join a labor union, but must be represented by the union. These workers are often referred to as "free riders" because they pay no dues.

The 20 states that have envoked section 14(b) of Taft–Hartley are referred to as "right-to-work" states. Supporters of such laws claim that it is a basic American right not to join an organization if one so desires. They claim that this is a fundamental of democracy. Opponents of right-to-work laws say just the opposite, that in America a majority rules. For example, if a Republican president favors a tax increase even his Democratic opponents must pay their share when enacted. One cannot advocate individual rights to the IRS and refuse to pay.

Results of these right-to-work laws have had a serious negative impact on the trade union movement. Most states that have envoked 14(b) are in the South and Southwest. It is not surprising that the wage rates in Mississippi, North Carolina, and South Carolina are so low. These states rank 48, 49, and 50 when computing total union membership as a percent of employees in nonagricultual workplaces[17] and have a per capita income that is $2585 below the national average.[18] These are truly "right-to-work for less" states.

[16] Rayback, op. cit., p. 400.

[17] AFL–CIO Department of Research, "Union Membership and Employment 1959-1979," p. I-27.

[18] *AFL*–CIO News, December 8, 1984, p. 10.

Another significant portion of Taft–Hartley gives employers a wide range of subtle threats when a union representation drive is going on. The employer is now free to say "the plant *may* close if the union gets in." Under the Wagner Act, that type of statement would have been an unfair labor practice. The employer is free to imply that labor unions are corrupt, racist, violent, and self-serving. Employers are also free to call for an election in a union shop to see if the workers would rather decertify the union. This has spurred on the creation of labor-relations consultants, sometimes referred to as "union busters," to help the employer and to coach employees on how to go through the decertification process legally or take a few chances and go outside the law.

There are other sections of Taft–Hartley that deal with national emergency strikes, featherbedding, picketing, secondary boycotts, and termination of the agreement. These are all interesting aspects of the law, but time and space only permit mentioning the most controversial: union unfair labor practices and the right-to-work portion of the law.

## LANDRUM–GRIFFIN: MORE UNION CONTROLS

Twelve years passed before another major piece of labor legislation was enacted. The Labor–Management Reporting and Disclosure Act (LMRDA), more commonly known as the Landrum–Griffin Act, was passed in September 1959.

Although Taft–Hartley slowed the rate at which unions grew, organizing was still taking place and the number of workers seeking organized strength continued to grow. With the size of unions taking on more prominence, unions also got more attention from the media, especially with television coming into its own in the 1950s. The difficulties between the AFL and CIO were being worked out, and the two labor organizations merged in 1955 to form the modern-day AFL–CIO. Suddenly, some 15 million workers were under one umbrella and the nation became alarmed. Labor was immediately faced with a challenge from Senator Barry Goldwater of Arizona and other legislators who feared that the unions had too much political influence.

For some time there had been charges of internal union problems, including mishandling of funds, corruption, and undemocratic election procedures. Because unions were relatively small, little attention was paid to the charges. In 1957, the problem of union corruption got national attention when the Senate established a special committee. Senator John McClellan of Arkansas chaired the committee to investigate racketeering in the field of industrial and labor relations.[19]

While the committee made a number of findings that confirmed union corruption and racketeering, it should be pointed out that its findings were based primarily on research of *only five unions*. There were over 200 national unions

[19] Rayback, op. cit., p. 432.

during this time, but Congress thoroughly investigated only the Teamsters, Bakery and Confectionary Workers, United Textile Workers, Operating Engineers, and Allied Industrial Workers.[20]

After almost two years of hearings, investigations, and research, the McClellan committee made a number of findings and recommendations. The more notable ones were:

1. There has been widespread misuse of union funds through poor auditing procedures.

2. International unions have raided local union treasuries by wrongfully placing them under trusteeships.

3. Sweetheart contracts have been arranged for by corrupt management and labor officials.

4. Unions have been infiltrated by gangsters.

5. Union members were kept in line through acts of violence.

Based on their findings, the McClellan committee made recommendations to regulate the internal affairs of all unions. These regulations sought to ensure union democracy, regulate union funds, and keep neutral employers from being hurt economically during a strike or boycott.

## Title I:  The Bill of Rights

Title I of Landrum–Griffin is often referred to as the "bill of rights" section of the law. Senator McClellan was determined to create minimum democratic standards that all unions involved in the private sector must adopt.

Title I provides that every member of a labor organization shall have equal rights and privileges to nominate candidates, to vote in elections, and to attend and participate in membership meetings. However, these rights are subject to reasonable rules and regulations as provided for in the union's constitution and bylaws.

Prior to LMRDA, no standards addressed dues increases. Today, dues can only be increased by secret ballot at meetings at which the membership knows in advance that the increase will be acted on. Dues may also be increased at a national convention, but the delegates to the convention must be elected by secret ballot. The key is that dues cannot be arbitrarily increased without some membership input.

Title I also covers the right to sue a labor organization, provided you exhaust internal union remedies for up to four months before going to court.

---

[20] Taylor and Witney, op. cit., p. 508.

## Title II: Reports by Officers

Every organization covered by the act must submit very detailed financial reports to the U.S. Department of Labor. These reports are lengthy and often require professional preparation. Under certain circumstances, employers and labor-relations consultants must also file these reports. Once filed, they are public information and available for inspection.

Along with these financial reports, unions are required to file copies of their most recent bylaws and constitutions. The reporting requirements do not usually apply to central labor unions, district councils, state federations, or public-section unions.

The annual financial reports are the LM-2 for organizations whose gross receipts total $100,000 or more and the shorter LM-3 for smaller organizations. Among other things, these reports contain the local union's assets, liabilities, receipts, salaries, and allowances of officers for the fiscal year. Organized labor protested about the disclosure information, but has learned to live with it. In fact, between 1959 and 1977 there were only 115 civil actions to compel reporting compliance, or an average of only 6 per year.[21] Union compliance over the years has appeared to be excellent.

Penalties for noncompliance with reporting or outright corruption can range up to $10,000 and one year in jail. Other infractions include bribery, embezzlement, and coercion. At any one time there are approximately 350,000 union officers to whom the LMRDA applies. Between 1959 and 1977 only 933 union officers were convicted of any criminal offense under the law.[22] This record is an outstanding testimony as to the relative honesty of labor union officials.

When Landrum–Griffin was enacted, there was a great deal of concern on the part of bonding companies as to how they should rate union officials and what their premiums should be. Because of the McClellan hearings and the widespread accusations that were made based on the five unions under investigation, the premiums were very high. Over the years those premiums have come down in cost to the point where union officials now rate as well or better than clergy and Red Cross administrators and considerably less than almost all white-collar fiduciaries.

## Employer and Consultant Reports

Both employers and labor-relations consultants may also be required to file disclosure forms if they attempt to have the union decertified or persuade employees not to join a union. This sounds good, but union busters (consultants) have been using a LMRDA loophole to avoid filing with the Department of Labor. Landrum–Griffin states:

---

[21] Benjamin J. Taylor and Fred Witney, *Labor Relations Laws,* 4th ed. Prentice-Hall, Englewood Cliffs, N.J., 1983, p. 607, as quoted from U.S. Department of Labor, Labor-Management Services Administration, Compliance, Enforcement, and Reporting, 1977, p. 22.

[22] Ibid., p. 608, as seen in Compliance, Enforcement, and Reporting, p. 39.

Nothing in this section shall be construed to require any employer or other person to file a report covering the services of such a person by reason of giving his advice to such employer . . . .

If the consultant deals with the employer only (not the workers), he is operating within the guidelines of the law. This loophole has enabled the growing field of union busters to escape investigation by the labor movement. If the consultants had to report in the same way that unions do, it would be easier for labor organizations to inform employees about the finances of the consultant firm and discredit the decertification effort.

## Title IV:  Union Elections

Title IV of LMRDA deals with union elections and attempts to make them democratic. Accusation of wrongdoing, before or during elections, goes back into the early 1900s, but little was done because of the relative weakness of the trade-union movement.

Landrum–Griffin provides certain minimum standards that labor unions must adhere to, such as:

1. Secret ballot elections every three years for local unions, four years for intermediate bodies, and five years for international unions.

2. Notification mailed to the last known address of the member.

3. Candidates can have observers at all poll locations.

4. Each member in good standing is entitled to vote.

5. Opportunity to nominate must be given.

6. Election records must be kept for one year.

Candidates may have to meet certain constitutional or bylaw requirements. The courts have consistently held minimum requirements to be valid, provided that they were reasonable. For example, the local union may require candidates to attend one-half the regular union meetings for one year prior to nominations. Rules like this are usually reasonable under the law. However, a 50% attendance for three years prior to elections might not be valid.

Should there be a problem with election results, the complaining union member must exhaust internal union procedures in order to correct the problem. After three months, the member may call in the Department of Labor to investigate the election and its results.

This is a startling difference between Title I and Title IV. With a Title I or a "bill of rights" complaint, the member, upon using all internal remedies, must turn to the courts to seek justice. This means hiring a lawyer and a potential for large out-of-pocket expense. Title IV violations are dealt with by the Secretary of Labor and that tab is picked up by the government.

This was done by design to keep the membership from raising frivolous charges against the local union and its officers. Presumably, if a member's rights have been trampled, she will seek justice through the courts and risk the expenses. On the other hand, if there has been an election violation, the lawmakers viewed it as serious enough to bring the Department of Labor and its officers into the alleged violation.

Again, evidence points to the relatively good compliance record that unions have had during elections. From 1965 to 1977, some 57,000 labor organizations were covered by the law. During that time there were 2038 complaints alleging violation of election standards as mandated by LMRDA. For these, only 235 new elections were ordered by the courts. This is a remarkable record because during this time about 195,000 elections were held.[23]

Although the labor movement fought the passage of Landrum–Griffin, it has been a law that it can live with. Ultimately, it is difficult to argue that labor unions would rather be less democratic. The ideas of free speech, assembly, honest elections, and financial safeguards for union members are all inherent in our nation and should be present in labor organizations as well.

Some local unions have been infiltrated by organized crime, but during a recent congressional investigation that number was put at about 300.[24] While this may sound like a lot, one has to realize that there are approximately 65,000 local unions in the nation. This includes unions from the AFL–CIO and independent labor organizations. These figures break down to approximately a corruption rate of 0.046% or 1 in every 217 labor organizations.

These calculations would also support the findings of Bok and Dunlop, who stated:

> The overwhelming majority of labor leaders are honest men who take seriously their obligation to represent the interests of members who have elected them to office.[25]

It would appear that union leaders are far more honest than their counterparts in business. A 1980 *Fortune* magazine survey revealed that 117 or 11% of large corporations studied were involved in corporate corruption, which included among other things bribery, kickbacks, and fraud.[26]

These figures suggest that on the whole the American trade union movement and its leadership stands head and shoulders above the corporate world when it comes to fiscal honesty and integrity.

[23] Ibid., p. 623, as seen in Compliance, Enforcement, and Reporting, 1974, op. cit., p. 4, 5, and 8.

[24] Baker A. Smith, "Landrum–Griffin after Twenty-One Years: Mature Legislation or Childish Fantasy." *Labor Law Journal,* May 1980, p. 276.

[25] Derek C. Bok and John T. Dunlop, *Labor and the American Community.* Simon and Schuster, New York, 1970, p. 69.

[26] Irwin Ross, "How Lawless Are Big Companies?" *Fortune,* December 1, 1980, pp. 57–64.

## Labor Law Reform

In July 1977, President Jimmy Carter announced legislation that was intended to modernize and streamline the Wagner Act. The changes had the full support of organized labor. The following October, the House of Representatives passed its version of the bill by a 257 to 164 majority. However, when the Senate companion bill emerged from committee it was greeted with endless amendments which led to a filibuster. What Carter thought to be a piece of "necessary and moderate"[27] legislation turned into a national battle between labor and management.

Some of the highlights of the bill were:

1. Expand the NLRB from five to seven members to speed up unfair labor practices cases.

2. Representation elections would take place within 30 to 45 days after membership cards were signed.

3. Grant back pay of up to one and one-half times to workers judged to have been fired for union activity.

4. Allow union organizers equal time to address workers about organizing.

5. Provide for a loss of federal contracts to law violators.[28]

The key provision for labor in the bill was to speed up representation elections. The delay tactic has been used by management to discourage organizing drives, along with firing union sympathizers and activists. Under current law, back pay and job reinstatement for fired workers can take years.

Proponents of both sides of the issue were paraded before Congress in an attempt to persuade legislators in their vote. First came a cadre of workers who had been discharged for union activity; they thought they were protected from firing under the law. Along with workers, international unions brought testimony about the delays that companies sought after authorization cards were signed.

The corporations spent about $5 million in an attempt to defeat labor law reform.[29] Realizing that the reform bill could not be defeated outright in the Senate, the strategy for defeat by filibuster was drawn by Robert Thompson, a South Carolina lawyer who has worked for J.P. Stevens and the National Chamber of Commerce. Thompson received help from both Goodyear and Bethlehem Steel.[30]

[27] George Meany, "For Working Americans, Time for Justice." *AFL–CIO American Federationist*, June 1978, p. 1.

[28] Tom Nicholson and others, "Labor's Push for Reform." *Newsweek,* March 20, 1978, p. 57.

[29] Juan Cameron, "Small Business Trips Big Labor." *Fortune,* July 31, 1978, p. 81.

[30] Ibid., p. 80.

The amount of money apparently was not as valuable as the filibuster that was used in the Senate. This strategy was also used in 1965 when labor, with the help of President Johnson, sought to repeal section 14(b) of Taft–Hartley. In both cases cloture could not be invoked and the business community was successful in beating back attempts to reform the law. Labor had the numbers to pass amendments to Taft–Hartley, but was defeated by the Senate filibuster.

## PUBLIC EMPLOYEES

As the nation grew, so did federal, state, and local governments. The need for collective bargaining and workplace democracy is as precious for public employees as those in the private sector. The states had been free to draft laws that permitted public employees the right to form labor organizations. However, the federal government discouraged any form of collective bargaining until the 1960s.

In 1962, President Kennedy issued Executive Order 10988. This order established the basic framework for collective bargaining in the executive branch of the federal government. In 1970 and again in 1975 Presidents Nixon and Ford made additional amendments with their executive orders. These orders became the framework for the Civil Service Reform Act (CSRA) of 1978.

The CSRA covers most federal employees, now giving them protection under statute rather than executive orders. The law is administered through the Office of Personnel Management, the Merit System Protection Board, and the Federal Labor Relations Authority. Of these three agencies, the FLRA is very closely modeled after the National Labor Relations Board and processes unfair labor practice complaints.

Several groups of federal employees do not have protection under CSRA. These groups include all military personnel, employees engaged in national security, and those who administer labor-relations law.[31]

Federal employees have grievance and arbitration procedures, but are forbidden to strike. This provision was soundly enforced in 1981 with the firing of some 12,000 members of the Professional Air Traffic Controllers Organization, which represented the nation's air traffic controllers. These workers went on strike in August 1981 over pay and safety issues. Within a few days, President Reagan had them all dismissed and barred from future jobs within the federal government.

Federal employees are also greatly limited in their ability to call traditional job actions such as slowdowns, work stoppages, and picketing. In some cases, informational picketing is permitted, provided the action does not interfere with the agency's operation.

[31]Taylor and Witney, 1983, p. 638–640.

## Postal Workers

The U.S. Postal Service is not subject to CSRA, but does fall under the Postal Reorganization Act of 1970. The National Labor Relations Board oversees the various postal workers' unions as they move closer and closer to resembling private-sector unions. The biggest difference is that postal workers are also forbidden to strike. Postal employees must submit their demands to final and binding arbitration upon reaching impasse. Even though postal workers are forbidden by law to strike, they did walk off their jobs in 1970. The action taken against Professional Air Traffic Controllers Organization (PATCO) has no doubt tempered the militancy of these employees, as well as those of other federal unions.

## State, County, and Municipal Employees

State, county, and municipal employees outside of the federal government have a very mixed bag of collective bargaining relationships under their respective laws. These laws vary from very mature and well-established rights to organize and bargain to an outright ban on organizing and a status of "collective begging."

Some states have drawn up statutes that closely resemble the National Labor Relations Act (NLRA) and even permit a limited right to strike for some workers. Most states have drawn the line at striking when it reaches "essential employees." The definition of essential employees is usually police and fire-fighters. Other states extend the definition to include sanitation workers and teachers. The question still remains that, even if forbidden by law to strike, will public employees obey the law?

Some states permit a union-shop agreement, others have an agency shop, and still others forbid any form of union security or dues checkoff. Disputes can be handled in a number of different ways, with some form of arbitration the final step in most cases.

Public employee organizing is certainly increasing. With this growth, the various laws that have evolved are beginning to resemble those that govern the private sector.

The competition to organize public workers is fierce, and unions with once clearly defined jurisdictions are leading the assault. This competition will no doubt bring about promises from the respective organizations as to who can deliver most of the economic pie. In the end, the public worker will be better served if the organizing is a cooperative effort by the interested unions, rather than competitive.

## IMPLICATIONS FOR LEADERSHIP

Laws are not created in a vacuum nor do they spring from the air. There are reasons why events happen the way they do. The Wagner Act was a reaction to the decades of frustration that workers faced when they tried to organize. It was the result of an evolutionary process that saw yellow dog contracts, blacklisting, labor injunctions, company unions, and many other employer tactics to repel collective bargaining. No other group of employers in the free world fought worker organization like the American corporation.

From 1935 to 1947 with corporate power held in check, the American labor movement grew very rapidly. Taft–Hartley slowed that growth rate very sharply. Perhaps labor was too successful during those 12 years in flexing its economic and political strength that the courts and big business had restrained for over a century. In the search for individual freedom, labor must tolerate section 14(b) and other antiunion portions of the law.

A dozen years would go by again before Landrum–Griffin was enacted. While this law was soundly denounced by organized labor, it has demonstrated that the trade union movement is relatively free of corruption, embezzlement, and financial wrongdoing. This is especially true when compared to white-collar (traditionally nonunion) jobs.

What lies ahead for labor and the law is a whole new agenda. To enact pro-union legislation, the American labor movement will have to build a broad-based coalition and demonstrate to the general public that it is not the ogre that has been portrayed over the years. Labor must demonstrate that what it wants for its members it wants for all workers. Labor must also demonstrate that members of trade unions do not belong to a special-interest group, but are indeed part of Main Street America. To complete this agenda, local union leaders must understand the history of economic and legal change and how each change has produced a corresponding change in the purpose and structure of unions. More changes are coming. Good local union leadership consists of those managers and administrators who understand this fundamental aspect of union organization, government, and purpose and choose to deal with this daily challenge head on.

## CHAPTER TEST

Choose the answer that seems most appropriate and place the letter in the space provided.

1. _____ The single toughest obstacle that the worker faced when trying to organize was the _____ .
   a. employer                    c. yellow dog contract
   b. strikebreaker               d. labor injunction

2. _____ The _____ Act viewed labor unions as an entity to actually help promote interstate commerce and industrial peace.
   a. Wagner                      c. Norris–La Guardia
   b. Clayton                     d. Railway Labor

3. _____ In 1935 there were about 4 million workers organized. By 1948 that number had grown to _____ million.
   a. 7             c. 13
   b. 10            d. 16

4. _____ Besides the employer, unions and workers also had to fight the _____ when trying to organize.
   a. strikebreaker      c. labor spies
   b. courts             d. injunction

5. _____ Public employees differ from private-sector workers because not all of them have the right to _____ .
   a. file grievances    c. strike
   b. arbitrate          d. job slowdowns

Put a T (true) or an F (false) in the space provided.

6. _____ The Wagner Act assures the right of the individual rather than the group.

7. _____ Section 14(b) of Taft–Hartley makes provisions for "free riders" in unions.

8. _____ President Truman favored the passage of Taft–Hartley.

9. _____ During the McClellan Anti-Racketeering Committee hearings, a large number of unions were investigated.

10. _____ Union leaders have shown over the years that they are just about as honest as business leaders.

11. List the four tactics that employers used to keep workers from organizing.

12. Which branch of government was trying to respond to the need to organize? Why would it be responsive while the others were not?

13. Describe why the Roosevelt Administration might have favored passage of the Wagner Act.

14. What are the most important sections of the Wagner Act? Why?

15. What events led to the passage of the Taft–Hartley Act?

16. What is the most controversial portion of Taft–Hartley?

17. Compare and contrast Titles I and IV of the Landrum–Griffin Act.

# GLOSSARY

**American Plan:** The open-shop campaign of American corporations during the 1920s. Corporations spread propaganda that stated it was unpatriotic to join a trade union.

**Civil Service Reform Act (1978):** The act that replaces the various executive orders granting federal workers the right to collective bargaining.

**Commonwealth v. Hunt:** A landmark case in labor law by which unions were declared to be lawful institutions in 1842. This case overturned the Conspiracy Cases.

**Cordwainers Conspiracy Cases:** A series of court decisions prior to 1842 that ruled labor unions to be unlawful organizations. The courts ruled that if two or more workers joined together to raise wages it was a "conspiracy in restraint of trade."

**Executive Order 10988:** The order issued by President Kennedy in 1962 that established the basic collective bargaining framework for federal workers.

**industrial democracy:** Worker input at his or her place of employment. This term is generally associated with the ability of the employee to affect decisions at the workplace.

**interstate commerce:** Trade or commercial relations between parties in two different states.

**labor injunction:** An order by a judge directing a person or organization to pursue or refrain from a course of action.

**Labor Management Relations Act (1947):** The basic law regulating private-sector labor-management relations. This act enabled states to outlaw the union shop and become known right-to-work states. It is more commonly known as the Taft–Hartley Act.

**Labor–Management Reporting and Disclosure Act (1959):** A federal statute establishing rules concerning the internal operations of unions and standards of conduct for union officers, employers, and labor-relations consultants. The law is more commonly known as the Landrum–Griffin Act.

**Landrum–Griffin Act:** See *Labor-Management Reporting and Disclosure Act.*

**National Industry Recovery Act (1933):** An early New Deal piece of legislation that helped establish the right of workers to join unions and elect their own representatives. Although it was ruled unconstitutional, it did help pave the way for the passage of the Wagner Act.

**National Labor Relations Act (1935):** The first comprehensive law that established the rights of workers to organize, bargain collectively, and elect their own representatives. This act also created the National Labor Relations Board to enforce the provisions of the law. It is commonly known as the Wagner Act.

**National Labor Relations Board:** The board that oversees enforcement of the Wagner Act. The two main functions of the NLRB are to supervise the selection of bargaining representatives by workers and to oversee unfair labor practice charges.

**New Deal:** A term commonly used when referring to the Franklin Delano Roosevelt administration (1932–1945).

**open shop:** A workplace where employees are not bound to join a union but must be represented by the union for collective bargaining and grievance procedure purposes.

**Railway Labor Act (1926):** An act that allowed workers on the railroads to join unions and elect their own representatives. This act now also applies to workers in the airline industry.

**right-to-work laws:** State laws that outlaw the union shop. These laws are permitted under section 14(b) of Taft–Hartley.

**scab:** A worker who will not join a labor organization or who takes another's place during a strike. Also see *strikebreaker.*

**strikebreaker:** A person who helps to break up a strike of workers by taking a striker's job or by supplying workers who will do so. Also see *scab.*

**Taft–Hartley Act:** See *Labor Management Relations Act.*

**union shop:** A contract clause that requires an employee to join a union and remain a member as a condition of employment after a probationary working period, usually 30 days.

**Wagner Act:** See National Labor Relations Act.

**yellow dog contract:** A contract that a worker had to sign as a condition of employment stating that he or she was not a member and would not become a member of a labor organization. If the worker did join a union, that was grounds for firing. This contract was outlawed in 1932 by the Norris–LaGuardia Act.

# CHAPTER 8

# Conducting Union and Committee Meetings

Perhaps the single greatest vehicle for effective local union leadership is the general membership meeting. Here, more than with any other union activity (on a regular basis), the fullest range of managerial and leadership skills and behaviors can be displayed before the most people. And yet these managerial and leadership skills seem to be used with less than full effectiveness by many union managers. It is imperative that local officers and members alike learn the fundamentals of meeting conduct and participation. Organizational and personal power bases both will increase as a result.

By the same token, committee meetings should be the spearhead for intensive and wide-ranging education and discussions by their members on behalf of the entire local membership. Committee members are charged with bringing informed recommendations to the local on how it can best go about achieving its goals. Since committees are composed of local members, it is surely the best case of members of an organization serving themselves for the common good of all that can be found.

An effectively managed and administrated union consists of officers who know how to conduct democratic yet efficient meetings and members who know how to fully participate in both general and committee meetings, as well as how to chair a committee. Such active involvement increases the number and quality of local union leaders, and that is what this book is all about in general, and this chapter in particular. The skills of determining follower readiness and the proper use of power, or the perception that it will be used in the course of influencing a follower holds true just as positively in knowing how to conduct and participate in meetings. Perhaps the judgments might be more complex because of the larger numbers involved and a greater variety of influencing factors, but the need for successful and effective leadership remains the same. Chapter 8 is a modest guide for those officers and members who wish to learn how to increase this area of critical leadership development.

Regardless of its size, each union meeting should seek to move the organization and its members toward their goals. A successful meeting accomplishes this movement in at least five ways. First, a meeting must communicate information. Members should leave the meeting with a feeling that they know more than when they went in. They should know more about the union, the issues, and each other.

Decisions need to be made at meetings. The authors are sure that at some point in your life you have been to a meeting, quite possibly for hours, where there was nothing but talk. No action took place and no decision was reached. The inclination is not to return.

Members should also leave the meeting feeling that they contributed to the progress of the meeting and moved the organization forward in some way. They should feel this accomplishment by openly voting on various motions and by participating in the discussions that led to the votes. And as the reader will find out later, many of these efforts at membership involvement begin prior to the opening of the meeting.

Solidarity ought always to be a product of a union meeting. That decisions reached were those of the group and that these decisions will help build the union will increase individual commitment. Members should feel closer to the union, with a greater sense of what the organization does, what it stands for, and where it is going.

Finally, meetings should be educational. This education can take many forms—organizational, political, community, contract, grievances, arbitration awards, the parent union, other employers/industries/agencies doing the work you do, and a host of other issues (refer to Chapter 5). The members should leave the meeting with more than just facts. They should head for their homes with a feeling of *knowing* more than when they left for work that morning.[1] It is the duty of union managers—officers—to develop personal communication techniques and democratic meeting procedures that assure maximum goal direction, participation, and education at general membership meetings.

## GENERAL MEMBERSHIP MEETINGS

The core of a good meeting comes from its planning. It takes the efforts of all the officers to sit down and plan what it is that the local needs to do in the coming year. It takes even more effort to figure out how these goals can be scheduled

[1]Si Kahn, *Organizing: A Guide for Grassroots Leaders,* 1982, pp. 130–136. Adapted with permission from McGraw-Hill Book Company.

into future meetings to ensure maximum membership input and guidance. The officers should represent a healthy cross section of their membership. This representation will help ensure that the pulse of membership's wants, needs, and desires is being considered in the planning of future local meetings. Through cooperation and collaboration, the officers can work up a meaningful agenda from month to month and, more importantly, on an annual basis. An annual agenda might seem to be a case of overload; however, the authors believe that the local's managers and administrators ought to have a special meeting, perhaps in December, to plan an entire agenda for the coming year. Such an agenda will surely change, but at least there is a statement of goals and intentions that can be measured against during the course of the year. Locals rarely set such goals down on paper, and even more rare is the day that a careful evaluation is conducted (see Chapter 3).

## Planned Meetings Make Better Meetings

Meetings that attract people and make them want to return do not just happen. They are the result of both long- and short-range planning (see Chapter 3). Long-range planning is for the entire fiscal or calendar year. (American Federation of Government Employees, AFL–CIO, does this with their financial budgets. Yet it seems that their goal is more fiscal soundness than meeting effectiveness. At any rate, more unions should follow their example.) Table 8-1 is a sample one-year planning calendar. Short-range planning is for the immediate meeting only.

Long-range planning includes the obvious consideration of general arrangements, but it also involves knowing where the union is going and how the union's leaders plan to get there (a goal statement, Chapter 3). It involves a commitment by the executive board and committee chairpersons to look ahead at least one year, instead of on the usual meeting-by-meeting system. Outlined next are some examples of long-range planning items.

Make the hall attractive and keep restrooms clean.

Buy a loudspeaker so everyone can hear and have microphones around the hall if needed.

Pass a rule that no one can speak for more than five minutes without special permission from the body.

Promote meetings on a regular basis.

Spend more time on educating members than on feeding them.

Buy a movie projector and ½-inch videotape player and monitor.

Arrange for a series of speakers.

Draft a series of educational programs.

Set up regular political action reports.

**TABLE 8-1.** Programs for the Coming Year

| SUBJECT | OBJECTIVE | TYPE OF PROGRAM (MEDIUM) | FOR WHO? | WHEN |
|---|---|---|---|---|
| Labor history | Show members the contributions of workers | Educational (*The Inheritance*) | General membership | February |
| Negotiations | Find out what members want from new contract | Informational (informal notified meeting) | General membership | March |
| Grievance procedure | Help stewards understand grievance investigation and writing | Educational (chief stewards) | Shop stewards | April (stewards meeting) |
| Vacation planning | Show membership types of regional vacations available | Informational (guest speaker from ABC Travel Co.) | General membership | May |
| Labor and politics | Teaching lobbying and communication to Political Action Committee | Educational (legislative aids) | Political Action Committee Members | August |
| Local union dance | Honor retirees | Social gathering | Entire membership and special guests | November |

Short-range planning sets up the next meeting. A meeting of the executive board or local officers an hour before the regular meetings can decide what will come up and when, its order of business. Items covered should include:

What correspondence is important.

Who will introduce the speaker.

Preparing the movie projector or the audiovisual requirements.

What important motions will come up, who will make them if they are not introduced from the floor, and who will speak on them to get the ball rolling.[2]

Remember, prior long-range planning has already scheduled special issues or topical portions of the meeting.

## Why Meetings Fail

Meetings fail for six basic reasons:

1. *Poor planning.* The officers did not set an agenda, did not establish objectives, and the location and time need to be changed (poor managerial planning).

2. *Failure to recognize the human needs.* Compliments are not given to those who deserve them or members are embarrassed by those who choose to only ridicule and be sarcastic.

3. *Loss of control.* A few dominant members are outspoken and are allowed to overwhelm the majority, who are generally timid.

4. *Poor leadership.* A dominant leader may try to make others follow and be manipulative. He or she constantly starts and ends late and uses vague or misleading language. Speakers are allowed to wander off the subject and are repetitious.

5. *Meetings are too long.* Generally, any meeting that goes beyond two hours will lose all its interest, even for the most ardent members.

6. *No teamwork atmosphere in the local.* The leadership, committee members, and rank and file are acting as separate and distinct groups. All three components are important to the whole, with some more active than others, but all contributing a portion.[3]

---

[2] UAW Department of Education, *Workbook for the Union Meeting: How to Participate,* May 1976, p. 8.

[3] Martin Jones, *How to Organize Meetings.* 1980, pp. 125–126. Adapted with permission of the author.

## Avoiding Conflicts in Meetings

Disagreements between individuals are inevitable. A union's general meeting or a committee meeting can be like a battleground because that is where policy is debated and often made. However, there are some techniques that a union manager can use to keep disagreements and disruptive forces to a minimum. First, if you are chairing a meeting and someone makes a false statement, how can you correct the situation without putting the union brother or sister down?

The first thing to consider is whether or not it is important to correct the mistake immediately. If the correction is unimportant, the matter can probably be handled after the meeting. This approach would avoid having the member feel foolish in front of his colleagues and go a long way toward gaining an ally.

However, there are times when you might feel yourself being drawn into a conflict. It is important to keep calm and be level headed. Remember the conflict management skills outlined in Chapter 1. During a disagreement one response might be: "If it's all right with everybody, I'd suggest that we continue this discussion after I've had time to study my files and come back with more details." Another choice might be: "This discussion has been time consuming; why not get together after the meeting and talk it over further?"

Disagreements are difficult to handle and even more difficult when the integrity of you and your officers might be threatened. There might be an antagonist who insists on putting you and the other officers down. The gut reaction is usually to snap back and hurt that person right back as a method of repayment. Such a response serves little purpose and will only harden the lines of conflict between you and the opposition.

It is hard not to respond in such a manner, but one should resist the impulse. A quick and terse response would gain a short-lived victory. What is needed is a long-term victory. A few seconds of silence might work wonders. During the silence at least two things will happen. You are gaining your composure and your antagonist is standing alone and just might be feeling slightly foolish for her remarks.

This technique is usually effective. However, the authors do not mean to suggest that officers allow themselves to be continually berated. Standing up strongly for yourself and the other officers may be necessary sometimes. A tougher approach might become necessary if this soft method fails.

An experienced chairperson is one who understands situations and the emotions that sometimes surround them. Sometimes some effective lobbying before a controversial matter comes up can be very useful. One will find that time spent in communicating ideas to key members or committee people will help in getting membership approval. To avoid a conflict on the floor of the general membership meeting, one must have the support going into the meeting. Time must be given to either *selling* or *participating* leadership communication in advance of the meeting (Chapter 1). These leadership behaviors will help to ensure the goal of meaningful meetings.

## Why Don't They Come?

An age-old problem for union managers is why more people do not attend meetings. The answer is complex, but, first, people do not attend meetings because they are usually boring. This is right, boring. We have all been at meetings with a long-winded reading of the minutes, reports, and financial presentations. If it is permissible, why not have these reports printed beforehand and distributed to the members as they come into the room? Such a move would eliminate the verbal presentations that so many members drift off during anyway. It would also provide a permanent copy for members to take home or back to their respective workplaces for other members to look over.

Another idea to help streamline meetings would be to eliminate "talka-thons" that tend to frustrate the average member. The chairperson should allow full debate on an issue; however, this should not provide a license for someone to monopolize the floor. Speakers should be limited in the amount of time they can speak on an issue and in the number of times they may speak on an issue. To see the same faces making the same arguments on the same issues will discourage most members.[4]

Local union officers have struggled with meeting attendance for generations. Many locals have tried various things to increase attendance (e.g., refreshments, raffles, 50/50 drawings, movies, uniform cleaning coupons, free tools). These devices usually have some short-term benefit, but eventually the numbers will be back to normal (low) in a short time.

All the preceding does have a small place in the scheme of meeting attendance, but here are some ideas that may also work:

1. Make sure members know the time, date, and place where the meeting will take place.
2. Use reminders on bulletin boards, newsletters, post cards, and radio announcements.
3. Ask your regular attendees to bring other members.
4. Run efficient, democratic, and lively meetings.
5. Have something interesting going on. If you show a long movie, spread it out over another meeting.
6. Ask stewards to talk it up in the shop and make personal contacts with others.[5]

---

[4] *Workbook for the Union Meeting,* op. cit., pp. 2–22.

[5] *IAM Officers' Guide,* International Association of Machinists, Education Department, p. 40.

## Make Sure Meetings are Interesting

The annual meeting agenda provides a blueprint for the coming year. It must be put into action. Remember, an agenda does not have to contain only union items. At least quarterly there should be guest speakers, films, or other presentations on subjects that the members need information on.

Program features can be on negotiations, skills training, vacations, basic automotive repair, home gardening, labor history films, safety and health slide shows, an attorney to speak about prepaid legal fees—almost anything. The union can be turned to for many, many reasons. It is after all a social organization. It is about time it started acting like one.

Interesting meetings do bring out more people. Workers will become involved if the debates and reports are lively, concise, and informative. The officers must be sure that each agenda has enough attractive items and make sure the members know about them in advance. See Exhibit 8-1 for a union meeting checklist.

All the newsletters and flyers that one can make, mail, and post are not as effective as personal contact. Encourage stewards, committee members, and other officers to personally remind their co-workers of upcoming meetings and that their attendance and participation are important. A simple verbal reminder might show surprising results. Not all leadership acts are complex. Some of the most successful are simple and personal.

---

EXHIBIT 8-1
### Checklist for Union Meetings[6]

1. Have the officers met to plan the agenda?

2. Have notices been sent to the members?

3. Have the officers and committee chairpersons been asked to make a report?

4. Have reports been streamlined, typed, and copied?

5. Is all the correspondence ready for presentation?

6. Have the letters and requests been reviewed and condensed?

7. Are the various committees ready?

8. Is the meeting hall ready? (heat, lights, chairs, ventilation, restrooms, podium, tables, flag, ashtrays, cleanliness)

9. Is all special equipment ready to use? (blackboards, flip charts, movie or slide projectors, microphones, video player)

10. Have the pamphlets or movie arrived?

[6]UAW Department of Education, *Parliamentary Procedures: Discussion Workbook*, May 1976, p. 31.

11. Are materials ready for distribution? (agenda, financial reports, minutes of last meeting, minutes of previous executive board)

12. Have all arrangements been made for guest or special speakers? (Where and when will the meeting be held? What is expected of them?)

13. Have refreshments been provided for?

## Some Do's and Dont's at Meetings

The business that comes before the general membership should be important or interesting to the majority of the meeting. Long discussions involving only an individual that are full of petty details usually discourage members from participation in the meeting. These singular conversations will put members to sleep or drive them away from further meetings. Be careful of the following:

1. *Individual grievances.* Every union member wants his grievance settled, usually now. However, the other members do not want to sit through long-winded discussions that affect only individuals. Individual grievances should come before the membership only if they involve questions of basic policy.

2. *Department grievances.* These should be settled within the department or with the aid of the grievance committee.

3. *Correspondence.* The recording secretary and executive board should get together before the membership meeting and condense correspondence to a reasonable length. The executive board can decide what should be considered at all. Routine letters, ads, donation requests can merely be announced and filed. Longer correspondence should be condensed and briefly explained. However, letters from the international and other important correspondence should be read entirely. Again, what should be read, condensed, filed, or thrown away should be up to the recording secretary or the executive board.

4. *Limit debate.* Some members talk too much, others too little. Adopt a rule that limits debate to a certain amount of time or allows the same speaker on the floor no more than two times per motion.

5. *Encouraging debate.* The chairperson is encouraged to draw upon the shy member. The timid member might be the best thinker in the group. After all, one learns more by listening than by talking.

6. *Auditory problems.* If people cannot hear, they certainly cannot listen. If there are sound problems, invest in a good public address system or rent one. At large gatherings, the officers and members should address the group from a microphone.[7]

[7] Ibid., pp. 28–29.

## OFFICER ROLES AND DUTIES

If the two toughest jobs in America are being president of the United States and mayor of New York City, then the third toughest job has to be that of the local union president. She or he must chair meetings, initiate new members, aid in the planning of social and educational programs, investigate grievances when they reach the higher levels of the grievance procedure, prepare cases for arbitration, act as an ex-officio member of committees, serve as the primary union public-relations person with the media and the public, and undertake many other important tasks and activities. Again, going back to the first chapter, the president is more than an officer; she is the local's primary manager in most cases.

Each of the other officers of the local also carries a set of roles and duties. These officers usually include the vice-president, recording secretary, financial secretary, chief steward, sergeant-at-arms, and trustees. For the purpose of this chapter, which is to better understand how to conduct a good local union meeting, the authors will confine their remarks only to the president through the financial secretary. Starting with the president, an outline of meeting roles and duties is provided for each.

### President

To acquire a working knowledge of parliamentary procedure and a thorough understanding of the constitution, bylaws, and standing rules of the union.

To appear at the rostrum or at the front of the meetroom a few minutes before the meeting is scheduled to begin.

To have on hand a list of committees for a guide in naming new appointees.

To preside over the meeting and maintain order.

To explain and decide all questions of order.

To announce all business to the membership.

To be informed on the communications.

To entertain only one main motion at a time and state all motions properly.

To permit no one to debate motions before they are seconded and stated; to encourage debate and assign the floor to those properly entitled to it. (No member may speak twice on the same motion if there are others who wish to claim the floor.)

To put all motions to vote and give the results.

To remain seated while discussion is taking place or reports being given.

To enforce the rules of decorum and discipline.

To talk no more than necessary when presiding.

To refrain from discussing a motion when presiding.

To vacate the chair if personally involved in the discussion.

To be absolutely fair and impartial.

To extend every courtesy to the opponents of a motion, even though the motion is one that the chairperson favors.

To give his signature when necessary.

To show appreciation to officers and chairpersons of committees for their service.

To perform such other duties as are prescribed in the bylaws.

### Privileges of the president

To debate motions before the membership, if essential; however, he must surrender the chair until the vote has been taken. The vice-president, then, is asked to take the chair until action on the motion is completed.

To use "general consent," which saves much time when routine matters are considered. Example: "If there is no objection, we will . . . ." If there is an objection, the chair must take the vote.

To preside during nominations and elections, even if she is the candidate. When the president is the sole nominee, the vice-president, merely as a matter of delicacy, puts the question of the president's election to a vote.

### Vice-president

In the absence of the president, presides and performs the duties of the president. If a vice-president is not willing to perform the duties of the president during his or her absence or when circumstances make it necessary to assume the presidency, the vice-president should resign from the office.

To head an important committee as outlined in the bylaws.

### Recording secretary

To be prepared before the start of each meeting

To keep the minutes of the meeting.

To take the roll call and mark the absentees at the executive board meeting.

To read the minutes of the last meeting.

To summarize correspondence, except for important letters and notices.

To prepare the local's correspondence in a logical order of presentation.

To record the name of the member who introduces a motion. It is not necessary to record the seconder.

To notify committees of their appointees and business.

To provide ballots when secret balloting is called for.

To hold all voted ballots until they are permitted to be destroyed.

To take charge of all documents belonging to the union, when requested.

To have on hand a copy of the local's constitution and bylaws during the meeting.

To sign official documents of the local when requested.

To call a meeting to order, in the absence of the president or vice-president, and preside until the election of a chairperson, pro tem. (The election of the pro tem should take place immediately.)

To assist the president in the preparation of the meeting agenda and with maintaining the order of business during the meeting.

Treasurer

To give a statement of finances to the membership as required.

To be able to handle membership inquiries about past receipts and disbursements.

Financial secretary

To make provision for collecting dues (where there is no checkoff) at the meeting.

To report to the membership the status of paid-up members.

All officers who have a part in the conduct of a membership meeting should prepare well for their tasks. While the president is usually seen as the one person moving the meeting along, it is actually a leadership team effort. To the degree that the other officers have readiness levels of R4 (see Chapter 1), the president will have to provide little guidance and support. But they will not all be R4s. In fact, the authors would be surprised if there were more than two R4s in an entire union leadership team at the local level. It is more likely that the readiness levels run the length of the readiness spectrum. The idea is to make the most of what one has. An effective situational leader will be able to cope with the variety of emotions found at a local meeting, in part because she has other union managers and administrators to help out.

## THE ROLE OF MEMBERS AT MEETINGS

Every member has an obligation to help determine the policies and activities of the union in which he holds membership. These policies are determined by the vote taken on various motions that come before the group for action. The member who remains silent is acting selfishly by shifting the responsibility for decision making to those who do vote. Unfortunately, it is this type of member, the nonvoter or nonparticipator, who is likely to do most of the complaining about the organization. Participating is a special privilege, and everyone should take advantage of it whenever the opportunity presents itself.[8]

Contrary to popular opinion, the role of the union member is not to monopolize discussion, remain silent on important matters, complain after the meeting, stay at home, or be a barrier to progress. Actually, being a good union member who participates at meetings takes a certain amount of effort. The authors list next some of your rights and responsibilities as members.

Rights

To offer any motion that is fitting for the local.

To explain or discuss that motion or any other matter properly before the meeting.

To call a point of order, if necessary. A point of order can interrupt a speaker. It is raised to ensure orderly procedure, particularly when there is a break or violation.

To hold the floor when legally obtained until through speaking (within time limits).

To appeal the decision of the chair to the membership.

Responsibilities

Know the rules of your organization.

Keep informed on current issues.

Listen to others and their point of view.

Keep awake.

[8] Marie H. Suthers, *The New Primer in Parliamentary Procedure.* Dartnell Corporation, Chicago, IL, 1965, pp. 54–55.

Object at the meeting if something is improper or unwise.

Address the chair and get recognition when necessary.

Debate the issue, not the person who presents it.

Yield the floor on calls of order.

Ask for information if in doubt.

Enter the debate only if you feel that you have something important to say.

Show a willingness to serve on committees.

Show openness to ideas.

Do not talk too long or too frequently.

Assume your share of responsibility for actions the group takes.

Refrain from side conversations and irrelevant issues.

Be respectful of others and their opinions.

Express opinions *at* meetings.

Display regular attendance and thoughtful input at meetings.

If possible, arrive early.

Remain for the full meeting.

Try to be a worker rather than a joiner.[9]

## CHAIRING MEETINGS

In a local union, the president usually chairs the general membership and executive board meetings. The main responsibilities that the chair has are to see that meetings are both democratic and efficient. This can be a very difficult task. The need for democracy is at the very roots of the trade-union movement. Yet there is an equally important task of keeping meetings efficient. How can these seemingly different ideals come together and be treated equally? Perhaps one answer comes in the form of proper use of and skill in parliamentary procedure. These rules of order make it possible to get business done in an organized and fair way.

Most deliberative bodies use either *Robert's Rules of Order* or *Demeter's Manual of Parliamentary Law* as parliamentary procedure guidelines. Strict use of either book can be intimidating to even veteran meeting goers. It is not necessary that the chairperson memorize and use the rules of either Robert or Demeter. However, the chairperson should have a sound knowledge of the rules of order and apply them only in the interest of efficiency and democracy.

The four basic principles of parliamentary law are:

[9]Ibid., pp. 21–22.

1. The rules are the same for everyone.

2. Only one thing at a time can be discussed.

3. Majority rules.

4. The minority has a right to be heard.

## Handling Motions

A chairperson has a duty to help members with motions. Business is conducted and the union moves forward by making, discussing, and passing motions on the floor of the assembly. Many members have trouble expressing themselves in the form of a motion or expressing almost anything before the body. It is incumbent on the chairperson to help members with poorly worded, confusing, or even obscure motions and discussion. Most often the wording of the motion is poor because the person is inexperienced or timid. It is up to the chair to reword or walk that member through exactly what he wants to propose.

## Parliamentary Law for the Inexperienced Chairperson

The use of parliamentary law will vary from local to local. As a general rule, its application will increase as the size of the meeting increases. Small meetings and committee meetings can usually stay informal without much parliamentary law application. Some locals are informal and work better without leaning on good old *Robert's*. However, when there are some members who are sharp in their parliamentary knowledge, the chairperson must be just as sharp and work within those conditions.

When chairing a meeting, have beside you the local's constitution, bylaws, and rules of order,[10] all of which should be studied until they are quite familiar. One should have a working knowledge of the list of ordinary motions arranged in their order of precedence, and should be able to refer to the Index of Rules of Robert or Demeter so quickly that there would be little or no delay in deciding all points contained in it; and you should know all the business to come regularly before the meeting and call for it in its regular order. Have a list of members of all committees to guide you in nominating new committees.

As soon as a motion is made and seconded, distinctly restate the motion to the membership. When a vote is taken, announce the result and also what further question, if any is then pending. Never wait for routine motions to be seconded when you know no one objects to them.

If a member unknowingly makes an improper motion, politely suggest the proper one. If a motion is moved "to lay the question on the table until 3 P.M.," you might then ask if the intention is "to postpone the question till 3 P.M." If it is moved simply "to postpone the question" without stating a time, do not rule it out of order, but ask the maker of the motion if she wishes "to postpone the

---

[10] *Robert's, Demeter's,* or whatever your constitution calls for.

question indefinitely" (which kills it) or "to lay it on the table" (which enables it to be taken up at any other time); then state the question in accordance with the motion she intended to make.

The chairperson should not only be familiar with parliamentary usage, but should be a person of leadership ability, capable of influencing people; and it should never be forgotten that, to influence others, it is necessary to understand one's self and one's leadership style.

A chairperson should not permit the object of a meeting to be defeated by a few factious persons using parliamentary forms with the apparent motive of obstructing business. In such a case he should refuse to entertain the dilatory motion. If an appeal is taken, the chairperson should entertain it. If the motion is sustained by a large majority, the chairperson can afterward refuse to entertain even an appeal made by the obstructing faction. But the chair should never adopt such a course merely to expedite business when the opposition is not hostile. It is only justifiable when it is perfectly clear that the opposition is trying to obstruct business.

Know parliamentary law, but do not become technical or more strict than is absolutely necessary for the good of the meeting. Judge the readiness of the membership. A strict enforcement of the rules, instead of assisting, may greatly hinder business. On the other hand, in large assemblies where there is much work to be done, the only safe course is to require a proper observance of the rules.

A chairperson will sometimes become confused with the many difficulties involved in the position; in such cases he or she will do well to heed the advice of a distinguished writer on parliamentary law and recollect that:

> The great purpose of all rules and forms is to subserve the will of the assembly rather than to restrain it; to facilitate and not to obstruct, the expression of their deliberate sense."[11]

## PARLIAMENTARY PROCEDURE AND UNION MEETINGS

"Parliamentary procedure" or "parliamentary law" are misnomers, incorrect titles or terms. When those who assemble at deliberative meetings use this term, they are referring to the rules of conducting a formal meeting, not a governmental procedure. But we are stuck with this term, and we can thank our then Vice-President Thomas Jefferson for it.

When our country was formally institutionalized as the United States and Congress was convened, there was no code or method of conduct on which our elected representatives could base their actions. Jefferson, who presided over the U.S. Senate, sought to remedy this situation by writing a manual of conduct for the Senate based on the procedures used by the British in their parliament.

[11] General Henry M. Robert, *Robert's Rules of Order*. William Morrow and Co., New York, 1979, pp. 242–244.

Jefferson then wrote his famous *Manual of Parliamentary Practice,* which is still in use today; hence, parliamentary procedure.

If, as citizens, we often have difficulty understanding the actions of Congress, then it is no small wonder that we would likewise have difficulty understanding our nation's congressional procedures. Realizing this difficulty, U.S. Army officer Henry M. Robert condensed and simplified the federal procedural rules so that group meetings and other forms of gatherings could be conducted on both a rational and orderly basis. His simplification has become known as *Robert's Rules of Order.* Parliamentary procedure, as refined by Robert and others, has become the framework by which one conducts a union meeting because such a meeting should be both democratic and efficient:

> *Democratic* in that it provides for the rule of the majority at the same time that it protects the rights of the minority, and
>
> *Efficient* in that while it provides for full discussion of all matters, it limits group consideration to one subject at a time and requires an orderly disposition of each item of business before taking up another.

Union meetings are not normally known to be exciting and action packed. However, special meetings concerned with new contract discussions or recommendations, elections, concessions, plant closings, or other key issues draw vocal and often overly zealous union members. It is at meetings such as these that some form of order needs to prevail. "The main objectives of parliamentary rules are to guard against hasty, ill-conceived action, to give each member an equal right to be heard, to determine the will of the majority, and to protect the rights of the minority."[12] Note the following principles guiding the conduct of a union meeting:

1. Only one question can be considered at a time; only one amendment can be considered at a time.

2. No one can speak until they have risen, addressed the presiding officer, and been "recognized."

3. No one can speak a second time on the same question as long as another wants to speak for the first time.

4. When two or more members rise to speak, the chairperson should recognize the one who opposes the preceding speaker, and preferably one who has not spoken previously.

5. Noting previous points 3 and 4, each proposal coming before the meeting shall be freely debated with meaningful discussion and the will of the majority be sought, but a minority or minorities have the right to present a case.

---

[12] J. Jeffery Aver, *Essentials of Parliamentary Procedures.* Prentice-Hall, Inc., Englewood Cliffs, N.J., 1968, p. 3.

6. Each member has rights and responsibilities equal to those of every other member.

7. The desires of the membership should move along in such a way that the welfare of the union, as a whole, is served.

Union democracy and parliamentary procedure go hand in hand. Properly utilized, parliamentary rules of order allow a union meeting to be both democratic and efficient. Improperly handled or technically abused, these same rules can demean the purpose of a meeting and impose unwanted decisions on officers and members alike.

A perfect parliamentary body would be a democracy in miniature with every member a "Respected Fellow-Worker." Each member's rights are to be useful and unlimited, but their opportunities for being a nuisance curbed; no one has a right to prevent needed action by sulking or yelling. The officers receive special power from the member, but the member retains the right to control the decisions of the organization. Each member gives of their ability, and shares in the strength of the whole group.[13]

## Components of a Union Meeting

The structure of a union meeting varies from international to international, from central labor body to central labor body, and from local to local. Even with this variety of form, there are certain aspects of conduct and activity that should be common to all union meetings, no matter what the level. These components are:

1. Constitutional and bylaw requirements
2. Nature of the meeting and the need for an order of business and agenda
3. Taking of minutes
4. Role of officers at meetings
5. Role of members at meetings
6. Role of committees at meetings

## Constitutional and Bylaw Requirements

Every labor organization that is recognized under a law operates its meetings by some set of rules of conduct, be it *Robert's Rules of Order, Demeter's Manual of Parliamentary Law,* or something else. Regardless of which authority is used, the local's constitution and/or bylaws should state clearly which authority is to be used and how some aspects of the rules have been altered to fit the needs of the local or the parent union. Therefore, it is important that all members be aware of which rules are being used and how they might differ because of local requirements. Such knowledge is essential if the members are to participate in full and

[13]*Parliamentary Procedure and Union Meeting Manual,* Labor Education Program, University of Missouri, pp. 1-2.

open discussions at the meeting. (All this assumes, of course, that the officers desire such "full and open discussion." The authors suggest that effective situational leaders do want this level of participation.)

## The Nature of the Meeting and the Need for an Order of Business and Agenda

There is a prevalent misconception about union meetings: they must be dull. The reality of this problem is that they do not have to be this way. Union meetings can be turned into major educational/informational, decision-making, and social events if local managers and members alike contribute their fair share toward better planning and communication.

First, make sure that the local has an established order of business to follow at the meeting. Again, such a structure of events is usually contained in the locals constitution and bylaws. If it is not, one should be constructed and approved.

If the *order of business* can be considered the framework for conducting a union meeting, then the *agenda* can be considered the "business" to be conducted within the order of business. The difference is important; yet it seems that it is precisely this difference that most union managers miss completely. The order of business is not by itself the whole content of the meeting. It is not the topics, concerns, wishes, and needs of the membership to be discussed. The business of the meeting is contained in its agenda. The agenda is the formal listing of committee reports, communications, officers' reports, educational presentations, guest speakers, and time for anticipated action and discussion from the floor. All the meeting's activities take place at various times *within* the local's standing order of business. Thus, the agenda is the meeting's plan for action for the conduct of pertinent union and membership matters. The order of business makes sure that the agenda gets covered.

Consistent effort is needed by union managers and administrators to plan new and varied agendas so that members will continue to want to come to the meetings. Union management, in an effort to solve the age-old union meeting attendance problem, must spend some time creating long- and short-range agenda ideas.

The authors have listed in Exhibit 8-2 a typical order of business containing its agenda items. Numbers 1 to 12 represent the order of business and the letters the agenda items.

---

### EXHIBIT 8-2
### Meeting Order of Business and Meeting Plan

1. Call to Order

2. Pledge of Allegiance to the Flag

3. Roll Call of Officers

4. Reading of Minutes from Previous Meeting and Executive Board

5. Reading of Correspondence

6. Reports of Officers
   a. President: report on negotiations
   b. Vice-president: report on new labor/management committee
   c. Treasurer: financial summary and bills*
   d. Business manager: report on district organizing efforts

7. Committee Reports
   a. Political Action Committee: Julie Edwards†
   b. Grievance Committee: Sam Steward
   c. Education Committee: Morgan Alexander
   d. Trades and Label Committee: Cary Edwards
   e. Bargaining Committee: Vera Hooper
   f. Social Committee: Jan Gunderson

8. Delegate Reports
   a. State AFL–CIO: President Jacobs
   b. Maple Grove Central Labor Body: Anne Johnson
   c. Union district delegate: Jo Nabors

9. Unfinished Business
   a. Continue discussion on quality circles as proposed by the employer

10. New Business
    a. Education Committee: Film, *Comparable Worth*‡
    b. New business from the membership

11. Good and Welfare

12. Adjournment

*Equipment needed:*

*Overhead projector to show transparency of treasurer's statement and diagrams the vice-president has on employer's quality-circle proposal. Also, chief steward Quincy has summary of grievances to show.

†½VCR and monitor for Political Action Committee to show 6-minute segment during its report (LIPA).

‡16-mm projector, screen, film, and extension cord. The education committee will have a brief handout.

## The Taking of Minutes

The recording secretary is responsible for the writing of local union minutes and the reporting of the same back to the members at the next meeting. Minutes are the only source of information as to what has been done in the past. They also serve as a reminder for future action. Minutes are the only permanent record a local union has of activities and actions over time. As such, members, officers, and outside parties such as the Labor–Management Services Administration will look to the minutes for an *official* record of what the union has voted to do. Because writing minutes is important, 11 suggestions for their writing are provided.[14]

1. Show clearly in the minutes what business was brought up at the meeting and what action, if any, was taken. Each order of business should be recorded. Where no action was taken, the word "None" should appear. Remember: minutes record what was done, not what was said. Under no circumstances should the recording secretary comment in the minutes either favorably or otherwise on anything said or done at the meeting.

2. Record each motion as stated by the chair. The exact wording of each motion must be written down and the recording secretary should be asked to read the motion aloud before the vote. If the chair rewords a motion to clarify it, that becomes the way the motion is recorded in the minutes. A motion that has been withdrawn should not be recorded. All resolutions that have been adopted must be entered in the minutes, in full.

3. Record the wording of the motion and the action taken on it. Every motion that is voted on must be written out in the minutes, and whether or not it passed must be indicated. If the voting on a motion is counted (ballot, roll call, or count of hands), the minutes should reflect the exact count. Action taken by the local by "unanimous consent" should also be noted.

4. Record the names of members making the main motion. Recording the member who seconds the motion is optional. It is advisable to record the seconder for future reference, especially if a correction is called for at the next meeting.

5. Take the roll call of officers and note the number of members present when there is not a quorum present. The minutes must show if a meeting was not held because of a lack of a quorum.

6. Use as few words as possible when writing the minutes, but include enough detail so that the members who missed the meeting will understand what took place. Emphasize what was done and decided at the meeting, not what was said. Record the details of a speech, report, or discussion only when it is felt that they are important for future reference.

7. Attach to, or file with, the minutes, and so note in the record, any document which was presented to the meeting and which might need to be referred to in its entirety. Examples are: written reports of local committees,

[14] International Association of Machinists, *Manual for Lodge Recording Secretary,* IAM Department of Education.

text of the remarks of a speaker, and prepared statements which members may ask to have made part of the record.

8. Briefly summarize the reports and recommendations of the local's committees and delegates. Show what action was taken on reports, if any.

9. Take careful notes during the meeting as each item on the agenda is handled. This will be easier if a copy of the order of business is available for immediate clarification.

10. It is handy to know shorthand, but not necessary for keeping accurate minutes. Any form of abbreviations or longhand will work, provided one can write fast and possesses good recall.

11. Write a draft of the minutes while the meeting is still fresh in mind. Make a new paragraph for each subject and each order of business.

Minutes should be kept in a bound ledger called the Journal of the Union. This ledger should have a border on one side of the page where corrections can be noted. Minutes should be written in black ink and all corrections should be lined out but still left legible. If the membership prefers to have the minutes typed, this is acceptable provided that these pages are numbered, dated, and periodically bound for the sake of security. Binding can take place annually or at the end of each term of office.

A correction or addition to the minutes should be written in completely on the last page of the minutes that require changing. All corrections must be initialed. Minutes may be approved and corrected by the group whose record the minutes reflect. For example, the executive board must approve and correct its own minutes. A motion to correct the minutes may be either for a deletion or an addition. The minutes may be corrected whenever an error is noticed, regardless of the elapsed time. However, after minutes have been adopted, their correction requires a two-thirds vote for passage.

The minutes of the preceding meeting are read at each meeting. The chairperson asks if there are any corrections or additions. If none are voiced, the chair then states that the minutes stand approved as read. If a correction is given but not disputed, use the method of noting the changes as provided in the previous paragraphs. When minutes are approved, it should be noted in the margins of the minutes with the initials of the recording secretary, the word "approved," and the date.

Of the six components of a meeting listed previously, the authors have discussed all but one, the role of committees at membership meetings. Since we are devoting a major portion of this chapter to making committees work, the discussion of committees as a part of the general meeting must wait for a few pages more. It is now time to turn to some fundamentals of parliamentary procedure.

# PARLIAMENTARY PROCEDURES AND RULES

## Motions

The motion is the basis for all action at a membership and formal committee meeting. Membership decisions to take action on an issue or a problem come in the form of a motion. The motion is the cornerstone of all meeting rules of order.

Without a motion, no report can be handled, no new business introduced, no discussion closed, no meeting adjourned, and no future meeting established. In short, without the motion, nothing can take place at the union meeting.

Motions are relatively simple, with problems arising only when they are either presented in a complicated fashion or when they become complex after alterations to the motion are offered. The next several pages highlight how a member or a chairperson handles motions in a formal meeting setting. The authors suggest a class in the subject if more depth is needed. Role playing would be particularly helpful.

## How Motions are Made

A member desiring to present a motion or speak on a motion must first be recognized by the chairperson. Anyone may speak once they have been "given the floor" by the person who is in charge of the meeting. A member desiring to speak before the membership:

1. Gets recognized by raising his or her hand or by standing and addressing the presiding officer: "Mr./Madame Chairperson . . . ."
2. After addressing, wait for recognition.
3. Chairperson recognizes by name or title: "Sister or Brother . . . ."
4. After recognition, the member has the floor, and may:
   a. offer a motion, or
   b. discuss any motion made and seconded.

The person making the motion is usually given the first opportunity to speak and argue for support of the motion. After the mover has made her arguments for the motion, the floor is open for further debate.

It is good practice for the chairperson to alternate speakers both for and against a motion. However, no member should be permitted to speak twice until all others have been given a chance to speak. It is also suggested that preference be given to members who seldom speak over those who speak frequently. In the case where two or more potential speakers address the chairperson at the same time, the chair should ask if the member wishes to speak for or against the motion. If the previous speaker was in favor of the motion, the next speaker should be one who is in opposition, unless there is no one opposed who wishes to be recognized.

## Stating a Motion

Most motions come about after considerable discussion on a particular issue. That is, a member is recognized by the chair and begins to speak about something. After sitting down, another member also speaks to the same issue, and so on. After the discussion runs its course, someone frames the essentials of the discussion in the form of a motion. This procedure is all wrong, even if it does suit the chair's needs and makes for some effective decision making.

The proper method of making a motion and then discussing it starts with the member being recognized by the chair. The member then makes the motion: "I move that Local 5097 hold the annual union picnic on June 1 . . . ." The motion should then be seconded by another member. Any member can make the second except for the maker of the main motion. "I second the motion" or "Second" or "So moved."

We are not even to discussion yet. No motion can be considered unless it receives a second. The reasoning here is that if a motion cannot obtain a second it is neither worthy of discussion nor efficient to do so. Some incidental motions, such as "point of order" and "point of information," do not require a second.

When the motion is made, the chairperson asks for a second ("Is there a second?" or "Do I hear a second?") if the main motion was not immediately followed by a second from the membership. (Most locals have someone who is the "automatic seconder." This person's sole reason for attending meetings seems to be seconding in a split-second fashion any motion coming to the floor.) After the motion has been seconded, the chair should repeat it clearly, politely making any confusing wording more clear. If the chair believes the motion to be out of order, she should rule so immediately and provide a brief explanation. (The mark of an ineffective leader of meetings is one who is quick with the gavel and an "out of order" without a brief explanation.) In repeating the motion to the membership, the presiding officer may ask the recording secretary to read it, especially if the motion is a difficult one.

## Discussion

After restating the motion, the chair asks for discussion: "It has been regularly moved and seconded that we hold the union picnic on June 1. Is there any discussion on the motion?" If no member rises to speak to the motion, the chairperson then says: "Hearing no discussion, the vote is on the motion that we hold the union picnic on June 1. Those in favor of the motion say Aye. (pause) Those opposed, No."

The chairperson decides the weight of the votes and declares: "The Ayes have it and the motion is carried," *or* "The Noes have it and the motion is lost." At this point the meeting moves on to the next motion or order of business.

## Changing the Motion:  Amendments

If discussion on the motion is extensive and ultimately makes the original motion unclear, a member might want to change it. A change in the motion might also be warranted because the discussion has brought to light some qualifications that ought to be included in the motion. In any case, one may move to amend a motion by: *adding, striking out, inserting, striking out and substituting,* or *dividing* the motion. "Mr./Madame Chairperson (pause for recognition), I move that we amend the motion by adding the words: between the hours of 10 A.M. and 6 P.M."

An amendment may be moved at *anytime after* a motion has been seconded and *before* the vote is taken. And just as with the main motion, an amendment must receive a second before it can be considered. An amendment should be clear and specific as to what portion of the motion it applies. If the proposed amendment is contrary to the spirit of the pending main motion, the chair will rule it is *out of order* (with an explanation). For example, if the motion "to have a picnic June 1" is on the floor, the amendment cannot state "not to have the picnic on June 1."

Thus, an amendment must be related to the motion to which it applies. It simply cannot be contrary to the motion's intent. Once a proper motion to amend is seconded, it can be discussed. Once the discussion is completed, the *amendment* is voted on. If the amendment passes, discussion on the main motion *as amended* resumes. If the amendment fails, discussion on the *original motion* continues.

## Substitute Motions

Handling an amendment takes some skill and practice, but it is not overly hard to understand and remember the rules for completing the work on an amendment before the business of the main motion can be completed. Confusion can arise rapidly, however, as soon as a member seeks to *amend* an *amendment* to the main motion. When this happens, it is not out of order for the chairperson to suggest a substitute motion be made. The maker of the main motion and the members who are offering the various amendments are asked if they would accept a new motion, a substitute motion. If they all agree, the chair then rephrases all the elements and asks for a member to offer the substitute motion. If all goes well, a member will so move and a second will be heard. Discussion then starts on the *new* main motion. Life is made easier for both the chairperson and the membership. But if any one of the parties to the motions and amendments refuses to allow a substitute motion, each amendment must be handled separately.

## Closing Debate

When it appears that no one else wants to discuss a motion or its amendments, or if discussion has continued sufficiently long for all the points to be made, the chairperson or any member may "call for the question." When this is done, the chairperson asks, "Are you ready for the question?" or "Are you ready to vote on the motion?"

This question from the chair requires a second but is *not debatable*. Upon hearing the second, the chair puts the request for a vote on the motion to an immediate vote. If the call for the question passes, the chair then repeats the motion (or has the recording secretary read it) and conducts the vote on the motion. On the other hand, if the call for the question (sometimes stated "move the question" or "move the previous question") fails, discussion on the motion continues. *Robert's Rules of Order* calls for a two-thirds positive vote for closing debate. The percentage may, however, be modified to some other figure, which should be found in the local's constitution or bylaws.

## Voting

When the membership is ready to vote, the recording secretary reads the motion if the chair chooses not to repeat it. One or the other should do it. Voting on a motion takes place in one of five ways:

1. *Voice vote*
   a. "All those in favor of the motion, please say Aye."
   b. "All those opposed to the motion, please say No."
   c. "The Ayes have it and the motion passes," or "The Noes have it and the motion is defeated."

2. *Show of hands or rising vote.* This method is used when the outcome of a voice vote is uncertain. In this case, a count of those in favor and those opposed to the motion is made and the number is usually recorded in the minutes. Either raised hands are counted or the members are asked to stand and be counted.

3. *Division of the house.* If a show of hands or a standing count still leaves some question or doubt as to the outcome of the vote, a *division* is called for. In this case, those in favor of the motion are asked to go to one side of the room while those who are opposed are asked to stand on the other side of the room.

4. *Roll call.* Used generally only in committee meetings, each member is called on by name and the vote is taken and recorded by the recording secretary.

5. *Secret ballot.* This method of voting is used when a show of hands or roll call vote might cause undue pressure on members to "vote with the crowd."

Although this method is time consuming, it provides for the most honest and least embarrassing method of expressing one's opinion. The local union's constitution or bylaws should outline under what circumstances a secret ballot is used.

## Point of Order

While the point of order is not a motion in the most strict sense, it is an action that helps keep order at a meeting. It is used whenever a member believes that the chair has let the discussion on a subject drift. The point of order is also used when a member believes that the chairperson has made a mistake in judgment or a wrong decision.

The point of order may be used at any time, even when another member has the floor or when a vote is being taken. The point of order is decided by the chair, subject to appeal by the membership. The point of order must be raised immediately after an error has been made, except in the case of a constitution or bylaws violation. During a point of order, the member who has the floor must yield until action has been taken on the point by the chair.

A member can call for a point of order[15] by rising and, after being recognized by the chair, state:

Member: "Mr./Madame Chairperson, I rise to a point of order."
Chair:    "Sister, what is your point of order?"

The member then states the point of order and the chair responds, "Your point is well taken" or "Your point is not well taken."

It is important to note that the point of order should not be used to criticize, slow down meetings, or interrupt speakers at will. Once the point of order is made, handled by the chair, and acted on by the membership if necessary, the meeting should resume where it left off before the point of order was offered.

## Appeals

If a member has been ruled out of order or his point of order is not accepted by the chair, an appeal can be made. Immediately after the decision of the chair, the member should say to the assembly, "I appeal the decision of the chair."

Some unions require the chairperson to vacate the presiding officer's chair at this point. The member takes the floor and presents his or her reasons for the appeal. The chair, in turn, states his or her reasons and has the right to discussion like any other member during the appeals process. The vice-president or chairperson pro tem asks the membership for a ruling once discussion is over. "Shall the ruling of the chair be sustained?" The vote on the question is taken

---

[15] The point of order is one of the few motions that does not require a second.

and the chairperson returns to conduct the meeting, regardless of the decision on the appeal.

The appeal, which does not take place too often, is a necessary check on the power of the chairperson. An appeal is in order only immediately after the chair has made a decision, but any member can call for the appeal.

## Point of Information[16]

When a member feels that he needs more information about the motion or discussion, a direct inquiry to the chair can be made. It is not unusual to hear a point of information come from the membership during an officer's report or the report of a committee.

All requests and answers to the point of information must be made through the chair. Again, as with the point of order, the questioner may interrupt a speaker and the chair has to recognize the member making the point. But unlike the point of order, the speaker being interrupted *does not* have to yield the floor. The chair asks if the speaker will yield. If the answer is a no, then the chair directs the speaker to resume.

The point of information can also be used by a member who seeks to *add* information to the discussion. This is done when the person holding the floor or the chairperson is not in possession of some information pertinent to the discussion.

## To Limit Debate

The membership may desire to limit debate on a question, and this procedure can be done in one of several ways:

1. Prescribe the number of speakers, pro and con.

2. Set a time limit for each speaker.

3. Set a time limit for calling the question.

4. Allot a specific amount of time for each side of the question.

5. Establish general rules limiting talk on all questions before the membership. These are sometimes established in the bylaws.

6. Limit each speaker to one time unless there are no objections by the membership.

The motion to limit debate can be on a specific question. "Mr./Madame Chairperson, I move that debate on this motion be limited to five minutes per speaker" or "that the debate close promptly at ten o'clock on this motion."

---

[16]The point of information is similar to the point of order and is handled in a like manner.

## Nominations and Elections

There are three ways that a person might be nominated to run for local office. These nominations usually "come from the floor." In larger organizations, such as the parent union, the nominations can come from a report of a nominating committee. The third method of nomination for office is the petition. In this case, a group of local members "draft" a candidate for office by circulating a petition.

When using the nomination committee system, take pains to ensure the committee's impartiality. The best way to do this is to have the committee elected by the membership. In any case, as president of the local do not nominate the committee yourself. This system has an advantage in that the committee can get advance commitment from potential nominees, once selected, as to whether or not she or he will indeed run for the office. Finally, even if the committee system is used, it is not a bad idea to permit members to be nominated from the floor.

During a meeting where nominations are coming from the floor, the chair must exercise extreme caution when suggesting that nominations be closed. Make sure that all members seeking to nominate another member be given the opportunity to do so. The motion "to close nominations" is out of order until the membership is apparently ready to have them closed.

When there are two or more nominations for an office, the motion to close nominations requires a two-thirds vote to pass. A negative vote on this motion is a clear-cut criticism that the chairperson has been premature in closing the nominations.

If the motion to close the nominations comes from the membership, the chair should ignore that motion until absolutely certain that there are no other nominations waiting to be put forward. The chair is especially responsible for protecting the rights of any minority membership groups.[17] If there is only one candidate for the office in question and it is obvious that there is not opposition, the recording secretary may be instructed to "cast a ballot," sometimes called a "white ballot," for the nominee. While it is not an official ballot, the action is recorded in the minutes of the meeting so that there is a permanent record of the action taken by the membership. The vote on a white ballot must be unanimous. If *anyone* votes in the negative, it is presumed that there is someone in the membership who desires to be a candidate for office.

Once the nominations for an office have been closed, the recording secretary should read back to the membership the names of the candidates. At this time each candidate should indicate either acceptance or rejection of the nomination. Sometimes candidates are given a future deadline to indicate their decision, a time still well in advance of the election. With acceptance or rejection of

---

[17] For a more detailed description of nominations and elections, the authors suggest that the reader consult O. Garfield Jones, *Parliamentary Procedure at a Glance,* Hawthorn Books, Inc., 1971, pp. 21–21L and XXX–XXXVII.

the nomination, the process of candidate nomination is over and the election is held in accordance with the local union's constitution and bylaws.

## CLEARING THE MUDDY WATERS

For several reasons, local union leaders generally do an inadequate job of membership meeting planning, both in the short and long range. Couple this deficiency with the almost zealous way the secrets of parliamentary procedures are guarded by union managers (we don't want any "know-it-all" members changing the way *we* run *our* meetings) and it is no small wonder that the few workers who belong to unions do not care if they ever attend a meeting.

The authors hope that they have managed to clear up a bit the muddy waters that swirl around the specter of lifeless union meetings and the fear of an active union membership. The general membership meeting can be a stage for successful leadership behavior that can reach more people faster and with greater intensity. It can provide communication and motivation for both the members and their officers.

Poor meeting planning and method of conduct (authoritarian versus democratic) can be changed or improved, as the case need be. We feel the concepts of leadership and the personal skill chapters (writing and speaking) presented in this text give the reader a framework for revamping and improving the quality of local union meetings. It will, of course, take leadership.

## MAKING COMMITTEES WORK

As promised earlier in this chapter, it is time to discuss the one remaining component of the general membership meeting—the role of committees. Committee reports can be the highlights of any general meeting, but usually they are more like a litany of tired reruns of past reports. Members often cannot wait for this part of the meeting to pass. Since committee reports and activities at the general meeting are so important, the authors have decided to devote the balance of this chapter to supplying the reader with some insights on how local union committees can be made to fulfill their role.

Committees are important because they encourage a greater degree of specialization and concentration of effort, which is so essential to efficient operations. Committee names usually reflect their immediate jurisdiction: grievance committee, safety and health committee, education committee, community services committee, political action committee, women's committee, and so on.

Committees give a needed continuity to union values. Through dedicated volunteers, committees stimulate and focus energy and attention on issues that go to the very heart of union ideals. Some of these concerns include fair and equal laws, economic well-being for all, equal access to education, justice and dignity in the workplace, the right to a safe and healthy workplace and community, and so on.

One of the oldest jokes in a local union, and probably in most other organizations, is that, if one wants to kill an issue, submit it to a committee and it will die a certain, if not slow, death. Committees need leaders to manage them. Here are some hints that might make the effort somewhat easier.[18]

## TYPES OF COMMITTEES

First, *a committee is a group of members charged with specific duties and responsibilities.* There are two major types of committees in local unions, standing and special committees.

*Standing committees* are those mandated by the local's constitution and/or bylaws. Some of the more common committees include the grievance committee, education committee, community services committee, political-action committee, and safety and health committee.

*Special committees* are created as the need arises. While a bargaining/negotiating committee may be a standing committee in some locals, it is often a special committee. Strike assistance committees and unemployed assistance committees are two examples of special committees formed to meet a special need. Where locals have not yet made women's committees permanent, they exist as special committees. Finally, while the organizing committee, like the women's committee, should be a standing committee, it is often only a special committee formed to handle a particular campaign.

In addition to special committees, local unions often appoint what are known as ad hoc committees or task forces. Like an ad hoc committee, a task force is usually a small group of members appointed to undertake some specialized function for a limited period of time. While standing committees are appointed to serve a period of time that coincides with the term of elected union officers, an ad hoc committee or task force is disbanded after completion of its assigned task. Ad hoc or special committees are often formed to plan union social functions or to study particular issues and turn over their findings.

Some locals elect the members to their committees. Others ask for volunteers. In other locals, the president appoints the committee members. No matter how the committee gains its members, the purpose of a committee is to assist the president or other managers and administrators in meeting the goals of the local or its members.

Committees do not make policy. They make recommendations to the membership or the executive board. The officers and the members make policy, often with the technical assistance of the local's committee structure.

[18] Pages 279-286 adapted with permission from *Getting Things Done Through Local Union Committees*, United Steelworkers of America, Education Department.

## Executive Board

Local unions have a governing body made up of members. This group is known as the local's executive board. The operations of the board are dictated by the membership's size and the traditions of the local and parent unions. Some executive boards include all elected officers, while others limit the board membership to the five top officers. Some executive boards are empowered to act on behalf of the membership between membership meetings. Such a power is a good management tool; however, there needs to be the proviso that the executive board must report its interim actions to the membership at the next general meeting for approval or disapproval.

Executive board deliberations and decisions can be enhanced by effective committee work. Before taking action on a given issue, a report from someone on a committee can provide board members with much needed information and expertise. The final decision belongs to the board, but the quality of the decision often rests with sound committee work. It is good management to use all one's resources.

Finally, a local's executive board should instigate an annual review of the union's progress toward its goals. It should survey the welfare and needs of its members. This process seems most often to be done only at an informal level. As described earlier in this chapter and in Chapter 3, goal setting and review are a much needed area of union management improvement.

# CHARACTERISTICS OF EFFECTIVE COMMITTEES

The old maxim that offers that "two heads are better than one" is the foundation for the operation of a committee. The more angles a problem or issue can be viewed from, the more likely a sound solution will result. There are at least five characteristics of smoothly functioning and productive committees.

1. Committee discussion encourages the sharing of opinions and the exchange of ideas. Through the give and take of group deliberations, a cross-fertilization of ideas usually results. One proposal sparks another. Suggestions are combined, extended, elaborated, and refined.

2. Serious committee discussion tends to minimize personal competition and judges an idea on its merit. There is a greater chance that within the group setting ideas are seen as belonging to all members and not the exclusive property of just one or two.

3. Compromise and consensus are easier to reach through face-to-face deliberations. Committee members are in a position to see common threads among ideas as they are developed through discussion. Usually there are committee members who can serve as mediators and help bridge differences, while moving discussion toward agreement.

4. While no guarantee can be given by the authors, it is more likely that committee recommendations will produce a greater degree of acceptance among local union members than suggestions offered by a single individual.

5. Referring an issue to a committee for additional study gives a proposal more "breathing room." Referral to an appropriate committee acts as a safeguard against hasty action, especially action taken in the absence of all available facts.

## HOW A COMMITTEE PLANS A LOCAL PROJECT

Frequently, a local union president will request a standing committee and, on some occasions, appoint a special committee or task forces to plan and undertake a project. As the following list indicates, special projects and programs cover a wide range of possible activities.

Registration and get-out-the-vote campaign

Occupational alcoholism program

Preretirement planning

New-member program

Consumer counseling

Training and education classes

Sports programs

Credit union

Food commissary

Health screening tests

Tax counseling service

Local union newsletter

Labor Day program

Local union picnic/Christmas party

Family night/local union open house

Union counseling program

Hospital visits

Blood bank

Services for the unemployed

Special conferences

If asked to plan one of these above projects, how does a committee go about its work? What does it mean to "plan"? What is involved in the planning process?

Among other things, good planning is the development of a realistic overview that provides a start-to-finish picture of the entire proposed project. In the beginning, it may be difficult to comprehend all the parts and details of a project and how they fit together. The committee must generalize who and what is involved, time requirements, resources, possible obstacles, and any other intervening factors. Such a master plan will serve to remind committee members of the original mandate and provide them with a schedule by which progress can be measured.

Good planning is also attention to detail. It is the effort given to anticipating the consequences of both acting and not acting. It is the ability to subdivide a specific action or phase of a program into logical units and steps. Good planning is the ability to outline a sequence of actions in a step-by-step fashion, seeing how each stage of the project links with the others. Good planning is the ability to delegate responsibility.

## QUESTIONS THE COMMITTEE SHOULD ASK ITSELF

The following questions are designed to help committee members think through the progressive steps needed for effective project planning.

1. *Nature of the project.* Does it comply with union policy? Can one pinpoint specific objectives, including a brief description of the program?

2. *Problems, needs, interests.* Why is this particular project needed? What is it the committee is seeking to resolve?

3. *Duplication.* Could any ready-made opportunities that already exist within the local be adapted or used for the same purpose? Is there a danger of duplication of existing activities?

4. *Target group.* Who is the project designed to reach or serve? Is it new members, the entire membership, members of a particular group, or members with particular interests?

5. *Involvement.* Is the project being planned for a target group or with a target group? Who will become involved with the project and why?

6. *Time span.* What is the time schedule for this committee project? When does it start and when will it finish?

7. *Resources.* What resources are required for the successful implementation of the project? Money? People? Facilities? Supplies?

8. *Publicity.* By what method will the project be publicized? Newspaper? Mail? Steward system? Personal contact?

9. *Administration.* Who is responsible for what in the implementation of the project?

10. *Evaluation.* Will it be possible to measure the success of the projects? Were the goals obtained?

## HOW WELL IS A COMMITTEE FUNCTIONING?

Aware of the need to keep its programs vital, a responsible union will assess how well its committees are functioning. Exhibit 8-3 is a checklist for measuring local union committee effectiveness.

EXHIBIT 8-3
**Committee Effectiveness Checklist**

|  | YES | NO |  |
|---|---|---|---|
| 1. | | | Are members willing to exchange ideas freely and become involved in committee deliberations? |
| 2. | | | Are members willing to accept personal responsibility for committee actions and not depend exclusively on the chairperson? |
| 3. | | | Do all members have a clear understanding of the committee's responsibility and goals? |
| 4. | | | Are committee objectives, meeting schedules and procedures realistic? |
| 5. | | | Does the committee hold regular meetings and maintain some form of minutes, especially a record of its recommendations? |
| 6. | | | Does the committee use the skills and abilities of its members? |
| 7. | | | Is full consideration given to minority points of view? |
| 8. | | | Does the committee make frequent progress reports of its activities and recommendations at membership meetings? |
| 9. | | | Is it possible for the committee to look at itself critically to improve its procedures and deliberations? |
| 10. | | | Does the local union sponsor some form of recognition program to acknowledge the work of committees? |

## FIVE STEPS TO EFFECTIVE
## COMMITTEE OPERATION

### Step 1: Committee Purpose

Elementary as it may seem, the first step toward making a committee effective is defining the scope of the committee's inquiry or action. Much time and effort will be saved if the committee's membership confines itself to its defined area of authority. What is the committee's jurisdiction? What has the local's president or constitution and bylaws defined as the purpose of the committee?

### Step 2: Committee Meeting and Discussion

There is no substitute for vigorous and searching discussion. A committee meeting is a valuable clearinghouse for the airing of ideas and the sharing of information. More importantly, a committee meeting provides an ideal forum for the distribution and assessment of proposed solutions to problems. A consensus should emerge. If not, complete majority and minority reports for consideration by the local's members and managers should be provided.

### Step 3: Committee Agenda

A simple agenda prepared by the committee's chairperson prior to the meeting will greatly facilitate the business of the committee. Meetings are less likely to be rambling and time consuming when members are mindful of the essential questions to be considered. Free-ranging debate is desirable on many occasions, but it is equally important to keep discussion on track without confusing digression into irrelevant matters.

### Step 4: Finding Solutions and Planning Projects

Ultimately, the test of an effective committee is the quality of its decisions and recommendations. Unfortunately, there is no precise formula for the creation of fruitful discussion or practical wisdom. Perhaps the most valuable function of a committee is the generation of new ideas and fresh approaches. Three techniques for generating new ideas are group discussion, brainstorming, and attribute listing.

#### Group Discussion

Perhaps the most time-honored of all methods of idea generation is the group discussion. There may or may not be a discussion leader. There certainly should be a recorder. Committee members voice their observations, convictions, and reflections in an attempt to work the committee toward an answer it can support. Group discussion efforts can wander if someone does not take the lead in sparking the committee on. Another problem often found with group discussion is that the members are not always challenged to come up with new or novel ideas. Brainstorming might be the solution to this problem.

### Brainstorming

As a method of generating ideas, brainstorming calls imagination into play and encourages the free association of ideas. For a period of 10 to 15 minutes, committee members are urged to voice as quickly as possible *any thoughts* on the subject that come to mind. During this period of uninhibited imaginings, all should refrain from analyzing or evaluating the ideas. Someone from the committee acts as a recorder of the ideas and another acts as the traffic director, making sure everyone has as many chances as possible to contribute. When it seems that the committee has run out of ideas, then and only then does the screening and evaluating of the ideas begin. Without a doubt, many of the more "interesting" ideas will be discarded. But those that remain often pose fresh and exciting suggestions for dealing with the project.

### Attribute Listing (Inventory)

When the well of inspiration has seemingly run dry, it is often useful to list the essential attributes or properties of the subject under discussion. Reducing a subject to its basic components or characteristics may enable committee members to gain a better perspective on how to handle it. For example, a committee considering a more efficient and profitable use of the union hall might draft the following attributes of the hall.

| | |
|---|---|
| Location | Lighting |
| Value | Heating |
| Age | Storage space |
| Type of construction | Parking |
| Number of rooms | Accessibility to public transportation |
| Seating capacity | Conference room facilities |
| Fixed or movable seats | Ventilation |
| Number of exits | Acoustics |
| Platform or stage | Relation to workplace |
| Restroom facilities | Rental possibilities |
| Kitchen facilities | |

The simplicity of making such a list overshadows its value. The cataloging of the characteristics of persons, events, objects, and programs will usually deepen the committee's understanding of the subject and result in meaningful changes and improvements.

## Step 5: The Committee Recommendation

When a committee has examined the subject of its inquiry in sufficient depth, it then must present its conclusions to the local union president or executive board with recommendations for the most advantageous course of action. If, as often happens, the committee cannot achieve unanimity after its discussions, alternative opinions must be presented to enable the local officers to choose the most promising option or options.

Within its formal recommendations, the committee should state clearly what it believes should be done, what the outcomes ought to be, and what pitfalls must be avoided. Whenever possible, both short- and long-range results of a recommended action should be cited, including costs, time to achieve the goal, and the number of people required.

## COMMITTEE REPORTS

When a committee report is delivered to the executive board or the membership, there is often confusion as to what should be done with it. Simply put, the report is either *accepted* or *adopted*. To accept means to take or receive. To adopt means to take, receive, and make it your own.

If the local agrees with a committee report and/or agrees with the recommendations and wishes to be bound by them, then the membership or executive board moves to adopt the committee report. If the local wishes not to be bound by the report of the committee, or if it wishes to wait and examine or act on the report at a later date, the motion to accept the report is made. Either acceptance or adoption of a committee report relieves the committee of the subject at hand; furthermore, if the committee is special or ad hoc, the action dissolves the committee.

One sure way of ensuring the best possible consideration of a committee report is to spend some time drafting an informative and useful report. Consider the following suggestions:

Sketch in some background facts about the report. What is the report about?

Talk the report through. Do not mumble along, translating one's notes or trying to decipher someone else's notes. Put the main points in your own words.

If there is nothing to report, say so and sit down.

In the first part of the report, outline the points to be made so the members can follow the report better.

Come to the main point or points as quickly as possible.

Let the content of the report suggest its tone.

Organize the report in some logical manner (dates, events, people, etc.).

Report only the high spots. Do not relive every moment of the committee's work.

Keep the report objective.

If the committee wishes to propose some course of action, make this recommendation as a motion separate from the report.

Encourage questions.

Remember that a report on information need not be accepted or rejected. Or, if you are making a progress report on some project, it need not be acted on.

## COMMITTEE AND DELEGATE REPORTS

An active local will have delegates that represent the membership in other organizations. These assignments might include delegates to the central labor council, building trades council, district or state union council, or even a local labor-management committee. The membership is entitled to hear reports from the representatives sent to these groups. These reports should be crisp and mention the highlights of various meetings and activities that might affect the local. If some action is needed from the membership on a delegate report, then that person should say so, either with or without recommendations.

Committee reports can be delivered by anyone on the committee. It might be a good idea to have a different person give a report each month so that the membership gets to know the different members of the committee. Such a simple move gives a committee more visibility and credibility with the membership.

## THE REWARDS OF COMMITTEE WORK

The authors have thus far said nothing of the genuine psychic and spiritual rewards of committee participation. There is the justifiable pride of serving one's union—one's friends and co-workers. Today, as never before, unions need informed guidance and committed leadership. The dedicated member who contributes time and energy to strengthening the local union is not likely to succumb to the feeling of political powerlessness that afflicts the life of many organizations.

Moreover, serving on a committee can be quite educational. The committee member must often grapple with abstract concepts on one hand and stubborn facts on the other. The task of imposing harmony on chaotic circumstances will clarify one's thought processes. Similarly, when battered by conflicting opinions as to what should be done, the committee member learns that honorable compromise is the mainspring of democracy.

Perhaps the best single reward comes from the knowledge that the committee member has joined with others in the constant struggle to preserve their mutual economic well-being and to ensure decent conditions in the workplace. With a proper mixture of good humor and tolerance, the joint efforts of working on a committee can be a rewarding adventure in human relations.

## CHAPTER TEST

Answer the following questions by inserting T for true and F for false.

1. _____ During a meeting, the member should address all questions about committee action to the chairperson of that committee.

2. _____ It is a good idea for a new chairperson to do what the previous chairperson did to conduct union meetings.

3. _____ The main purpose of the committee is to involve as many members as possible in the union.

4. _____ When a member disagrees at what is being said, she should debate the person with whom she differs.

5. _____ A good union member objects when he believes that something improper is happening at the meeting.

Circle the proper answer or answers.

6. Attendance at union meetings is poor because of
   a. parliamentary procedure       c. poor facilities.
      and confusion.                 d. uninteresting meetings.
   b. sports events.

7. If you are the chairperson of a committee and have nothing to report, you should
   a. fake it.                       c. say so, then sit down.
   b. be absent.                     d. ask another committee member
                                        to report.

8. The most powerful unionist at the local meeting is the
   a. president.                     c. chairperson of the executive board.
   b. treasurer.                     d. member.

9. Local union minutes are kept because they
   a. recap the previous meeting's highlights.
   b. provide an official means for showing the action taken by the assembly.
   c. give the recording secretary something else to do.

10. If the membership wishes to be bound by a report of a committee and move

on its recommendations, the membership moves to (circle one) *accept* or *adopt* the report.

11. The major purpose of union meetings is to
    a. understand management.
    b. discuss grievances.
    c. solve problems.
    d. have a night out.

12. Consulting other members and officers, and seeking their _____ is a good way to accomplish goals.

13. A suggestion for streamlining union meetings might be to
    a. set a time limit for reading the minutes.
    b. have written reports.
    c. refer committee reports to the executive board.
    d. use *Robert's Rules of Order*.

14. A good way to increase attendance at meetings is to
    a. have raffles with big prizes.
    b. have a dues rebate for attendance.
    c. have stewards emphasize the importance of attendance.
    d. send a notice in the union newsletter.

15. Meetings can be successful if
    a. the officers work on interesting agendas.
    b. the members are encouraged to participate.
    c. new members are encouraged to come.
    d. the international minds its own business.

16. Officers and membership working together in free discussion to improve the organization is an example of
    a. a lofty goal.
    b. teamwork.
    c. an impossible dream.
    d. a joke.

Discuss the following:

17. Is it always necessary to have an agenda that contains only union business? Why or why not?

18. If you were planning an annual agenda, how would you change this plan to make meetings more interesting?

19. Can the chairperson enter into a debate on a motion? If so, how is this best accomplished?

20. List three reasons why members fail to attend meetings.

21. List three ways to keep the concerned members, and interest other members in, coming to meetings.

22. Discuss the word "apathy" as it applies to union members and their organizations.

## GLOSSARY

**agenda:** A list of things to be dealt with or brought before a meeting. The agenda is the needs and desires of the membership that are built into the order of business.

**amendment:** A change that is offered to a motion by adding, omitting, or altering the original language.

**appeal:** A motion that asks the assembly whether or not a decision made by the chairperson should be upheld or overturned.

**auditor:** A person who examines and checks the financial accounts of the organization.

**bylaws.** The laws of a labor organization that govern its own affairs and conduct. These laws are secondary to the organization's constitution.

**call for the question:** A subsidiary motion used when someone in the assembly has heard enough debate and wants to vote on the pending motion. When the question is rightfully called for, the vote taken will be on whether or not to close debate.

**chairperson:** The person who presides at a meeting.

**committee:** A group of persons, who are usually appointed by the president, to carry out an assigned task. There are special (one time) committees and standing (continuing) committees.

**correspondence:** The letters and notes that are sent to a local union and reported on by an officer; usually the recording or corresponding secretary.

***Demeter's Manual of Parliamentary Law:*** A textbook written and compiled by George Demeter that deals with parliamentary procedure and standard rules of order at meetings.

**democracy:** A form of government that is run by the people who live under it. In a democracy, decisions are made either directly by the members (such as a union meeting) or indirectly through representatives of their choosing.

**efficient:** The ability to produce a result without wasting time or energy.

**executive board:** A group of elected officers who act on behalf of the members between regular meetings. The executive board is usually composed of the chief officers of the union.

**expenditure:** The act or process of spending money on behalf of the organization.

**incidental motion:** A motion that arises out of another question that is on the floor. This motion should be decided before the main motion is further acted on.

**lay on the table:** A subsidiary motion used to delay action on the pending motion while more research is done.

**main motion:** The motion that is the basis of all action at a meeting. It has the lowest precedence and yields to all privileged, incidental, and subsidiary motions.

**minutes:** A written summary of the actions and events that took place at a meeting. They are usually kept by the secretary and are a legal record of what took place.

**nomination:** The act of naming a member to be a candidate for office

**officer:** A member who has been elected by other members and has certain duties to carry out. Typical officers in an organization are president, vice-president, treasurer, secretary, executive board member, and trustee.

**order of business:** The sequence of events that are regularly scheduled to take place at a meeting. These might include call to order, credentials, old business, new business, good and welfare.

**parliamentary law:** A body of rules recognized for preserving order and regulating debate and procedure at meetings.

**parliamentary procedure:** See *parliamentary law.*

**point of order:** An action that helps keep order at the meeting. It is used whenever a member believes that the chair has let discussion on a subject drift off the topic that is on the floor.

**privileged motion:** A motion of such importance to the assembly that it should be acted on at once.

**question of privilege:** A privileged motion that relates to the rights of the assembly, such as the ability of the members to properly hear the speaker.

**quorum:** The smallest number of members who lawfully meet and transact business that will be binding on the entire group.

**rescind:** A motion that seeks to repeal some action already taken by the assembly.

***Robert's Rules of Order:*** A textbook written by General Henry M. Robert that simplifies the parliamentary rules that had been passed down through English law. This is the text that most organizations are governed by regarding the rules of conduct at meetings, how business is to be conducted, and how to participate in meetings in both a democratic and efficient manner.

**subsidiary motion:** A motion to modify, postpone, or refer action on a main motion.

**union constitution:** The rules and regulations that govern the behavior and conduct of the membership with its parent organization (usually the international union).

# CHAPTER 9

# Personal and Public Communication Techniques

Communication is any local union's primary activity and any local leader's means of influence. All the service functions, bargaining, organizing, and political education of unions take place through interpersonal communication. This has always been so; the only difference in the present lies in the greatly expanded types of communication media at one's disposal. This expanded range of media presents the local union leader with the challenge of enlarging his own personal range of communication abilities. Audiences large and small have come to demand "performance" from those who ask for their attention. Therefore, as someone whose leadership effectiveness will depend on an ability to reach people, engage their attention, and persuade them to take action on behalf of union goals, one must devote considerable time and energy to the improvement of verbal communication skills and abilities. (Written skills are discussed in Chapter 10.)

This chapter will focus on both verbal and nonverbal communication skills. It will help the reader evaluate personal skill areas and introduce current perspectives on communication and how they relate to accomplishing trade union goals—accomplishing effective local leadership. The chapter first focuses on personal communication strategies, then on ways one might improve communications within the local, and, finally, on improved preparation and delivery of public presentations to help the reader reach a broader public with a trade union message.

Union officials at all levels are in the seemingly unique position of being able to develop and use a wide range of verbal communication techniques. There is scarcely another institution in America whose lay members are provided with the range of opportunity to express themselves before various groups on policy issues in public forums, in intense one-on-one exchanges where the outcome is so weighty in terms of individual fates, or in small groups whose decisions may have considerable impact on the community. Trade unions (both here *and* abroad) have for that reason long been a source of recruitment to public office, and remain one of the few institutions in America where ordinary citizens can receive training in the skills of citizenry that enable them to play significant roles in the public lives of their communities and their country.

Yet the "training" for political and community involvement provided by unions has been almost entirely unstructured "learning by doing." This has been undeniably effective and has produced some fine public speakers and skilled community organizers. Yet such informal training has its limits, particularly today with the electronic media and with the extensive formal training available to those against whom unionists often find themselves locked in debate. This chapter suggests that a systematic approach to improving verbal communication, with emphatic local union support, can go far to help union leaders attain a polished and effective communication style that will bring benefits not only to individuals, but, more importantly, to local unions across the country.

## DIALOGUE: THE ESSENCE OF COMMUNICATION

Contemporary research on interpersonal communication rests on a perspective stressing the two-way nature of communication: it must be a genuine dialogue in which a sent message is received and a response is perceived, taken into the communicator's receptor system, and integrated into the next outgoing message. Interpersonal communication, in other words, is not comparable to what happens when a radio or TV station sends out a signal, which is passively received with no feedback. That is failed communication, on the interpersonal level, unless one has previously prepared the listener for maximum receptivity. Why failed? Because communication, as the root of the word suggests, is a communal, shared activity, carried on between involved, engaged parties.

The psychological reality behind this view of communication is important for trade unionists: a great deal of what we call communication is really *persuasion*. Certainly this is true of most union communications: union activists are called on to be persuaders as a regular part of their union duties—you want to persuade new employees to join the union; convince someone to talk on a committee assignment; change the supervisor's mind on a grievance; convince a member that her complaint is a gripe rather than a grievance; help someone understand why his grievance does not warrant arbitration; get someone to agree to participate in a voter registration campaign; persuade an unregistered member to register to vote; turn around a member's thinking on a political issue—the list could go on and on.

One form of communication, however, *can* be a one-way signal. That is the simple imparting of information. Certainly this is part of what unionists do, but it is far more difficult to make up a list of communication functions that involve pure information delivery without a persuasion dimension. Union officers often have to explain things to members: here is the new overtime clause; here is the NLRB ruling; here is the union-endorsed list of candidates. But most information delivery is accompanied by "therefore please vote for (the contract, the dues increase, the candidate, the motion under consideration)."

Where dialogue and feedback are essential to persuasive communication, "packaging" or extrinsic interest is important in straight information delivery. *Extrinsic interest* means simply imparting to your material an interest that is not intrinsic to or inherent in the information itself, that is, making it more palatable or attractive than it might be in unvarnished form. Here communication *style,* as opposed to interaction with the audience, becomes key. Both aspects of communication are important, and since the two (information delivery and persuasion) are so closely intertwined in your daily work as a union officer, we will talk about both style and dialogue throughout this chapter, whether we focus on persuasion, information, public presentations, or one-on-one communications.

## EVALUATING YOURSELF AS A COMMUNICATOR

Your skills are related closely to the experience you have had; few people are born great communicators—nearly everyone can develop considerable proficiency in communication *with practice.* Answering the following questions with the help of someone close to you can measure your current skill level in both public and personal communications areas.

### Checking Your Skill Level

|  | Yes | No |
|---|---|---|
| 1. Can you speak to a group using notes rather than a written-out speech? | ____ | ____ |
| 2. When you read a speech, do you maintain eye-contact with the audience so that some people don't know you are reading? | ____ | ____ |
| 3. Can you tell when your audience is really with you? | ____ | ____ |
| 4. When talking one-on-one, do you give other people enough opportunity to speak? | ____ | ____ |

5. Do you sometimes ask people for their opinions before offering your own, when you have a strong opinion about something?   _____ _____

6. Do you speak clearly, and vary the speed, volume, and inflection of your voice and words?   _____ _____

7. Do you use appropriate, natural-looking hand and body movements when you speak?   _____ _____

8. Have you ever asked anyone for feedback on your speaking style or content? Both?   _____ _____

9. Are you able to disagree with people without alienating them?   _____ _____

10. Are you able to ask for something you want without embarrassment or apologizing?   _____ _____

11. Are you able to move people to your way of thinking?   _____ _____

12. Are you considered a good listener by your friends?   _____ _____

These questions, although few in number, point out several important areas in communication techniques. They suggest your skill level with regard to both style (or packaging) and dialogue, and also indicate how you are doing in a couple of other areas central to effective communication: self-confidence and assertiveness.

## PERSONAL COMMUNICATION

Leading and managing an organization requires the development of superior one-on-one and small-group communication styles. Your personal communication style reflects your awareness of the other person's unique perspective, what that person has to contribute, and the likely possibility that she will differ with you on what course of action to take in a particular situation. Unions are filled with much inevitable conflict. Serious work on specific communication skills can mitigate much of this. We want to focus here on several aspects of personal communication that can greatly enhance your effectiveness as a union leader. We want to begin with a discussion of how you respond to other people when communicating with them.

### "Helping Talk"

Dialogue in communications comes about when you are aware of and responsive to your communication partners. The *way* you respond to your partner(s) is called your response *mode,* and one speech researcher has identified six modes or kinds of "helping talk."[1]   You can become a more effective communicator when you become aware of what these ways of talking are, when you are using them, and how they affect your conversations in small groups or in one-to-one conversations.

### Questions

Try using more questions to get at other people's meanings and states of mind. Open-ended questions are more effective than closed-ended questions in facilitating dialogue and exchange. "How do you feel today?" rather than "Is your cold gone today?"; or "What did you think of the movie?" rather than "Did you like the movie?" Give people a chance to expand on their experiences.

### Advice

Even when people ask for advice, they often have mixed feelings about getting it. Most people do not want advice unless it is from an expert. What they really want is verification from you that what they are doing is already right. Before giving advice, ask yourself what special competence do you have that makes your advice worth taking. If you do not see any, think twice before offering advice. Most people just want someone to listen to them.

### Spacing

Include lots of pauses in your conversation, especially if you tend to be a dominant conversationalist. We all know people with whom it is difficult or impossible to "get a word in edgewise." They are not very satisfying conversation partners. (If you do not know anyone like that, you are probably such a person yourself!) Try hard to change this; you will get instant positive feedback from those you usually swamp with your opinions.

### Interpretation

Pay attention to the meaning behind the words of the other person and try to figure out if you are understanding exactly what is meant. Does the person use a jargon you are not entirely familiar with? Does the person assume you know more than you do? Does the person use words incorrectly? There are many roadblocks to understanding. Trying to interpret the other person means paying attention to nonverbal cues as well as the spoken word. If there is a conflict between the words and the nonverbal cues, you should pay close attention to the cues. (We discuss these later.) They may convey important signals to aid you in interpreting what the other person means.

---

[1] Gerald Goodman, cited in Tom Greening and Dick Hobson, "Communication Blocks," in Joseph A. DeVito, *Communication Concepts and Processes,* 3rd ed. Prentice-Hall, Inc., Englewood Cliffs, N.J., 1981, pp. 29–33.

### Self-disclosure

Do not be afraid or hesitant to reveal things about yourself, especially things that the other person is mirroring. The "me-too" response is one that can bring you much closer to the other person. "Hey I had that same impression . . ." or "I'm confused by this . . ." or "What you just said really got to me . . . ."

### Reflecting Feelings

The most helpful aid to communication is also the least used, according to the experts. Seeing into people's states of mind and feelings and letting them know you understand what they are feeling is a powerful way to get in touch and clear away communication roadblocks. Another name for it is *active listening,* and it deserves a more extended discussion.

## Active Listening

We all know how to listen—or so we think. But are we listening or just "hearing"? Do we in fact take in what the other person is saying, grasp it from his or her perspective so that we truly understand what was meant by that statement? Consider how often you do some of the following things when engaged in a conversation:

1. Focus on what you are going to say next, rather than what your partner is saying.

2. Let your emotional response to what a person is saying drive all thoughts from your mind except "I've got to counter that!" or "How can I respond to that in a way that makes me look good?"

3. Interrupt the other person on some pretext or other: "I don't think you heard me correctly" or "Let me state my point another way." These interruptions are usually grounded in your assumption that, if the other person has not agreed with you, he must not have heard or understood you; therefore, you must correct the misapprehension before the other person continues.

By learning to use the art of active listening you can replace the old style of interruptions and conversational dominance and achieve the same end, *persuasion.* Active listening has also shown dramatic ability to change the behavior of the person listened to.

Active listening involves increasing your concentration powers during a conversation in order to plan your own remarks while at the same time keeping track of the other person's basic attitudes. It requires your ability to get inside another person—what we call empathy, the basis of human compassion, but the foundation as well of the art of persuasion, because you are able to start from *their* starting point and therefore sense what needs to be said and done to move them in the direction you want them to go.

Active listening demands sustained mental and even physical energy over a long period of time: during an entire conversation or throughout a meeting. Passive listening, on the contrary, is nothing more than hearing—letting messages pass through the ear and into the brain uncritically, without attempting to get at the emotional or psychological state of the person sending the message.

Active listening has two major principles: first, you must listen for feelings, not just words, or rather, you must listen for the feeling *behind* the words. A new steward comes up to you and says, "Well, I asked the supervisor for the absence records as you suggested, and she just laughed at me and said she would have to have a written request from you." As a busy officer you might respond with, "Why can't the steward handle this herself?" or "Another flap with management over getting information relevant to grievance handling," or "Now I'll have to put in another call to the international about a possible unfair labor practice," or even, defensively, "So you think I don't know the system here?"

It is only natural to think in terms of tasks, function, and structure in such a situation—to hear and respond to the verbal content of the steward's statement and to overlook completely the feeling behind the facts. But communications experts say that "feelings are facts," and very important ones in interpersonal relationships. This steward would have to be a very tough person indeed not to feel embarrassed and demoralized by this encounter with the supevisor in her new union role. But your main goal, building an organization and organizational loyalty, requires in this situation that your response take account of the feeling of the steward. She must be reassured that her request was in order and made properly, that she performed well, that you understand her embarrassment, anger, or chagrin.

The second principle of active listening involves the supportive response you can give the speaker to indicate your empathy and your willingness to suspend for a moment your task orientation and identify with her pain, anger, or frustration. What we suggest here is that you identify the emotion of the speaker that lies behind her words and that you verbally indicate to her your understanding of that feeling. You are willing, you in effect tell her, to suspend for a moment your own pressing agenda of action. You are willing instead to take some time to interact with her on a personal, caring level. Responses to the new steward might include, "I can tell that you feel slighted by her brush-off," or "Sounds as if you're pretty angry about that . . . ." Under certain circumstances, a reassuring touch, an understanding look, and head gesture might do the trick; or you may sense that the steward needs to talk about it over a cup of coffee.[2]

Active listening and helping talk are the building blocks for improved interpersonal communication. They are also very important to the health of the organization. We want to discuss two additional personal communication strategies that have important implications for the organization: personal assertiveness and persuasion skills.

[2]Carl R. Rogers and Richard E. Farson, "Active Listening," in DeVito, op. cit., pp. 137–147.

## Assertion Tips for Local Union Leaders

The women's movement has helped us realize that many of us need to gain assertiveness, that is, to be better able to speak up on our own behalf in a way that clearly states our position without needlessly stepping on anyone else's legitimate rights. Women have often been taught by society to avoid confrontation and social unpleasantness, and thus they tend to need help in learning how to state what they want without making apologies. Men may have been taught to be needlessly aggressive and competitive—seeing conflict where there is none and being excessively demanding of their rights without always taking account of the rights of others. But many men, finding themselves in a subordinate position, as at work, also find it very difficult to assert their rights in a calm and effective manner. Assertion training aims to find the middle ground between passivity and aggression. Both sexes can learn from a few tips developed by people who conduct assertion training courses.

Assertion is most frequently needed in (1) saying no to unreasonable requests and (2) making requests yourself. The application of these skills in work situations is quite clear; in a local union setting, perhaps less so. But think of the situation in your union when you find yourself asked to take on more work than you can expect to accomplish without serious infringement on your personal life or serious compromise of the quality of your work. It is vital that union activists learn how to say no, both to prevent burnout in themselves and to force the local to look elsewhere for people to draw into union activism. Learning how to say no in such a way as to build the local instead of creating distrust of yourself and your motives can be an important skill. On the other hand, being able to state a request for something that you want can be difficult, particularly for those who have always given so much of their time and energy. Unions are filled with people who are wonderfully skilled at making requests for other people, but who feel too "selfish" when they ask for something for themselves.

Here are some guidelines for building assertiveness skills.[3]

1. Clearly identify your goal in the situation. Exactly what is the issue?

2. Will assertive behavior here help you achieve this goal?

3. What would you normally do at this point to avoid asserting yourself?

4. What are your rights in this situation? Are you sure of them? Do they infringe on anyone else's?

5. Are you anxious about asserting yourself? What might be the worst possible result? Is that really very likely?

6. Do you have all the facts you need to present your case for saying no or for making your request?

7. Do you feel able to listen to the other person and let him know that you understand his position?

[3] See Lynn Bloom, Karen Coburn, and Joan Pearlman, *The New Assertive Woman*. Dell Publishing Co., New York, 1975.

The simple formula for stating a request or a rejection bears a remarkable resemblance to the formula for grievance writing (situation, contention, remedy). In educational programs conducted by the Cornell Institute for Education and Research on Women and Work, it has proved to be astoundingly effective. Women who used it to change their work situations described it as "absolute magic."[4]

The key steps are simple:

1. State the issue (the situation).
2. Explain your thinking about the issue—why it is important to you (the contention).
3. State what you want (the remedy).

A *refusal:*

1. "I'd like to talk to you about that committee assignment you asked me to take on." (the situation)
2. "I believe that if I were to accept that position, my work on the grievance committee would really suffer." (contention)
3. "I'm afraid I'm going to have to decline." (remedy)

A *request:*

1. The situation: There is a collective bargaining class being offered at the university.
2. Your contention: "I think it would really help me polish my skills for the upcoming bargaining in the fall."
3. Your request: "I would like the local to pay my tuition and lost time for the course."

If the formula sounds like shorthand, it is, because you must often get your statement out in full at one shot or it gets sidelined by protests or interruptions from the other person. But you should have your facts ready, just as in a grievance meeting, to follow up this initial statement in a discussion. In these communications, as in all, it is important to use controlled body language so as not to appear nervous, guilty, or ready for rejection. Those who act, speak, or look like victims usually get victimized. Another hint is that you should state your position and requests in the first person: "I want"; "I believe"; and avoid starting with "you." Use of the first person makes your statement much more forceful. It shows that you are ready for (but not inviting) confrontation. And it prevents putting your partner on the defensive. Remember that nearly any statement that starts with addressing a person directly by name or with the

[4] Communication from Anne Nelson, March 1981.

pronoun "you" puts him or her immediately in a defensive stance. If you are approached by someone who begins with the first person "I," your defenses are usually down.

What makes this formula for assertiveness so attractive is exactly that it is nonmanipulative and nonaggressive toward other people and their rights. This form of communication emphasizes the dignity and equality of both parties and the use of reason rather than force or manipulation. We offer it here as a way of making local union interactions more responsive to the rights of all parties.

## PERSUASION SKILLS[5]

Changing people's minds on a single minor point is one thing; changing their minds on more deeply held values and positions is quite another. Both forms of persuasion, however, are what union leaders are often called on to do as a regular part of their jobs. Findings from the numerous studies conducted since the end of World War II may help you increase your effectiveness in this area. Persuasiveness has become an art, and manipulation of large bodies of people is now commonplace. The political success of Nazi Germany, as well as that of the advertising media in this country in mobilizing public opinion, has stimulated studies that can help union leaders in their difficult job of moving opinion within local unions—at times in directions running directly contrary to prevailing public opinion and the mass media's often hostile view of the labor movement.

### One-on-One Persuasion Efforts

Let us start small, with the kind of shop-floor (or union-hall) discussions that so often occur with regard to politics or current issues within the local. Here are six hints for more successful persuasion or conversion efforts. Try your next persuasive conversation using these guidelines.

1. Try to get a handle on the other person's basic attitudes. Ask questions: "Why do you think that?" "Could you explain what you mean by that?" This helps you target your strategic approach.

2. Try to find a common ground that you share with the other person. What do you both genuinely agree on? "Inflation really hurts." "Our people need jobs." "The roads and bridges in our state need repair." This gives you a foundation on which to build toward compromise and agreement.

3. Try to guide the discussion in the direction you want it to go, where you feel you have the best facts to build a persuasive argument. "I've read that a major cause of inflation is military spending. Are you familiar with that argument?" Do not hesitate to bring your dialogue partner back to your position if she gets off in an area you are unsure of. "We might discuss gun

[5]This section is based on persuasion research reported in a classic study: Carl I. Hovland, Irving Janis, and Harold H. Kelley, *Communication and Persuasion, Psychological Studies of Opinion Change.* Yale University Press, New Haven, Conn., 1953.

control on another occasion, but I'd like to get back to what you said about inflation." (Notice that if you bring the other person back to your area by citing with approval something said earlier, she is much more likely to follow your lead.)

4. Remain calm and factual and try to keep personal egos and feelings out of it. It helps to rely on facts, rather than your personal opinion if you can do so. Not "I think the flat tax is really unfair," but "Here are some figures which show that the flat tax really hurts people who earn less than $15,000 annually." Not "I think you're dead wrong on that," but "That's an interesting view. I'd like to see your figures on that, because I've read just the opposite." Remember the cardinal rule for debaters: never argue about facts that are indisputable and can be looked up. Many arguments are about just that and should be avoided by checking the facts.

5. Do not make up facts or exaggerate what you do know to be true. Do not feel inadequate if you don't know everything. No one does. So do not be afraid to admit it. You can always look up the missing information. You only damage your credibility by faking.

6. Conclude the conversation with an open channel of communication that leaves room for continuing the discussion. "I'll try to find that reference (or those statistics)," or "I'd like to talk about this again after I've thought over what you've said," or "This has been interesting . . . let's do it again."

Remember that total persuasion of another person is unlikely, particularly in your first conversation, and particularly if your differences touch on deeply held values, attitudes, prejudices, or beliefs. So let your goals be modest at first:

1. Try to get the individual to open his mind and let you plant a few seeds of doubt about his own position.

2. Be friendly and gain the confidence of the other person that *you too* have an open mind and are not interested in mere confrontation and winning an argument.

3. Try to maintain an ongoing dialogue in which you both participate and to which you both contribute.

## Some Strategies for Changing Attitudes

Changing people's deeper attitudes—about the union or about politics—requires almost an entire campaign strategy. Psychologists studying communication and persuasion have come up with some considerations you might bear in mind when attempting to effect more profound changes in people's attitudes.[6]

1. How much change in attitude is desired? Obviously a 180-degree attitude change is more difficult than simply getting more commitment and energy

[6] Ibid.

from someone already friendly to your cause. If the 180-degree turnaround is your goal, think carefully about whether you really have the time and energy to invest in this effort. Make sure your target person is worth the effort!

2. How to work toward effecting a 180-degree change: It has been found to be more effective to begin by advocating moderate change, in the hope of gradually moving the person to a different position. It is also better to talk to the person in terms of a two-sided (pro and con) presentation. These approaches may help to avoid the boomerang effect of entrenching the person more deeply in her position, and help create the trust that you are a reasonable person.

3. Preferred approaches to effecting congruent change (or getting greater commitment from someone already close to your own opinion): Here it is not necessary to start with the pro-and-con approach; you may be more effective by using a stronger initial statement. You may also feel more confident in advocating more dramatic action right away.

4. Use positive arguments or material first: People have a habit of ignoring unpleasant accounts or information. If you have two main arguments, for example, you want to argue against a certain course of action, because you fear it could (a) bankrupt the local union and (b) you want to save money to build a new union hall, you should use argument b first and the threat second. Your audience will, say the scholars, be more likely to listen to your whole presentation and retain it longer if you start with the positive.

5. Use dialogue—not a lecture. What we have said about dialogue throughout this chapter is most important when it comes to effecting attitude changes in people. They must get involved, speak their minds, and feel part of a mutual exchange. Otherwise, they will go away secretly still harboring their initial views: "If I had said *my* piece, she would have seen that I was right!"

6. "You become what you do." Sometimes it is most effective to get people involved in union or political activity first and let their attitudes fall into place later. People naturally seek harmony and consistency in their lives and beliefs; they cannot for long act against their beliefs without getting into an uncomfortable psychological state of tension. Either they change their actions or their beliefs. Find ways to get your members active in behavior that is related to the changes you want. If someone is not yet willing to help write the newsletter, ask him just to help you with distribution. Before long, you have someone who sees himself as part of the newsletter team.

7. Perceived consensus or the bandwagon effect. If, in group discussion, persons holding one view perceive that the great majority of the group holds opposite opinions, they feel pressure to change or at least to modify their views to conform to those of the majority. The group should be one with which they have a long-term relationship and one that is of importance to them. That is why it is sometimes helpful to bring potential members or

activists to union functions. Let them feel part of a larger group that is strongly pro-union. Public speakers often attempt to create a bandwagon effect by asserting or implying that the audience already holds the view they are espousing. Whether true or not, the dissenters in the crowd suddenly feel uncomfortable or out of place.

8. Your personal credibility: Your own physical appearance, projected personality, and credentials are crucial ingredients in making your attempt to influence your audience successful. If you have *membership characteristics* (share attributes of the audience), your chances of success with your listeners will also increase. That is why speakers so often stress their connection with the audience or the geographic area in their opening remarks. Campaigning politicians are masters of this: "My parents were working class," "I grew up in this neighborhood," "The last time I was in this part of the country . . . ."

9. "What's in it for me?" If you can point out to your listener that changing her attitude will result in a positive benefit, you are far more likely to win the point, and the person. Every persuasion effort should contain this element. It may take some thought, but a union message will generally address, on some level, the broad concerns of most ordinary citizens. We all have to pay taxes, want to own homes, care about our families, hope for secure retirements, want our towns and states to flourish. The common ground upon which you started your discussion can also serve as a point of departure for a joint effort in the direction you advocate.

Persuasion often seems terribly difficult, almost like magic; yet remember it goes on in front of millions of American television sets daily and nightly. It is not magic, it is simply communication carefully planned and based on an acute understanding of human psychology—of the vanity, greed, and desire to belong and gain approval that is a part of all of us. It is also, however, based on an appreciation of the powers of human reason and response to facts and solid argument. You can learn these skills and use them to promote the interests of your local labor union and the goals your union stands for.

## COMMUNICATING UP AND DOWN
## THE LEADERSHIP STRUCTURE

Communications analysts have discovered some facts about the special way communications work within organizations that can help unionists attempt to tighten lines of communication. Their basic insights stem from the entertaining parlor game "gossip." Why does an original message, when passed through a series of communicators, become simplified, lose important elements, pick up not only details but even large general patterns that were not there in the original, and get changed in so many odd ways? At a party this phenomenon can be amusing; in a union or any other organization, it can be disastrous.

*Serial communications*—those passed through several communicators—fall victim to some normal human traits that account for these changes in messages. Most people apparently desire to *simplify messages* to make their job of transmitting the message easier. Passing along a complex piece of information about the way the new overtime clause is to be applied asks a great deal of grievance committee persons, chief stewards, and the stewards who have to explain it to members and even supervisors. It becomes simpler if some details are omitted—especially those we assume everyone already knows. Omission of detail for purposes of simplification is done unconsciously, but universally.

A second motive is the desire most of us have to *convey a sensible message*—one that we grasp completely and that we can make intelligible as we relay it. Complex information and special twists that are not fully understood may be subject to a steward's desire to "make sense of it" before she tells members about it.

A third reason messages may get distorted is the desire to *convey pleasant news.* No one wants to share the fate of the messenger who was executed for bringing the king bad news. We all hate to upset people to whom we are responsible, and psychologists have pinpointed this trait as leading to distortion. A divisional steward may hear from a departmental steward that his members are upset with the current leadership over a recent grievance settlement and that they have contacted a lawyer to file suit against the union for failure to represent. By the time the business agent hears this message, it can have been watered down to "A few of the folks over in department B weren't too happy with that grievance settlement."

Understanding the all-too-human motives for the unconscious distortion of messages can help you correct this problem. Dealing with conscious, willful, and malicious distortions is another problem, and must be handled with other methods than those we suggest here. Our point is, however, that you should never jump to the conclusion that the distortions are conscious.

Communications experts suggest some ways of correcting the innocent, even well-meaning distortions we have discussed here. Four of these are especially helpful:

1. Encourage your "transmittors" to double-check the message if they have the slightest doubt as to whether they fully understood it. Encourage them to restate it to you as they might transmit it, and give them positive feedback for asking for a restatement—never make them feel stupid for not getting it the first time through.

2. Try to reduce the links in your chain of communication if possible. We are not suggesting a complete structural reorganization (although you might benefit from one), but rather that you might, for example, consider calling a stewards' meeting to announce anything very complex, rather than relying on your committee members or chief stewards to relay the message. When

you do undertake such short circuits, be very careful that you are not undermining the position of your important organizational middlemen, such as the chief stewards, executive board, or other officers.

3. Try using what the experts call "dual media" to get the message across when it is complex enough to give you cause for concern. This means that when you give a message you might also provide a handout that lists the major points you want made. If you are in a meeting, try using an overhead projector and some transparencies or even a chalkboard to make important points.

4. Use the "preview and review" approach. This is the familiar rule for speakers and teachers: "Tell them what you're going to tell them, then tell them what you told them." In your initial relaying of the information—even in a one-on-one situation—you can follow this pattern. Studies have shown a far higher degree of retention by people who have received information in this fashion.

These suggestions and insights can be a vital aid to a local union in reducing misunderstandings and increasing the effectiveness of the local's communication channels.[7]

## MANAGING CONFLICT THROUGH IMPROVED COMMUNICATION

Research on organizational behavior has discovered some of the sources of conflict within groups. Understanding their sources can help you handle more effectively the inevitable conflict that arises within local unions as different groups strive for different goals or the same goal is sought by all, but in different fashions.[8] Five major sources of conflict within groups have been identified. Learning to recognize them can help you to see how inevitable a part of local union life conflict is and can help you reduce its negative consequences, while exploiting the positive that can come from healthy conflict. (Refer to the conflict management portion of Chapter 1 and the conduct of committees in Chapter 8.)

One source of conflict comes from disagreement among members as to the proper goals of the organization (Chapters 1 and 3): what is the organization for? Does the union, for example, exist solely to negotiate and administer contracts, or does it exist to serve a broad range of members' social and personal needs? Does it exist to function as an agent working for social change in the direction of greater

---

[7] For a more detailed treatment of this theme, see William V. Haney, "Serial Communication of Information in Organizations," in DeVito, op. cit.

[8] "Managing Conflict," in Michael Ruffner and Michael Burgoon, *Interpersonal Communication,* (Holt, Rinehart and Winston, New York, 1981, pp. 243–257; and Richard L. Weaver II, "Overcoming Barriers: Coping with Conflict," in DeVito, op. cit.

justice and equality? Disagreement on organizational, group, and personal goals can create factions within the local.

A second source of conflict arises when normal communication channels are impeded, when people stop talking to each other or stop checking with the business agent or local president. Even if this happens accidentally or as a result of an intentional structural change, blocked communication channels can create conflict where none need exist.

Members' perception that normal methods of internal discipline are no longer effective can be a third source of conflict. More serious is the situation that arises when the norms or principles of the group conflict with those of individuals. This is hardest on the group when those individuals cannot pull out. We see this in the labor movement during election years, for example, when candidate endorsements by internationals or federations conflict with strongly held contrary views of individuals or constituent local unions. Resignation is not an option for most in these situations, and wounds inflicted can be quite vicious and leave long-lasting scars.

A fifth common source of intragroup conflict is the extreme competitiveness for office or status within the group. When factions form around candidates, the competition can become intense and potentially dangerous for the local union.

Is all this conflict permanently damaging to the local union? Experts say not necessarily. Conflict within a group can lead to impeded efficiency and damaged morale. Worse, it can create distrust, eroding the group solidarity so important to unions, which count on their ability to mobilize members in common defense of the goals of the organization. But there are benefits to be derived from conflict if it is handled creatively.

Healthy conflict can prompt change and improvement of the organization. It can, if brought into the open rather than being suppressed, clarify issues and situations within the local and even forge closer friendships and loyalties within the group.

Some tips on handling conflict include:

1. Get it out in the open. Suppressed conflicts can fester and cause irreversible damage. State the conflict openly; define the differences. Are there resentments against inadequate service from the international? If left unattended, these can tear a local apart. A large international union, recently struck by an agonizing round of concession bargaining, massive plant shutdowns, and job blackmail from employers, has experimented with opening up the conflict. Efforts by the international to save standards in the industry by resisting concessions were met in many local unions with resentment and even revolt. The international, attempting to get these differences resolved, sent a high-level representative around the country for an intense series of meetings and informal discussions with members. It is doubtful if these efforts ended the differences, but the increase in trust and the higher level of communication

that followed was widely recognized. All parties had the chance to air their views, fears, hopes, and goals. Simply laying out the conflicts had a highly beneficial "air-clearing" effect.

2. Look at the conflict as a *mutual problem,* rather than the problem of just one of the parties. There are always two sides to an issue, and ordinarily no one is exclusively to blame, particularly where people of good will are dealing with tough, often externally imposed problems. It can help in a discussion of the conflict to start with a statement of your overall shared goal, which may be as basic as "to save this local union." Stating the shared goal and admitting that the problem is joint can pave the way for compromise.

3. Get feedback and check your perceptions. Are you sure that you really understand what the other party is feeling and thinking? Could the conflict be resolved just by clearing up a misunderstanding? Once you grasp all the possibilities for crossed signals that come from communicating through channels in a local union, you can see that wrong information is a very likely source of needless conflict.

4. Admit when you are wrong; be honest with the other party. When you do see that you have been in error, admit it openly and thereby set an example that others may be willing to follow. If you begin with an agreement that the conflict is a joint problem, others may be more willing to follow your lead in being honest. If you find it very hard to admit you are in the wrong, admitting errors can be a surprisingly positive experience for you and for the group. If someone else admits being wrong, *don't gloat.* Deny yourself the pleasure of "I told you so" in the interest of helping the union.

5. Use problem-solving methods. Work through an orderly process to get at the underlying problem and attempt to resolve it. John Dewey's famous six steps to problem solving have long been used by groups trying to get problems resolved efficiently and democratically: (1) define the problem in a way both sides will agree to (e.g., assume your problem is intense competition and rivalry for union office); (2) analyze the problem with regard to its history and causes, its effects and extent (it originated when maintenance people lost an election three terms ago, which caused a break-off faction among maintenance and skilled craft people); (3) agree on the criteria for possible solutions (the local will remain integral; democratic election processes will be maintained; the solution must be acceptable to the majority; maintenance will get a voice of some sort); (4) generate and evaluate possible solutions, perhaps with the use of brainstorming (establish a quota of officers for maintenance; create a new second vice-presidency for maintenance; create a skilled trades committee, etc.); (5) select the best solution, the one most acceptable to all parties and that meets the criteria laid out; (6) establish a plan of action (educate membership; determine need to change

bylaws; get clearance from parent union if necessary; call special membership meeting, etc.).[9]

Remember that though conflict is inevitable, it can be worked through and
the local can emerge more united than before. Whether the conflict to be
resolved is on a one-to-one basis as in Chapter 1 or on a group basis as presented
here, open communication, dialogue, and feedback are the keys to a satisfactory
(and effective) outcome.

## ELIMINATING SEXISM IN LOCAL UNION COMMUNICATIONS

Most union officers are by now familiar with the general movement in our
society toward sex-neutral nouns, pronouns, and modes of address. Not all
unionists—men and women—approve of this trend, and there is considerable
opposition to it within the ranks of officers who are expected to show the way by
adopting such terms as "chairperson" instead of "chairman" or "committee person" or "committee member" instead of "committeeman." "Workmen's compensation" persists within union ranks even when the government has officially
moved to "workers' compensation." This resistance to change is understandable,
and our purpose here is not to argue the point, except to point out what many
union leaders have already recognized: the unorganized masses upon whose
movement into unions the future of organized labor in this country depends are
increasingly female. Many of them—the white-collar, clerical, and service
workers of the unorganized sectors—are increasingly assertive of their rights
within organizations. Unions that remain adamantly opposed to making changes
in communication styles to reflect the new realities in the workplace may be
hard-pressed to persuade these women that they are indeed welcome in the ranks
of labor. For those union leaders who are concerned about their communication
styles and want to work toward eliminating sexist language, we offer a few
pointers.

We will discuss two related ways in which language reflects sex roles
demeaning to women. One is in the exclusive use of male-oriented nouns and
pronouns (such as "chairman" or reliance on "he" to refer to the generic steward
or member). The other is the different communication styles of men and women,
which can subtly erode women's effectiveness as union activists.

### Male-oriented Language

How can we make our language gender-neutral and still retain some grace and
fluency? Some suggestions have been offered by concerned parties, such as the

---

[9]Ruffner and Burgoon, op. cit., pp. 227–228. Refer to Chapter 1 for additional suggestions for
effective conflict management.

McGraw-Hill publishing company, which we list here for your consideration. (See Chapter 10 for making your writing gender free.)

1.  Use the plural when possible, without falling into ungrammatical failures of agreement between verbs, nouns, and antecedents. Instead of "The steward should fill out *his* fact sheet," try "Stewards should fill out *their* fact *sheets.*" But not "The steward should fill out *their* fact *sheet.*"

2.  Use the definite article "the" instead of the personal pronoun when possible: "The steward should fill out *the* fact sheet."

3.  Alternate gender references. In an extended talk or piece of writing it is possible to simply alternate use of *he* or *she* every other paragraph or every other major example.

4.  Assemble a list of alternate pronoun references: "one," "you," "he or she," "she or he."

5.  Be aware that women may get tired of being continually left out of references to union members. Even union women who would never define themselves as feminists may surprise you one day. At the very least, be prepared for this eventuality and be ready to move with the situation—the conflict.

Remember that the issue of changing "chairman" to "chairperson" is really of slight overall importance when compared with the overwhelming need for women to feel at home and respected in their local labor organizations.[10]

## Sexism in Communication Styles

Sex role socialization refers to the way we learn to act like men or women as we grow up. Those lessons are reflected in the way we sit, stand, eat, laugh, hold cigarettes, in how close we sit or stand to each other, how much we touch each other, and the way we speak. Often when we say a man is effeminate or a woman is masculine we are talking about only superficial mannerisms. Researchers have found that women and men have characteristic ways of communicating that combine verbal and nonverbal cues to express their sexuality quite unconsciously. Women's communication modes are often such as to be *reactive*— to be good listeners, to stroke egos, to reduce tension, to facilitate good feeling, and to smooth conversational difficulties. Men are socialized so as to be *proactive* in communication—to take the lead, to be confrontative and analytical, to control the discussion, to change the subject, to interrupt the partner.

Women tend to construct their sentences differently than men. They are more likely than men to express a declarative statement (such as "Help me with this") as "Would you mind helping me with this?" or "Why don't you help me

---

[10] Barbara Eakins and R. Gene Eakins, *Sex Differences in Human Communications,* Houghton Mifflin, Boston, 1978; and "Guidelines for Equal Treatment of Sexes in McGraw-Hill Company Publications," McGraw-Hill Book Company, New York, n.d..

with this?" This has been called the W-imperative. They also tag on more questions to their declarative statements: "Management is sure dragging its feet on this grievance, *isn't it?"* or "Don't you think that . . . ." This form of communication has the effect of heading off disagreement and direct confrontation and keeping the conversation safely pleasant and agreeable.[11]

Even when women do make a direct declarative statement, they tend far more than men to intone the statement so as to make it sound like a question, and thus head off confrontation. And women are less likely than men to use humor to dispel aggression or confrontation.

Is this necessarily bad? Not at all. In fact, much of what we recommend here as good communication technique builds on these qualities: sensitivity to the other person's response and on avoidance of needless confrontation. The disadvantage to women (and to the unions that want to see them play more forceful roles in the organization) is that it can become difficult for women to engage in direct and forceful confrontation when it *is* necessary.

For those women and men who want to increase their effectiveness, we recommend adopting some of the communication styles of the other sex! Women could use more humor, listen to themselves more carefully, and control their use of tag-ons and the questioning mode when they want to declare facts and opinions forcefully. Men, on the other hand, might try using some of the more sensitive behaviors of women, might concentrate on developing their ability to listen actively, and might note the other person's emotional state in a conversation.

## Sex Jokes and Flirtation

An attempt to eliminate sexism from union leadership communication styles must include a careful reconsideration of the use of sexual jokes and flirting behavior. If you are a man, analyze your sex jokes before repeating them: they are not all alike! Some are friendly to women, some are sadistically demeaning. Consider what you want to communicate to women and other men about your view of women. Many women will laugh at all sex jokes—but more and more are protesting against the hurtful ones.

Flirtation has its place in normal interaction between men and women, and few people want to eliminate it entirely, even from work or professional relationships. But you should be aware that to treat women in a flirtatious, sexual manner makes it difficult for them to function as effectively as they might without that approach.

You will probably not get a direct yes from any woman of whom you ask, "Does this flirting bother you?" But women deeply appreciate being taken seriously and not having to cater to the disruptive, even childish behavior of the man who can only relate to women in a flirtatious manner. If your overall goal is maximum effectiveness of the local union, try dealing with all people equally as respected members of the union team.

[11] Robin Lakoff, *Language and Women's Place.* Harper and Row, New York, 1975.

## COMMUNICATIONS AND RACE

As the United States more and more becomes a home for various ethnic groups from around the world, our culture changes. Not only do we have more interesting cultural diversity in our cities, but we have the challenge of overcoming racial stereotypes in our thinking and racial references in our verbal communications. The labor movement of this and every country has long been plagued with the disruptive specter of racism, and employers have often consciously divided the work force along race lines so as to control it more easily.

When jobs are scarce and employment opportunities are shrinking, the tensions and anxieties of the workplace move all too easily into the local union, where racial animosity can replace union solidarity. It is therefore incumbent on the leadership of the local union to act firmly to reduce and eliminate racial slurs and jokes from the union environment. It has been shown repeatedly that workers in this country who are ethnic minorities are willing to be active fighters in the labor movement. As growing income gaps threaten to make us a nation of rich and poor, the division of the labor movement along racial and ethnic lines will be a tragedy of great dimensions for all workers and for the labor movement. A prime test of leadership quality in this decade will be the commitment of union officers to race and sex equality in their own organizations, as well as in society.

## NONVERBAL COMMUNICATIONS

Gaining an awareness of the role and function of the nonverbal aspects of communication can greatly expand and enhance your effectiveness as a communicator. The nonverbal realm includes in the broadest sense everything one does when communicating in addition to the actual spoken words. The experts talk about "metamessages," "paralanguage," or "extra verbal" communications to denote particular aspects of the nonverbal world of communication. They study the fields of kinesics (body movement), proxemics (spatial relationships between people), chronemics (the use of time in communicating), and haptics (the use of touch). Their most important finding is that "the nonverbal channels carry more social meaning than do the verbal channels."[12] If we understand this nonverbal world, we can gain far greater insight into verbal messages others are sending us, and we can strengthen and clarify the messages we are sending.

There are several ways nonverbal cues complement the verbal messages they accompany. They *accentuate* the message, as when you hold up both fingers while saying "I want to make two points . . .," or when you pound the table during negotiations. These cues *elaborate* the message, expanding on or modifying it, as, after a difficult talk with a son, the father says "Hey, are you okay about this?" and accompanies it with a gentle hand on the back or a touch on the

[12]Gary Cronkhite, *Communication and Awareness.* Cummings Publishing Co., Menlo Park, Calif., 1976, p. 295.

arm. The touch carries a far more powerful request for reconciliation than do the words alone.[13]

Nonverbal cues can even *substitute for* the verbal message if they are powerful and unambiguous enough, as when an emblem is displayed and words become unnecessary. Think, for example, of the most powerful scene in the movie *Norma Rae*—when the protagonist climbs on the table and slowly rotates, holding up her hand-made sign UNION so that all workers can see the physical demonstration of the idea of unity against the employer. Tears can substitute for words (and also make them impossible!), as when a beloved union leader says goodbye and retires. When the long-time head of the Minnesota AFL–CIO rose to give notice that the 1984 state convention would be his last, he could not continue because his tears spoke with more eloquence of his feelings about the labor movement than the words he had written.[14]

The most revealing function of nonverbal cues, however, is when they actually *contradict* the verbal message they are accompanying. We are all familiar with sarcastic comments where the tone of the voice belies the words: "Management sure is generous with us." It is perhaps not necessary to point out to union officers that such comments lend themselves to media disasters. The newspapers may not report, and may *not even hear,* the sarcastic intonation. Voice inflections are highly individual and take a while to get to know. It is best to use the sarcastic comment only with people who know you well. Other nonverbal cues that contradict the spoken message are more interesting because they are *nonintentional* and can tell you the real state of mind of the person with whom you are communicating.

Studies[15] have shown that the body language signs that we interpret favorably are the following:

> *Eyes:* occasional head-on glances, direct gaze, few shifts in glance.
>
> *Hand gestures:* quiet, composed hands, wide slow, and easy gestures.
>
> *Face:* smooth brow, chin slightly tilted upward, slightly raised brows to accompany some statements.
>
> *Breathing:* slow and regular.
>
> *Voice quality* and *fluency:* resonant, moderate speed, natural pauses, no stuttering or frequent use of "um's" or "uh's."

These are the nonverbal cues that you might want to adopt to conceal your agitation, anger, or uncertainty in a difficult verbal exchange, as when engaged in bargaining, grievance meetings with management, or news conferences. Practice on these can help them become second nature to you and can allow you to make forceful statements with greatly increased power and authority. It appears to

[13] Ruffner and Burgoon, op. cit., p. 71.

[14] See file videotape of the 1984 Minnesota AFL–CIO convention, prepared by Martin Duffy and John See of the University of Minnesota Labor Education Service, Industrial Relations Center, Minneapolis, MN, 1984.

[15] Rowland Cuthill, "How to Read the Other Guy's Silent Signals," in DeVito, op. cit. pp. 105–111.

your listener that you are not bluffing and that you probably have the backup support (facts, member solidarity, etc.) to give you the confidence you exhibit.

On the other hand, of course, nonverbal cues can give you away (or, used to your advantage, enable you to "read the other guy's silent signals"). A word of warning: interpreting body language requires some familiarity with the other person and his habitual use of hands, eyes, posture, and so on. Be wary of interpreting a complete stranger's nonverbal cues. But in the settings where you find yourself, dealing with familiar personalities on a regular basis, you may find these tips helpful, for they are based on typical American uses, learned in the same way we learn table manners or how to show affection.

Consider posture. Seated posture is regarded as especially indicative of a person's attitude: leaning forward is said to suggest interest; a backward sprawl, disrespect; an erect back, caution or wariness. But what about the person with a bad back? Or the person in an uncomfortable chair? One helpful suggestion is to note the way the person is sitting at the beginning of your conversation and then look for shifts as you get into the heart of your discussion.

One signal most researchers agree is almost universally interpreted (in America) is crossed legs and folded arms. This signals that the person is turning you off, cutting you out; she has become defensive, is perhaps cueing you that you have invaded personal territory (either physically or psychologically). On the other hand, outstretched arms with the palms or hands up and open signal understanding, participation, giving oneself up in trust. Outstretched arms with the hands down, perhaps on a desk or table, suggest calm and tranquility.

In the United States, the most important nonverbal signal comes through eye contact or lack of it. Since our culture places a very high premium on distance and avoidance of close contact with strangers, we have become extremely responsive to eye contact for many cues that in other cultures are given through touch or physical proximity. Studies of eye contact and conversation have revealed the vital role of direct eye contact in establishing oneself as a good listener. The good listener fastens his eyes on the speaker's eyes or lips constantly. The speaker, on the other hand, shifts the gaze as she speaks from the listener to the table, the wall, the air, back to the listener. Direct eye contact from the speaker is interpreted as too intimate or threatening; it signals a stronger emotion: love, passion, family-level intimacy, anger, rage.[16] Eye contact is so important to humans in judging how the other person is responding to us that we have developed an amazing ability to judge the direction of another's gaze. Even in a large crowd and from considerable distances, we can tell the object of another person's attention.[17]

Since normal "listening eye contact" is very direct, failure of the listener to maintain eye contact can signal us that the listener is bored, guilty, uncomfortable, unfriendly, or hostile. When we put the wandering gaze together with other body language—shifting weight, perhaps an erect sitting posture—we gain important clues as to how we might interpret the verbally transmitted message.

---

[16] George A. Miller, "Nonverbal Communication," in DeVito, op. cit., pp. 97–104.

[17] Ibid., p. 99.

Learning to read body language can make us much more effective communicators. As we become aware of our own signals, we can learn to accentuate our verbal statements and elaborate on them through the use of smiles, frowns, and touches, or, should we choose, to disguise our true feelings in order to achieve an important aim. As we learn to read the body language of other people, we can become more sensitive, active listeners and thus more able to respond to what the person is *really* saying.

## PUBLIC SPEAKING

"Better to keep one's mouth shut and be thought a fool than to open it and remove all doubt." This maxim is dear to the hearts of many otherwise talented and assertive unionists when it comes to "opening one's mouth" in front of a large group—especially an unfamiliar one. Yet the ability to speak effectively in a public forum is perhaps as important now as at any time in the history of the labor movement. And many of the communication skills that you already use in one-to-one or small-group interactions can serve you well before a large audience. Still, of the expressed fears of unionists in labor-education speech courses, "looking bad" is by far the greatest. Here we offer some suggestions to help you to gain more self-confidence about your speaking skills.

Perhaps the first guideline to remember in thinking about public speaking is that "the primary difference between an extended monologue and other communication formats is that of *organization.*"[18] This means preparation, the single most important aspect of public speaking. The amount of preparation you do varies with the importance of the presentation you are making. Your "prep" can consist of four points scribbled on an envelope just after a motion has been placed on the floor for discussion or several days of library research for a presentation to a legislative committee. The reward of making speeches is that you have control over your material and your (silent) audience in a way you do not have in the one-to-one dialogues we have discussed previously. It is difficult to steer a genuine dialogue (although we have suggested that you try). But in a speech, you do *all* the steering because of the restricted feedback the audience is allowed.

Here are ten steps to preparing a speech or public presentation.

1. Select your topic—do not make it too broad.

2. Analyze your audience and tailor your approach to it.

3. Write out the goal of your speech: After my speech I want the audience to . . . .[19]

4. Research your topic; collect the facts you will need.

---

[18]Cronkhite, op. cit., p. 323. Author's emphasis.

[19]William I. Gordon, *Communication Personal and Public*. Alfred Publishing Co., Sherman Oaks, Calif., 1978, p. 217.

5. Design the speech. Here are three of the main design formats for speeches; pick the one best suited to your audience and topic.[20]
   a. the topical: organized around three or four important ideas.
   b. the question and answer format: designed around questions you think your audience may have about your topic and your answers to them.
   c. the problem and solution: organized around a problem and a possible answer to it.

6. Lay out the body of your speech according to the design you have chosen.

7. Work out an appropriate introduction. This is important and warrants considerable thought. Here is where you establish rapport with the audience, build your credibility, and establish a common ground (your membership characteristics) so as to create maximum receptivity for your message. You also want to "tell them what you are going to tell them" in a brief forecast of what you will talk about and why they should listen.

8. Work on the internal transitions and summaries after your main points.

9. Work out your conclusion. This, like the introduction, is also strategic rather than substantive. You want to leave the audience with a favorable impression, while at the same time summarizing, "telling them what you told them," and reinforcing its importance to the audience.[21]

10. Look over what you have written and ask yourself if it will achieve the goal you stated: "After my speech, I want my audience to . . . ."

Now that you have the speech composed, you are ready to move to the final stages of preparing for delivery and for the delivery itself. Gordon has put together seven tips for the delivery of a speech.[22]

1. Read aloud to yourself just the central idea and the supporting points of the speech; then talk to an imaginary audience from the introduction to the conclusion, using simple language. Translate your speech into a keyword outline and practice before a mirror, using this outline only. Do this at least twice, using bodily gestures that seem natural to you. Select dress in which you feel comfortable and in which you feel you look your best.

2. At the meeting, move toward the podium with confidence when you are called.

3. As you arrive at the platform, greet the chairperson and any others with a nod or handshake.

4. Look out at the audience and pause to collect yourself. Then begin without looking down at your notes. Address yourself in the first few words to one

---

[20] Ibid., pp. 234–236.

[21] Ibid., p. 261.

[22] Ibid., p. 276–277.

person in the middle of the audience; then move your attention gradually to the rest of the room.

5. As you move into the body of your speech, increase your body language, making sure that it is natural and feels right.

6. If you note feedback from the audience, adjust your remarks. If there are signs of confusion, enlarge with an illustration or example. If you note signs of boredom or fatigue, change your pace; even alter your remarks if possible.

7. In your conclusion, signal your audience with nonverbal cues—a change of your rate and intensity of speech, a different volume, reduced body language. Close firmly with a nod and a "thank you."

## Coping with Speech Fright

Most of us experience some degree of speech fright, although it will often diminish markedly with repeated speaking experience. But even some noted actors never quite get over severe panic or anxiety attacks. We offer some basic hints on how to minimize their effect on your performance.

First, identify the physical symptoms of speech fright in yourself. Is it hands trembling? Knees weakening? Voice tightening up? Shortness of breath? Blushing? Once you identify them you can take measures to conceal these effects—from makeup to massaging your throat and neck area before you go on. You might also arrange your physical environment so as to compensate for trembling hands (rest them on the podium or keep them in your pockets) or weak knees (lean against the podium or ask for a high stool).

Speakers often use two techniques that are very useful to counter the excess adrenalin in your system and the muscle contractions that can cause shortness of breath and panting. One is to engage in deep-breathing just prior to going on the speaker's platform. To do this, simply fill your lungs from bottom to top very slowly, hold the breath a moment, and then exhale again slowly and regularly. Repeat this several times, slowly so as not to hyperventilate. The second is to perform some form of intense isotonic muscle exercise: if you are seated, pull up on the seat of your chair with both hands as strongly as possible without attracting attention. Push down on a table or press your feet to the floor, holding and repeating the exercise several times. Try turning your head slowly as far to the right and left as you can, again slowly and naturally. Try to avoid the appearance of writhing in agony! An advantage of these exercises is that they can be done surreptitiously, even when you are seated on the platform awaiting your turn to speak. Perhaps even more importantly, they take your mind off your imminent performance and focus it on your body and your concealment strategies. When you stand to approach the podium with confidence, you have had a few moments of a clear mind, oxygen-filled lungs, and energized muscles.

## CREATING OPPORTUNITIES FOR IMPROVED COMMUNICATIONS

This chapter has outlined an exhaustive program for improving communication skills within the local union. As a local union leader, you will want to work on your own personal communication skills, but you will also want the members of your local union to become more expert communicators, both within the local in committee work and union administration and at the workplace in dealing with management. You will also recognize the benefits for the local union if members with facility in communication can play roles in community and political life.

It is possible for the local union to provide many structured opportunities for communications skill building of members. Some locals run communication classes or send members to outside communication courses. A democratic style at union meetings can encourage members to speak there. Union committees and boards can provide opportunities for work on small-group discussion and problem-solving techniques. The local can organize a speakers' bureau where members agree to address community groups when spokespeople are needed to provide labor movement perspectives on social or political issues. These speakers' bureaus can easily be turned into support groups where members practice speaking skills and get feedback and constructive criticism from other members.

Improved communication skills can help your local union. With their emphasis on improving the dialogue element in interpersonal relations, they can greatly enhance the democratic spirit of the local union. Leaders and officers who understand the importance of active listening and who practice it will be in close touch with members' needs and interests. Members who are listened to trust and respect the officers who take time to understand their situations. Leaders who understand that some conflict is healthy and natural and can lead to beneficial change will be able to create new bonds of solidarity and cohesiveness within the local union. Individuals who come to see the local union as an institution where they can express themselves and grow personally, while assisting a collective movement for positive social change and human dignity, will be more loyal members. If the American labor movement is to survive and grow in a changing environment, local unions must start to tap into the sources of increased member activism, which can be found in better personal and organizational communications.

## DISCUSSION QUESTIONS

1. Outline and prepare for delivery a speech on one of the following topics:
   a. An appeal addressed to new employees, urging them to join the union.
   b. An appeal to union members to support the United Way Drive.

    c. Support for a dues increase at a local union meeting.

    d. Ask for a positive strike vote at a local union meeting.

2. "The most effective union leader is the person who understands and has mastered persuasive communication." Explain this statement, using concrete examples from union life.

3. Identify three main sources of conflict within a local union and lay out a specific communication plan to try to manage that conflict.

4. Discuss the need to eliminate sexist and racist language within local unions. Do you agree or disagree with the position taken in this chapter?

## GLOSSARY

**active listening:** Listening for feelings in the communication partner as well as words, and providing a supportive response to the feelings behind those words.

**assertive communication:** Communication of one's legitimate desires and demands in a way that respects the rights of others while maintaining one's own.

**helping talk:** Use of questions, empathy, self-disclosure, frequent pauses, and the reflection of the feelings of the person with whom one is talking to facilitate understanding, exchange, and genuine dialogue.

**interpersonal communication:** Two-way communication between two or more individuals, characterized by dialogue and exchange, both verbal and nonverbal.

**nonverbal communication:** Messages communicated by physical signals other than words, such as body language, eye contact, and physical distancing.

**serial communication:** A message passed verbally through a series of people or levels of an organization. Such a message is subject to extreme distortion, omission, and simplification.

## ADDITIONAL RESOURCES

Bloom, Lynn, Karen Coburn, and Joan Pearlman. *The New Assertive Woman.* New York: Dell Publishing Co., 1975.

DeVito, Joseph A., and Richard Weaver II. *Communication Concepts and Processes.* Englewood Cliffs, N.J., Prentice-Hall, Inc., 1981.

Perlow, Austin H. *Basic Communications Skills: A Handbook for Unions.* Washington, D.C., Bureau of National Affairs, Inc., 1981.

# CHAPTER 10

# Effective Writing Skills

People often assume that since someone has completed high school or even college, he or she is able to write effectively. The truth of the matter is that most people do not write either clearly or precisely. This malady affects women and men of all ages and all ethnic backgrounds. Neither social status nor income are predictors of good writing.

Some professional writers believe that "he who writes badly thinks badly."[1] While the authors do not fully endorse this extreme notion, we do believe that an understanding of basic writing principles ordinarily brings to one's mind a sense of critical thinking and logic. Given an idea or a belief, good writing can bring substance to chaos, order to rambling ideas.

We write poorly because we do not write enough. Our world is increasingly a visual and verbal one. Writing, while still important, has been largely supplanted by the telephone (instead of a letter), the television (instead of the newspaper), and the radio (when one cannot get to the television). Computers and word processors give their operators greater access to and control of thousands upon thousands of words. But the program really does the work. We just punch a command key.

Much of union leadership is verbal and this aspect of leadership communication was dealt with in Chapter 9. Yet much of what union managers and administrators do in the formal performance of their duties is in the written

---

[1] William Cobbett, as quoted in "The Linear Camel," William Safire, *New York Times Magazine*, December 9, 1984, p. 18

form: grievances, the contract, local constitution and bylaws, articles and features for the local's newsletter, letters to the parent union and the employer, arbitration briefs, and more. Just as a key element to effective leadership is the ability to flex *styles* to fit the situation, an important element in leadership behavior is being able to flex to the proper *mode of communication* to fit the situation. Having covered the verbal mode of leadership communication, it is now time to turn to the written word as a form of communication leadership.

Writing can be improved quite simply: write, rewrite, rewrite, and rewrite again.[2] First, write letters: to friends, to relatives, to political representatives, and to the local newspaper editor. Write articles for the local union newsletter; or submit them to the international's paper. If you are on the negotiating committee, handbills and leaflets; or on the resolutions committee, resolutions.

"Communication is a triad: speaker or writer, listener or reader, and the matter."[3] In written communication, the writer controls *what* matter is presented. The readers determine *how* it will be presented. How one writes, then, is determined by the intended audience. Know your audience: membership, employer, or public? Although your audience may be different, your goal remains the same: you want your readers to see what you saw when they read what you wrote. So "Say what you mean, mean what you say, and mean it!"[4]

## TOOLS FOR THE WRITER[5]

Keep a dictionary handy when you write. It not only has definitions, but can help you with spelling, word division, word usage, plurals, synonyms, pronunciation, and word roots.[6] We recommend a hardcover, unabridged version, but a paperback can also be useful.

If you have trouble finding the right word to express your thoughts, get a copy of *Roget's Thesaurus,* or Funk and Wagnalls' *Standard Handbook of Synonyms, Antonyms and Prepositions.*

If you write speeches, you may want to have a copy of *The Oxford Dictionary of Quotations* or Edmund Fuller's *2500 Anecdotes for All Occasions.*

Two excellent books you can use to improve your writing skills are *Writing with Precision* by Jefferson D. Bates and *Write to the Point* by Bill Stott.

There is no shortage of reference and how-to books to assist you. Check your bookstore or library. But remember, no book can help you improve your writing skills if you do not practice writing.

---

[2] *Rewrite again* is redundant. The writing lesson begins.

[3] Edward D. Johnson, *The Handbook of Good English.* Facts on File Publications, New York, 1982, p. 193

[4] Michael J. Wakeriak, ninth-grade algebra teacher of one of the authors.

[5] Obviously, pens, pencils, paper, and maybe even a typewriter are necessary.

[6] Jan Venolia, *Better Letters: A Handbook of Business and Personal Correspondence.* Ten Speed Press, Berkeley, Calif., 1982, p. 4.

# GRAMMAR

The word usually brings back bad memories from high-school English classes. Most people would like to forget those days. Grammar has never been the favorite subject of students. Rules like

> The number of the subject determines the number of the verb.[7]

or,

> Use the present participle and present infinitive to indicate time that is the same as the time of the main verb, whatever the tense of the main verb is; use the past participle and the past infinitive to indicate time previous to the time of the main verb.[8]

will scare away even the bravest writers.

This section covers the basics of grammar. It is not meant to scare you away, but to help you to use grammar to your advantage in writing.

You can improve your writing by being *clear* and *precise*. Clear writing has two main components: choosing the best words to express your ideas, and arranging the words to help the reader grasp your ideas.[9]

This section borrows heavily from Jefferson Bates's book, *Writing with Precision*. Bates has outlined 10 principles for improving clarity and precision in writing. Unlike many rules of grammar, they are simple to understand and apply. Use these principles in your writing for the union.

The 10 principles for improving clarity and precision of written documents are:

1. Prefer the active voice.

2. Don't make nouns out of good, strong "working verbs."

3. Be concise. Cut out all excess baggage. Keep your *average* sentence length under 20 words.

4. Be specific. Use concrete terms instead of generalizations.

5. Keep related sentence elements together; keep unrelated elements apart. Place modifiers as close as possible to the words they are intended to modify.

6. Avoid unnecessary shifts of *number, tense, subject, voice,* or *point of view.*

---

[7] William Strunk, Jr., and E. B. White, *The Elements of Style,* 3rd ed. Macmillan Publishing Co., New York, 1979, p. 9.

[8] Johnson, op. cit., p. 37.

[9] Venolia, op. cit., p. 4

7. Prefer the simple word to the farfetched and the right word to the almost right.

8. Don't repeat words, phrases, or ideas needlessly. But don't hesitate to repeat when the repetition will increase clarity.

9. Use parallelism whenever it is appropriate—that is, when you are expressing similar thoughts, make sure you write your sentences so that the elements are in similar or parallel form. But do *not* use parallel structure when expressing thoughts that are not truly similar.

10. Arrange your material logically. Always begin with ideas the reader can readily understand. If you must present difficult material, go *one step at a time*. Do not skip any steps. Arrange your format to give the reader every possible chance to understand the material.[10]

### Prefer the Active Voice

Writers agree that using the active voice makes writing stronger and more concise than using the passive voice. Here are examples of both. Which do you think is the stronger?

Active voice: The members debated and voted on the issues.

Passive voice: The issues were debated and voted on by the members.

The first example is not just stronger, but also more concise. Do you always want to use the active voice? It depends. Bates says:

If the person or thing receiving the action is more important than the person or thing doing the action, use the passive. If the person or thing doing the action is unknown or unimportant, use the passive.[11]

Decide which you want to emphasize. In the previous examples did you want the reader to know that the *members* were exercising their democratic rights? (Use the active voice.) Or do you want the reader to know that the *issues* were important? (Use the passive.)

### Don't Make Nouns Out of Good, Strong "Working Verbs"

*Organize* is a good, strong "working verb."

The CIO *organized* workers on an industrial basis.

*Organization* of the workers was accomplished by the CIO on an industrial basis.

Which of the two is stronger? Do not weaken your verbs with endings like *-ion, -tion, -ment, -ance, -ancy,* and *-zation.*

---

[10] Jefferson D. Bates, *Writing with Precision.* Acropolis Books Ltd., Washington, D.C., 1982, p. 16.

[11] *Ibid.,* p. 23.

*Negotiations* of the contract were conducted by a committee.

This should be:

A committee *negotiated* the contract.

Express action with your verbs. Do not change them into nouns. Using verbs as verbs also makes your sentences shorter and more concise.

### Be Concise. Cut out All Excess Baggage. Keep Your Average Sentence Length under 20 Words

Long sentences are hard to read and understand. The mind of a reader will shut off somewhere in the middle of a long sentence. If you *have* to write long sentences, break them up with commas, semicolons, or dashes. Otherwise, you will only confuse your reader.

Don't be redundant or wordy:

Redundancy is repeating things over and over again.

Wordiness is due to the fact that most people can't express themselves with less than a multitude of words in a sentence.

These should read:

Redundancy is repetition.

Wordiness is too many words.

Get the picture? Write short sentences. Do not repeat yourself. Use as few words as possible.

He was a *conservative type* of union leader.

He was a *conservative* union leader.

By interpreting carefully the last article under the seniority clause, you find that it applies in this case.

Article 5, Seniority, applies in this case.

### Be Specific. Use Concrete Terms Instead of Generalizations

Avoid abstract words. If you mean to call someone a liar, do not say, *"I believe that you are misrepresenting the facts."* Read the following grievance.

It's clear from the grievance that we submitted last week that management violated Article X, Section 6, of the Labor Agreement. We have not received any reply yet. Basically, what happened was that we three utility men were laid off from the county highway department, Section #7, by Sam Cloud, even though we have way more seniority than some of the other guys who did not get the axe. We ask that we be made whole and that this grave injustice be corrected.[12]

Can you determine what happened? Use the Five W's to rewrite the grievance.

> On December 9, the County Highway Department, Section #7, laid off Jim Jones, Jack Jensen, and John Johnson. This action violated Article X, Section 6, Layoffs and Seniority. The Union requests that the grievants be reinstated to their positions with full back pay and benefits; and be made whole in all respects.

Be specific. Use abstract words only when you want to disguise your meaning.

### Keep Related Sentence Elements Together; Keep Unrelated Elements Apart. Place Modifiers as Close as Possible to the Words They Are Intended to Modify

*Where* you put words or phrases in a sentence can change *what* the sentence means. This is especially crucial when you write collective bargaining agreements or union bylaws.

> The Employer agrees to grant a leave of absence without pay to any worker *who* is obligated to attend active duty with a duly constituted military reserve unit.[13]

Does this sentence mean something different than:

> The Employer, *who* is obligated to attend active duty with a duly constituted military reserve unit, agrees to grant a leave of absence without pay to any worker.

You bet! Now the employer is obligated to attend active duty instead of the worker.

**Modifiers.** Do not modify words you want to leave alone. Do not misplace, dangle, or squint your modifiers.

1. Misplaced:

> Wilma Denton was called back to work after 9 months unemployment due to improved business conditions.

> Was Wilma laid off because conditions improved?

> Due to improved business conditions, Wilma Denton was called back to work after 9 months unemployment.

---

[12] David C. Spencer, *A Steward's Guide to Contract Administration.* Indiana University Labor Education and Research Center, Bloomington, Ind., 1977, p. 44.

[13] Lawrence Stessin and Len Smedresman, *The Encyclopedia of Collective Bargaining Contract Clauses.* Business Research Publications, Inc., New York, Clause 29, p. 18.

2. Dangling:

   Having no money in the strike fund, their threats were not taken seriously by management.

   Do threats have a strike fund? No, the union does.

   Since the union had no money in the strike fund, management did not take their threats seriously.

3. Squinting:

   Members only may vote at union meetings.

   Does this mean *only members may vote or members may vote only at union meetings?* Write it to say what you mean:

   Only members may vote at union meetings.

As a general rule, put your modifiers near the words they modify. In the case of *only*, put it before the word or phrase it modifies.[14]

## Avoid Unnecessary Shifts of Number, Tense, Subject, Voice or Point of View

### Number

*Everyone* wants to improve *their* wages and working conditions.

Everyone is singular, their is plural. This is an unnecessary shift of number. Change it to:

*Everyone* wants to improve *his or her* wages and working conditions.

Although this is accepted and nonsexist, too many sentences using *his or her* can be awkward to read. A more effective way of writing this sentence would be to use the plural consistently.

*All of us* want to improve *our* wages and working conditions.

*All workers* want to improve *their* wages and working conditions.[15]

### Tense

After the grievants *reported* for work, the company *refused* to pay them.

[14]Sylvan Barnet and Marcia Stubbs, *Practical Guide to Writing*. Little, Brown and Company, Boston, 1977, p. 243.

[15]See the section on nonsexist writing for more examples.

This is a very common mistake made by writers. Keep the tense consistent throughout the sentence.

> After the grievants *reported* for work, the company *refused* to pay them.
>
> After the grievants *report* for work, the company refuses to pay them.[16]

### Subject

> The *union* wants higher wages, but *job security* can substitute for it.

Can job security substitute for the union? This sentence would read more clearly written like this:

> The *union* wants higher wages, but *it* will settle for job security.

### Shift of Voice

> When *workers want* justice on the job, *organization* must *take* place.

If you are writing in the active voice, do not shift gears in the middle of a sentence to the passive voice.

> When *workers want* justice on the job, *they* must *organize.*

### Shift in Point of View

> When *you read* the statistics, *unemployment is* on the rise.

Unemployment does not rise because you read the statistics. It will rise or fall regardless of what you read.

> When *you read* the statistics, *you* can *see* that unemployment is on the rise.

## Prefer the Simple Word to the Farfetched and the Right Word to the Almost Right[17]

Use simple, descriptive words. Do not try to impress your readers with your vast vocabulary. Remember, understanding is your object. If your reader has to spend time looking up words you have written, there is no understanding and, therefore, no communication.

---

[16] Although technically correct, this sentence is not appropriate for grievance writing. Use instead the past tense.

[17] See the section on words and phrases for exmples of simple and right words.

> Providing meaningful jobs for the unemployed will ameliorate a difficult situation and will help reduce the unemployed worker's sense of impuissance.[18]

This could have been written:

> Providing meaningful jobs for the unemployed will ease a difficult situation and will help reduce the unemployed worker's sense of impotence.[19]

Can you simplify the sentence even more?

Writing simply, however, does not mean that you should write as you speak. Conversational English does not translate very well onto the written page, especially when it is spiced with local speech inflections.

> "Jeet jet?"
>
> "No, j'ew?"[20]

This is an example of how someone in Pittsburgh might ask

> "Did you eat yet?"
>
> "No, did you?"

Perhaps the example is a little farfetched, but it makes the point: write in formal English, not in conversational English.

How do you find the *right* word? Use your reference books. They can give you the connotation of the word as well as its denotation.[21]

> Are unions *affected* or *effected* by right-to-work laws?
>
> Does the contract *infer* or *imply* that overtime is mandatory?
>
> Does past practice *complement* or *compliment* unclear contract language?

Make sure you know the definition *and* connotation of words before you use them. Take the time to look them up. Similarly spelled words can have vastly different meanings.

Avoid using jargon or cliches. Jargon is the "technical terminology or characteristic idiom of a special activity or group."[22] If your readers are not part of

---

[18] Louis Hampton, Jr., "Additional Exercises" in Bates, op. cit., p. 198.

[19] Ibid., p. 209.

[20] Sam McCool, *Pittsburghese: How to Speak Like a Pittsburgher.* Hayford Press, Inc., Pittsburgh, Pa., 1982, p. 19.

[21] Denotation is what a word *means;* connotation is what a word *suggests.*

[22] *Webster's Ninth New Collegiate Dictionary.* Merriam-Webster, Inc., Springfield, Mass., 1983, p. 647.

the "activity or group," they may not understand what you are trying to tell them. Even if they are part of the group, do not assume that they think the same as you do.

> The local union *interfaced* its *c.b.* activities with *the international.*

This sentence would confuse all but the most "in" group of readers. What does *interface* mean? Most people do not know. Does *c.b.* mean collective bargaining or citizens' band? What is *the international,* a union or a song?

> The local union *coordinated* its *negotiations* with the *international union.*

A cliche is a "trite phrase or expression."[23] Cliches are stale and unoriginal. Your readers will appreciate a fresh approach.[24]

> *Union demands; management offers.*

Not only are these stale and unoriginal, they imply that the union always takes and management always gives. Try instead:

> *Union offers; management demands.*

Or use something entirely different.

Avoid using legalese,[25] especially when you write contract language. Since it is the language of attorneys, only they can understand and interpret it. Your union cannot afford to pay for law degrees for your stewards.

Use concrete words.[26] Be specific. Unless ambiguous language is necessary, do not use it. Make your meaning clear.

> Due to the absence of contract language in this particular problem area, the prevailing practices of the participating parties to this agreement will take precedence.

This language can be rewritten to be less confusing:

> When the contract is silent, union and management will rely on past practice.

Use short, familiar words.[27] If you know a lot of multisyllable words, fine. Impress your family and friends when you play Scrabble™. Do not confuse your readers with:

---

[23] Ibid., p. 248.

[24] A *fresh approach* is a cliche; avoid it.

[25] *Legalese* is jargon; don't use the word.

[26] Venolia, op. cit., p. 7.

[27] Ibid., p. 9.

> Unless the respective representatives have an understanding of the complexities and vagaries of the labor–management agreement, neither will be able to administrate it effectively.

Neither one would be able to read that sentence either. Rewrite:

> If the stewards and supervisors don't know the contract, they can't enforce it.

### Don't Repeat a Word or Words Unnecessarily. But Don't Hesitate to Repeat When the Repetition Will Increase Clarity

Professional writers hesitate to repeat words in a sentence and, sometimes, in a paragraph. This is the combination of the advice against using cliches and being redundant. Try to use a different word if necessary; but do not change the meaning of a sentence by avoiding a repetitious word. On the other hand, if you want to emphasize a point, you may *want* to repeat the word.

### Make Sentence Elements That Are Parallel in Thought Parallel in Form. But Do Not Use Parallelism to Express Thoughts That Are Not Parallel

Do not be scared by the seemingly complexity of this principle. It is not that confusing.

What is parallelism or parallel construction? It is simply using the same or similar grammatical construction in your writing.[28] For example:

> Contract administration is the process of *amplifying, interpreting,* and *application* of the agreement.

Sound awkward? Add some order to the sentence:

> Contract administration is the process of *amplifying, interpreting,* and *applying* the agreement.

Why do people violate the principle of parallel construction? Perhaps they think that the variation will make their sentences more interesting and impressive.[29] By bringing order to the parts of sentences or paragraphs, parallel construction adds balance. Parallel construction should be used for more than sentences and paragraphs. It can also be used in outlines:

> The duties of the steward include:
>
> (a) processing grievances;
> (b) organizing nonmembers;

[28] Bates, op. cit., p. 67.
[29] Johnson, op. cit., p. 10

(c) *education* of members.

Improve this outline:

The duties of the steward include:

(a) processing grievances;
(b) organizing nonmembers;
(c) *educating* members.

Even reports and books can be improved by the proper use of parallelism. When a book is written by more than one author, the skill of the editor is crucial in defining the relationships between the chapters.

### Arrange Your Material Logically. Always Begin with Ideas the Reader Can Readily Understand. If You Must Present Difficult Material, Go One Step at a Time. Do Not Skip Any Steps. Arrange Your Format To Give the Reader Every Possible Chance to Understand the Material

How many times have you begun reading a book, only to put it down because you could not "get past the first chapter?" It could have been that the author presented you with a difficult idea too early.

When *you* write, start with a basic idea. This is especially true when you are dealing with a complicated issue that your readers are unfamiliar with. Let your readers understand what you are talking about from the beginning. From that common understanding, you can begin to lay out and explain the details.
begin to lay out and explain the details.

You can arrange your material using any of a number of different methods. The purpose of your writing should determine which method you need to use.

Analytical order

Alternative order

Cause-and-effect order

Chronological order

Conclusions order

Criteria order

Deductive order (also known as general-to-specific)

Geographical order

Hierarchical order

Inductive order (specific-to-general)

Spatial order[30]

A letter to the editor may call for a cause-and-effect order, a deductive order, or an inductive order. A grievance may require a chronological order or a conclusions order. Articles in the union newsletter may use a number of different methods, depending on the subject about which you are writing.

## Conclusion

The *Ten Principles* that Bates has outlined can help you to write more clearly and more precisely. Use them. They will not make your writing more creative, but they will help your reader to understand what you are trying to communicate.

## PUNCTUATION

Does it really matter if you do not punctuate correctly, or punctuate at all?

> When you read a sentence without punctuation because there are no commas semicolons or periods you will find it difficult to understand despite how smart you are or how simple or short the sentence may be It will make very little sense

Did you get lost reading the last sentence? Think of your writing as a series of roads on which the reader is traveling. Your goal is to direct them to understanding. "Punctuation helps to keep the reader on the right path . . . . The right punctuation enables the reader to move easily through the sentence."[31] Punctuation should assist reading, making it easier and more enjoyable. It should make your writing clearer, not more ambiguous.

How do you know when and when not to punctuate? Some experts advise reading your writing aloud, that punctuation can be "heard."[32] A common usually indicates a pause, a question mark a rising tone . . . ."[33] And a period means stop when you run out of breath. The way you structure your sentence also determines how much you have to punctuate. So, if you write simple sentences, you will not have to worry about having to punctuate very much; right? Not necessarily. Some simple sentences have more punctuation than their more complex brothers and sisters.

---

[30] Bates, op. cit., pp. 71–72, and Candace L. Kumerfield, "10 Guidelines for Better Business Writing: Guidelines for Writing and Revising," University of Minnesota MBA Communication Skills Program, Minneapolis, 1984, p. 7.

[31] Barnet and Stubbs, op. cit., p. 288.

[32] Johnson, op. cit., p. 56.

[33] Ibid.

There are many rules and principles of punctuation. Fortunately, there is not enough space in this chapter to cover them all. We say *fortunately* because a complete list would only confuse the subject. Colwell and Knox[34] have developed some useful guidelines. They are short, concise, and easy to understand. We have added a few comments to their outline to clarify, not to confuse, the principles of punctuation.

## Comma

"A comma is a punctuation mark, a coma is a state of unconsciousness."[35] The comma is the most used, most overused, and most abused mark of punctuation. Because commas are needed to prevent run-on sentences, many people litter their writing with them, resulting in the problem known as comma splice.[36] So use commas, but use them only when you need them.

You *should use* commas in a series:

> The safety committee listed noise, dust, heat, and toxic chemicals as the biggest problems in the plant.

Do not use commas if the words in a series are connected by *and*. Some writers also eliminate the comma after the next-to-last item in the series. You can do it either way. Whichever way you do it, be consistent and do it that way throughout your writing.

Use commas after an introductory word, phrase, or clause:

> Remember, all supervisors are human.

> Despite her small size, Vickie was able to lift the heavy metal casting.

> Having spent all night cleaning up the oil spill, the workers were glad to go home this morning.

If an introductory phrase or clause is short, the comma may be omitted, provided the omission does not result in ambiguity.

Use commas between independent clauses:

> Most of the members attend meetings at contract time, but would rather watch television during the rest of the year.

> The committee discussed the issues, and they decided what to do.

Use the comma if the clause is not short and if it is connected by a coordinating

---

[34] C. Carter Colwell and James H. Knox, *What's the Usage?: The Writer's Guide to English Grammar and Rhetoric.* Reston Publishing Company, Inc., Reston, Va., 1973, pp. 164–192.

[35] Rudolf Flesch, *A Deskbook of American Spelling and Style.* Barnes & Noble Books, New York, 1981, p. 81.

[36] Comma splice is the misuse of commas between two independent clauses not joined by a coordinate conjunction.

conjunction (*and, but, or, nor, for, yet, so*).

Use commas to enclose parenthetical expressions[37] (word, phrase, or clause):

> The president, *nevertheless,* vetoed the jobs bill.
>
> The president, *despite the congressional pressure,* vetoed the jobs bill.
>
> The president, *exhibiting a conservative philosophy,* vetoed the jobs bill.

Make sure that you do not leave out one comma and keep the other unless the parenthetical expression comes at the end of the sentence.

> The president vetoed the jobs bill, *despite congressional pressure.*

Use commas between adjectives of equal weight:

> The Teamsters have always been considered a big, rough, tough union.

Note that no comma follows the last adjective before the noun.
Use commas with quotations (direct conversation):

> The supervisor said, "Obey the order or don't come in tomorrow."
>
> "Obey the order," the supervisor said, "or don't come in tomorrow."

Note that if the comma is part of the quotation, it falls inside the quotation marks. Do not use commas if you are describing indirect conversation.

> The supervisor said to obey the order or not to come in tomorrow.

Use commas to separate dates, places, and numbers:

> The agreement was ratified on December 22, 1984.
>
> The author was born in McKees Rocks, Pennsylvania.
>
> The local, which once had 2,500 members, was now down to 1,100 members.

Dates use no or one comma; places use one comma; but numbers may use two or more commas. More information on how to write numbers is in the section on style.
Use commas to avoid confusion (comma splices and run-on sentences):

> The worker came to me with a grievance, I went to see the supervisor.

---

[37] A parenthetical expression is nonrestrictive. In other words, the sentence has meaning without it. All it does is to modify or add to the sentence.

This is an example of a comma splice. *The worker came to me with a grievance and I went to see the supervisor* are independent clauses. But the comma is not strong enough to separate them. Eliminate the comma and see what happens.

The worker came to me with a grievance I went to see the supervisor.

We have created a run-on sentence. You can correct these faults by doing one of the following:

Use a period and write two sentences: The worker came to me with a grievance. I went to see the supervisor.

Use a semicolon to separate the clauses: The worker came to me with a grievance; I went to see the supervisor.

Use a coordinating conjunction with the comma: The worker came to me with a grievance, and I went to see the supervisor.

Make one of the clauses subordinate: Because the worker came to me with a grievance, I went to see the supervisor.

## Semicolon ;

"Typographically a semicolon is part comma, part period; and it does indeed function as a strong comma or a weak period. It can never function as a colon."[38] The semicolon is not used as frequently today as it has been in the past. Some writers have replaced it with periods and commas. Nevertheless, it is still around and has some useful functions.

1. Between clauses (as a strong comma or weak period):

When human flesh and blood could stand no more it got up at five in the morning as usual and put on its work clothes and went into the mill; and when the whistle blew it came home."[39]

2. To correct comma splice and prevent run-on sentences: (see the examples in the comma section).

3. Between words or phrases in a series (when there are commas within that series):

The executive board included Duffy, the president; Hillman, the treasurer; Joyce, the secretary; and four at-large members.

4. To avoid confusion in the sentence:

[38] Barnet and Stubbs, op. cit., p. 291.

[39] Thomas Bell, *Out of This Furnace*. University of Pittsburgh Press, Pittsburgh, Pa., 1976, p. 48.

Beneficial to organized workers, almost always; beneficial to the economy, in many ways; but harmful to the bottom line of company balance sheets: this is the paradox of American trade unionism, which underlies some of the ambivalence of our national policies toward the institution.[40]

Try writing that sentence with commas instead of semicolons. The semicolon is much better than the comma to separate major breaks from minor ones.[41]

## Colon :

"A colon tells the readers that what follows is closely related to the preceding clause."[42] The primary use of the colon is to introduce something that follows. In addition, it can follow after some things. And, in some cases, it comes between things.

1. To introduce a list or series:

   The workers organized to achieve their goals: justice, better wages, and job security.

2. To introduce a long or formal quotation:

   Henry George pointed out: "A house and the lot on which it stands are alike property, as being the subject of ownership, and are alike classed by lawyers as real estate. Yet in nature and relations they differ widely. The one is produced by human labor, and belongs to the class in political economy styled wealth. The other is part of nature, and belongs to the class in political economy styled land."[43]

3. To introduce an emphatic word or phrase or clause:

   Management's demand met with one word: no!

   The president rallied the members: "Hit the bricks!"

   Management laid down the gauntlet: They brought in strikebreakers.

Follow colons with lowercase letters, unless you begin a new sentence following the colon.

1. To introduce a summary or amplification:

---

[40] Richard B. Freeman and James L. Medoff, *What Do Unions Do?* Basic Books, Inc., New York, 1984, p. 190.

[41] Johnson, op. cit., p. 88.

[42] Strunk and White, op. cit., pp. 7–8.

[43] Page Smith, *The Rise of Industrial America,* volume 6. McGraw-Hill Book Company, New York, 1984, p. 205.

The economic news was good: employment up and inflation down.

2. To introduce a new paragraph:

The following resolution was adopted:
  Whereas . . .[44]

3. To follow *as follows* or *the following:*

Our remedy includes the following: reinstatement with full back pay, restoration of seniority, and make whole in all respects.

4. To follow a formal greeting in letters:

Dear Brother Moore:

5. To come between chapter and verse and hours and minutes:

The minister quoted Matthew 5:3-6 in his address to the unemployed workers.

It was 11:30 when the meeting was finally adjourned.

## Dash  —

"A dash is a mark of separation stronger than a comma, less formal than a colon, and more relaxed than parentheses."[45] Like commas and parentheses, it can set off parenthetical expressions; and like a colon it can introduce a summary. Two hyphens (--) equal (=) one dash (—) on a typewriter. Use the dash:

— As informal parentheses:

However, most could—and did—cite numerous disturbing examples of the displacement of workers by machines.[46]

— To mark an abrupt break in a thought:

Management announced it would give up its demand for wage concessions—"ice in the winter" we thought.

— To summarize or rephrase:

Review the information on the grievance fact sheet covering the five W's—the

[44] Flesch, op. cit., p. 80.

[45] Strunk and White, op. cit., p. 9.

[46] Thomas R. Brooks, *Toil and Trouble: A History of American Labor.* Dell Publishing Co., Inc., New York, 1971, p. 264

Who, When, Where, Why, and What of the grievance.[47]

There were 150 members at the Christmas party—a good time was had by all.

— To show that a sentence is unfinished:

If the boss only knew—

— To list items (as we have just done).

Never use a dash with a comma. Use dashes as little as possible and only when another mark of punctuation will not do the job. In informal letters, however, dashes can make the tone more relaxing, just like friendly conversation.[48]

We enjoyed the convention—you know how much I like Atlantic City—the weather was beautiful, the water warm—we did get some work done.

## ''Quotation Marks''

"Quotation marks may be double (" ") or single (' ')."[49] The British use double quotation marks like the Americans use single quotation marks, and vice versa. We will follow the American method.

Use quotation marks to enclose direct quotations (spoken or written):

"Only scabs cross picket lines," she said.

James K. Galbraith, in *Working Papers,* wrote, "By itself, the bill would neither end unemployment nor bankrupt the Republic; it did not deserve either the accolades or the ridicule with which it was widely received."[50]

When you quote more than one paragraph, you need to put quotation marks at the end of *only* the last paragraph. But use quotation marks at the beginning of *all* the paragraphs you quote.

Use quotation marks to enclose titles of short stories, songs, short poems, chapters from books, essays, and newspaper or magazine articles:

I especially liked Jack London's "The Apostate."

The crowd arose as one and sang "Solidarity Forever."

"Effective Writing Skills" is the title of this chapter.

Did you read the article, "Why We Have No Full Employment Policy"?

[47] Bob Repas, *Contract Administration.* BNA Books, Washington, D.C., 1984, p. 99.

[48] Johnson, op. cit., p. 92.

[49] James M. McCrimmon, *Writing with a Purpose.* Houghton Mifflin Co., Boston, 1963, p. 481.

[50] "Why We Have No Full Employment Policy," *Working Papers: For a New Society,* March/April 1978, p. 29.

Use quotation marks to enclose words or expressions being used in a special way:

> In our union strikebreakers are called "scabs."

> The process of negotiating and administering a contract is known as "collective bargaining."

Do not overuse quotation marks to indicate something special. Especially don't use to indicate slang. Slang should be able to stand on its own.

Use quotation marks to enclose words used as words or letters used as letters:

> What does the word "disaffiliation" mean?

> Use the letters "cb" to abbreviate collective bargaining.

Use quotation marks to enclose definitions:

> Joe found that it meant "Withdrawal of a local union from a national or international union, or of a national or international union from a federation."[51]

Single quotation marks—or inverted commas[52]—are used to enclose quotations within quotations

> "In the words of Gompers," he said, " 'Labor wants more.' "

The use of quotation marks with other marks of punctuation often causes confusion. Keep the following in mind when using quotation marks. Put quotation marks:

1. Outside commas and periods.

2. Inside semicolons, colons, and dashes.

3. Outside question marks and exclamation points if they are part of what is quoted.

4. Inside question marks and exclamation points if they are not part of what is quoted.

## Apostrophe's[53]

"Strictly speaking, the apostrophe is not a mark of punctuation but a part of the

---

[51] Austin Perlow, *Basic Communications Skills: A Handbook for Unions*. BNA Books, Washington, D.C., 1981, p. 294; *disaffiliation* defined.

[52] H. W. Fowler, *A Dictionary of Modern English Usage*. Oxford University Press, New York, 1965, p. 591.

[53] The *apostrophe's use* (possessive) or the *apostrophe is* (contraction).

spelling of a word; it occurs as part of the word, not as something between words."[54] Apostrophes are not quotation marks or accents. Their primary uses are:

1. To show possession:

The steward pursued Jill Anderson's grievance.

It was everyone's grievance.

What about names that end in *s* or *z*? Writers are divided. The traditional method is to add an *s:*

Ethel Jones's grievance

Bernie Schwartz's office

Other writers see no need for the second *s:*

Ethel Jones' grievance or Bernie Schwartz' office

Whichever you use, be consistent. For proper nouns with more than one syllable, ending in *s* or the *s* sound, use only an apostrophe (unless you want to pronounce the *siz*). Read the following aloud:

Marcus' bid for the treasurer's office fell short.

Marcus's bid for the treasurer's office fell short.

To form the possessive of plurals, add only an apostrophe when the plural ends in *s:*

Workers' rights are paramount.

"Ladies' night out" might be construed as sexist by some people.

Others' grievances are as important as ours.

The Joneses' house was next to the Jameses' house.[55]

For plurals that do not end in *s*, add apostrophe and *s.*

The men's room is down the hall from the women's room.

July 19 was the strike alumni's fiftieth anniversary.

When you form the possessive of compound nouns or indefinite pronouns, put

---

[54] Johnson, op. cit., p. 126.

[55] Note that the plurals of Jones and James are formed by adding *es.*

an apostrophe in the last word.

> The sergeant at arm's duties were to guard the door and keep out company goons. (Singular)
>
> The sergeants' at arm's duties were to guard the door and keep out company goons. (Plural)
>
> The AFL–CIO's political agenda was nonpartisan.
>
> We discussed each other's grievances.

When you want to indicate *joint* possession, put the apostrophe in the last word.

> Joyce and Vickie's union was AFSCME.

However, if there is no joint possession:

> Joyce's and Vickie's unions had overlapping jurisdictions. (Joyce and Vickie obviously belong to two different unions.)

Gerunds[56] also need apostrophes.

> I can't stand Keith's *griping.*
>
> Do you think Mary's *negotiating* was effective?

Use *no* apostrophes with personal, relative, or interrogative pronouns to show possession.

> Its primary function is economic.
>
> "Whose jacket is this?"
> "It's hers."
>
> The union is ours, not theirs.

Use apostrophes with these pronouns *only* to form contractions.

2. To show contractions (omission of letters in words or numbers):

> He wouldn't come because he couldn't come.
>
> She does not believe in unions, and she won't help.
>
> The arbitration hearing began at ten o'clock in the morning.
>
> The older members vividly recall the strike of '59.

---

[56] A gerund is a verb form used as a noun.

Avoid mixing contractions with the written-out forms in the same clause. They look awkward together.

"You could not, or you wouldn't?"

3. To form plurals of numbers, letters, abbreviations (and sometimes, words):

The six figures in his salary are six 6's.

Industrial unionism grew rapidly in the late 1800's.

Remember to cross your t's and dot your i's before you sign the contract.

No if's, and's, or but's, this is our final offer.

The UAW's position was well known.

# Hyphen (hy-phen)

"The hyphen is the only mark of punctuation that has the specific function of joining words together."[57] Its origin is the Greek expression for "in one" or "together."[58] Use hyphens:

1. To divide a word at the end of a line.[59]

We were much better prepared for these negotiations than we were for the last contract talks.

Divide words between their syllables. Do not divide one-syllable words. Your dictionary will help you.

ne go ti a tion

Words with suffixes should be divided like this:

A word to the wise: be careful of double cross-
ing the union at the bargaining table.[60]

Try to put more letters (at least three) after the hyphen than before it (at least two).

[57] Johnson, op. cit., p. 134.

[58] Barnet and Stubbs, op. cit., p. 306.

[59] Although you're *dividing* a word, you're *joining* it to another line.

[60] Make sure that the word can stand alone without its suffix.

un-

unsuc-

unsuccess-

successfully;

cessfully;

fully;

not

unsuccessful-

ly.

2. To attach prefixes from root words. There is no hard-and-fast rule. Writers tend to avoid doubling a consonant. However, many previously hyphenated words have been combined. For example,

| | | |
|---|---|---|
| re-elect | is now | reelect |
| re-employ | is now | reemploy |
| non-union | is now | nonunion |

However,

| | | |
|---|---|---|
| co-opt | is not | coopt |
| anti-inflation | is not | antiinflation |

Be careful to check your dictionary for the correct form. If it looks like this:

*co-op,* hyphenate.

If it looks like this:

*co op er ate,* don't hyphenate.

If you can't find the word you want in your dictionary:

*co-ownership,* hyphenate.

Remember:

A co-op (not a coop) means co-ownership and cooperation.

Do not triple a consonant; use a hyphen.

The supervisor was well-liked (not wellliked).

Use a hyphen when the root word begins with a capital letter.

It's not anti-American to be pro-union. (or is it prounion? Check your dictionary!)

3. To form compounds (adjectives, nouns, and numbers):

Adjectives:

The union wanted an across-the-board increase. (But, as a noun, the increase was across the board.)

Nouns or capitalized words:

She ran for the office of secretary-treasurer.

Organized labor opposed the Taft-Hartley Act.

Numbers:

One-half of fifty is twenty-five.

Hyphenate fractions and compound numbers between twenty-one (21) and ninety-nine (99).[61]

Numbers as measurements and adjectives:

three-year contract

60-year-old man

4. To show distance or span of time: Although it is preferable to write

1980 to 1984, and pp. 228 to 332;

it is acceptable to write

1980-84; and pp. 228-332.

5. To avoid confusion:

Will the steel industry ever recover?, but an upholsterer will re-cover your chair.

The employees are unionized, but the atoms are un-ionized.[62]

[61] Flesch, op. cit., p. 191.
[62] Ibid.

## Parentheses (and [Brackets])

"The most common problem with parentheses is not how or when to use them but how to use other punctuation—commas, periods, question marks, [and brackets]—with them."[63] If parentheses enclose a whole sentence begun with a capital letter, punctuate inside the parentheses; if they enclose a simple parenthetical expression, punctuate outside the parentheses. Simple enough?

"The breakdown in negotiations," said the union spokesperson, "came from the other side of the table." (Management representatives were unavailable for comment.)

"The breakdown in negotiations," said the union spokesperson (comments from mangement representatives were unavailable), "came from the other side of the table."

Use parentheses:

1. To enclose interruptions or comments:

If wages were raised across the board (as the authors advise), the most productive and/or innovating capitalists could adjust (the authors claim).[64]

The owner (a tight-fisted woman) would not give in.

2. To enclose numbers, dates, and references:

Jimmy Hoffa was a young man (18) when he led his first strike at a Kroger warehouse in Detroit.

Enclosed is a check for eight hundred dollars ($800.00) to cover the union's half of the cost of arbitration.

The sit-down strike in Austin (in 1933) set the stage for organizing packing-house workers around the rest of the country.

Feldacker outlines the steward's right to free expression (see p. 147) as part of the right of concerted activity.[65]

3. To enclose illustrations, definitions, explanations, or other information not a main part of the main structure of the sentence:

Ronald Reagan won the electoral votes of all the states but one (Minnesota) in the 1984 election.

---

[63] Johnson, op. cit., p. 96. Note that insertions into quoted material are enclosed by brackets (not parentheses).

[64] Jim O'Connor, "High Wages and Plenty Don't Mix," *In These Times,* vol. 8, no. 32 (Aug. 22–Sept. 4, 1984), p. 15

[65] Bruce S. Feldacker, *Labor Guide to Labor Law.* Reston Publishing Co., Inc., Reston, Va., 1983.

The duty of fair representation was developed through case law (court interpretations), but its basis is in statutory law (legislation).

The American Federation of Government Employees (AFGE) began a campaign to organize air traffic controllers.

John rose and spoke to the motion (he seldom speaks at union meetings), and urged the members to vote for it.

4.  To enclose numbers or letters in a list:

Being politically active is (1) registering voters; (2) handing out leaflets; (3) putting up lawn signs; (4) phoning potential voters; and (5) voting.

"Seniority will govern, subject to:
(a)  ability,
(b)  fitness, and
(c)  work record."

Do not use too many parentheses in your sentences. It makes the sentence hard to follow. Never use parentheses to explain pronouns.

He (Humphrey) was a champion of organized labor.

If you mean Hubert Humphrey, say so; do not use *he*.

Humphrey was a champion of organized labor.

## [Brackets]

Brackets should not be substituted for parentheses. They should be used:
1.  To enclose your own words within a quotation to clarify or to add to a quotation:

The local president said, "Hubert [Humphrey] was a champion of organized labor."

Or, if the president said, ". . . *he* was a champion of organized labor," and you wanted to identify *he* as Hubert Humphrey:

The local president said, "[Hubert Humphrey] was a champion of organized labor."

Or if the president used a nickname:

The local president said, "The Happy Warrior [Hubert Humphrey] was a champion of organized labor."

If you want to add your own comment to the president's remarks:

The local president said, "Hubert Humphrey [former vice-president and senator] was a champion of organized labor."

2. To enclose parenthetical material within parentheses: Try to avoid using brackets as parentheses within parentheses, as they tend to be confusing. Use commas or dashes instead. But, if you have to:

"The breakdown in negotiations," said the union spokesperson (comments [favorable or unfavorable] from management representatives were unavailable), "came from the other side of the table."

## Exclamation Point    !

"The exclamation point is to be reserved for use after true exclamations or commands."[66] Stop! Do not overuse the exclamation point![67] Overuse will disguise your *true* exclamations. Use an exclamation point:

1. After strong commands:

"Take your proposal, and shove it!"

"Hit the bricks!" the president cried.

Don't use a comma or period with the exclamation point. If the exclamation is part of the quote, enclose the exclamation mark.

2. After emphatic words, phrases, or clauses:

Help!

Oh, no!

Save me!

3. After interjections:

Whoa! Where do you think you're going?

Uffda! That's a heavy load.

4. Within sentences to call attention to a certain word:

Fay was the only (!) one who supported the president.[67]

## Question Mark    ?

"The question mark is probably the most heard of the marks of punctuation. The voice rises to it.'[68] Read this aloud:

---

[66] Strunk and White, op. cit., p. 34.

[67] Overuse also includes using more than one (!!!!!) per sentence.

[68] Johnson, op. cit., p. 101.

What did you say?

Did you hear your voice rise? Use questions marks:
1. To ask a direct question:

Who is the steward in your section?

You called the steward, didn't you?

2. To phrase a question as a statement:

You don't want me to handle the grievance?

Management thinks we're kidding?

3. To show uncertainty about what has just been said:

Two (?) weeks ago I asked her about the status of my grievance.

The impartial (?) arbitrator issued his award.

Do not use question marks with indirect questions.

Indirect: Jane asked what was wrong.

Direct: Jane asked, "What is wrong?"

If the question is part of the quotation, enclose the question mark; if not, place it outside.

Did I hear you say, "nothing's wrong"?

## Ellipsis  . . .

"Ellipsis means the omission of words."[69] Points of ellipsis may look like periods . . ., but their function is different. Use points of ellipsis:

1. To omit words from a quoted sentence:

"Obviously, actions taken by management will directly affect the number of grievances filed."[70]

At the beginning, no points of ellipsis are needed:

Repas writes, "actions taken by management will directly affect the number of grievances filed."

[69] Flesch, op. cit., p. 129.
[70] Repas, op. cit., p. 113.

In the middle:

> "Obviously, actions . . . by management . . . affect the number of grievances filed," Repas writes.

At the end:

> Repas has written, "Obviously, actions taken by management affect the number of grievances . . . ."

At the end of a sentence, add a fourth dot to serve as a period.

2. To show pauses:

> We saw the foreman approach the picket line . . . carrying a club . . . . He was obviously upset . . . . We held our breath . . . .

3. To omit a paragraph or a line of poetry:

> "I was in this 24-hour a day plant
> . . . . . . . . . . . . . . . . . . . . . . . . . . .
> just like I am every night--
> chained to small parts and metal."[71]

## Period  .

"The period says, 'Full stop.' "[72] We are coming to the end of punctuation. Finally. Use periods:

1. To end most sentences:

> Declarative sentence:  Joan is the best steward we have.
>
> Imperative sentence:  Clean up that scrap.
>
> Indirect question:  Ray wanted to know if he could leave early.

2. After abbreviations:

> Mr. and Mrs. Doe
>
> Minn., Ia.
>
> Ms., not Miss or Mrs.

3. After sentence fragments:

> Hello.

[71] Joy Walsh, "Second Shift," *Mill Hunk Herald,* Fall 1982, p. 15.
[72] Perlow, op. cit., p. 93.

Goodbye.

How did you get to the rally? By bus.

4. To indicate decimals and dollars and cents:

The C.P.I. went up 3.5% this quarter.

Our pay increased an average of $3.50 per worker.

PUNCTUATION IS DONE.

## STYLE

Writing style shows the writer's attitudes to the reader. Every writer has his or her own style, which has been developed over time. All writing style is made up of certain elements (those things that when added to grammar and punctuation improve readability). Most writers keep style books, references they have developed to help their writing. Style books cover things like when to capitalize, how to abbreviate, and how to write numbers and dates. The *Steelworkers Style Book* is an excellent example. We have borrowed their list of elements and added others. This listing should give you a start on developing your own style book. Some of our inclusions might be considered punctuation in the strictest sense, but we think they fit comfortably into either punctuation or style. The guidelines provided here are not the *last word* on style. Bend them to fit your writing and to develop your own style book. And remember, whatever style you develop, be consistent in applying it.

### Abbreviations and Acronyms[73]

Do not overabbreviate. It chops up smooth writing. Also, do not assume that your reader knows what your abbreviations or acronyms mean. You may have to explain them. Here are some things to keep in mind:

1. Write out the full name of the organization first, then abbreviate. Identify it unless you're sure all of your readers know what the abbreviation stands for.

   The United Steelworkers of America can be referred to later as simply USWA.

2. Use periods in your abbreviations for dates, places, and people.

   Oct. 4, 1948
   15th St. N.W., Washington, D.C., U.S.A.[74]
   J. R. Ewing

---

[73] An acronym is formed by using the first letters from each word in a group. For example, the National Organization for Women (NOW).

[74] Some people shorten this to USA.

3. Don't use periods for organizations and other acronyms with all capital letters.

AFL–CIO
OSHA
CPI
UCLEA
BLT[75]

You can also abbreviate:

1. The names of months when you use them as exact dates (except March, April, May, June, and July):

Dec. 7, 1944
April 1, 2001

2. Corporation, company, and incorporated when they follow a name:

International Harvester Corp.
Citgo Petroleum Co.
The New York Times, Inc.

but not,

Corp. for Public Broadcasting

3. States when they follow cities:[76]

New York, N.Y.; Tampa, Fla.

4. Street, avenue, boulevard in specific addresses (when they follow the name)

15B Baker St.
2233 Industrial Blvd.
2563 Avenue of the Americas

If the use is nonspecific, then write the word out.

The plant is on Helen Street.

5. Abbreviate some titles:

Ms., Mr., Mrs., Dr., Prof., and Rev.

[75] The first three acronyms are well known. UCLEA is the University College Labor Education Association, and BLT is bacon, lettuce, and tomato.

[76] On envelopes use the two-letter abbreviation. Postal union members will appreciate it.

Write the person's full name first to identify him or her. From then on, you can use the title.

William Winpinsinger becomes Pres. Winpinsinger

Avoid abbreviating:

1. People's names: Chas. or Geo. for Charles or George
2. And so on (etc.), in other words (i.e.), namely (viz.), for example (e.g.), except in informal writing.

## And/or

June and/or Jerry will be coming.

This means that both and/or either can happen. It can be confusing. Try writing without it.

June or Jerry, or both, will be coming.

## Asterisk *

An asterisk used to mean that something was omitted from a sentence. Today we use points of ellipses . . . . Asterisks are also used as informal footnotes, especially if there is only one footnote in the paper. If you have more than one footnote, use numbers.

## CAPITAL LETTERS

Capitalizing the first letter in a word gives the word more importance. So if in doubt (after consulting your dictionary), don't capitalize. You should capitalize all proper nouns. This includes names of particular people, places, and titles.

Alfred Parsons
Haymarket Square
Machinist (when referring to a member of the IAM[77])
machinist (when referring to the occupation)
Doctor Johnson
*The Washington Post*

Generic terms are not capitalized.[78]

A *lake* is a generic term.
*Lake Erie* is a particular location.

[77] International Association of Machinists and Aerospace Workers.

[78] Johnson, op. cit., p. 164.

People drink *cognac.*
It may have come from *Cognac,* France.

Trademarks are usually capitalized.[79] Over time, however, many trademarks have become ordinary working words.

She works for *Xerox.*

Will you *xerox* this page for me?

Proper names of particular items are capitalized when you first introduce them to your reader. But in their subsequent use you do not have to capitalize, especially when they are nonspecific.

The City Civil Rights Commission
The commission decided . . . .

Chief Steward St. Clair said . . . .
The chief steward said . . . .

The General Electric Co. offered . . . .
The company offered . . . .

The Austin Central Labor Union . . . .
The central labor union . . . .

This rule is true for *most* of the following examples. The exceptions are noted. Capitalize the initial use of:

1.  Buildings (union offices), colleges, universities, hospitals, parks, and public places:

    Solidarity House
    Slippery Rock State University
    Eye & Ear Hospital
    Yellowstone Park
    Biltmore Hotel

2.  Companies, committees, commissions, and councils:

    Pepsi Cola Co.
    Negotiating Committee
    Warren Commission
    Council for a Union-Free Environment

[79] Ibid., p. 165.

3. Courts (from the highest to the lowest):

U.S. Supreme Court
Eighth Circuit Court of Appeals
Ramsey County Small Claims Court

4. Departments (of unions or the AFL–CIO):

Research and Education Department
Building and Construction Trades Department

5. Educational courses:

Languages are always capitalized: Italian, French

Other subjects are capitalized as part of formal titles: Economics 101; but not when just economics.

6. Geographical names and terms:

California, Arkansas, Oklahoma
Sacramento, Little Rock, Oklahoma City
the Northeast, the Midwest, the Sunbelt
the state of Tennessee

Don't capitalize directions as part of a place.

southern California; northern Maine

Don't capitalize compass directions.

goin' south; north by northwest[81]

7. Government and politics:

United States government
federal government

state of Connecticut
state government

city of Phoenix
municipal government

---

[80] The U.S. Supreme Court should always be capitalized, even when referred to only as "the Court."

[81] Don't capitalize unless they are parts of titles.

8. Government bodies:[82]

   U.S. Senate
   House of Representatives
   U.S. Congress
   Canadian Parliament

9. Government departments:

   Department of Labor
   Department of Economic Security
   Human Rights Commission

10. Groups:

    Board of Overseers
    Committee on Fine Arts

11. Officeholders:

    Senator Robert Packwood (R-Ore.)
    Representative Byron Dorgan (D-N. Dak.)
    Minn. State Senator James Ulland (R-St. Louis)
    Minn. State Representative Ken Nelson (D-Hennepin)[83]

12. Political parties:

    Citizens' Party, Communist Party, Democratic Party, Fascist Party, Progressive
    Party, Republican Party, Socialist Workers' Party

13. Historical events:

    World War II, Vietnam War
    Memorial Day Massacre, Age of Enlightenment
    the Sixties
    the Great Depression

14. Holidays:

    Fourth of July
    Veterans' Day
    Christmas
    election day (not usually capitalized)

---

[82] These should be capitalized when used alone: Senate, House, Congress, and Parliament.

[83] State senators and representatives are usually identified by the county in which their district lies.

15. Institutions and organizations (including unions):

Veterans of Foreign Wars
Salvation Army
Common Cause
United Mine Workers of America
65th Constitutional Convention
Joint Council 32
Local Union 7263
District 33
Metal Trades Council

but

UMWA headquarters
Joint Council 32 office

16. Publications:

*Public Employee*
*The Nation*
*Branch Nine News*

17. Race/nationality:

Black, Eskimo, German, Mexican, Ukrainian (but white)

18. Religion:

United Jewish Appeal
Roman Catholic
Lutheran Synod
Episcopal Church[84]

19. Seasons: Don't capitalize the seasons unless they are part of a title or name:

Princess Summer-Fall-Winter-Spring[85]

20. Time:
    a. Days of the week: Monday, Tuesday . . .
    b. Months of the year: January, February, June, or July . . .
    c. Time zones: Eastern Standard Time, Central Daylight Time . . .
    d. Don't capitalize years, period of the day, or time segments:

[84] Religions and members of religions are always capitalized. Church used alone is not.
[85] More mature readers will remember the *Howdy Doody Show.*

nineteen eighty-four, twenty-five B.C.[86]
morning, afternoon, evening, night
hours, minutes, seconds

21. Titles:

Mayor Cermak
Chief Steward Kelly
Supervisor Stone
Senator Kennedy
Judge Edwards
Governor Thompson
Prime Minister Thatcher
President Reagan, president of the United States (but *former president* Reagan in 1988)
Doctor Davis
Professor Finkelman[87]

22. Forms of address:

Mr. James Boyd
Ms. Sally Mackenzie
Mrs. Anna Weiss

Initially identify the person by using first and last names. You can refer to them later with a form of address and the last name, or the last name only.

Sally Mackenzie; then Ms. Mackenzie or Mackenzie

If the person is well known, you can use the last name.

Nixon, Kissinger, Stalin, Hitler

Avoid sex or class distinctions. Do not write:

Mr. Bundy told Mary . . . .

Write:

Mr. Bundy told Ms. Shuster . . ., or

Leroy told Mary . . . .

Avoid using chairman or chairwoman (unless that particular person wants

---

[86] *B.C. (before Christ) is always capitalized.*

[87] If a professor has a Ph.D the title *Dr.* is appropriate, even if the *Dr.* is not an *M.D.*

to be called by either). Instead use chairperson or chair to refer to a man *or* woman.

Use *Brother* or *Sister* in internal union communications, but avoid using either address in external publications. Titles add stature to a person. Dr. Davis sounds impressive. If you wish to lessen someone's importance, don't use a title. Instead of Dr. Davis, say Mr. Davis, or Davis.

## Dates and Times

Use cardinal numbers when you write dates:

Contract negotiations begin on May 16. (not May 16th or May sixteenth)

1. Use noon and midnight (instead of 12 P.M. and 12 A.M.):

Negotiations began at Noon and ended at 9 P.M.

2. Don't be redundant:

We took a recess at 10:45 A.M. (Don't say 10:45 A.M. this morning. That's redundant.)

3. When you use time zones:

The president's address will be on the air at 7:00 P.M. Mountain Time.

## Datelines

1. If the city or town is not well known, write:

Ludlow, Colo.; Sudbury, Ont.; Rapid City, S. Dak.

2. If it is well known, you only need to write:

Philadelphia, Buffalo, Pittsburgh[88]

## Footnotes[89]

## Headings

Center headings at the top of page 1. Do not use a period after the heading. You

---

[88] Don't write it this way if you mean Philadelphia, Miss.; Buffalo, Minn.; or Pittsburg, Kan.

[89] Use footnotes for quotes if you don't cite the author in the body of your text. Also use them to identify sources, add comments, or to provide details. You can put them at the bottom of the page or at the end of a chapter. You can also use abbreviations such as *pp.* for pages and *vol.* for volume.

can, however, use a question mark or exclamation point, or points of ellipses.

Puckett Wins Local Presidency

Does Management Want a Settlement?

To Strike or Not to Strike . . .

## Italics and Underlining

Most typewriters do not have *italic* type. If yours does not, you can show italics by underlining. In fact, underlining is used by editors to tell the printer to use italic type. Use italics or underlining for:

1. Newspapers, magazines, and books (except the Bible):

   The Des Moines Register, Newsweek, A History of Organized Labor[90]

2. Movies, plays, TV programs, and record albums:

   Norma Rae, Steeltown, Skag, Hobo's Lullaby

3. Paintings, sculptures, and musical compositions (except single songs):

   The Gleaners, Venus de Milo, New World Symphony

For chapters, poems, short stories, articles, or songs, use quotation marks. You also use italics:

1. For foreign words not considered part of the English language:

   Carol brought me a bottle of vinho verde from Portugal.

   She had the savoir faire of an experienced negotiator.

2. Instead of quotation marks for something you want to call attention to

   One of the worst things that can happen to a union is decertification.

3. For emphasis:

   The members are not represented by the union; they are the union.

Do not overuse italics for emphasis; overuse deemphasizes.

[90]When the *The* and *A* are part of the title, underline them.

## Margins of Letters and Newsletters

Both the right and left margins should be about the same width.

## Numbers

The general rule is to spell out numbers from one to ten, and use figures for numbers from 11 to 999,999. For numbers over 1 million you can use a combination of figures and written-out numbers. Here are some other guidelines for spelling out or using figures. Be consistent.

Spell out:

1. Numbers (except for years) that begin a sentence:

   Twenty-two workers signed the petition.

   1982 was a bad year for industrial workers.

2. Ordinal numbers:

   Larry was first, Arnie was second, and Liz was third.

3. Fractions that stand alone:

   There were one-tenth as many volunteers the second time around.

4. Indefinite amounts and numbers:

   There were five or six thousand people at the rally.

   He lost millions on the stock market.

5. Numbers in dialogue:

   "If I've told you once, I've told you a hundred times."

6. The time of day with *o'clock:*

   The meeting begins promptly at seven o'clock.

   or the time of day alone

   The meeting begins promptly at seven.

7. School grades under ten:

He spent two years in the sixth grade.

8. The plurals of numbers:

Walter Reuther was in his early sixties when he died.

They came by the thousands to see the first female vice-presidential candidate.

9. Dates and years on formal invitations:

the twenty-second of June,
nineteen hundred and fifty-five.

Use figures:

1. For street numbers and addresses:

224 72nd St. S.W.

2. For highway routes and road numbers:

Highway A1A

3. For chapter and page numbers:

Chapter 11, page 35

4. For article and section numbers in union contracts:

Article IV, Section 3

5. For ages:

Walter Reuther was 26 and Victor Reuther 21 when they went to Gorky in the Soviet Union.

but

Walter Reuther was a twenty-six-year-old man . . .

6. For percentages (unless starting a sentence):

The recession cut our membership by 50 percent. (or %)

Fifty percent was a large number.

7. For numbers with fractions:

It was 1¼ times the size that they wanted.

8. For decimals:

The CPI rose 0.3% during the month of August.

9. For sums of money:

The minimum wage was $2.25 per hour when I entered the work force.

but

Their pay was only 12 cents above the minimum wage. (Spell out cents.)

or

His contract was worth $3 million.

10. For headlines:

Strike Support Demo Draws 10,000!

11. For dates and time of day:

June 11, 1963
The 1950s were conservative years.
6 A.M.

12. For temperature degrees:

We were on the picket line when the temperature was 35 degrees below zero. That's cold!

13. For school grades over ten:

She had an 11th-grade education to fall back on.

14. For voting results and sports scores:

The vote was 325 to 1 in favor of the union.
The first shift defeated the second shift 6-3 in softball.

15. For numbers with abbreviations:

She was going 85 mph when the state trooper pulled her over.

Use of Roman numerals:

1. Contract articles
2. Volumes in a set or chapters in a book
3. An introduction or table of contents
4. Page numbers in a preface
5. Acts in a play[91]

Use of *th* or *rd*:

1. Add them to figures over ten:

   13th floor
   25th anniversary
   65th Constitutional Convention

2. Don't add them to calendar dates. It's redundant.

   March 15, not March 15th

Use of the hyphen or *to* and *from* for ranges:

1. When you ratified your contract, did wages increase:

   (a) from $10-$12 an hour;

   (b) from $10 to $12 an hour;

   (c) by $2 to $12 an hour?

Which is correct? It depends on what you mean. What was the wage level before you ratified the contract? Did wages increase *by* $10 or $12 an hour; or did wages increase *to* $12 an hour? Answer *(a)* is incorrect. Never substitute a *hyphen* for *to* with *from*. If you meant $10-$12 to be the range of increase

   The range of wage increases was $10-$12 an hour.

If your wage level was $10 before the contract and $12 after, the *(c)* is the proper way to write. Answer *(b)* implies that your increase *alone* was $10-$12.

## Proofreading/Editing

One of the best ways to improve your writing is to edit it. Too many times people write something and send it out without proofreading it. The person who receives it may be amused or confused, or both. By proofreading, you can step

---

[91] Perlow, op. cit., p. 275.

back and take a more objective look at what you said. You can be critical, and you can use your criticism to improve your writing.

## Slash /

The slash has traditionally been used as a way to separate things:

apples/oranges/bananas/grapes;

or to mark the end of a line of poetry when the lines are run together in text. It is used most often today in abbreviations. The use of the slash for abbreviations is not suitable for formal writing. You can use it to speed up your writing. Some of its uses include:

$8.00/hour ($8.00 an hour)
55 miles/hour (55 miles per hour or 55 mph)
w/ (with); w/o (without)
c/o (in care of)

## Spelling

"I've never been a good speler," complained the student; "and I've tried everything. It must be in my jeans." It's not in your genes. Anyone can become a good speller. Is there a foolproof way to learn how to spell better? Are there any simple rules to follow? No. There are plenty of courses and books around that can help, but the best way to learn to spell is to learn to read. Read everything you can. Learn new words. Keep a dictionary near, or write down a word you don't understand. It's not easy; it takes time and effort.

When you write, use your dictionary often to make sure your spelling is correct.

And remember, "It's *i* before *e,* except after *c,* or when sounded as *a* in neighbor."[92]

*receive,* not recieve
*grievance,* not greivance

For a listing of commonly misspelled words, see the section Words and Phrases.

## Style Book

If you write often for the union, you should develop your own style book. This chapter is a beginning for one. You can add to it. You might want to follow the format of the *Steelworkers Style Book,* the handy pocketbook on which this topic is based.

[92] Perlow, op. cit., p. 67.

| Helpful hints and editor's notes | **Numbers** |
|---|---|
| _____ | Spell out (write out) numbers up to nine (four committee members, two-year contract, nine saw it), but use figures for 10 and more (A full committee of 10, there were 50 at the meeting, more than 200 members voted). |

*Helpful hints and editor's notes*

### Numbers

Spell out (write out) numbers up to nine (four committee members, two-year contract, nine saw it), but use figures for 10 and more (A full committee of 10, there were 50 at the meeting, more than 200 members voted).

Use figures, even under 10, for street numbers (The address is 9 Birch), page and chapter numbers (page 6, chapter 4) and ages of persons (Susan Smith, 16 and her sister, Helen, 3), except when writing "Sixteen-year-old, Susan and three-year-old, Helen."

Use figures in headlines, tabular matter, percentages, date of the month, time of day, highway and road numbers, degrees of temperature, school grades and years, but write "third term, fourth form, second semester."

Do not use figures to start a sentence (200 delegates took part). Instead write "Two hundred delegates took part" or, "About 200 delegates took part" or "There were 200 delegates."

Use figures for whole number and fraction combinations (7½, 6¼) and use figures for decimals (0.3, 3.8,

In addition to outlining how to write numbers, it gives the writer space to add his or her own comments or notes. That allows the writer to develop a personal style in addition to what is in the book.

## NONSEXIST WRITING

More and more women are entering the work force, and this trend is likely to continue. "In November 1984, they were 43.3 percent of the labor force and Government labor experts calculate they will get the majority of the new jobs over the next 20 years. Further, much job growth has come in the service sector.[93] Historically, manufacturing industries have provided the membership base for unions in this country. In recent years these industries have declined and, along with them, union membership. To stay strong, unions will have to organize the service industries. This means that they must convince women workers that unions can give them an effective voice both in dealing with the employer and within their own unions.

The ranks of women within organized labor have swelled. One out of every 3 union members is a woman, according to the AFL-CIO, and women account for half of the total increase in union membership in the past 20 years. More than 7 million women belong to unions—up from approximately 4 million a decade

---

[93]"White Men Discover It's a Shrinking Market," *New York Times*, Sunday, December 9, 1984, p. 2E.

ago."[94] In addition to joining unions, women are also assuming leadership positions in many unions.

With more women in the work force and more women in unions, why do unionists (male and female) continue to use sexism in their writing? The excuse of *tradition* is no longer valid. A new tradition is forming, and women (unlike the past) will take a credited leadership role in that tradition. Union writing should reflect this change.

Another reason given for continuing to use sexist terminology in writing is that it looks awkward to use pronouns such as *he and she*, *his and hers*, and *herself and himself*. Writers can desex their writing without an excessive use of gender pronouns.

If unions expect to organize women workers and activate women unionists, they will have to be able to communicate better. One of the basic elements of communication is *knowing* your audience. Using sexist language could mean that you do not know your audience, let alone how your audience feels.

Sexist writing has been around a long time. It can be changed. There are a number of books on desexing writing.[95] We advise the union writer to add at least one to his or her library of resources and references. Old habits die hard, but through practice sexist writing can be put to rest. Editing for sexism will also improve your overall writing.

This section is designed to assist the union writer in desexing writing. It covers some problems encountered in unlearning bad habits, along with providing some answers and suggestions to learning how to write a nonsexist way.

## Pronouns

The most common misuse of pronouns is using them generically.

> A manager should know what *his* responsibilities are.

> A nurse knows that *she* is not paid enough for *her* work.

How can you correct those mistakes?

1. Use pronoun pairs (his/her/his or her; he/she; her or his, her/his[96])

> A manager should know what *his/her* responsibilities are.

> A nurse knows that *he/she* is not paid enough for *her/his* work.

> If *he/she* and *her/his* seem awkward to you:

---

[94]"Women Flex Muscles in Union Movement," *U.S. News & World Report*, October 29, 1984, p. 76.

[95]Two good resources are Bobbye D. Sorrels, *The Nonsexist Communicator*, Prentice-Hall, Inc., Englewood Cliffs, N.J., 1983; and Casey Miller and Kate Swift, *The Handbook of Nonsexist Writing*. Barnes and Noble Books, New York, N.Y., 1980.

[96]You can reverse the order. His, him, and he don't always come first.

2. Use plurals:

> Managers should know what *their* responsibilities are.
>
> Nurses know that *they* are not paid enough for *their* work.

3. Use *you* or *one*.[97]

> As a manager, *one* should know what *one's* responsibilities are.
>
> As a nurse, *you* know that *you're* not paid enough for your work.

4. Repeat the noun (if enough words come between the nouns):

> A manager should know what a *manager's* responsibilities are.
>
> A nurse knows that *nurses* are not paid enough for *their* work. (A combination of repeating the noun and using plurals.)

5. Eliminate the pronouns:
   a. substitute *the, a, an* for pronouns

> A manager should know what *the* responsibilities are.
>
> A nurse knows that *the* pay is not enough for *the* work.

   b. Rewrite the sentence:

> A grievant should never handle a grievance *himself.*

>     Rewritten:

> A grievant should never handle a grievance alone.

>     Rewrite:

> Nothing comes between the worker and his union.

>     Rewritten:

> Nothing comes between the worker and the union
> Nothing comes between worker and union.

There are more ways to avoid pronoun problems.

1. Alternate pronouns:[98]

---

[97] One sometimes sounds stilted. Be careful in its use.

[98] If you alternate your pronouns, be careful that you don't make your sentences confusing. Alternate at natural breaks.

A steward should never let her emotions get in the way. Her primary purpose is to win the grievance. Second, a steward should never let the emotions of his grievant get in the way.

2.  Use the passive voice:[99]

    The steward represents all the members. He plays no favorites.

    Rewritten:

    All the members are represented by the steward. There is no favoritism.

3.  Use *their* with a singular noun:[100]

    Everyone gets *his* just due.

    Rewritten:

    Everyone gets *their* just due.

    Although it is not grammatically correct, you can use the plural with the singular in informal writing.

## Writing Letters

*Dear Sir:*
*In response to your inquiries about using sexist salutations in letter writing, the correct salutation is:*

    Dear Sir or Madam (Madam or Sir)

*Dear Gentlemen* is passe and can now be written:

    Dear Ladies or Gentlemen (Gentlemen or Ladies), or Gentlepeople or Dear People

Or address people (men and women) by their title or company:

    Dear Supervisor, Dear District Director
    Dear Phelps Dodge, Dear United Airlines

    For titles:

    Use *Mr.* for *men*

---

[99] Sorrels, op. cit., p. 24.
[100] Miller and Swift, *The Handbook of Nonsexist Writing,* 1980, p. 38.

Use *Ms.* for *women* (unless they prefer *Miss* or *Mrs.*)

If you are unsure of the gender, use:

Mr./Ms. J. F. Kennedy

Use a married woman's first name, not her husband's.

Mr. John and Ms. Joan Kennedy (Mrs. Joan Kennedy), or
Ms. Joan and Mr. John Kennedy

For closings, eliminate the titles of Ms., Mr., and Mrs., unless the reader might be confused about your gender.

Sincerely,          Sincerely,
John Kennedy        (Ms.) Terry Kennedy

For memos, when using titles:

To:   Ms. Terry Kennedy
From:   Mr. John Kennedy

If it is an internal memo:

To:   John
From:   Terry

Never write:

To:   Terry
From:   Mr. Kennedy

This last example talks down and is sexist.

## Stereotyping

We have traditionally stereotyped females and males. This has prevented many men and women from achieving their fullest potential in a role or occupation not suited for them. You avoid stereotyping individuals by portraying them in non-traditional occupations or by a complete reversal of traditional roles in your writing.

All men are not strong, smart, aggressive, dominant, chauvinistic pigs. All *policemen,* welders, hockey players, and presidents are not men.

All women are not weak, compassionate, timid, submissive, emotional, pretty, ladylike things. All nurses, teachers, homemakers, and cheerleaders are not women.

Men can stay at home and rear children. Women can lead the union.

## Words and Phrases[101]

There are common words and phrases everyone uses to stereotype men and women into male and female roles and occupations. We have listed some of them along with suggested alternatives.

| SEXIST | IMPROVED |
|---|---|
| actress | actor |
| airline steward, stewardess | flight attendant |
| alumni of a school | alumnae and alumni |
| anchorman | anchor |
| aviatrix | aviator |
| bachelorette | unmarried (if it's anyone's business) |
| black labor leader | labor leader |
| black presidential candidate | presidential candidate |
| businessman | businesswoman, executive |
| cameraman, cameragirl | camera operator |
| chairman | chairperson, chair, chairwoman |
| charwoman | charworker |
| clergymen | clergy |
| congressman | congresswoman, representative, member of Congress |
| councilman | councillor, council member, councilwoman |
| craftsman | craftswoman, craftsperson |
| delivery man | delivery person |
| directress | director |
| draftsman | drafter, draftsperson, draftswoman |
| effeminate | (do not use) |
| Englishmen | English (you do not say Italianmen, do you?) |
| executrix | executor |
| farmerette | farmer |
| fellowmen | fellow citizens |
| female | (don't use, unless as counterpart of male) |
| female presidential candidate | presidential candidate |
| feminine | (don't use) |
| fisherman | fisher |
| forelady, foreman | supervisor |
| forefathers | predecessors |
| freshman | first-year |
| girl | young woman (unless you mean the counterpart of boy) |
| God | God |

---

[101] These words and phrases have been collected from many sources.

| <u>SEXIST</u> | <u>IMPROVED</u> |
|---|---|
| god/goddess | god/goddess |
| good-old-boy network | cronyism |
| hat-check girl | hat-check attendant, person |
| heroine | hero |
| hostess | host |
| King's English | Queen's English (depending on who is sitting on the throne) |
| lady | woman |
| laundress, laundryman | laundry worker |
| layman/laymen | layperson/laypeople |
| lineman | line installer, line repairer |
| lion stalks *his* kill | lion stalks *its* kill[102] |
| longshoreman | stevedore |
| maid | house worker |
| maiden name | birth name |
| male hairdresser | hairdresser |
| male nurse | nurse |
| man in the street | average person |
| mankind | humankind, humanity |
| man-hour | work-hour |
| manmade | manufactured, synthetic, artificial, handmade |
| manpower | personnel, staff, workers |
| mistress of ceremonies | master of ceremonies |
| Mother Nature | (don't use) |
| motherhood/fatherhood | parenthood |
| mothering/fathering | parenting |
| office boy, girl | office helper |
| policeman | police officer |
| pressman | press operator |
| repairman | repairer, service rep |
| salesman | sales agent, sales rep, salesperson, saleswoman |
| seamstress | sewer, mender, tailor |
| spokesman | spokesperson, representative, spokeswoman |
| statesman | diplomat, statesperson, stateswoman |
| statesmanlike | diplomatic |
| suffragette | suffragist |
| they *manned* their work stations | they *ran* (staffed, operated) their work stations |
| unwed mother | mother, parent |
| usherette | usher |
| watchman | guard |
| weatherman | weathercaster |
| woman attorney | attorney |
| woman superstar | superstar |
| womanly | (don't use) |
| working man | worker |
| working father/working husband | working parent |
| working mother/working wife | working parent |
| workmanlike | skillful |
| workman's compensation | worker's compensation |

[102] *Unless you are sure of an animal's sex, don't assume that it* is male or female. In this case, females do the hunting.

## MISUSED WORDS AND PHRASES

A word on words.[103] Words convey meaning. They can be used as tools or weapons. Your choice of words should reflect what you think and feel when you write. Words can persuade, ridicule, flatter, cajole, motivate, anger, insult, or confuse your readers.[104] You should choose them carefully. Every word you use should have a purpose. All too often, however, writers:

Use too many words

Use the wrong words

Use cliches or jargon

Misuse words

Misspell the correct words

In this section we have compiled lists of misspelled words, misused words, and unnecessary words and phrases. The lists are not original or complete. You have probably seen some of the examples and can probably add some of your own.

## Spelling

Why spell corektly? If you mispell wordes, you're reader wil fiend it hard to follough watt your saying. Mispeling a worde can allso change it's meaning. If your writting for the union, mispelling ownly adds to the stareotipe that union leaders are an iliterate, borish lot.[105] Use your dictionary to help you spell correctly.

The following are commonly misspelled words. Study them so you can spell them correctly.

abbreviate, abbreviation
absence, absent
acceptable
accidental, accidentally
achieve, achievement
accommodate, accommodation
accompany, accompanies (d),
   accompanying
accurate, accurately, accuracy

acknowledged, acknowledging,
   acknowledged
acquiesce, acquiescent, acquiescence
across
address
aggravate, aggravation
aggressive
aging
agree, agreed, agreeing, agreement,
   agreeable

---

[103] This is an example of an acceptable sentence fragment.

[104] Some of the words in this sentence could *confuse* your readers.

[105] Rewrite this paragraph with correct spelling.

allege, alleged, alleging, allegedly
alleviate
allot, alloted, alloting, allotment
announce, announcement
annul, annulment, annulled, annulling
appall, appalled, appalling
apparent
arctic
arduous
argument
attendance
basically
believe
beneficial, beneficiary
calendar
caprice, capricious
ceiling
changeable
chief
choose, chose
circumstantial
collateral
collectible
column
commission
commit, committed, committing,
  commitment
committee
competent, competence
comprehensive, comprehensible
concede
conceive
concur, concurred, concurring,
  concurrent, concurrence
condemn
confer, conferred, conferring
conscience
conscientious, conscientiousness
conscious, consciousness
consensus
control, controlled, controlling,
  controller, controllable
dais
deceit, deceitful, deceive
defer, deferred, deferring
desire, desirable
deter, deterred, deterring, deterrent
die, dies, died, dying
dilemma
disagree, disagreement, disagreeable
disappear, disappearance
disappoint, disappointment

discipline, disciplinary
discriminate, discrimination,
  discriminatory
dispel, dispelled, dispelling
dissatisfy, dissatisfied, dissatisfying,
  dissatisfaction
eighth
embarrass, embarrassment
efficiency, efficient
enforceable
enroll, enrolled, enrolling, enrollment
equip, equipped, equipping, equipment
err, erred, erring
especial, especially
exaggerate, exaggeration
excel, excelled, excelling
exhort, exhortation
existence
exonerate
exorbitant
favoritism
forty
friend
fulfill
fuse, fusion
gas, gases, gassed, gassing
gauge
government
grateful
grievance, grievant, grieve, grieved,
  grieving
guarantee
half, halves
harass, harassment
height
her, heroes
hindrance
Hippocratic
homogeneity, homogeneous
hoof, hooves
hundredth
hurry, hurried, hurrying
hypocrisy, hypocritical
ice, icy, icing
ideal, ideally
immaterial
immediately
impanel, impaneled, impaneling
impel, impelled, impelling
inaccessible
inaccuracy, inaccurate

inadmissible
inappropriate
inaugurate, inauguration
incidental, incidentally
incompetence
inconsistency, inconsistent
incur, incurred, incurring
innocence, innocent
interruption
innumerable
interpretation
irreconcilable
irregardless (does not exist!)
irrelevance, irrelevant
jeopardize, jeopardy
judge, judged, judging, judgment
kerosene
kneel, knelt, kneeling
knowledge, knowledgeable
label, labeled, labeling
language
lay, laid, laid, laying
length, lengthened, lengthening
libel, libeled, libeling, libelous
lie, lay, lain, lying
likelihood
livelihood
logically
magazine
magically
maintain, maintenance
malleable
manage, manageable, managed,
    managing
maneuver
meanness
meant
memento, mementos
memorandum, memorandums (or
    memoranda)
merchandise, merchandised,
    merchandising
merit, merited, meriting, meritorious
metal, metaled, metaling
metallic, metallurgical, metallurgy
minimum
mischief, mischievous
misdemeanor
mispronounce, mispronunciation
misspeak
misspell
misstate, misstatement

model, modeled, modeling
naive, naivete
necessarily, necessary
negligence, negligent
negligible
negotiable, negotiate
noticeable
nullify, nullified, nullifying
occur, occurred, occurring
oily, oilier, oiliest
OK, OKs, s/he OK's, OK'd, OK'ing
okay, okays, okayed, okaying
omission
omit, omitted, omitting
parallel
parliament, parliamentary,
    parliamentarian
parenthesis, parentheses (plural)
pastime
perceive, perception
permit, permitted, permitting, permission
picnic, picnicked, picnicking
plumb, plumbed, plumbing
politically, politicked, politicking
possess, possession
prefer, preferred, preferring, preference
prejudice, prejudicial
privilege
proceed, proceeding
psychiatric, psychiatrist, psychiatry
psychological, psychologist, psychology
pursue
qualify, qualified, qualifying
questionnaire
quiz, quizzed, quizzing, quizzical
rebel, rebelled, rebelling, rebellious
rebut, rebutted, rebutting, rebuttal
recede
receipt
receive, receivable
recession
recommend, recommendation
recur, recurred, recurring, recurrence,
    recurrent
refer, referred, referring, reference
referendum, referendums (or referenda)
regret, regretted, regretting
relief, relieve
remit, remitted, remitting, remittance
repel, repelled, repelling, repellent
representative
reprieve

revolutionary, revolutionize
rhythm, rhythmic, rhythmical,
   rhythmically
ricochet, ricocheted, ricocheting
riot, rioted, rioting
rise, rose, risen
rival, rivaled, rivaling
roof, roofs
roommate
rumor
scab, scabbed, scabbing
schedule
secede, secession
seize, seizure
sentence
separable
separate, separation
sergeant at arms
shellac, shellacked, shellacking
shield
shrink, shrank, shrunk
shy, shier, shiest, shied, shying, shyly,
   shyness
siege
sieve
signal, signaled, signaling
skillful, skillfully
slur, slurred, slurring
sly, slier, sliest, slyly, slyness
solely
sovereign, sovereignty
special, specially
specialization
spring, sprang, sprung
statute, statutory
stink, stank, stunk
stop, stopped, stopping, stopper
strength, strengthen
strenuous
strike, struck, struck (stricken)
substance, substantial
success, succession, successor
suddenness

sufficiency, sufficient
supersede
suppose
suppress
surprised
surround
synonymous
temperament
tendency
till
thorough
transfer, transferred, transferring,
   transference, transferral
truly
try, tries, tried, trying
unaccommodating
unavailable
uncommitted
uncommunicative
undoubtedly
unforeseeable
unforgettable
unforgivable
unintelligible
unmanageable
unnecessary, unnecessarily
unnegotiable
unthinkable
until
unusual, unusually
usage
useful
valuable
vengeance
warrant
weird
willful, willfulness, willfully
withhold, withholding
worse
worship, worshiped
write, wrote, writing, written
yield
zinc, zinced, zincing

## Misused Words

Many words sound the same or are spelled similarly,[106] but have different meanings. Other words do not look the same but have similar meanings.[107] Finally, there are words that are not spelled similarly, do not have the same meaning, but are

---

[106] Homonyms.

[107] Synonyms.

incorrectly used interchangeably. Make sure you use the correct word, for a wrong word can change the meaning of the entire sentence. If you are unsure of the word you need, look it up. The authors have provided some homonyms and other pairs of words. Look up their meanings. You can use them in your writing.

a/an
ability/capacity
accede/exceed
accelerate/exhilarate
accept/except
adapt/adopt
adverse/averse
advice/advise
affect/effect
afflict/inflict
aggravate/irritate
aisle/isle
all ready/already
all right/alright
all together/altogether
allude/elude
allusion/illusion
ally/alley, allies/alleys
altar/alter
alternate/alternative
alternately/alternatively
alternative/choice
alumna/alumnae, alumnus/alumni
amend/emend
among/between
amoral/immoral
amount/number
analysis/analyze
ante/anti
anticipate/expect
anxious/eager
any body/anybody
any one/anyone
arbiter/arbitrator/mediator
arouse/rouse
arrant/errant/errand
ascent/assent
assume/presume
avenge/revenge
avocation/vocation
avoidance/evasion
award/reward
bad/badly
bated/baited
bazaar/bizarre
because/since
beside/besides
bi-/semi-
biannual/biennial

breadth/breath
break down/breakdown
broach/brooch
callous/callus
can/man
canon/cannon
canvas/canvass
capital/capitol
casual/causal
censer/censor/censure
certainty/certitude
check off/checkoff
choir/quire
cite/sight/site
climactic/climatic
climb/clime
coarse/course
colonel/kernel
compare/contrast
compare to/compare with
compose/comprise
compulsive/compulsory
confidant/confident
confound/confuse
connote/denote
consul/counsel/council
continual/continuous
coolie/cooly
coral/corral
corps/corpse
councilor/counselor
credible/creditable/credulous
currant/current
cut off/cutoff
cymbal/symbol
dairy/diary
dammed/damned
data/datum
deduce/deduct
deduce/induce
defective/deficient
definite/definitive
delusion/illusion
deprecate/depreciate
desert/dessert
desperate/disparate
device/devise
deviser/devisor
die/dye

dinghy/dingy
discover/invent
discreet/discrete
disinterested/uninterested
distinct/distinctive
divers/diverse
drier/dryer
dual/duel
dully/duly
dying/dyeing
each other/one another
economic/economical
effective/effectual
elicit/illicit
emigrant/immigrant
eminent/imminent
empathy/sympathy
endemic/epidemic
ensure/insure
envelop/envelope
eruption/irruption
especial/special
ethic/ethics
elegy/eulogy
every one/everyone
exalt/exult
exceedingly/excessively
exercise/exorcise
explicit/implicit
explosion/implosion
extant/extent
facial/facile
fair/fare
faker/fakir
farther/further
faint/feint
fewer/less
flammable/inflammable
flotsam/jetsam
florescence/fluorescence
flier/flyer
forceful/forcible
forego/forgo
foreword/forward
forth/fourth
fortuitous/fortunate
gate/gait
get/got
good/well
gild/guild
gorilla/guerilla
hangar/hanger
hardly/heartily

hear/here
heroin/heroine
historic/historical
hoard/horde
hoarse/horse
holly/holey/holy/wholly
homely/homey
hoping/hopping
hypercritical/hypocritical
imaginary/imaginative
immanent/imminent
impassable/impassible
imply/infer
incredible/incredulous
indiscreet/indiscrete
indict/indite
indoor/indoors
inedible/uneatable
ineffective/ineffectual
inapt/inept/unapt
inequity/iniquity
infarction/infraction
ingenious/ingenuous
inhuman/inhumane/unhuman/nonhuman
innervate/enervate
inside/inside of
insoluble/unsolvable
intellectual/intelligent
intense/intensive
interment/internment
interstate/intrastate
it's/its
judicial/judicious
kind of/sort of
laudable/laudatory
lay/lie
lay off/layoff
lead/led
leak/leek
lean/lien
leave/let
lectern/podium
lend/loan
lessen/lesson
levee/levy
liar/lyre
libel/slander
lightning/lightening
literal/littoral
llama/lama
load/lode
loath/loathe
loose/lose

loose/loosen
luxuriant/luxuriate/luxurious
magazine
magnate/magnet
majority/plurality
mantel/mantle
marital/martial
marquee/marquis
masterful/masterly
material/materiel
may be/maybe
mean/median
mean/mien
medal/meddle/metal
media/medium
metal/mettle
mil/mill
militate/mitigate
miner/minor
missal/missile
moral/morale
no body/nobody
no one/none
a number of/the number of
obligated/obliged
observance/observation
official/officious
on to/onto
oral/verbal
ordinance/ordnance/ordonnance
pair/pare/pear
parameter/perimeter
parol/parole
partially/partly
passed/past
patience/patients
peace/piece
people/persons
peremptory/preemptory
perpetrate/perpetuate
persecute/prosecute
personal/personnel
perspective/prospective
perspicacious/perspicuous
phenomena/phenomenon
poll/pool/pole
populace/populous
practicable/practical
pray/prey
precede/proceed
precedence/precedents
precipitate/precipitous
prescribe/proscribe

prescription/proscription
presence/presents
presentiment/presentment
preventative/preventive
price/prize
principal/principle
prostate/prostrate
quiet/quite
quotation/quote
rack/wrack
rain/reign/rein
rap/wrap
rational/rationale
really/rely/relay
rebut/refute
receipt/recipe
reduce/lessen
relaid/relayed
remediable/remedial
repairable/reparable
repel/repulse
resin/rosin
resister/resistor
resort/resource/recourse
right/wright/write
role/roll
rye/wry
scene/seen
seasonable/seasonal
secede/succeed
secession/succession
sensible/sensitive
sew/so/sow
shall/will
should/would
sprain/strain
stationary/stationery
statue/stature/statute
straight/strait
strategy/tactics
substitute/replace
subtlety/subtly
summarily/summary
take/bring
taught/taut
than/then
that/which/who
their/there/they're
theirs/there's
threw/through/trough
till/until
tinge/twinge
to/too/two

tortuous/torturous
translucent/transparent
trooper/trouper
tycoon/typhoon
undue/unduly
unexceptionable/unexceptional
unionized/un-ionized
vain/vane/vein
varies/various
venal/venial
viable/workable
vial/vile/viol

vice/vise
vicious/viscous
waist/waste
waive/wave
ware/wear/where
weak/week
weather/whether
were/we're
who/whom
whole/wholly
whoever/whomever
whose/who's

## Unnecessary Words, Jargon, Cliches and Phrases[108]

One of the best ways to write concisely is to use as few words as possible to tell your story. Unfortunately, most people do not follow that guideline. The result is not better understanding by the reader, but confusion. Avoid using words and expressions like the following. If you can, substitute other words or phrases, or eliminate them all together.

| *POOR* | *BETTER* |
| --- | --- |
| above-mentioned | (avoid using) |
| according to our resources | we find |
| add together | add |
| adequate enough | adequate |
| advance planning | planning |
| afford an opportunity | let, allow |
| aforementioned | (avoid using) |
| ain't | am not, are not, aren't |
| all but | almost |
| all of | all |
| along these lines | to the same effect |
| and also | also |
| and, etc. | etc. |
| as good or better than | as good *or* better than (not both) |
| as of this date/day | today |
| as per | under |
| as to whether | whether |
| as yet | yet |
| assemble together | assemble |
| at all times | always |
| at a later date | later |
| at an early date | soon |
| at the present time | now |
| at this point in time | now |
| awesome | (avoid using) |
| basic fundamentals | basics *or* fundamentals (not both) |
| be in a position to | can |

[108] These words and phrases were selected from a number of sources.

| _POOR_ | _BETTER_ |
|---|---|
| because of the fact that | because |
| being as/being that | since |
| between _you_ and _I_ | between _you_ and _me_ |
| big in size | big |
| bitter end | (avoid using) |
| bottom line | (avoid using) |
| busy as a bee | (avoid using) |
| by leaps and bounds | (avoid using) |
| came to the realization that | realized |
| captain of industry | (avoid using) |
| capitalist | (avoid using) |
| cease and desist | stop (unless a legal term) |
| center of attraction | (avoid using) |
| of a . . . _character_ | (avoid using) |
| commingle | mingle |
| company goon | (avoid using) |
| concerning the matter | about |
| conclusive proof | proof |
| connect together | connect |
| connect up | connect |
| consensus of opinion | consensus |
| contact | call, speak to, write |
| continue on | continue |
| at your earliest _convenience_ | (be more specific) |
| cope | cope with |
| count your chickens . . . | (avoid using) |
| despite the fact that | because |
| due to/due to the fact that | because |
| during the course of | during |
| each and every one | each one _or_ every one (not both) |
| earliest practicable date | soon |
| eleventh-hour bargaining | (avoid using) |
| enclosed herewith | enclosed |
| enclosed please find | enclosed |
| enthused | enthusiastic |
| entirely completed | completed |
| equally as willing | equally willing |
| every now and then | now and then |
| every so often | sometimes, now and then |
| exactly identical | identical |
| expired and terminated | expired _or_ terminated (not both) |
| the _fact_ that | that |
| few and far between | few |
| finalize | finish, end |
| first began | began |
| first and foremost | first _or_ foremost (not both) |
| food for thought | (avoid using) |
| for the period of | during |
| for the purpose of | for |
| for the reason that | because |
| former/latter | (avoid using) |
| forthwith | at once, immediately |

| POOR | BETTER |
|------|--------|
| fullest possible extent | as much as possible |
| furnish us with | send us |
| general consensus | consensus |
| goodly number | number |
| had ought to | should |
| have reference to | mean |
| have the desire to | want |
| heated argument | argument |
| hereafter | from now on |
| heretofore | until now |
| hit the bricks | (avoid using) |
| hitherto | up to now |
| however | but (in some cases) |
| I am of the opinion | I think |
| I came to the realization | I realized |
| if and when | if *or* when (not both) |
| impact | affect |
| implement | carry out |
| in an effort to | to |
| in a number of cases | some |
| in a nutshell | (avoid using) |
| in a satisfactory fashion | satisfactorily |
| in all cases | always |
| in case of | if |
| in length | (avoid using) |
| in lieu of | instead |
| in most cases | mostly |
| in order that | so, so that |
| in rare cases | rarely |
| in receipt of | we have |
| in regard to/in relation to | about/on |
| in terms of | (avoid using) |
| in the amount of | for |
| in the course of | during |
| in the event that/of | if |
| in the last analysis | (avoid using) |
| in the matter of | in |
| in the nature of | like |
| in the near future | soon |
| in the neighborhood (of) | nearby, (about) |
| in the process of . . . doing | doing |
| in the vicinity of | around |
| in this connection | regarding |
| in view of the fact | as |
| inasmuch as | since |
| innumerable number of | a number of, many |
| input | (avoid using) |
| inside of | inside |
| insightful | perceptive |
| interface | (avoid using) |
| irregardless | regardless |
| irrespectively of | irrespective of |

| _POOR_ | _BETTER_ |
|---|---|
| is often the case | often |
| is where | is |
| it goes without saying | (avoid using) |
| it is my opinion | I feel |
| kind of/sort of | rather/something like |
| labor boss | (avoid using) |
| a large amount | a lot |
| last but not least | last |
| little did I know | (avoid using) |
| little doubt what | little doubt |
| locality/location | place |
| locate | find |
| -ly | (avoid using to form adverbs) |
| magnitude | size |
| maintain | keep up |
| major portion of | most |
| manufacture | make |
| marathon negotiations | (avoid using) |
| materialize | show up, happen |
| maximum possible amount | maximum amount |
| meaningful | (avoid using) |
| might possibly | might |
| modern world of today | today |
| and moreover | moreover |
| moreover | also |
| most all | almost all |
| most unique | unique |
| motivation | reason |
| mutual advantage of both | mutual advantage |
| my personal opinion | my opinion |
| near future | soon |
| necessary requisite | necessary |
| necessitate | call for |
| new beginners | beginners |
| nonetheless | but |
| notation | note |
| notification | notify |
| notify | let know |
| not in a position to | can't |
| not too distant future | soon |
| not to exceed | up to, no more than |
| notwithstanding | despite, in spite of |
| null and void | null _or_ void (not both) |
| ojective | goal |
| obliterate | wipe out |
| occupation | job |
| off of | off, from |
| of late | recently, lately |
| is of the opinion | thinks |
| oftentimes | often |
| on a few occasions | occasionally |
| on a monthly basis | monthly |

| POOR | BETTER |
|---|---|
| on behalf of | for |
| on or about | on (unless you're not sure) |
| on the basis of | for, by |
| on the grounds that | because |
| on the part of | by |
| only | (Be careful. Where you put it changes the sentence's meaning.) |
| open-ended | (avoid using) |
| orchestrate | lead |
| -oriented | (avoid using as a suffix) |
| other than | except |
| owing to the fact that | because |
| perpetrator | criminal, etc. |
| peruse | read |
| please be advised that | (avoid using) |
| please do not hesitate to | please |
| please find | here is |
| point in time | now, then |
| possess | have |
| powers that be | (avoid using) |
| predominant | main, chief |
| prejudicial | harmful |
| prepared to | willing to |
| previously | earlier |
| prior to | before |
| problem is when | problem is |
| promulgate | issue |
| provided | if |
| purport | claim |
| for the *purpose* of | for |
| pursuant to | under |
| the reason . . . is because | because |
| refer back to | refer |
| reiterate again | reiterate[109] |
| relative to/in relation to | on, about |
| repeat again | repeat |
| reply | answer |
| respective/respectively | (avoid using) |
| response | answer |
| as a *result* of | because of |
| return back | return |
| round-the-clock negotiations | (avoid using) |
| same identical | same *or* identical (not both) |
| secondly, thirdly | (avoid using) |
| secure | get |
| seldom ever | seldom |
| short but sweet | (avoid using) |
| similar to | like |

[109] Technically, *reiterate* is redundant. Iterate is sufficient. *Book of the Month Club,* November 1984, pp. 29–30.

| *POOR* | *BETTER* |
|---|---|
| slowly but surely | (avoid using) |
| sources close to | (avoid using) |
| spill the beans | (avoid using) |
| state | say |
| statute | law |
| stick to our guns | (avoid using) |
| still remains/persists | remains, stays/persists |
| stonewall | (avoid using) |
| struggle for existence | (avoid using) |
| subject to | open to, under, depends on |
| submission | sending, filing |
| subsequent/subsequently | later |
| subsequent to | after |
| substantial | large, great, big |
| substantiate | prove, back up |
| successful achievements | achievements, successes |
| such as | like |
| such is the case | it is so |
| suchlike | similar |
| surrounding circumstances | circumstances |
| take one's word for | believe |
| take under consideration | consider |
| terminate | end, fire, kill, neutralize[110] |
| than him/than her, etc. | than he/than she, etc. |
| thanking you in advance | (avoid using) |
| that | (avoid overusing) |
| if . . . *then* | if |
| thenceforth | from then on |
| thereabouts | so |
| thereby | by it |
| they are both alike | they are alike |
| thunderous applause | (avoid using) |
| thusly | thus |
| time-honored | (avoid using) |
| to all intents and purposes | in effect |
| to the extent that | as far as |
| transpire | happen, occur |
| true facts | facts |
| the *truth* is . . . | (avoid using) |
| try and | try to |
| 'twas | it was |
| -type | type of |
| ultimate/ultimately | final/in the end, finally |
| union demands/company proposals | union proposals/company demands |
| unless and until | unless *or* until (not both) |
| unravel | ravel |
| until such time as | until |
| usage | use |
| use of | (avoid using) |

[110] In CIA terminology.

| <u>POOR</u> | <u>BETTER</u> |
|---|---|
| utilize | use |
| verbalize | say |
| verification | proof |
| viable | (avoid using) |
| whence/from whence | from where |
| -wise | (don't use as a suffix, e.g., price*wise*) |
| wish to advise | (avoid using) |
| with a view to | to |
| with regard to/respect to | about |
| with the result that | so that |
| words fail me | I'm speechless |

## COMMUNICATION MAKES IT WORK

Once a leadership style is adopted in a situation, the union leader then attempts to influence the other parties. Communication can transmit these behaviors in either a positive, neutral, or negative manner. This is why three of the four skill chapters in this unit focus on behavior delivery—communication. The authors hope that, having read this chapter on writing and the other two chapters on conducting meetings and verbal communications, union leaders can properly select the most effective means of communication to be successful in a leadership situation.

Successful leadership behavior has been the focus of Unit Three, or, perhaps more correctly, the four personal skills that enhance one's ability to influence others. It does one little good to understand the leadership models of Unit One if they cannot be implemented in the day-to-day life of union management. Anyone can learn the framework. It is the learning of the personal skills, however, that is the most difficult: the intricacies of labor law, the nuances of making meetings work, and how to communicate sincerely and clearly in either the written or verbal form.

Of the first three units in this book, Unit Three is the hardest to follow. Part of this is by design. The authors hope that this unit will serve as a reference guide in the future for those managers and administrators who have questions on labor law principle, how to conduct a meeting or manage a committee, and how to speak and write more effectively. Why memorize rules and such when they can be looked up? Place this book on your local union's library bookshelf and use it often.

## DISCUSSION QUESTIONS

1. Write a short paragraph describing your union activities. Use the 10 principles of writing as outlined in this chapter.

2. Rewrite the following grievance using correct grammar, punctuation, style, and spelling.

on or about april thirtieth nineteen eighty two madeleine johnson was suspended for one week for excessive absenteism by her imediate supervisor rory right the union contends that management has violated the spirit of the agrement including but not limited to artical fourteen disipline and discharge and the abcence policy the union demands that madelein johnsons suspention be revoked that her personel file be cleared of this matter that she be reinstated to her regular shift and that she be made hole in every way for lost wages benefits seniority and any other rights.

3. Correct the following:
   a. The Recording Secretary announced that senator Smith was scheduled to speak at 7 p.m. this evening.
   b. "Its true," she cried. "The plant has announced it's plans to close its doors."
   c. 55 out of one hundred and three was 53–54% of the members voting. The officers had hoped for eighty percent.
   d. Members of the IAM, AFSCME, AFT, and other AFL–CIO unions came to D.C. to protest the cuts in DOL, OASDI, and OSHA budgets by the admin.
   e. The members were excited this was our first contract.
   f. She (Madeleine Johnson) was the greivant.
   g. The contract was signed at 11:55 pm Thursday February 14 in Pawtucket RI.
   h. The Company moved it's operations to Southwest Texas on thanksgiving day: what a turkey!
   i. The Chairman, Brother Etheridge announced that the committee completed its business at twelve p.m.
   j. I got there promptly at 6 o'clock a.m. I was 2nd in line in front of one hundred fifty other job seekers.

4. Plan an educational program for your new members. Write a letter to your international union education and research department. Request information relating to your union's history, structure, and function.

5. Using the techniques outlined in this chapter, rewrite the following, eliminating the sexist writing from this steward manual.

### THE STEWARD: HE IS THE CORNERSTONE OF THE UNION

As representative of his union in his plant, the steward is the key man in the relationship between the union and the foreman, and the union and the members. Upon him depends, in large part, the success or failure of collective bargaining in his plant. Collective Bargaining is a constant process and the steward will be doing the day-to-day bargaining. Without him, and others like him, even the best contract is meaningless. He gives it life, he makes it work. The wisest union leader, the most effective administrator cannot build the union, and make it function efficiently without his help. The union depends on him and his fellow stewards for future leadership. The men who will in the future represent labor in industry-wide conferences and at national policy-making conventions will come from the ranks of those men who are adjusting plant grievances and collecting union dues. He should do what he thinks is right. He should be fair in his judgments and he will win the respect of all the men concerned.

6. Spell the following misspelled words correctly.

| | | |
|---|---|---|
| favortism | comission | parlimentry |
| seperate | harrass | recuring |
| alledged | managable | disiplinairy |
| greivance | unecessary | judgeing |
| preferrence | strenth | accross |

## GLOSSARY

**acronym:** An abbreviation formed by the first one or two letters of a name or title (e.g., NOW, HUD).

**active voice:** Using a verb form where the subject "acts" (e.g., *She wrote the article*).

**antonym:** A word that means the *opposite* of another word (e.g., *love* and *hate*).

**cardinal number:** A number that is used in counting (e.g., *one, 15;* written or figure). *Ordinal* numbers are those used in a series (e.g., *first, second, 15th*).

**cliché:** An expression that is overused and not very original (e.g., a *mountain out of a molehill*).

**compounds:** (a) A sentence with two or more main clauses, or (2) an unhyphenated word that was formed by two words (e.g., *checkoff*).

**dateline:** The geographical place and time used to identify where and when a letter or news release originated (e.g., *Chicago, May 31, 1985*).

**generalization:** An assertion based on specific instances, which may be true or just an opinion (e.g., *Everybody generalizes*).

**homonym:** A word that is spelled differently than another word(s), but pronounced the same (e.g., *lean* and *lien*).

**jargon:** Technical vocabulary (e.g., *job specs, legalese* and *computer talk* are forms of jargon).

**modifier:** Adjectives and adverbs that "modify" nouns and, therefore, the meaning of sentences (e.g., *Being* inexperienced, the union negotiating team revealed its final position too soon).

**parallelism:** Expressing a similar relationship between articles, prepositions, and conjunctions by using similar grammatical forms (e.g., He wrote letters *to* the union, *to* management, and *to* his congressional representative).

**passive voice:** Using a verb form where the subject is "acted upon" (e.g., *The article was written by her*).

**sexist writing:** Writing that puts males and females into roles based on their sex alone (e.g., *The best way a nurse can get better wages is if he joins a union*).

**stereotyping:** Putting people in roles based on a fixed idea or notion (e.g., *Women are compassionate, while men are unfeeling*).

**style:** (1) Your personal style of writing (e.g., a recognizable quality), or (2) the style of writing (rules and the like in your stylebook).

**synonym:** A word that has the same or similar meaning as another word (e.g., *strike* and *walkout*).

**tense:** A verb form that shows time (e.g., *He is steward, was steward, and will always be steward*).

---

## ADDITIONAL RESOURCES

Apps, Jerold W. *Improving Your Writing Skills: A Learning Plan for Adults.* Chicago: Follett Publishing Co., 1983.

Brigham, Nancy. *How To Do Leaflets, Newsletters and Newspapers.* Boston: Popular Economics Press, 1982.

Colby, Constance T. "Writing and Study Skills." Ithaca, N.Y.: Cornell University Trade Union Women's Studies, 1974.

Follett, Wilson, edited and completed by Jacques Barzun. *Modern American Usage.* New York: Hill & Wang, 1966.

Fowler, H. W. *Dictionary of Modern English Usage,* 2nd ed. New York: Oxford University Press, 1965.

Government Employee Relations Report, Reference File No. 2, *Glossary of Collective Bargaining Terms.* Washington, D.C.: Bureau of National Affairs, Inc., 1977.

Kelly, Saundra. "Effective Letter Writing for Union Women." Ithaca, N.Y.: Cornell University Trade Union Women's Studies, 1976.

Leggett, Glenn, C. David Mean, and William Charvat. *Prentice-Hall Handbook for Writers.* Englewood Cliffs, N.J.: Prentice-Hall, 1970.

Mencken, H. L. *The American Language,* 3 vols. New York: Alfred A. Knopf, Inc., 1945; abridged, 1963.

Roberts, Harold S. *Roberts Dictionary of Industrial Relations.* Washington, D.C.: Bureau of National Affairs, Inc., 1971.

Roman, Kenneth, and Joel Raphaelson. *Writing That Works.* New York: Harper & Row, 1981.

Shaw, Harry. *Writing and Rewriting.* New York: Harper & Row, 1973.

Thatcher, Rebecca. *Academic Skills: A Handbook for Working Adults Returning to School.* Ithaca, N.Y.: Cornell University Press, 1975.

Zuckerman, Marvin. *Words Words Words.* Beverly Hills, Calif.: Glencoe Press, 1974.

# UNIT FOUR

# A SYNTHESIS
# AND SOME ADVICE

- *Leadership case study: the steward system*
- *Coping with stress*

# CHAPTER 11

# Leadership Case Study: The Steward System

The steward system is usually regarded as the heart of the local union organization, by the membership at least, if not the officers. Yet this subsystem of the organization receives surprisingly little nurturing by local officials beyond some lip service and an occasional stewards' recognition event. This chapter looks at the steward system as an integrally linked component of the local union and suggests methods of management and administration that will nurture the system so that it operates as a healthy organic part of a living and growing local—an open natural system operating as it should. Managing such a subsystem requires sound *managerial* skills and effective *leadership* behaviors. This chapter is what this book is all about.

## THE STEWARD SYSTEM

Locals that have paid little attention to the way their stewards communicate with each other, with members, and with officers are surprised to find out that even they have a *system*. It may be unstructured, haphazard, or in disrepair, but every local whose contract provides that the grievance procedure starts with the departmental or area steward does have a system with communication channels and lines of authority—authorized or (and here is the problem) unauthorized. Thus there exists a starting point for systematic improvement and change. Creating a *directed* steward system that serves the overall goals of the union should be the aim of the local's leadership.

## Purpose and Function of a Directed Steward System

In a directed steward system, the elected officers *plan* and maintain *control* of the activities and communications of the stewards (recall Chapter 3). Lest this sound too authoritarian, let's look at the typical undirected system. In such a structure, stewards, left to their own devices to handle problems, tend to seek out advice and guidance from personal friends, old-line and highly placed local officers, or even former leaders. In this system, guidance is not coming from the wellsprings of workplace democracy. A directed steward system enables officers to create environments where stewards have access to new ideas, have a chance to share experience with each other, and are able to stay close to the resources and agendas to create an environment within which the steward may seek educational opportunities and personal growth and development while serving the needs of work colleagues and the local union.

This vision may sound idealistic, but is it any more so than the many steward training manuals that lay out a range of "roles of the steward" from organizer to educator, from grievance handler to political activist, which are seldom filled by any but the most exceptional steward? Most local unions, facing steward apathy, ignorance, and turnover, are delighted if the steward is willing simply to keep and distribute grievance forms to aggrieved employees. The "roles of the steward" *beyond* grievance handling evaporate. A system that can encourage stewards to start fulfilling these other roles and to perform their duties with enthusiasm and dedication must provide information, protection, and rewards, as well as wider learning opportunties for stewards. These four elements of a directed steward system grow out of a recognition of the psychological component of union activism.

## PSYCHOLOGY AND STEWARDSHIP

The desires for individual recognition and achievement that motivate all of us also operate in the person who accepts the job of steward. In addition, stewards, possibly even more than other union officials, may be motivated by a keen sense of their own rights and self-worth, by the desire to help other workers stick up for their rights, and by an enjoyment of an adversarial stance with supervisors. (Many stewards "get there" by first fighting for their own grievance.)

But not long into their stewardship, stewards begin to feel the pressure of failure and frustration. They are expected to know the contract (and often don't), and they are expected to "talk down" the supervisor (and often can't). They all too often lose track of the grievances they have initiated as those grievances move up the process, and they are left to field all too many questions on collective bargaining, labor law, and internal union activities and policies without adequate information. Perhaps most frightening of all, they are too often left unprotected in the face of petty management harassment and humiliation.

In such a situation, the job of steward is more likely to frustrate than to reward normal human desires for recognition and accomplishment. St. Peter's greeting to the shop steward entering heaven, "Come in and choose your harp 'cause you've had your share of hell," rings all too true to many a loyal union steward.

There are, however, important ways in which local officers can restructure the environment for stewards so as to make possible the psychological rewards of stewardship, and thereby combat steward apathy and cynicism and act to stem turnover among stewards.

## INFORMATION

The starting point of a directed steward system is an adequate flow of information. The steward's job can be made personally more rewarding and institutionally far more useful if each steward is provided with *all* the information necessary to do the job. First, this refers to information on the contract and the enforcement mechanisms within the local, including past grievance and arbitration settlements, past practices, and clear information on how the local machinery functions and where each of the steward's own grievances is within the system at any given moment.

### The Grievance File

"A local union is only as good as its filing system," said one veteran local union official commenting on the ability of a union to enforce and administer the collective bargaining agreement. Files are essential. We speak elsewhere of the efficiency possible to locals able to computerize their operations. Computerized grievance files are a splendid tool in the hands of local union grievance handlers, but even locals that are unable to computerize can multiply the amount of information available to stewards and grievance committee members through a simple filing and cross-referencing system.

The method of filing depends on the size of the local union and the complexity of the bargaining unit it represents. A chronological file of grievances by department can well serve a local of 2000 to 3000 members. Department or divisional stewards may know their grievance histories well enough to locate past departmental grievances quickly. But these only become accessible to the entire steward system when they are cross-referenced in a notebook organized by contractual provisions and discipline/discharge categories. Grievances from the chronological file are entered by number in the notebook under the proper category as they are filed. One advantage of this simple system is that it can be started immediately without a complete redoing of the existing method. Periodic house cleanings can remove settled grievances to another location, which is organized on the same principles and remains accessible for research.

Accessibility is a key concept when evaluating the utility of a grievance file. The file represents the collective property and experience of the local union. It should be open to all stewards, who should be introduced to it when they first take office and encouraged to use it for research into grievance cases and to build it for those who come after them. One local union proudly displayed its tidy filing system to visitors; past officers were given full credit for initiating the system. Here completely open files had given way to a tighter security system, and stewards were allowed free access only in the presence of an elected officer of the union. Although access and security may raise problems, they are solvable ones, and experience shows that stewards with the research capability of a local grievance file will generally respond to the challenge and the increased responsibility given them by an open system.

## Contents of a Grievance File

The active grievance file should be created first by the steward. It should be clearly spelled out that it is her responsibility to accumulate the basic information needed to evaluate and process the grievance. The steward should be schooled as to the need for immediate interviews with the grievant(s), the supervisor involved, and other witnesses. These should be dated and clearly signed by the steward, although they can be handwritten notes. Each local should have a grievance fact sheet (Exhibit 11-1), possibly several for varying types of grievances, and stewards must be repeatedly schooled in the importance of carefully and candidly filling out these sheets. The grievance fact sheet should be reserved for the internal use of the union officers involved in grievance handling. It is a vital document. Properly used, it can provide third- and fourth-step union officers invaluable information as they prepare and evaluate grievances.

In addition to interview notes and the fact sheet, the active grievance file should also contain documents received from management or outside agencies (e.g., OSHA) relevant to the grievance. A well-kept grievance file, carefully maintained and open to stewards, can help the local to win grievances and, of even greater long-term significance, to develop active and responsible stewards who understand the procedure, are able to research grievances, and have a sense of helping to contribute to a more efficient local union.

Beyond the grievance file, other information is also important to stewards, including the activities of the local with regard to collective bargaining, arbitration, political action, and community activities. This information is ordinarily available to all rank and file members through newsletters, bulletin boards, and rank and file meetings. The motivated steward will seek out this information and be able to pass it on to the members he or she represents. Some locals may put out a "steward's update" when special news flashes in crisis situations are needed, and stewards can then pass on this emergency news to their members. Our suggestion here, however, is that information on the grievance system and open grievance files are the basics, which, because they enable the steward to do a better job, draw the steward more closely into involvement with the entire organization.

EXHIBIT 11-1
## GRIEVANCE INVESTIGATION FACT SHEET

Department _____    Date _____

Shift _____    Steward _____

Name of employee(s) _____

Classification _____    Seniority date _____

Name of supervisor _____

*WHAT HAPPENED:*

Employee story:   When _____    Where _____

What _____

_____

_____

_____

_____

Date of interview with employee(s) _____

Supervisor story:   When _____    Where _____

What _____

_____

_____

_____

_____

Alleged contract/rule violation _____

Date of interview with supervisor _____

*WITNESSES*

Name(s)                                    What they witnessed

_____                    _____

_____                    _____

_____                    _____

*DOCUMENTS NEEDED* (Check "yes" when received and attach to fact sheet)

_____ Attendance record.    Date requested _____    Date received _____

_____ Work record.    Date requested _____    Date received _____

_____ Medical record.    Employee permission _____

Date requested _____    Date received _____

_____ Other grievances filed by this employee

Additional helpful information: _____

_____

_____

***USE BACK OF THIS FORM
TO RECORD ADDITIONAL PERTINENT INFORMATION***

## PROTECTION

Under U.S. labor law, stewards have considerable protection (although less than in many European countries) against discrimination as they perform their representational functions. Most stewards have additional negotiated contractual rights that enable them to perform their duties more conveniently. In a good many workplaces with established bargaining relationships, stewards also have customary rights that may reach far beyond anything guaranteed them by law or contract, including considerable on-the-clock problem-solving and grievance investigation. By the same token, however, some employers have limited the legal rights of stewards through practice accepted by both parties, either out of ignorance or indifference to the issue of stewards' rights. Many of the unfair labor practice cases arising under those sections of the Taft–Hartley Act that protect stewards come from workplaces where employers have long denied stewards clearly recognized rights, such as the right, for example, to receive from management information relevant to grievance handling.

### Educating Stewards on Their Responsibilities and Rights

Stewards may be unaware that their roles have been specifically addressed and certain of their rights secured by national labor policy. A clear explanation of these statutory rights to stewards when they first take office has been a source of considerable informational power for many stewards and should occupy a leading place in any steward training program. These basic rights protected by the National Labor Relations Act are:[1]

1. The right to police the contract, solicit grievances and represent employees through the grievance procedure free of harassment or discrimination from supervisors.

2. The right of free speech, or the right freely to speak their minds while fulfilling their representational roles.

3. The right to request and get from the employer information that is relevant to the grievance at any point during the grievance process, including prior to filing a formal grievance.

4. The right to be present during a predisciplinary investigatory management interview with an employee if the employee requests representation.

5. The right to assist the employee during such an interview through helping clarify and giving advice.

6. The right to meet with the employee prior to such an interview to become familiar with the basic facts of the case.

[1] Bruce Feldacker, *Labor Guide to Labor Law,* 2nd ed. Reston Publishing Co., Reston, Va., 1983, especially Chapter 4.

7. The right to sign up new members and, within legitimate workplace distribution rules, to distribute union literature.

These rights adhere to every private-sector steward (and, since state law for public-sector unions generally follows NLRB precedent, for many public-sector stewards as well). Negotiated rights that can expand on these statutory rights (or in some cases limit them) differ from contract to contract. They can include:

1. The right to investigate grievances on paid work time.
2. The right to circulate in the work area to police the contract.
3. The right to take paid time for posting union notices.
4. The right to talk with new hires at the time of their orientation.
5. The right to unpaid (or paid) leave for union business, including education for union duties.
6. The right to be notified of discipline of bargaining unit members.

Whatever the rights secured by contract, and whatever customary rights have grown up over the years, these should also be made clear to stewards as they take over their positions. Unscrupulous supervisors do not hesitate to attempt to narrow the rights of the new and inexperienced steward ignorant of statutory, contractual, or customary rights. Self-assertion of these rights by the new steward is far preferable to having higher union officers step in just as the new steward is attempting to gain credibility (power). Intervention by higher-level officers is often necessary and can be a positive experience for the unsure steward, but it should be reserved for serious cases that cannot be handled by the steward alone.

## PARTICIPATION STRUCTURES AND THE UNION STEWARD

A new threat to the integrity of the steward system and the grievance-handling role of the steward lies in the quality-of-work-life programs (under whatever name) and the workplace teams, steering committees, and other new workplace institutions that have proliferated in U.S. workplaces in recent years. Stewards and the entire grievance-handling system must be protected against the possibly insidious effects of a competing workplace representation and problem-solving structure, for it can, if not closely watched, erode and even replace the steward's role as problem solver.

Workplace participation teams handle production problems, housekeeping matters, and a wide range of other items usually defined, in a unionized setting, as outside the bargaining or grievance area altogether. Advocates of these programs argue that dividing problems between those subject to the formal grievance process and those not, actually benefits the local union in that it clears the grievance procedure of the many nongrievance items that can otherwise clog it up. The steward is then free to handle true grievances more effectively.

In theory, such a freeing up sounds most appealing, particularly in workplaces where poor labor-management relations have indeed clogged the procedure with numerous grievances. In practice, however, the steward's problem-solving role in the workplace has always extended beyond pure grievances. All types of workplace problems and gripes have been brought to stewards for resolution both through the grievance procedure and by informal conciliation and bargaining. A very significant if nonmeasurable part of the stewards' actual functioning in the workplace has occurred outside formal structures, and those wide-ranging problem-resolution activities have been a great source of union strength and steward prestige in countless workplaces.

The steward who successfully intervenes to settle a three-way dispute between two workers and a supervisor over "the right way" to perform a job may be acting unconventionally and even outside the contract in terms of traditional labor–management roles, but she is strengthening worker and union power in the workplace and bolstering her own importance and credibility in the eyes of workers and supervisor. Quality circles or work teams remove that extra-contractual dimension of the stewards' work and correspondingly weaken his or her position.

A more direct challenge to the grievance system as a whole comes when the participation teams begin to discuss and resolve matters that are mandatory subjects of bargaining such as safety and health. That is a frequent object of work team discussion and action, and since it is one that joint union–management safety and health committees address, it seems natural that the work team would take it up. Once this area has been acted on, it is not clear what stops the work team from taking up other bargaining areas. And in fact many have interfered in the grievance area, occasionally solving problems far more quickly than the traditional union mechanism. Why and how? Because any management unit that wishes to discredit the union-negotiated grievance procedure in favor of a management-initiated employee participation program can easily allow problems to be settled with dispatch through the favored structure while not yielding on the same issue in the grievance procedure.

How can the grievance procedure be protected in an employee participation situation? Unions have experimented with several types of safeguards. The standard is to declare all mandatory subjects of bargaining off limits for discussion. For this safeguard to work, well-trained union representatives must sit in on each committee and be alert for even marginal topics and issues. It is important in this situation that management be willing to participate in stating that the issue is one appropriate to the grievance procedure, rather than blaming the union for blocking a quick solution by insisting on use of a "less effective" mechanism.

One union had special training sessions for stewards on their roles in a quality-circle program when it was suspected that management was considering a Quality of Work Life (QWL) program. The local president sees a direct causal relationship between those early sessions and management's ultimate decision against the program.

Stewards who understand the history, nature, purpose, and possible abuses of employee participation are far more able to monitor their functioning and protect the grievance system. Some of the abuses and dangers of quality circles and employee participation teams are:

1. Discussion and quick solution of grievance items.
2. Competition for participation and allegiance of talented rank-and-file members.
3. Bypassing of the union in communicating management positions and arguments during or prior to collective bargaining.
4. Undermining the union during bargaining. ("We would like to accept that idea and implement it, but with the union's position on wages, we just can't see our way clear . . . .")
5. Turning young and old workers against each other.
6. Dividing departments or plants in a chain operation by introducing competition regarding productivity.
7. Pushing the idea that loyalty to the union divides workers from management and militates against maximum cooperation and productivity.
8. Filling participation teams with those dissatisfied with the union or, in right-to-work states, with nonunion members.
9. Encouraging worker complaints against other workers for not pulling their weight.

Safeguards of local grievance machinery to ask for when setting up joint participation teams include:

1. Union representative on each team.
2. On-the-clock training by union representatives of these union members.
3. No nonunion members on the team.
4. No contract or grievance issues can be discussed.
5. Shared responsibility to keep grievance issues out of discussion.
6. No discussion of personalities or union policies or politics.
7. Voluntary participation by employees.
8. Management agreement to facilitate grievance handling as a quid pro quo for union agreement to cooperate in the participation program.

None of these safeguards automatically guarantees protection of the grievance system. That depends on the loyalty of members to the union and on the commitment of stewards and their awareness of the dangers of the participation programs. Union officers faced with a QWL situation must look first to the health and strength of their grievance and steward systems. The grievance system—heart of the union in the workplace—can too easily atrophy in the face of a competing and active participation program. It behooves every union official to give special attention to the steward system if it is to coexist with an employee participation program.

## RECOGNITION

The third element necessary to a vital steward system is recognition of stewards for their services to the union. Recognition goes beyond, but may include, reward in terms of some form of payment for time spent in meetings. Each local must decide for itself whether to pay stewards. Payment is an acknowledgment of the considerable sacrifices that the job entails, but probably should be kept low enough so that it does not become a motive for accepting the position. Overcoming stewards' resistance to attending meetings may be achieved more readily by having short, well-planned meetings full of substance than by any form of financial or liquid reimbursement.

Steward recognition can certainly take the widely used form of yearly recognition dinner-dances and of "stewards' weeks" such as some international unions have celebrated in their national journals. But the local should not over-look the form of recognition that is most effective, if more homely. This is the recognition that salutes the stewards' good work before those he or she repre-sents in the workplace. Hours of hard investigative work and hard bargaining with management may not always result in a grievance victory, but they must be credited—publicly if possible. The disappointed grievant will not thank the ste-ward for this work. That is the job of the local officers. One survey of "you and your union" offered in the context of a union leadership educational program has for years asked the question, "Have you ever been publicly thanked for doing a good job for your local?" Only rarely to participants answer that question in the affirmative. In a volunteer organization run almost entirely by committed and universally overworked activists, it is natural to overlook the special per-sonal "thanks for your good work" that means so much. And in no office is that recognition as badly needed and as lacking as the stewards'.

A planned program of recognition for stewards who do the daily grinding work of solving problems at work is a must. If the steward structure allows, this could be the job of the chief steward or some designated member of the grievance committee who is aware of how well stewards are performing their many func-tions. A few moments spent at a Stewards' Council meeting commending Sandra for her tenacious seeking out and interviewing witnesses or Jim for his complete and detailed grievance fact sheet can pay off not only in terms of pleasing those two stewards, but as a means of educating other stewards as to what is expected of them in their grievance-processing roles. Role modeling is far easier than reprimanding as a means of improving stewards' performance. Another form of local recognition for stewards is to use the local's newsletter to print stories with photos, either on a regular basis ("Meet Your Steward") or for special recognition ("Steward's Work Gains Back Pay"). As a union-building strategy, it is more important to recognize the steward than the grievant in such a success story.

Nurturing the grievance procedure and the steward system is one way to help it flourish. Recognition must be planned, built in, and regular to make it work to build the entire system. But above all, it must be deserved! Although we are suggesting that a recognition program be part of a conscious effort to change stewards' behavior, we are not advocating the kind of mindless praise ("Everyone look at Johnny: he has all four legs of his chair on the floor!") that is part of some manipulative behavior modification approaches. Don't overdo it; but don't overlook it.

## PROVISION FOR WIDER
## LEARNING OPPORTUNITIES

Thus far we have discussed three components of a successful steward system: information, protection, and recognition. These may be the fundamentals, but the addition of a fourth dimension to the job of steward is what can turn a system around and make it a vital and constructively contributing part of a local union organization.

If we look at a steward system in terms of Abraham Maslow's familiar "hierarchy of human needs",[2] we can see that our first three elements fulfill basic needs for safety and belongingness (protection and information) and for esteem (recognition). But if local unions are to tap into the sources of human creativity and commitment that can lift their organization into a revitalized state, the system must also include the opportunity for stewards who so desire to develop personally in new and fulfilling directions (Maslow's "self-actualization" needs).

## AN EDUCATION PROGRAM
## FOR STEWARDS

A local union that intends to strengthen its grievance machinery must devote serious attention to steward education, both in the traditional sense of steward training and in a broader understanding of general educational opportunities made available to stewards with union financial support.

Every steward should be offered a steward training course at the time of assuming the position. This is the moment when the steward is most receptive to, even eager for, information on his duties and responsibilities and the various resources that can be called on to carry them out. The problem is that many

[2] A. H. Maslow, *Motivation and Personality,* 2nd ed. Harper & Row, New York, 1969.

stewards assume office at odd intervals when no school is scheduled. Some locals have stewards' schools at six- or twelve-month intervals. This means that the steward with an interim appointment may go for months without any formal training and, by the time a class comes around, will have lost the initial impetus, since the steward has been performing the job OK without a school. Worse, bad habits will have already been developed in grievance writing and investigation, which may later be very difficult to break. (Recall our example in Chapters 1 and 2.)

One solution to this problem is to videotape selected sections of an introductory steward training session, which an individual can watch as part of a private orientation. Such a tape would capture key skills of the steward's job—screening of gripes from grievances and grievance identification; proper investigation, including interviewing techniques and use of the grievance fact sheet; grievance writing, including several samples on different issues; and dealing with the supervisor, focusing on thorough preparation of arguments and facts. This solution is increasingly within the reach of even small local unions; but if it is not technically feasible, a second-best alternative would be a one-on-one session with a chief steward or equivalent officer. As personal resources, each new steward should be given a steward's tool kit consisting of at least the following items:

The contract

The local's bylaws and the International Constitution

Current seniority list

Employer rules, regulations, and policies

Job descriptions and wage rates for the steward's department

Grievance investigation forms and fact sheets

Grievance forms

List of union officers, their locations at work, and phone numbers

File of people in the department

Membership cards, Political Action Committee (PAC) checkoff cards

This list can be expanded to include information on relevant labor laws, including Title VII guidelines and workers' and unemployment compensation law.

Most international union offices have steward training materials, some of very high quality, which can be used in a local program. University or community college labor education programs are usually willing to share materials and help locals develop their own education programs, even if they are not always invited in to do the training. If local officers feel unable to conduct the training themselves, the district or regional union offices offer steward classes as part of their service to locals either by request or at intervals. University or college labor education programs nearly all offer steward schools, which can generally be tailored to a local's needs. Some local unions have established programs for stewards that involve a progression of classes in two or three stages, beginning with basic contract interpretation and grievance handling, then skill development, and perhaps finally political and economic issues and labor law classes.

If the local can make some of these classes mandatory for stewards, fine. But most locals cannot exercise this kind of suasion over stewards and at the most can offer lost time for stewards' schools and conduct powerful recruitment campaigns among stewards to encourage attendance.

Beyond a program focusing on skills and issues of direct relevance to the functional roles of the steward, a broader educational menu might be offered as part of the reward for performing the job of steward. The proliferation of adult and continuing education programs available in local communities has made a wide range of interesting classes available to working adults, from auto mechanics to philosophy and history courses. The acquisition of a broader liberal education for adults is now possible and increasingly attractive to working people. Many local unions have educational programs under which they reimburse members for community college or university credit and degree classes. These options could be directed specifically at stewards (while not necessarily excluding nonstewards) and made especially accessible to them by targeted advertising of available courses and perhaps other forms of special tuition reimbursement or scholarship arrangements.

A stewards' educational program should also include special consideration for stewards when the local is selecting members to attend conferences or seminars sponsored by outside institutions or universities and union leadership conferences. (A sample educational program is outlined in Exhibit 11-2.)

This fourth educational aspect of a directed stewards system can be the key to developing a superior cadre of stewards, some of whom will eventually emerge as local union leaders. But the real return on the local's investment in education will take the form of a vital steward system and an enhanced workplace presence for the local union.

The job of the steward must offer personal rewards to the individual asked to sacrifice so much time and peace of mind. The local union must be prepared to answer the "What's in it for me?" question when recruiting stewards just as when recruiting new members. We are suggesting an ambitious program for energizing steward systems. It might well take the full attention of a union officer to direct the overall program: the establishment and monitoring of the grievance file, the protection of stewards against both supervisor harassment and the erosion of duties through employee participation programs, the recognition of outstanding performance by stewards, and the establishment of a broad educational program. The goal is to make the position sought after and rewarding so that the union can demand and receive quality performance from stewards.

EXHIBIT 11-2
**Education Program for Local Union Stewards**

I. Basic Steward Training. Introduction to the Union (structure and history). Contract Interpretation and Grievance Procedure. Roles and Expected Duties of the Steward (including education and politics). Basic Steward Skills: What is a grievance? Use of the Fact Sheet. How to Write Grievances. Tips on Negotiating the Grievance.

II. Advanced Steward Training. Intensive Work on Fundamental Skills of Effective Grievance Handling: communicating with the grievant; use of resources such as grievance file, steward meetings; thorough investigation, including documentation and evaluation of evidence, use of witnesses, practice on grievance fact sheet; negotiating skills, including active listening, development of argument and facts; grievance issues, focusing on how to approach specific problem areas for the local such as absentees, drug/alcohol, insubordination cases.

III. Advanced Steward Training. Labor Law, Politics, Legislation, Economics, Labor History, Communication Skills incuding public speaking, writing and grammar, persuasion skills, organizing/motivating members.

IV. Attendance at specialized conferences or seminars offered by external institutions on labor topics.

V. Attendance at union conferences and conventions.

VI. Tuition reimbursement or scholarship program for community college or university continuing education or degree programs.

## OFFICERS VERSUS STEWARDS

The ranks of union dissidents as well as challenger electoral slates have often been filled from stewards' committees. This has perhaps naturally created a certain reluctance in some union officials to encourage union training and resource investment in stewards. Is the educated and informed steward more or less of a threat to local union unity and harmony? While we know of no quantitative studies of the connection between steward education and steward divisiveness, anecdotal evidence suggests that educated stewards are indeed likely to be critical and demanding of union officers and their political and bargaining agendas. But there is a crucial variable that holds the promise of channeling that criticism and helping it build rather than divide the union. That variable is open communication between the steward system and the officer corps. All too often the steward system and the local union management and administrative structures tend to function almost independently of each other. This is a source of weakness and disunity for the local union as a whole. A cohesive steward–officer system can help clear many of the problem areas that develop when rumor and competition rather than dialogue and sharing of problems prevail.

## STEPS TO IMPROVE INTERNAL COMMUNICATIONS

Improved communications within the local union involve several steps, the first of which is an *examination* and *evaluation* of the present system. An internal evaluation instrument can be developed and applied to any local union to permit evaluation of the system in place (see Exhibit 11-3).

EXHIBIT 11-3
**Evaluation of a Local Steward System**

1. *Representation ratios*
   Number of bargaining unit members   _____
   Number of stewards                  _____

| Department | No. Bag. Unit Members | No. Stewards | Ratio |
|---|---|---|---|
| | | | 1 to ____ |
| | | | |
| | | | |

   Are minority groups and women represented proportionately? _____

2. *Method of steward selection*
   Elected _____ Are elections contested? _____
   Appointed _____ Are candidates interested? _____ Reluctant? _____

3. 

| Vacancies | Department Name | Percent Vacancies |
|---|---|---|
| | | |
| | | |

4. 

| Department | No. grievances filed in last six months | No. grievances settled at step 2 |
|---|---|---|
| | | |

5. *Grievance filing system*

| | | By dept. | Entire workplace |
|---|---|---|---|
| Filed by steward's name | _____ | _____ | _____ |
| Filed chronologically | _____ | _____ | _____ |
| Filed by grievant name | _____ | _____ | _____ |
| Filed by subject or contract clause | _____ | _____ | _____ |
| Open to all stewards? | _____ | _____ | _____ |

   Who is responsible for maintaining grievance file? _____

6.  *Structure and communication channels*
    Departmental stewards _____
    Divisional (chief) stewards _____
    Chief steward for entire workplace _____
    Grievance committee _____

    | | By dept. | Entire workplace |
    |---|---|---|
    | Regular meetings of first-line stewards | _____ | _____ |
    | Regular meetings of divisional (chief) stewards | _____ | _____ |
    | Do elected officers attend any of these meetings? | _____ | _____ |

    Which officer? _____
    Does this officer report back to Union Executive Board? _____
    Is there dual membership between steward system and local executive board? _____
    Do representatives of stewards or Stewards' Council sit in on executive board meetings?
    _____
    Are stewards required to attend rank-and-file meetings? _____
    Percent of year? _____
    How do shift stewards normally communicate with each other? _____
    _____
    Does the local newsletter report on stewards or grievances? _____
    _____

7.  *Duties of first-line stewards*

    | | | Actually carried out? |
    |---|---|---|
    | Present grievance verbally at first step | _____ | _____ |
    | Investigate grievances | _____ | _____ |
    |     Interview grievant(s) | _____ | _____ |
    |     Collect documentation from management | _____ | _____ |
    |     Interview witnesses/supervisor | _____ | _____ |
    |     Fill out fact sheet | _____ | _____ |
    | Write grievance | _____ | _____ |
    | Present grievance at step 2 | _____ | _____ |
    | Attend step 2 meeting | _____ | _____ |
    | Attend step 3 meeting | _____ | _____ |
    | Inform grievant of grievance resolution | _____ | _____ |
    | Sign up new members | _____ | _____ |
    | Political action | _____ | _____ |

    Other _____
    _____

8.  *Steward training*
    Training offered for all new stewards _____
    Periodic training offered for all stewards _____

Progressive levels of training
   Two levels    _____
   Three levels _____
Is the schooling offered on lost time? _____
Number of current stewards who have attended stewards' school _____
   Percent _____
Do stewards' meetings have an educational segment? _____
Do stewards receive a steward's tool kit when they take office? _____
Does the national or international provide a stewards' manual? _____
Do all stewards receive it? _____

9. Recognition
   What form of regular recognition does the local union provide for stewards?
   — Banquet _____
   — Yearly stewards' week _____
   — Other _____

10. List major problems perceived in steward system:

| | By: | Local officers | stewards | members |
|---|---|---|---|---|
| _____ | | _____ | _____ | _____ |
| _____ | | _____ | _____ | _____ |
| _____ | | _____ | _____ | _____ |
| _____ | | _____ | _____ | _____ |
| _____ | | _____ | _____ | _____ |

If the examination shows that the system is not functioning as desired—if, for example, stewards are being bypassed, if some departments are out of touch with the rest, if the results of arbitration settlements are circulating by word of mouth or rumor, if officers are uninformed on major current grievance issues or workplace problems, then structural reform of the system might be considered (organizational development). It is important both informationally and strategically that steward input be an important part of the evaluation process that should precede any structural change (Chapter 3).

In attempting to increase communication between the steward and local officer systems, it can be very helpful to identify the existing informal channels of communication and determine if those are effective and desirable or if formal, regularized channels should be developed or encouraged. As a general principle, use of formal structures and discouragement of bypassing tends to encourage greater development of the role of the first-line steward. Where a free flow of information and expertise travels both up and down the structure between local officers and stewards, the grass-roots reach of the union is strengthened, and democracy and formal stratification can coexist.

Steward systems can take many forms and will vary with local circumstances, workplace layout, diversity of the bargaining unit, and so on. One system is diagrammed in Figure 11-1, with communication channels suggested by arrows.

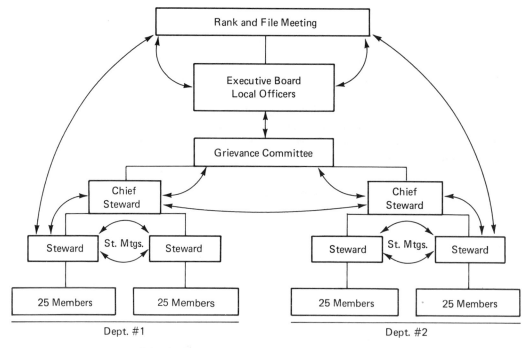

**FIGURE 11-1.** Outline of a steward communication system

## CONCLUSION

Given the central importance the role of contract administration plays in the life of the local union, managing the grievance system should be a major focus of local union officials. Often it is not. Grievance and arbitration cases undoubtedly occupy center stage, but the system that has been created to handle them is left to function on its own.

To many members, the union exists primarily for bargaining and enforcing the collective agreement. A union whose grievance system suffers from poorly trained and motivated stewards, from missed deadlines and inadequate investigation, is at serious risk of losing the support of its members. It is a truism that even the best contract is worthless without vigilant daily enforcement of the protections it has won for bargaining unit members. Yet too many local union leaders accept an apathetic and semicompetent steward corps as if this were as much a fact of union life as low attendance at rank-and-file meetings. But many local unions possess effective steward systems that they have achieved by investment of thought, time, and money. So much of the problem is simple neglect. If the present systems were merely brought into line with existing local and national union guidelines, many locals would see considerable immediate improvement in grievance handling and steward motivation.

The broader program we suggest is based on the experiences of local unions and close observations of grievance-handling problems in a wide spectrum of workplaces and bargaining unit constituencies. It may be that implementation of this program or some variation of it may require a specially designated union officer who gives full attention to this project alone. Is it worth this extra commitment? We believe that it is.

Stewards who are educated and caring can form the foundation of an entire internal union communication network. Their regular intimate contact and influence with rank-and-file members, if brought into the service of other local union projects, can enhance the performance of every one of the local union's committees. Recreation, political action, community services, civil-rights issues, all can be brought to the attention of that great majority of members who do not attend meetings.

As more and more unions turn their attention to legislation and politics, the education and mobilization of stewards appears increasingly as the key to union political effectiveness. The route to this *goal* lies through improving stewards' *desires* and their *ability to perform their primary tasks: grievance handling and contract enforcement.*

# CHAPTER 12

# Coping with Stress: The Forgotten Skill

Stress diminishes managerial and administrative leadership effectiveness. Therefore, it is proper that this book conclude with some suggestions, self-diagnosis instruments, and guidelines for coping with stress. As a managerial topic, stress is a relatively new discipline, and it is patently unlike the other topics or skills covered in this learning guide; yet its importance to the overall scheme of effective union leadership is paramount. As a local union leader, you are of little or no value to your membership or your parent union if your ability to make correct decisions and influence others is impaired or totally neutralized by stress and ultimately—burnout.

Life-style is the focus of this chapter. The authors believe that one should be prepared for a change in life-style if stress management is to work. We are talking about coping with the following living and working (union and/or workplace job) pressures: personal, cultural, creative, social, financial, and professional. The authors simply ask that you approach this topic with an open mind, accepting or modifying those suggestions that apply to your situation. If you do, stress levels should decline. Leadership effectiveness should increase.

*One caution must be exercised.* The ideas, suggestions, and procedures contained herein are no substitute for competent medical advice. All matters regarding one's health require medical supervision. This qualifier is especially true when one moves into the areas of relaxation, exercise, and diet. Finally, if you are on medication, have not done physical work in years, or are on a supervised diet, do not embark on a stress management program until a doctor has been consulted.

---

## STRESS AND JOB BURNOUT

### What is Stress?

In its medical sense, stress is essentially the rate of wear and tear in the body. Dr. Hans Selye has been called the father of modern stress research and has defined stress as "the nonspecific response of the body to any demand made upon it."[1] We have all felt some stress during our lives, and it can take place during both pleasant and unpleasant events. Almost every event in life causes stress according to Selye, and the only way we can rid ourselves of stress entirely is through death.

In his book, *The Stress of Life,*[2] Selye listed some common misunderstandings about stress and the correct concepts according to his research.

#### What Stress Is

Stress is the wear and tear on your mind and body caused by life.

Stress is the mobilization of the body's defenses that allows us to adapt to an event.

Stress is dangerous when it is prolonged, comes too often, concentrates on one part of the body, and is unnoticed.

Stress can be brought on by both pleasant and unpleasant events.

Stress can begin in either your mind or your body.

#### What Stress Is Not

Stress is not simply nervous tension.

Stress is not an emergency discharge of hormones from the adrenal glands.

Stress is not anything that causes an alarm reaction (that is the stressor).

Stress is not the influence of some negative occurrence.

Stress does not only result from bad events.

Stress is not something to be avoided.

### Three States Of Stress

In 1950, Selye published his first paper on stress, which he called the "General Adaptation Syndrome." His research over the years has shown there are three stages that follow a threatening experience:

[1] Hans Selye, *Stress without Distress.* New American Library, New York, 1974, p. 14.
[2] Hans Selye, *The Stress of Life.* McGraw-Hill Book Co., New York, 1978, pp. 57–67.

1. *Alarm stage:* When threat is perceived through the body's senses (sight, sound, smell, touch), a message is sent to the pituitary gland in the brain where the adrenocorticotrophic hormone (ACTH) is made. ACTH then travels by the blood to stimulate the adrenals (glands attached to and over the kidneys) that manufacture adrenaline and other hormones. Their job is to cause the body to increase breathing and heart rate, raise the blood pressure, release sugars and fats into the circulation, and tense the skeletal muscles. Such actions provide the fuel and oxygen for quick energy, prepare muscles for strenuous action, help increase blood clotting mechanisms to protect against cuts or lacerations, and improve the sight and hearing and other protective actions required for "fight or flight" and survival.

2. *Resistance stage:* After the immediate threat disappears, the body relaxes and returns to a normal state. The pulse, blood pressure, and breathing rate slow down and return to normal levels. The pupils that were enlarged to improve the range of vision become smaller. The tensed muscles of the legs and arms, ready to fight a foe or run away to a safer place, relax. The digestive system, which had ceased functioning so that extra blood could flow to the muscles and brain, resumes its normal movement and digestive functions. The bladder and kidneys, which had dramatically slowed down, now can speed up and return to their normal function, often bringing the strong urge to urinate.

3. *Exhaustion stage:* If the actual or perceived danger continues over a prolonged time, a new stage begins that can end in disease or in certain cases, death by exhaustion. Protracted wear and tear can affect any of the body's organs or systems. In the case of the arteries in the cardiovascular system, there may be such continuous spasm that a condition develops called hypertension (high blood pressure). The increased blood-clotting mechanisms may create a clot in a small vessel in the heart, leading to a myocardial infarction (heart attack). Other types of wear-and-tear problems depend on the physical and hereditary makeup of the individual. Examples include peptic or duodenal ulcers, heart rhythm abnormalities, diabetes, and nervous colon.

## Pleasant and Unpleasant Stress

Throughout all his writings and research Selye has emphasized that stress is not always bad for you. The alarm reaction is a physical response set off by what Selye calls a *stressor*. A stressor is defined as something that produces stress. If the stressor is present, the alarm reaction will follow.

As mentioned earlier, a pleasant event such as the birth of a child yields stress, but this is positive stress or *eustress*. An unpleasant event, such as an IRS audit, brings about negative stress or *distress*. Keep in mind that stress can be triggered by both sad or happy events. That will be important when you later go through the life event chart that will determine the possibility of you having a stress breakdown or illness because of stressful events in your life.

Most of us are at ease when our lives are stable, orderly, and predictable. When changes occur, we can go through either eustress or distress. When people go through many changes over a short period of time, studies have shown that they are more vulnerable to injury and infection, sickness, heart attack, and strokes.[3]

Thomas Holmes and Richard Rahe have devised a rating scale that measures life events and have shown how they can be scored. This scale will give you some predictability for sickness or worse if you score too high. See Exhibit 12-1.

EXHIBIT 12-1
**Score Yourself on the Life Change Test**

| LIFE EVENT IN LAST 12 MONTHS | VALUE | TIMES HAPPENED | YOUR SCORE |
|---|---|---|---|
| 1. Death of spouse | 100 | _____ | _____ |
| 2. Divorce | 73 | _____ | _____ |
| 3. Marital separation | 65 | _____ | _____ |
| 4. Jail term | 63 | _____ | _____ |
| 5. Death of close family member | 63 | _____ | _____ |
| 6. Personal injury or illness | 53 | _____ | _____ |
| 7. Marriage | 50 | _____ | _____ |
| 8. Fired at work | 47 | _____ | _____ |
| 9. Marital reconciliation | 45 | _____ | _____ |
| 10. Retirement | 45 | _____ | _____ |
| 11. Change in health of family member | 44 | _____ | _____ |
| 12. Pregnancy | 40 | _____ | _____ |
| 13. Sex difficulties | 39 | _____ | _____ |
| 14. Gain of new family member | 39 | _____ | _____ |
| 15. Business readjustment | 39 | _____ | _____ |
| 16. Change in financial state | 38 | _____ | _____ |
| 17. Death of close friend | 37 | _____ | _____ |
| 18. Change to a different line of work | 36 | _____ | _____ |
| 19. Change in the number of arguments with spouse | 35 | _____ | _____ |
| 20. Mortgage over $45,000* | 31 | _____ | _____ |
| 21. Foreclosure of mortgage or loan | 30 | _____ | _____ |
| 22. Change in responsibilities at work | 29 | _____ | _____ |
| 23. Son or daughter leaving home | 29 | _____ | _____ |
| 24. Trouble with in-laws | 29 | _____ | _____ |
| 25. Outstanding personal achievement | 28 | _____ | _____ |
| 26. Spouse begins or stops work | 26 | _____ | _____ |
| 27. Begin or end school | 26 | _____ | _____ |
| 28. Change in living conditions | 25 | _____ | _____ |
| 29. Revision of personal habits | 24 | _____ | _____ |
| 30. Trouble with the boss | 23 | _____ | _____ |
| 31. Change in work hours or conditions | 20 | _____ | _____ |
| 32. Change in residence | 20 | _____ | _____ |
| 33. Change in school | 20 | _____ | _____ |

[3] Martin Shaffer, *Life after Stress.* Contemporary Books, Inc., Chicago, 1983, p. 29.

| | | | |
|---|---|---|---|
| 34. Change in recreation | 19 | _____ | _____ |
| 35. Change in church activities | 19 | _____ | _____ |
| 36. Change in social activities | 18 | _____ | _____ |
| 37. Mortgage or loan of less than $45,000* | 17 | _____ | _____ |
| 38. Change in the number of family get-togethers | 15 | _____ | _____ |
| 39. Change in sleeping habits | 15 | _____ | _____ |
| 40. Change in eating habits | 15 | _____ | _____ |
| 41. Vacation | 13 | _____ | _____ |
| 42. Christmas | 12 | _____ | _____ |
| 43. Minor violations of the law | 11 | _____ | _____ |

Total score for 12 months _____

*Adjusted for inflation. The original instrument had a figure of $10,000.
Note: The more you change, the more likely you are to get sick.

Of those people with a score over 300 for the past year almost 80% get sick in the near future; for a score of 150 to 299, 50% get sick shortly; if you scored less than 150, there is only about a 30% chance of sickness in the near future. It is important to note that even pleasant changes can produce stress.

## The Hidden Epidemic

According to Herbert Benson in his bestseller "The Relaxation Response," the United States is in the "midst of an epidemic."[4] Benson says that the epidemic is hypertension, which is the medical term for high blood pressure. Hypertension makes one more prone to heart attacks and strokes. These diseases account for more than half the deaths in the United States annually.[5]

The theories that try to explain why Americans have such a high death rate due to heart failures include (1) inappropriate diet, (2) lack of exercise, and (3) poor family relationships. Benson claims that these are all valid, but he also says that the factor of environmental stress has been ignored and is poorly understood.[6]

Doctors have traditionally handled high blood pressure through medication, which is a polite term for drugs. The family doctor has been trained to treat the symptoms of the body and not the cause. On the other hand, the psychiatrist is concerned with the patient's psyche. One professional treats the body and the other cares for the mind. Stress is related to both the body and mind, and the patient needs a combination of both professionals for most cases of stress to be dealt with effectively.

[4] Herbert Benson, *The Relaxation Response*. William Morrow & Co., Inc., New York, 1975, p. 18.

[5] Ibid, p. 19.

[6] Ibid. pp. 20–21.

## Fight or Flight

All animals, including humans, react to stress in a rather predictable way. Certain instincts cause us to react to stressful situations by what has been termed the "fight or flight" response. That is, when we are faced with situations that require adjustment of our behavior, we choose to flee from or fight the situation. During this time an involuntary response increases our blood pressure, heart rate, respiration, muscle tension, and metabolism, preparing us for conflict or escape.[7]

If this condition occurs too often and is not relieved in some conscious way, the result might eventually lead to a heart attack or stroke.[8]

## JOB BURNOUT: WHAT TO LOOK FOR

Now that we have defined stress and shown what unrelieved stress can do to us, let's apply that to your job and the possibility of burnout. There is no doubt about it, your work can be hazardous to your health. Burnout has no respect for education, occupation title, age, or years of service. It can affect homemakers, secretaries, school teachers, coal miners, dentists, college students, and union officers. The time and emotional demands on a local union officer can be enormous, and he or she can certainly burn out or blow up.

The *primary cause* of job burnout is *unrelieved stress,* the kind that goes on day in and day out, month after month, year after year.

### Stages of Job Burnout

In their research on job burnout, Veninga and Spradley have found five stages before one is totally spent or "fried."

1. *Honeymoon stage:* A period of high energy and job satisfaction. During this stage we are still thrilled about having the job and develop habits of dealing with the stress. People are doing exactly what they want to do. It is almost like getting paid to sample chocolate or play baseball.

2. *Fuel shortage:* The honeymoon has ended. The challenge of work and your former enthusiasm have declined. This feeling can happen every few weeks or only a couple of times a year. There are five signs to look for: (1) job dissatisfaction, (2) inefficiency at work, (3) fatigue, (4) sleep disturbances, and (5) escape activities. All these early warning signals can alert you that work stress may begin to affect your health. During this fuel shortage stage, people begin to eat and smoke more.

[7] Ibid, p. 24.

[8] Ibid, p. 25.

3. *Chronic symptoms:* One begins to feel that "something is happening to me" and many people will visit the doctor. During this stage you might feel chronic exhaustion, physical illness, anger, and depression.

4. *Crisis:* This stage begins when symptoms become critical: bleeding ulcers, rapid heartbeats, long-term migraine headaches. People become obsessed with their problem; job burnout dominates their lives.

5. *Hitting the wall:* Victims of job stress can no longer function and their personal lives deteriorate. They can no longer adapt and have taken on the other problems of alcoholism, drug abuse, heart disease, and mental illness. Very few can reach this stage and recover.[9]

Certainly job burnout does not mean that in order to be "fried" you have to go through all five stages. Many people bounce between stage one and three for years. It might indeed take a long period of time to ever get to the later stages. The key is to identify the early warning signs or symptoms and treat them as listening posts and learn how to cope so as to prevent job burnout. Knowing which stage you are in is a big step in dealing with job burnout.

## Symptoms: The Signs of Danger

Your body is equipped with many warning signs to indicate that something might be wrong with you. What you have to do is pay attention to these signs, recognize that they might be stress related, and then do something about the stress. In his book, *The Stress of Life,* Selye points to many of these symptoms:

General irritability

Depression

Hyperexcitation

Pounding of heart

Dryness of throat or mouth

Impulsive behavior, emotional instability

Overpowering urge to cry or run and hide

Inability to concentrate, flight of thoughts and general disorientation

Feelings of unreality, weakness, or dizziness

Become easily fatigued

Floating anxiety; we are afraid, but do not know exactly what we are afraid of

Emotional tension and alertness; being keyed up

---

[9] Robert L. Veninga and James P. Spradley, *The Work Stress Connection: How to Cope with Job Burnout.* Ballantine Books, New York, 1982, pp. 37–70.

Trembling

Tendency to be easily startled

High-pitched, nervous laughter

Stuttering and other speech difficulties

Bruxism, or grinding of the teeth

Insomnia, usually because of being keyed up

Hypermobility, or an increased tendency to move about without any reason; you just can't sit still and relax

Sweating

Frequent need to urinate

Diarrhea, indigestion, queasiness in the stomach, and sometimes even vomiting

Migraine headaches

Premenstrual tension or missed menstrual cycles

Pain in the neck or lower back

Loss of or excessive appetite

Increased smoking

Increased use of legally prescribed drugs

Alcohol and drug addictions

Nightmares

Neurotic behavior

Psychoses

Accident proneness[10]

Of course, the more symptoms that appear, the more obvious it becomes as to whether or not you are suffering from too much stress. An important point to remember is that you can control all these symptoms by proper stress management. You can make a choice as to whether you will continue to suffer and possibly experience a genuine (hit the wall) breakdown or gain control of stress before it controls you.

Our bodies are always talking to us, and we have a responsibility to listen. Just as you would not ignore a bright red light on the car dash that says FUEL, OIL, BATTERY, it is wise to pay attention to our body's warning signals. With awareness and practice you too can listen to those signs. In order to cope, one must be tuned into those signals.

[10]Selye, *The Stress of Life*. pp. 174–177.

## Personalities

Your personality might be an indication of how well you are currently handling stress. Doctors Meyer Friedman and Ray Rosenman did a 10-year study and reported their findings in a book entitled *Type A Behavior and Your Heart.* They learned that a certain type of personality was three times more likely to get a heart attack. They discovered that attitude and temperament had much to do with a bad heart.

In his book entitled, *Stress/Unstress,* Dr. Keith Sehnert listed the characteristics of a type A personality:

1. Tendency to overplan: they develop time urgency. Even small setbacks can become a major disaster.
2. Multiple thoughts and actions: these people are habitually involved in many actions simultaneously: having a phone conversation, eating, opening mail, interviewing someone, all at the same time!
3. Need to win: they would rather die than lose.
4. Desire for recognition.
5. Overconcerned with earning money and collecting adult toys to constantly prove their success.
6. Impatient with delays or interruptions.
7. Overextend themselves: they will take on many projects and have difficulty in delegating work.
8. Sense of time urgency.
9. Excessive competitive drive.
10. Workaholics: they have no time for recreation, exercise, family, or friends.[11]

## Are You a Type A?

The self-test (Exhibit 12-2) and analysis that follows[12] will help you to determine whether you are a type A personality and, therefore, whether you face a high risk of cardiac illness or other stress-related disease.

As you can see, each scale is composed of a pair of adjectives or phrases separated by a series of horizontal lines. Each pair has been chosen to represent two kinds of contrasting behavior. Each of us belongs somewhere along the line between the two extremes. Since most of us are neither the most competitive nor the least competitive person we know, put a checkmark where you think you belong between the two extremes.

[11] Keith W. Sehnert, *Stress/Unstress.* Augsburg Publishing House, Minneapolis, 1981, pp. 43-48.

[12] Ibid., pp. 46–47.

EXHIBIT 12-2
## Self-Test for Type A Personality

1 2 3 4 5 6 7

| | | |
|---|---|---|
| 1. Doesn't mind leaving things temporarily unfinished | — — — — — — — | Must get things finished once started |
| 2. Calm and unhurried about appointments | — — — — — — — | Never late for appointments |
| 3. Not competitive | — — — — — — — | Highly competitive |
| 4. Listens well, lets others finish speaking | — — — — — — — | Anticipates others in conversation (nods, interrupts, finishes sentences for the other) |
| 5. Never in a hurry, even when pressured | — — — — — — — | Always in a hurry |
| 6. Able to wait calmly | — — — — — — — | Uneasy when waiting |
| 7. Easygoing | — — — — — — — | Always going full speed ahead |
| 8. Takes one thing at a time | — — — — — — — | Tries to do more than one thing at a time, thinks about what to do next |
| 9. Slow and deliberate in speech | — — — — — — — | Vigorous and forceful in speech (uses a lot of gestures) |
| 10. Concerned with satisfying himself, not others | — — — — — — — | Wants recognition by others for a job well done |
| 11. Slow doing things | — — — — — — — | Fast doing things (eating, walking, etc.) |
| 12. Easygoing | — — — — — — — | Hard driving |
| 13. Expresses feelings openly | — — — — — — — | Holds feelings in |
| 14. Has a large number of interests | — — — — — — — | Few interests outside work |
| 15. Satisfied with job | — — — — — — — | Ambitious, wants quick advancement on job |
| 16. Never sets own deadlines | — — — — — — — | Often sets own deadlines |
| 17. Feels limited responsibility | — — — — — — — | Always feels responsible |
| 18. Never judges things in terms of numbers | — — — — — — — | Often judges performance in terms of numbers (how many, how much) |
| 19. Casual about work | — — — — — — — | Takes work very seriously (works weekends, brings work home) |
| 20. Not very precise | — — — — — — — | Very precise (careful about detail) |

SCORING: Assign a value from 1 to 7 for each score. Total them up.

*Source: Reprinted with permission from* Stress/Unstress *by Keith W. Sehnert, Augsburg Publishing House, Minneapolis, Minnesota, 1981.*

## Analysis of Your Score

> ***Total score = 110 to 140: Type A1.*** If you are in this category, and especially if you are over 40 and smoke, you are likely to have a high risk of developing cardiac illness.

*Total score = 80 to 109: Type A2.*    You are in the direction of being cardiac prone, but your risk is not as high as the A1. You should, nevertheless, pay careful attention to the advice given to all type A's.

*Total score = 60 to 79: Type AB.*    You are a mixture of A and B patterns. This is a healthier pattern than either A1 or A2, but you have the potential for slipping into A behavior and you should recognize this.

*Total score = 30 to 59:  Type B2.*    Your behavior is on the less-cardiac-prone end of the spectrum. You are generally relaxed and cope adequately with stress.

*Total score = 0 to 29:  Type B1.*    You tend to the extreme of noncardiac traits. Your behavior expresses few of the reactions associated with cardiac disease.

This test will give you some idea of where you stand in the discussion of type A behavior that follows. The higher your score, the more cardiac prone you tend to be. Remember, though, even B persons occasionally slip into A behavior, and any of these patterns can change over time.

If you are a type A personality, you will want to do something about it. First, you must realize that type A behavior is, like all other behavior, learned. It starts at a very early age with parents rushing us off to school, teachers and their time tests and assignments that must be in by a certain day, our boss who makes time and productivity demands on us. In short, we are reinforced throughout our lives to develop type A traits. That may be fine when we are young and better able to handle stress. As we get older our routines change, and so must our behaviors. One might consider these suggestions by Friedman and Rosenman for modifying your type A behavior:

1. Recognize that life is always an unfinishedness. It is unrealistic to believe you will finish everything needing to be done without something else needing to be done presenting itself.

2. Listen quietly to the conversation of other people, refraining from interrupting them or in any other way attempting to speed them up.

3. Concentrate on one thing at a time.

4. Do not interfere with others doing a job that you think you can do faster.

5. When confronted with a task, ask yourself:
   a. Will this matter have importance five years from now?
   b. Must I do this right now?
   Your answers will place tasks in proper perspective.

6. Before speaking, ask yourself:
   a. Do I really have anything important to say?
   b. Does anyone want to hear it?
   c. Is this the time to say it?
   If the answer to any of these is no, remain quiet.

7. Tell yourself daily that no activity ever failed because someone executed it too slowly, too well.

8. Refrain from making appointments or scheduling your activities when unnecessary. Try to maintain as flexible a schedule as possible.

9. Remember that your time is precious and must be protected. When possible, pay someone else to do bothersome chores and save your time.

10. Purposely frequent restaurants, theaters, and other such places where you know there will be some waiting required. Perceive such occasions as an opportunity to get to know your companion better or, if alone, as a chance to get some "downtime" away from the books, phone, or people seeking your time.

11. Practice eliminating polyphasic behavior (doing two or more things at the same time) by reading books that demand your entire attention and patience. A several-volume novel that is complex would work well. Proust's *The Remembrance of Things Past* is recommended.

12. Plan relaxing breaks from activities you know will result in tension by nature of the time or effort required to do them. Plan these breaks to occur prior to the feelings of tension and pressure.

13. Engage in daily practice of a recognized relaxation technique (which will be discussed later)

14. Smile at as many people as you can so as to decrease free-floating hostility.

15. Thank people for nice things they have done.

16. Remind yourself daily that no matter how many things you have acquired, unless you have improved your mind or spirit, they are relatively worthless.

17. Consider most of your opinions as only provisionally correct, while maintaining an open mind to new ideas.

18. Seek some "aloneness" regularly.

19. Consolidate your relationships with some friends and acquaintances to make them more intimate and rewarding.

20. Spend time periodically remembering your past and the well from which you sprang.[13]

## MANAGING YOUR STRESS

### Changing Your Lifestyle

If you are like most people in leadership positions, you never seem to have enough time to get things done or keep putting things off that should be done. There is a constant battle for your time, energy, ideas, and body to be all things

[13] Meyer Friedman and Ray H. Rosenman, Type A Behavior and Your Heart. Alfred A. Knopf, New York, 1974, pp. 230–235.

to all people. Your job, house, union, spouse, children, co-workers, subordinates, boss, committeepeople, all want a piece of you.

According to Karl Albrecht, there is a steady-growing philosophy that human happiness, health, and well-being are a *holistic* aspect of life.[14] This holistic concept implies that you cannot be an *effective leader* and be an *ineffective person* in private life. Since your total life is a sum of the various parts of your life, a breakdown in one will sooner or later affect the others.

To be a truly effective leader, you have to be an effective person. The effective leader is an effective spouse, parent, committeeperson, companion, and friend. A holistic approach to effective leadership and life-style requires a balance of all dimensions of living and working.

Consider the following six dimensions of your life that Albrecht details in his research, *Stress and the Manager.*[15]

1. *Professional:* how you go about making your living; your relationship to the organization.

2. *Financial:* your salary, benefits, security, assets, and liabilities.

3. *Social:* relationships and activities you share with others; family, friends, organizations, colleagues, members of the opposite sex.

4. *Cultural:* movies, plays, television, traveling, adult education; anything that helps you grow into a more knowledgeable person.

5. *Creative:* hobbies, crafts, artwork, gardening, remodeling of your apartment or home.

6. *Personal:* your physical health and well-being; recreation to relax and bring relief from tension; exercise, diet, privacy. (See Figure 12-1.)

A holistic approach to managerial life-style requires a balance of all dimensions of living and working.

Take a pencil and paper and draw a circle approximately the size of Figure 12-1. Make six segments of a pie and draw them in according to how much effort you put into each of the six dimensions that we have just outlined. If some of the segments are only slivers or, worse, not part of the pie at all, you may need some reworking of your life-style and habits. The key here is to seek some form of balance. They cannot possibly all be equal, but you will now have an idea of where your general areas of living could use some attention and more balance.

[14] Karl Albrecht, *Stress and the Manager.* Prentice-Hall, Englewood Cliffs, N.J., 1979, p. 216.

[15] Ibid, pp. 219–220.

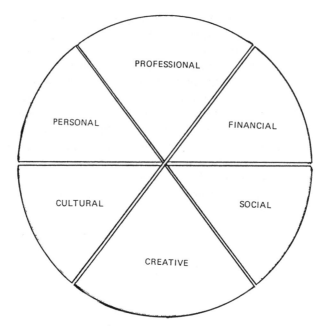

*Source: Reproduced with permission of Karl Albrecht,* Stress and the Manager, *Prentice-Hall, Inc., Englewood Cliffs, N.J., 1979.*

**FIGURE 12-1.** Dimensions of living and working

## The Wellness Triad

The holistic approach to stress management deals with balance, especially balance of the six general areas of living that you just sketched. (If you haven't sketched them, you're cheating and in too much of a hurry.) According to Albrecht, the wellness triad also deals with balance—the balance of *relaxation, exercise,* and *diet.* Albrecht unites these three factors and says that they must be dealt with as a synergistic whole—a wellness triad.[16] The following description will not be totally valid for all readers, but some of it is bound to apply. Albrecht frequently refers to this as his RED triad. A brief description follows:

1. *Relaxation:* anything you do, including deep relaxation practice, to relieve the stress accumulated through your daily activities. A good night's sleep; sitting in a quiet place and observing the silence; listening to relaxing music; taking a quiet walk by yourself; creating your own time out to put up your feet and relax; listening to a deep relaxation cassette tape or record (they are

[16]Ibid, p. 221.

available in most public libraries and many bookstores); meditating; thinking pleasant thoughts.

2. *Exercise:* anything you do that causes you to breathe heavily for more than three to five minutes. Jogging, swimming, fast walking, racquetball, bicycle riding, tennis; activities that arouse your whole body, use your muscles vigorously, make you breathe heavily, and make your heart pump more rapidly and strongly.

3. *Diet:* a good diet is made up of a balanced combination of foods that supply the basic ingredients of nutrition without too many fats, sugars, or calories; supplements taken in moderation; minimal use of "junk foods" and those overburdened with additives, colorings, and preservatives; alcohol in moderation; no use of tobacco or hard drugs; rare use of aspirin or pain medication unless required for medical management of a specific disorder; rare or no use of patent medicines such as antacids, cold remedies, laxatives; no use of tranquilizers, sleeping pills, or other central nervous system depressants; no or moderate use of caffeine (coffee, tea, or cola drinks).[17]

If one decides to adopt Albrecht's wellness triad and seek meaningful stress management, an important ingredient is to proceed slowly and cautiously. Many of the relaxation techniques that will be mentioned later you might find uncomfortable. Keep trying until you find one that works for you. Many of the exercises that are mentioned will not be right for you. Certainly a brisk game of golf can provide both relaxation and exercise, but how many of us become outraged when we slice a drive into the lake and avoid walking the course by renting an electric cart? Diet is another area where it is easy to develop bad habits. Probably all too frequently we eat "empty calories" in overprocessed foods or sweets that are intended to turn off the hunger switch in our minds.

Now that you are becoming familiar with Albrecht's wellness triad, let's look at Exhibit 12-3.

You can see that as you improve your old habits in the wellness triad, the other parts will also be enhanced. It is a snowball effect. One part enhances or supports the other. However, if one part is weak, it also weakens the others.

## Wellness Behavior Test

Albrecht has also developed a test to see how well your RED behavior really is. Use the wellness triad of factors as a checklist of your wellness behaviors. The term behaviors rather than habits is used because it strongly implies that they are

---

[17]Ibid, pp. 223-224.

EXHIBIT 12-3

**The Factors of Relaxation, Exercise, and Diet Form a
Synergistic Wellness Triad**

| THIS FACTOR | | ENHANCES THIS FACTOR | |
|---|---|---|---|
| Relaxation | Calmer attitude makes living more enjoyable; relaxation and recreation get higher priority. | Changes time priority; makes it easier to make time for exercise. | Reduces anxiety-related eating; increased body awareness and relaxation reduce over-eating at meals |
| Exercise | Improved physical condition enables the body to consume stress chemicals; makes relaxation skills easier to learn and maintain. | Improved physical condition raises energy level; makes more exercise easier and enjoyable. | Regular exercise burns calories, promotes gradual weight loss, increases metabolic level, reduces appetite. |
| Diet | Reducing consumption of alcohol, tobacco, and caffeine makes parasympathetic relaxation response easier. | High-quality diet increases energy level; exercise becomes easier as weight decreases. | Good eating habits become easier to maintain over time. |

*Source: Reproduced with permission of Karl Albrecht, Stress and the Manager, Prentice-Hall, Inc., Englewood Cliffs, N.J., 1979.*

voluntary. The following short quiz of a dozen items will tell you how well you maintain the most important form of personal capital you have—your own health.

Refer to the questions in Exhibit 12-4 and give yourself an A, B, C, D, or F, depending on your judgments. Be fair with yourself but be honest. After you have scored the test, you might want to compute the average grade. Assign four points to an A, three to a B, two to a C, and one to a D. If you flunk, you flunk—no points. Then add up all the points and divide by 12 to get your health grade-point average. Did you average at least a B-plus?

EXHIBIT 12-4
**Wellness Behavior Test**

*Relaxation:*

1. Do you take time to get completely away from work and other pressures to unwind?

   | | | | |
   |---|---|---|---|
   | Frequently | A | Seldom | D |
   | Fairly often | B | I "just can't" | F |
   | Sometimes | C | | |

2. Do you sleep well? Fall asleep easily? Sleep through the night?

   | | | | |
   |---|---|---|---|
   | Very well | A | Have trouble | D |
   | Fairly well | B | "Certified | F |
   | Not so well | C | insomniac" | |

3. Do you take, or feel you need, aspirin, tranquilizers, sleeping pills, stomach medicines, or laxatives?

   | | | | |
   |---|---|---|---|
   | Seldom or never | A | Quite often | D |
   | Occasionally | B | I'm hooked | F |
   | Fairly often | C | | |

4. Do you practice a form of deep relaxation (e.g., meditation, progressive relaxation, autogenic training, etc.) daily?

   | | | | |
   |---|---|---|---|
   | Nearly every day | A | Seldom | D |
   | Often | B | What's deep | F |
   | Occasionally | C | relaxation? | |

*Exercise:*

1. Can you run a mile (at any speed) without becoming exhausted?

   | | | | |
   |---|---|---|---|
   | Easily | A | Can't do it at all | D |
   | Fairly well | B | Can't walk a mile | F |
   | Can barely make it | C | | |

2. Can you play a fast game of tennis or other strenuous sport without becoming exhausted?

   | | | | |
   |---|---|---|---|
   | Easily | A | Get exhausted | D |
   | Fairly well | B | Wouldn't try it | F |
   | Get very tired | C | | |

3. Do you jog or engage in some other very active exercise several times a week?

   | | | | |
   |---|---|---|---|
   | Usually | A | Seldom | D |
   | Fairly often | B | Allergic to | F |
   | Occasionally | C | exercise | |

4. Are you fairly strong and physically able?

   | | | | |
   |---|---|---|---|
   | Very | A | Adequate for | C | in a strong wind |
   | Moderately | B | my purposes | | |

| Quite weak | D |
| I can't stand up | F |

*Diet:*

1. Are you overweight? (Just check to see how much surface fat is visible on your body.)

| Not at all | A | Quite a paunch | D |
| Mildly overweight | B | Butterball | F |
| Moderate amount of flab | C | | |

2. Do you smoke?

| Never | A | Pack or more a day | D |
| 2 or 3 a day | B | | |
| Half-pack a day | C | Chain smoker | F |

3. Do you drink liquor (including wine or beer)?

| Rarely or never | A | Several a day | D |
| Socially and seldom | B | I'm an alkie | F |
| One a day | C | | |

4. Do you drink coffee, tea, cola drinks, or other sources of caffeine and sugar?

| Rarely or never | A | Regularly, including with meals | D |
| 1 or 2 a day | B | | |
| Several a day | C | Can't do without it | F |

*Source: Reproduced with permission of Karl Albrecht,* Stress and the Manager, *Prentice-Hall, Inc., Englewood Cliffs, N.J., 1979.*

Putting these various models together—your grade-point average, your personal balance wheel, your life-stress score, and the present state of your health—will tell you most of what you need to know. In a sense, you are estimating your potential for handling stress and the amount of it you have developed in your overall patterns of living.

## Rebuilding Your Health

The following suggestions by Albrecht are based on the assumption that you scored poorly on the wellness behavior test. You may choose any of them to start to bring your stress under control. However, do not start out too ambitiously or quickly. Start slowly and achieve a few "victories" while building the confidence to adopt a good portion of Albrecht's suggestions.[18]

[18] Ibid., pp. 236–240.

### Relaxation

1. Buy a deep relaxation cassette for yourself, preferably the kind that helps the mind relax the body.

2. Use the tape once a day in private in order to learn to relax completely.

3. Start using momentary relaxation from time to time during the day. This will become more natural as you learn deep relaxation or visualization more thoroughly.

4. Take a course in meditation, autogenic training, or self-hypnosis that is oriented to relaxation training.

5. Program your thoughts with positive images of relaxation, tranquility, and pleasant human relations with others.

6. Do not change any of your medications without your doctor's concurrence.

7. Schedule specific times away from your work for real relaxation.

8. Find a certain amount of private time when you can be absolutely alone with yourself. You have a right to your own space.

9. Develop the habit of self-monitoring. Pay attention to your body signals as you go about the day's activities, and frequently de-escalate your internal level and relax your muscles.

10. Watch less television and read interesting books more often; watch fewer shows and movies with violent scenes or other anxiety-producing episodes; switch off radio news when it gives useless bad news.

11. Find a place that helps you to relax and detach yourself from the world for short periods. Visit a park, the beach, an untraveled back road, or a spot in the woods where you can feel remote from society and close to your own thoughts.

12. Start rethinking your time priorities and make time for regular periods of solitude and relaxation.

13. If you are heavily in the type A pattern, read *Type A Behavior and Your Heart* (Friedman and Rosenman, 1974). Follow the authors' advice and begin to impersonate a type B.

### Exercise

1. Do not increase your exercise activities without making sure you are in reasonably good health.

2. If you are over 35, have a thorough medical examination and get your doctor's permission before beginning any exercise program.

3. Find a healthy doctor who is in excellent physical condition (this may not be easy). Have the doctor administer a heart-stress test (sometimes called an

exercise physical) and give you an idea of your cardiopulmonary fitness level and heart condition.

4. Read a book on exercise and adult fitness. Begin to sell yourself on the importance of good exercise habits.

5. Join a class in slow, long-distance jogging and begin to build up your stamina in easy stages. This also lends itself to group support.

6. Never exercise so vigorously or for so long that you find it fatiguing and that you later are tempted to find many "reasons" to skip it "just this once." Make it so easy that you feel a sense of reward and accomplishment and want to do it again.

7. Take your time getting into shape. Don't become obsessed with the need to prove yourself or to get back into shape quickly. Again, make exercise a pleasant growth experience for yourself and welcome the challenge.

8. Give exercise the same priority as any other routine activity, such as grocery shopping, maintaining your car, cleaning or repairing the house, improving your education, tending to your investments, or even traveling to and from work.

9. Think about exercise as a long-term investment. Set an easily attainable goal for the next month and one for the next three months.

10. Exercise with other people if it helps you to find time for it. Associate with people who are trim and in good condition. Put yourself in situations in which you will be encouraged to engage in enjoyable physical activities.

### Diet

1. If you are extremely overweight, get your doctor's concurrence before you undertake any weight-loss program. Find a trim, healthy doctor and ask her or him to help you work out a sensible diet program that is best for you.

2. Otherwise, if you need to lose a moderate amount of weight, do not go on a crash diet—ever. Think of losing weight as a long-term process of readjusting your eating habits so that you take in fewer calories while still enjoying eating fairly well.

3. Consider joining a weight-reduction school or program, preferably one combined with an exercise program.

4. Make up your mind to be satisfied with a slow, steady loss of weight. A few pounds a month will soon add up to a respectable loss, and you will not feel as though you have tortured yourself to do it.

5. Resign your membership in the "Clean Off Your Plate Club." Learn to eat slowly until you feel your body's hunger signal turn off; then leave the rest. Understand that the waste of food took place when it came out of the kitchen, not when you left it on your plate. Select a few morsels you plan to leave on the plate before you begin eating.

6. Trick your mind into being less hungry when you sit down for a meal. You can do this by having a glass of tomato juice about 20 minutes before the meal. This caloric intake will make you less aggressive when you begin to pile food on your plate.

7. Read articles on diet, eating behavior, and losing weight to bring the subject to your attention from time to time.

8. Study your overall eating habits and decide for yourself what changes, if any, you should make. Begin to make them gradually and avoid the self-punishment syndrome of carrot sticks, skim milk, and black coffee.

9. Read some of the literature on nutrition and form your own theory about vitamin supplements in your diet. Don't be intimidated by some physicians (most of whom know very little about nutrition—or wellness, for that matter) who smile indulgently on vitamin users. And do not be bamboozled by health freaks who hop from one magical fad food or supplement to another, urging you to make eating a religious process through chemical manipulation of your body. Find your own middle road.

10. Make sure you have plenty of fiber (roughage) in your daily diet. You can easily and cheaply supplement it by taking a little bran with water now and then—a very effective and simple habit.

11. Pay attention to your feelings after meals. Begin to favor fresh or frozen vegetables, salads, and fresh fruits, all of which contribute to your energy and are easy to digest. Don't worship the thick steak as the epitome of eating pleasure. Balance meat with a variety of vegetables and do not settle for tired, canned vegetables. Demand good-tasting, well-prepared dishes, preferably steamed. Eat lightly in the middle of the day to avoid the heavy, tired feeling of satiety and to function well in the afternoon.

12. Keep careful tabs on the amount of junk food you eat. This practice will lead you to reduce it over the long term if you feel you should. (See Table 12-2.)

13. Start letting go of supersweet snacks or desserts at a comfortable rate. Replace them, for example, with sweet fresh fruits or other tasty but less fattening substitutes (not carrot sticks, unless you especially like carrots).

14. If you smoke, give it up completely. Read health articles, visit a healthy nonsmoking doctor, frighten yourself, associate with nonsmokers, take a no-smoking class or a clinical behavior conditioning program, or do whatever else you need to do to free yourself from this killer. You will probably find that the physiological changes brought about by jogging will help enormously in letting go of the habit.

15. If you drink heavily, cut back immediately. If you flunked the wellness behavior test on this item, see your physician immediately. If you only feel you drink too much, change your activity patterns to find sources of relaxation that make drinking unnecessary. Break the habit of having a drink

every day by making one day a week your "dry" day, and begin to cut down further from there. Use a relaxation practice to help you overcome the tension you have been drowning with liquor.

16. If you take recreational drugs, tranquilizers, or patent medicines more often than rarely, see a healthy physician who understands stress reduction. Have him or her supervise your program of substituting deep relaxation for the use of these chemical controllers.

17. If you drink a great deal of coffee, tea, cola drinks, or other sources of caffeine, start tapering off at a comfortable rate. Take a month or two to get your use down to the "occasional" level. Use a relaxation practice to get rid of the tension that leads you to overuse these stimulants.

## Stress Relief Safety Valves

Most electrical and mechanical devices have a form of safety valve so that the system they are involved with cannot destroy them. Humans also have a series of safety valves to avoid self-destruction. Sooner or later unrelieved stress will exploit a part of your physical or mental well being. In their book that deals with job burnout, Veninga and Spradley mention stress safety valves and their two important functions:

> they enable you to escape the direct pressure of work stress . . . and counteract the biochemical and psychological changes that occur when our bodies mobilize to deal with stress.[19]

They go on to point to numerous safety valves to help release stress. Again, not all will be right for you, so pick and choose to fit your needs.

1. *Changing gears:* In its worst form this involves changing jobs, but if you feel a total breakdown about to occur, the change might be worth it; develop or restart a hobby that you truly like; get involved in your children's school or some community project.

2. *Plan some fun:* If we can plan work, we can plan fun. Take out your pocket calendar, look for the next Saturday night and plan on going out to dinner, a play, the movies, bowling, ice skating, or for a long drive in the country. While looking through your calendar, we will bet you came across two dozen work-related items and dates. Now, plan some kinds of things that the whole family can be involved in from day trips to vacations. This can do wonders to reduce the stress levels within the family.

3. *Reduce work hours if they are excessive:* There is a law of diminishing returns and you just might owe it to yourself and your family to spend less time at work. Even if yours is the type of job where you must be in at 8

[19]Veninga and Spradley, op. cit., pp. 94-95.

A.M. and you are still on the move at 10 P.M., there may be a chance that you can get away during the day, if for no other reason than to break your routine. Go to a movie, take a walk, join a health club and exercise during the day.

4. *Exercise:* Dr. George Williams, Director of the Institute of Health Research in San Francisco, believes that exercise is one of the best ways to counteract stress. He says that exercise can relieve the accumulation of stress for the day and, therefore, put you in a better position to accept stress the next day.[20] If you have had a particularly stressful day, stop at your favorite bowling lanes and play a game or two. It is marvelous therapy to hit those pins and relieve your anxiety.

5. *Treat yourself good:* There are many ways in which you can be good to yourself. You might want to "have a night on the town." Go to the bank, take out $200, and go to the best restaurant, order the best meal and wine and enjoy! Purchase that new fishing rod that you've admired for some time. When it comes to pampering yourself, let your imagination run wild, and do it!

6. *Get a proper start on the day:* Many of us just get started poorly each day. We know it takes 30 minutes to get to work and so we arise at 7:25 and cram washing, breakfast, and dressing between then and 7:30 so that we can be in by 8. Of course, we are exaggerating, but this scenario is probably accurate in some phase of your life, perhaps when going to visit your relatives, to church, or to a sports event. When it comes to starting the day, allow enough time for a proper breakfast and extra time in case there are traffic problems. You will arrive at work much more relaxed and mentally ready to have a solid day. You should also know if you are a morning, afternoon, or night person. That is, know what time of day you can concentrate best and do your mental work; do the routine work at some other times. Don't try to do your high-stress jobs when you are tired; they just won't get done as effectively as when you are fresh.

7. *Learn how to relax:* Practice the relaxation techniques that are discussed later in this chapter.

## RELAXATION, EXERCISE, DIET

**Medical caution:** This section of the chapter will deal with some approaches to RED that may be entirely new to you or they may be things that you may not have used for years. Read through the remainder of the chapter, decide what is best for you, discuss your findings with a competent physician, and then move on to genuine stress management.

[20]"How to Deal with Stress on the Job," *U.S. News & World Report,* March 13, 1978, pp. 80–81.

## Relaxation

Dozens of books provide excellent details and suggestions for proper relaxation. We will not describe the relaxation techniques to any great extent. We will detail them briefly and point out some of their characteristics. Additional research will be up to you.

Because it is so popular and can be learned quickly and easily, meditation has become one of the most researched of the relaxation techniques. Researchers have discovered that proper meditation can reduce heart rates, slow respiration, decrease muscle tension, decrease anxiety, improve self-actualization, develop a more positive feeling toward a stressor, improve sleep behavior, decrease cigarette smoking, provide headache relief, and develop an overall positive mental attitude.[21]

### Meditation

In his book entitled *The Relaxation Response,* Herbert Benson says there are four basic elements to meditation:

1. A quiet environment, one that can be turned off to outside stimuli.
2. Have an object to dwell on (i.e., a word or sound, sometimes referred to as a mantra).
3. A passive attitude.
4. A comfortable position; sitting is usually recommended.[22]

There are many forms of meditation including transcendental meditation, Chakra Yoga, Rinzai Zen, Mudra Yoga, Sufism, Zen meditation, and Soto Zen. Regardless of the type of meditation that interests you, the four elements of Benson should apply.

Meditation can be quite pleasing and can help you better manage stress, but it does require time to do. Most experts recommend that you meditate twice a day for a minimum of 20 minutes each time. However, there are very few of us who would ever admit to having a spare 40 minutes daily. It should be emphasized that those who cannot find a spare 40 minutes daily to relax are the ones who need it most. The time is always available, we just choose to spend it differently. You have to find the time to do healthy things.

### Progressive Relaxation

This type of relaxation is directly opposite to meditation. In meditation we use the mind to relax the body. Progressive relaxation uses the body to relax the mind. This occurs through a series of exercises in which you tense muscles in one

---

[21] Jerrold S. Greenberg, *Managing Stress.* William C. Brown Co., Dubuque, Iowa, 1984, pp. 134–137.

[22] Benson, op. cit., pp. 110–111.

part of your body for a few moments, then release the tension. The purpose of first contracting the muscle is to teach people to recognize more readily what muscle tension feels like.

This relaxation technique has been proved effective and you do not need any special equipment. One can tense the various muscle groups by following a script or by purchasing a cassette that is made for progressive relaxation exercises. In any case, this method of relaxation can be easily learned and benefits can result in a few weeks of three daily practices of 5 minutes each.[23]

Research has discovered that there are both physiological and psychological benefits to progressive relaxation. Progressive relaxation has been shown to be effective in treating both tension and migraine headaches, backache, depression, anxiety, alcoholism, and drug abuse.[24]

As with other forms of relaxation, one should seek a quiet place and assume a comfortable position. Progressive relaxation can be done either by lying down or sitting in a hard chair. You can start with a group of muscles (e.g., your arms), then move to your face, neck, shoulders, and upper back, then move to your chest, stomach, and lower back, and finally the hips, thighs, and calves.

These exercises can be in one group of muscles that may be particularly bothersome or you can do all major groups for a total feeling of relaxation. An important point to remember, once you relax the muscle groups, is to concentrate on the feelings of that relaxation.

### Autogenic Training

Autogenic training is a relaxation technique that uses exercises to bring about feelings of warmth and heaviness throughout your body. Like so many other forms of relaxation, autogenic training has been proved to be effective in reducing heart rate, respiratory rate, muscle tension, migraine headaches, high blood pressure, ulcers, and lower back pain.[25] In short, this form of relaxation has had good results for problems of both the body and mind.

Again, numerous books on the market describe autogenic training, or you can buy a cassette tape that produces the same results through the use of imagery.

In his book entitled *Managing Stress,* Jerrold Greenberg takes you through a modified version of the six stages of autogenic training in which you focus on:

1. Sensations of heaviness throughout the arms and legs

2. Sensations of warmth throughout the arms and legs

3. Sensations of warmth and heaviness in the area of the heart

4. Your breathing

---

[23] John D. Curtis & Richard A. Detert, *How to Relax:   A Holistic Approach to Stress Management* (Palo Alto: Mayfield, 1981), p. 102.

[24] Greenberg, op. cit., p. 158.

[25] Ibid, pp. 144-145.

5. Sensations in the abdomen

6. Sensations of coolness in the forehead[26]

According to Greenberg, with experience in autogenics, it should take only a few minutes to feel the various aspects of heaviness, warmth, relaxation, and coolness through the parts of your body that are concentrated on. It could also take several months of regular practice to get to that point. Do not be overanxious, since trying too hard will interfere with the learning process. Proceed at your own pace, moving to the next stage only after mastering the previous stage.[27]

### Deep Breathing

Deep breathing is one of the quickest and easiest methods of relaxing. It is an exercise that does not require special training, tape players, books, or any paraphernalia. Deep-breathing exercises have been found to be effective in reducing anxiety, depression, irritability, muscular tension, and fatigue. They are used in the treatment and prevention of hyperventilation, shallow breathing, and cold hands and feet, which could be signs of stress and poor circulation. One can do deep-breathing exercises while either sitting, standing, or lying down.

Try to inhale slowly and deeply through your nose until you feel your chest fill. You can exhale through your mouth or nose in the same steady but slightly faster fashion that you inhaled. Try this for 10 to 15 breaths and see if you do not feel warm, pleasant, and less anxious. Concentrate on how good it feels as you exhale and let your body go limp and loose.

### Hypnosis

According to Benson, hypnosis is a widely known, but poorly understood, technique of relaxation.[28] The hypnotic procedure usually includes a comfortable position and suggestions of relaxation and drowsiness. When you first start, hypnosis requires a competent hypnotist to guide you through peaceful thoughts. After much training, it is possible to bring about relaxation through self-hypnosis.

If you are interested in learning more about hypnosis, contact your local medical professionals for recommendation of a reputable clinic or professional organization that has experience and has demonstrated positive results.

## Exercise

Exercise is the second portion of Albrecht's wellness triad. As a reminder, if you are over 35 or have not been physically active for some time, you should seek a doctor's advice before beginning any exercise program. A good exercise program

[26]Ibid, p. 148.

[27]Ibid, p. 149.

[28]Benson, op. cit., p. 101.

will help you to get rid of the by-products of stress—poor heart and respiratory rates, blood fats, excessive cholesterol, muscle tension—so that they are no longer a drain on your energy.

When we think of exercise, many of us remember the old physical education classes of our school days. This may bring back some terrible memories, but like it or not there are excellent physical and psychological reasons for exercise.

### Physical Health

When people speak of health, most often they are referring to physical health. Physical health is the status of your body and its parts. Vigorous exercise achieves the following:

1. Improves the functioning of the lungs and circulatory system so that transportation of food and oxygen to cells is facilitated.
2. Provides the lungs with greater elasticity to breathe in more air by expanding more.
3. Delays the degenerative changes of aging.
4. Increases the production of red blood cells in the bone marrow, resulting in a greater ability to transport oxygen to the parts of the body where it is needed.
5. Helps to maintain blood pressure at more healthy levels.
6. Results in a quicker recovery time from strenuous activity.
7. Strengthens the heart muscle the way other muscles are strengthened—by exercising it.
8. Results in a lower pulse rate, indicating that the heart is working more efficiently.
9. Burns calories, thereby helping to prevent hypertension, heart disease, diabetes, and other conditions related to excess body fat.
10. Accelerates the speed and efficiency with which food is absorbed.
11. Tones muscles to improve strength and create a more visually appealing physique.
12. Increases endurance.
13. Improves posture.
14. Decreases serum cholesterol.[29]

Depending on your need and what appeals to you, certain sports or activities will be better and more effective than others. Again, your doctor can help you select.

---

[29]George B. Dintiman and Jerrold S. Greenberg, *Health through Discovery*. Addison-Wesley Publishing Co., Reading, Mass., 1980, pp. 74–75; used with permission of Random House, Inc., New York.

Most experts agree that you do not have to run, bike, skate, or swim 50 miles a week to stay fit. Jack Kelly, director of the Human Performance Laboratory and the Adult Fitness Program at St. Cloud State University in Minnesota claims that burning 2000 calories a week should keep you in shape.[30] Kelly also suggests that most of us would be better off if we did not rely exclusively on running, but rather used a variety of exercises and activities.

Dr. Arthur Leon of the University of Minnesota's Division of Epidemiology has developed a table of activities and the number of calories you burn by doing them for an hour:

Badminton: 480 in competitive singles.

Bicycling: 240 at 5 mph, 300 at 8 mph, 420 at 11 mph, 600 at 12 mph, 660 at 13 mph.

Canoeing: 230 at 2.5 mph.

Cross-country skiing: 560 at 2½ mph, 600 at 4 mph, 700 at 5 mph, 1020 at 8 mph.

Ice skating: 400 at 10 mph.

Lawn mowing: 450 pushing hand mower (you burn 300 pushing a power mower, but you get minimal cardiorespiratory benefit).

Paddleball or racquetball: 600.

Raking leaves: 360.

Rope skipping: leisurely, 300; vigorously, 800.

Rowing machine: 840 at vigorous pace.

Running: 600 at 5 mph, 750 at 6 mph, 870 at 7 mph, 1020 at 8 mph, 1130 at 9 mph, 1285 at 10 mph.

Square dancing: 560.

Swimming: crawl, backstroke, or breast stroke, 360 to 750 at 25 to 50 yards per minute; butterfly, 840 at 50 yards per minutes; sidestroke, 660 at 40 yards per minute.

Table tennis: 360.

Tennis (singles): 420.

Walking: 300 at 3 mph, 360 at 3½ mph, 420 at 4 mph, 480 at 5 mph; hiking at 3 mph with 40-pound pack, 420.

Wrestling: 900.

(Caloric consumption is based on a 150-pound person. There is a 10% increase in caloric consumption for each 15 pounds over that weight, a 10% decrease for each 15 pounds under it.)[31]

[30]Gordon Slovert, *Minneapolis Star & Tribune,* February 26, 1984, p. 15C.

[31]Ibid., p. 15C.

Table 12-1 shows a rating scale that has been developed by Jerrold S. Greenberg. This should give you greater clarification as to what best suits you.

**TABLE 12-1.**    Physical Fitness Rating Scale

| | JOGGING | BICYCLING | SWIMMING | SKATING (ICE OR ROLLING) | HANDBALL/SQUASH | SKIING—NORDIC | SKIING—ALPINE | BASKETBALL | TENNIS | CALISTHENICS | WALKING | GOLF* | SOFTBALL | BOWLING |
|---|---|---|---|---|---|---|---|---|---|---|---|---|---|---|
| **Physical Fitness** | | | | | | | | | | | | | | |
| Cardiorespiratory endurance (stamina) | 21 | 19 | 21 | 18 | 19 | 19 | 16 | 19 | 16 | 10 | 13 | 8 | 6 | 5 |
| Muscular endurance | 20 | 18 | 20 | 17 | 18 | 19 | 18 | 17 | 16 | 13 | 14 | 8 | 8 | 5 |
| Muscular strength | 17 | 16 | 14 | 15 | 15 | 15 | 15 | 15 | 14 | 16 | 11 | 9 | 7 | 5 |
| Flexibility | 9 | 9 | 15 | 13 | 16 | 14 | 14 | 13 | 14 | 19 | 7 | 8 | 9 | 7 |
| Balance | 17 | 18 | 12 | 20 | 17 | 16 | 21 | 16 | 16 | 15 | 8 | 8 | 7 | 6 |
| **General Well-Being** | | | | | | | | | | | | | | |
| Weight control | 21 | 20 | 15 | 17 | 19 | 17 | 15 | 19 | 16 | 12 | 13 | 6 | 7 | 5 |
| Muscle definition | 14 | 15 | 14 | 14 | 11 | 12 | 14 | 13 | 13 | 18 | 11 | 6 | 5 | 5 |
| Digestion | 13 | 12 | 13 | 11 | 13 | 12 | 9 | 10 | 12 | 11 | 11 | 7 | 8 | 7 |
| Sleep | 16 | 15 | 16 | 15 | 12 | 15 | 12 | 12 | 11 | 12 | 14 | 6 | 7 | 6 |
| **Total** | 148 | 142 | 140 | 140 | 140 | 139 | 134 | 134 | 128 | 126 | 102 | 66 | 64 | 51 |

*A rating of 21 indicates maximum benefit. Ratings were made on the basis of regular (minimum of four times per week), vigorous (duration of thirty minutes to one hour per session) participation in each activity.*

*\*Ratings for golf are based on the fact that many Americans use a golf cart and/or caddy. If you walk the links, the physical fitness value moves up appreciably.*

*From Jerrold S. Greenberg,* Comprehensive Stress Management. *© 1983 Wm. C. Brown Publishers, Dubuque, Iowa. All Rights Reserved. Reprinted by permission.*

## Psychological Benefits

Besides the physical benefits of exercise, there can also be far-reaching psychological extras:

1. Greater self-esteem because you will look and feel better.
2. Others will view you as a person who takes pride in personal appearance.
3. You will feel more alert, awake, alive.
4. You will be a better worker by reducing absenteeism through less illness.
5. Decreased feelings of anxiety and depression.[32]

[32]Greenberg, op. cit., p. 189.

Assuming that your doctor gives you the OK on an exercise program, what should you do next? Simply, begin *slowly!* Do your exercises at a pace and frequency that make you healthy while you also have some fun. Enjoy what you are doing. Make a game and a challenge of it. Set realistic goals and shoot for them. Above all, do not make exercise a drudgery or surely you will never get into a routine and you will soon be back into the old routine of exercising only when you open the refrigerator.

### Exercise without Knowing It

If you just cannot get started with a regular program, the following list offers some suggestions for burning calories with only a slight change in your normal routine.

1. When you drive to the store, don't look for the closest parking space (especially not one for the handicapped!), but rather park at the far end of the lot and walk in, briskly.

2. If you take public transportation, get off a few blocks before your regular stop and walk briskly to the store or work.

3. On short trips, walk rather than ride.

4. Avoid using the elevator and walk up or down a few flights of stairs.

5. Sweep out your garage or the sidewalk.

6. When you go out with the family for the day, take along bats, balls, gloves, frisbees, or anything that will pull you into an activity.

7. Do yard work and house chores a little more lively and with bounce.

8. The next time your child or granchild wants to play some ball or go for a walk, put down the newspaper and do it.

## Diet

There is a wealth of information on proper nutrition. We will only outline some of the ideas that nutrition experts have been talking and writing about for years. An old expression says, "You are what you eat." The ability of your body to maintain adequate reserves of energy against stress depends largely on a well-balanced and appropriate diet. Our 1980s life-style does not always make proper nutrition easy, but again the choice is ours.

The convenience of fast foods either at home or out is well documented. Convenience has been made at a nutritional cost. With more homes having two incomes and the wife having less time to plan and cook, the age of nutritious, well-thought-out, and balanced meals on a regular basis is a thing of the past. It is very easy to slam down a doughnut in the morning, have a bologna sandwich on white bread for lunch, and stop at the local fast-food store for a burger and fries at supper time. Of course, in between meals there is nothing like a piece of chocolate cake, some popcorn, two cans of soda pop, and how about a large bowl of ice cream just before bed? Plenty of calories, but not much nutrition.

According to Shaffer:

> In general, people who eat too much also weigh too much. The body needs only so many calories for survival. Any calories above that level are stored as fatty tissue. When fat develops, the body accommodates by developing new blood vessels to feed that tissue. Thus, as weight increases, the heart must pump blood farther and thereby must work harder.[33]

Probably no subject is more misunderstood than nutrition. As consumers, we are deluged with information about fat, additives, sugar, flavorings, fructose, cholesterol, vitamins, and minerals. Should we have "natural," "organic," or "artifical" things added to our diets. Some doctors will have us take megadoses of vitamins A, B, C, calcium, iron, and zinc. The wizards of Madison Avenue will have you solving all your problems in pill form. It is an absolute jungle of confusion.

To try and start fresh, let's see what the U.S. Department of Health and Human Services and the Department of Agriculture have to say:

1. Eat a variety of foods.
2. Maintain ideal weight.
3. Avoid too much fat, saturated fat, and cholesterol.
4. Eat foods with adequate starch and fiber.
5. Avoid too much sugar and sodium.
6. If you drink alcohol, do so in moderation.

Good nutrition requires your diet to use the basic four food groups for a balanced diet.

Group 1: Dairy products: milk, cheese, yogurt, ice cream.

Group 2: Meats and protein: meat, poultry, fish, eggs, dry beans, and nuts.

Group 3: Fruits and vegetables: preferably fresh to avoid added sugar and salt.

Group 4: Breads and cereals: pasta, breads, crackers, biscuits, cereals.

Check with your doctor about vitamin supplements. Do not get carried away with vitamins and depend too much on them for nutritional needs. Remember a poor diet plus vitamins is still a poor diet.

---

[33]Shaffer, op. cit., p. 112.

The body provides clear warning signs when we are having nutritional problems and prolonged poor dietary habits. Indigestion, nausea, diarrhea, constipation, stomach pains, cramps, and gas are the body's chief distress signals. Do not ignore these signals; they are trying to tell you something.

## Calories and Fast-food Chains

Those of you who are in leadership positions are generally on the run and therefore have no time for thinking about nutrition. When it's 5:30 P.M. the alarm clock in your stomach says it's time to eat, even if you've been "trying to stick to your diet." Table 12-2 lists a number of fast-food chains and their specialties so you can get an idea about caloric consumption. Think about these foods and how quickly the calories add up, especially if your doctor has you on a 1500 calorie per day diet. These foods do not include condiments, such as mustard, ketchup, mayonnaise, or tartar sauce.

### TABLE 12-2

| WENDY'S | |
|---|---|
| Single hamburger | 470 |
| Double hamburger | 670 |
| Triple hamburger | 850 |
| Single with cheese | 580 |
| Double with cheese | 800 |
| Triple with cheese | 1040 |
| Chili | 230 |
| French fries | 330 |
| Frosty | 390 |

| BURGER KING | |
|---|---|
| Whopper | 630 |
| Whopper with cheese | 740 |
| Double beef whopper | 850 |
| Double beef whopper w/cheese | 950 |
| Whopper Jr. | 370 |
| Whopper Jr. with cheese | 420 |
| Hamburger | 290 |
| Cheeseburger | 350 |
| Double cheeseburger | 530 |
| French fries | 210 |
| Onion rings | 270 |
| Apple pie | 240 |
| Chocolate shake | 340 |
| Vanilla shake | 340 |

| ARBY'S | |
|---|---|
| Roast beef | 350 |
| Beef and cheese | 450 |
| Super roast beef | 620 |
| Junior roast beef | 220 |
| Ham and cheese | 380 |
| Turkey deluxe | 510 |
| Club sandwich | 560 |

| TACO BELL | |
|---|---|
| Bean burrito | 343 |
| Beef burrito | 466 |
| Beefy tostada | 291 |
| Bellbeefer | 221 |
| Bellbeefer with cheese | 278 |
| Burrito supreme | 457 |
| Combination burrito | 404 |
| Enchirito | 168 |
| Pintos 'n cheese | 168 |
| Taco | 179 |
| Tostada | 179 |

| MCDONALD'S | |
|---|---|
| Egg McMuffin | 327 |
| English muffin, buttered | 186 |
| Hotcakes with butter and syrup | 500 |
| Sausage (pork) | 206 |
| Scrambled eggs | 180 |
| Hashbrown potatoes | 125 |
| Big Mac | 563 |
| Cheeseburger | 307 |
| Hamburger | 255 |
| Quarter pounder | 424 |
| Quarter pounder with cheese | 524 |
| Filet-o-fish | 432 |

| Regular french fries | 220 |
| Apple pie | 253 |
| Cherry pie | 260 |
| McDonaldland cookies | 308 |
| Chocolate shake | 383 |
| Strawberry shake | 362 |

### BASKIN ROBBINS

| One scoop ice cream, all flavors | 133–148 |
| Sherberts and ices | 139 |

### DAIRY QUEEN

| Frozen dessert | 180 |
| DQ cone, small | 110 |
| DQ cone, regular | 230 |
| DQ cone, large | 340 |
| DQ dip cone, small | 150 |
| DQ dip cone, regular | 300 |
| DQ dip cone, large | 450 |
| DQ sundae, small | 170 |
| DQ sundae, regular | 290 |
| DQ sundae, large | 400 |
| DQ malt, small | 340 |
| DQ malt, regular | 600 |
| DQ malt, large | 840 |
| DQ float | 330 |
| DQ banana split | 540 |
| DQ parfait | 460 |
| DQ freeze | 520 |
| Mr. Misty freeze | 500 |
| Mr. Misty float | 440 |
| Dilly bar | 240 |
| DQ sandwich | 140 |
| Mr. Misty kiss | 70 |
| Brazier cheese dog | 330 |
| Brazier chili dog | 330 |
| Fish sandwich | 400 |
| Fish sandwich with cheese | 440 |
| Super brazier dog | 518 |
| Super brazier dog with cheese | 593 |
| Super brazier chili dog | 555 |
| Brazier fries, small | 200 |

| Brazier onion rings | 300 |
| Vanilla shake | 352 |
| Hot fudge sundae | 310 |
| Caramel sundae | 328 |
| Strawberry sundae | 289 |

### KENTUCKY FRIED CHICKEN

| Original recipe dinner | |
|    Wing and rib | 603 |
|    Wing and thigh | 661 |
|    Drum and thigh | 643 |
| Extra crispy dinner | |
|    Wing and rib | 755 |
|    Wing and thigh | 812 |
|    Drum and thigh | 765 |
| Mashed potatoes | 64 |
| Gravy | 23 |
| Coleslaw | 122 |
| Rolls | 61 |
| Corn (5½-inch ear) | 169 |

### PIZZA HUT

| 1/2 of 13-inch cheese pizza | |
|    Thick crust | 900 |
|    Thin crust | 850 |
| 1/2 of 15-inch cheese pizza | |
|    Thick crust | 1200 |
|    Thin crust | 1150 |
| 1/2 of 10-inch (thin crust) | |
|    Beef | 488 |
|    Cheese | 436 |
|    Pepperoni | 459 |
|    Pork | 466 |
|    Supreme | 475 |

## Nutritional Summary

Sound nutrition is necessary for successful coping and maintenance of energy levels. Ultimately, survival and avoidance of frequent illness and maintenance of energy levels are at stake.

In his book, *Life after Stress,* Shaffer suggests the following for sound nutritional living:

1. Listen to and learn from your body's signals.

2. Attend to how you eat. Eat slowly, chew fully, and enjoy the process of eating. Relax while you eat.

3. Stop eating when you begin to feel full, yet are still comfortable.

4. Avoid large meals in the evening, and avoid late evening snacks.

5. Eat in moderation.

6. Sample a variety of fresh foods. A daily diet should include items from all categories.

7. Take vitamin supplements according to your life-style.

8. Limit daily caloric intake to maintain a trim body. Few adults over the age of 40 need more than 1800 calories a day. From 30 to 40, few need more than 1800 to 2500, the amount depending on activity level. An active 20- to 30-year-old might need 2000 to 3000. You do not really need a scale. Look in the mirror.

9. Vary the amount you eat according to conditions. Under stressful conditions, including illness, eat less but selectively. Increase vitamin supplements of vitamin C, pantothenic acid, folic acid, and B-complex vitamins. Listen to your body and be flexible; nutritional demands are not static.

10. Eat to live and to laugh. Enjoyment and energy will follow.[34]

To combat stress, one's energy levels must be high and proper nutrition will build an energy reserve. Shaffer recommends three basic steps to maintain an effective energy barrier: (1) adequate sleep and rest, (2) an exercise program that will keep you in good physical condition, and (3) learning to eat a well-balanced, moderate, and healthful diet.[35] If you take these three points seriously, they will provide a foundation that will enable you to combat stress. Your resistance to stress will grow and you will be better able to cope with the day-to-day stressors that come into your life at home and work.

## TOWARD UNSTRESS

Stress is part of life and, as mentioned earlier, the only way to avoid it totally is by death. Since that may sound a little drastic, we suggest that you decide to control it before it controls you.

Remember in our work lives that there are two sets of stressors, those we *can* control and those we *cannot* control. Let's look at some examples. What should you do if you are caught in a traffic jam, or have to wait past your

[34] Ibid., pp. 124–125. Reprinted from *Life after Stress.* © 1983 by Martin Shaffer, with permission of Contemporary Books, Inc., Chicago.

[35] Ibid., pp. 124-125, used with permission.

appointment time at the dentist, or it rains on your day off? These are matters you cannot control, so why get worked up, upset, and stressed? If these things happen to you, just turn them around and enjoy some pleasant music while in traffic, bring something good to read while waiting for your dentist, or do something creative around the house until the rain stops. The thing you must do is plan ahead and expect the unexpected.

On the other hand, many things at work and in our private lives we can control. If you never learned how to relax, you might have to take a class at your local community college that will teach about the various relaxation techniques mentioned earlier. The same holds true for exercise and diet. Nobody makes you get out of shape and nobody else jams 4000 calories of empty nutrition into you daily. You control your intake and the energy that you expend. Take care of your RED and you will be much more prepared for those stressful and tense events that come up on a regular basis.

For those of you who believe you can't find the time to exercise or don't have the willpower to diet, we have listed next some things that are very easy to accomplish. Any one or a combination of these suggestions should help you to reduce stress.

1. Plan some unscheduled time every day. This is your slice of tranquility, at home and at work if possible.
2. Let others help you. Don't insist on doing everything yourself.
3. Talk out your problems to someone. This is the support that we all need from time to time.
4. Make time for fun and recreation.
5. Set priorities and do one thing at a time.
6. Read a book, take a class, or buy a tape that takes you through relaxation techniques.
7. Laugh more often.
8. Take a catnap if possible. Even a 10-minute nap can revitalize your energy levels.
9. Practice deep breathing.
10. Visualize yourself at your favorite vacation spot.
11. Massage your forehead and neck by making small circular motions with your fingertips.
12. Stretch away your tension by standing and reaching for the ceiling and then the floor.
13. Take a break. Walk around the block.
14. Go to a movie.
15. Plan your ideal vacation.

16. Give someone some attention—your spouse, children, a friend. That behavior is contagious and often reciprocated.

17. Read and learn more about stress.

18. Don't procrastinate. The longer one puts off unpleasant tasks, the more tense one becomes.

Whatever you do to reduce your stress levels, do not expect miracles overnight. It probably took a long time to develop poor habits and it will take time and patience to break them. Stress management takes time. Work on one thing at a time and do not get discouraged if there are not instant results.

Above all, keep in mind that we do have some control over what happens in our lives, be it stress management or developing leadership effectiveness. Simply remember: *Don't curse the darkness—get a flashlight.*

## CHAPTER TEST

Fill in the blank with the appropriate answer.

1. The alarm reaction stage is set off by a _____.
   (a) pleasant event          (c) change in life events
   (b) stressor                (d) hormone

2. Hypertension has traditionally been treated with the use of _____.
   (a) relaxation techniques   (c) hypnosis
   (b) jogging                 (d) medication

3. Job burnout is caused chiefly by _____.
   (a) long hours              (c) unrelieved stress
   (b) pressures at work and home  (d) hypertension

4. If you have a type A personality you _____.
   (a) should consider modifying your behavior
   (b) should socialize with type A's
   (c) are productive and in control
   (d) are managing stress well

5. According to Albrecht, you should seek a _____ approach in your drive to happiness.
   (a) balanced                (c) stress-free
   (b) holistic                (d) eustress

6. The wellness triad consists of _____.
   (a) relaxation              (c) physical fitness
   (b) proper nutrition        (d) RED

Place a T (true) or an F (false) in the space provided.

7. _____ Stress is brought on by both happy and sad events in our lives.

8. _____ A score of 285 on the life event test indicates an 80% chance of illness.

9. _____ A type A personality does one thing at a time in order to avoid mistakes.

10. _____ If you are under 35, you do not need a medical exam before starting an exercise program.

11. _____ Crash diets will usually help you lose weight and keep it off.

12. _____ The end result of vigorous exercise will be a higher pulse rate.

13. _____ For exercise to really help, you must be aware of what you are doing.

14. _____ The best way to help lower your blood pressure is through medication.

15. List and describe the three stages of stress.

16. List and describe the various stages of job burnout.

17. Briefly describe the wellness triad that Albrecht believes in.

18. Name four stress relief valves and describe how they may help you avoid job burnout.

19. Name and describe three forms of relaxation.

20. Name the four basic food groups.

---

## GLOSSARY

**distress:** The feeling of helplessness, desperation, and disappointment that comes about through unpleasant experiences.

**eustress:** Positive consequences of stress. This is the stress of achievement, triumph, and exhilaration brought on by happy events in our lives.

**fright or flight:** The human reaction during a stressful situation in which a person decides to fight the event or to run away from it.

**holistic:** An approach toward stress management that says in order to be an effective person you must have a balance in all dimensions of your life.

**hypertension:** The medical term for high blood pressure.

**job burnout:** A debilitating psychological condition brought about by unrelieved work stress. During this condition a worker has no energy, lowered resistance to illness, increased dissatisfaction, absenteeism, and inefficiency at work.

**nutrition:** The processes by which we take in the various food groups and the way the body uses them.

**physiological:** Having to do with the functions of the body.

**psychological:** Having to do with the functions of the mind.

**relaxation:** The act or process of loosening your muscles and mind through some form of a meditation, progressive relaxation, autogenic training, deep breathing, hypnosis, or other means that will make us feel more at ease with life.

**stress:** The rate of wear and tear on the body that is brought on by a stressor.

**stressor:** Something that causes stress (e.g., noise, cold, heat, a speech, an IRS audit, an examination).

**symptom:** A sign or an indication that often accompanies sickness; for example, a fever is a symptom of illness.

**type A personality:** A person who is always on the go. He or she has a time urgency, has a need to win everything, is impatient, and is very competitive.

**wellness triad:** The term that Karl Albrecht uses when he refers to stress management being possible through a balance of relaxation, exercise, and diet.

# INDEX

## About the Authors

Gene Daniels, formerly a local union member of the Machinists Union and later the Furniture Workers Union, is currently a labor educator with the Labor Education Service, Industrial Relations Center, University of Minnesota. He holds a bachelor's degree in labor studies from the Division of Labor Studies, Indiana University at South Bend, and a master's degree in industrial relations from the University of Minnesota. He is a co-author of the book *Labor Guide to Negotiating Wages and Benefits* and the article "The Lost Dream: Worker Control at Rath Packing." Mr. Daniels is a member of Workers' Education Local 189, University and College Labor Education Association, Midwest Labor Press Association, and AFSCME Local 1164.

Roberta Till-Retz is currently director of the Labor Center at the University of Iowa. She holds a Ph.D. in European social history and a master's degree in industrial relations, both from the University of Oregon, and a master's degree in American history from Harvard University. She is co-author of the chapter "Labor Education and Women Workers: An International Comparison" in Barbara M. Wertheimer's *Labor Education for Women Workers.* Ms. Till-Retz is a member of Workers' Education Local 189, University and College Labor Education Association, and the Cedar Rapids Federation of Teachers, AFL–CIO.

Larry Casey has been a trade unionist as a member of the International Brotherhood of Electrical Workers since 1964. He worked as an apprentice, journeyman wireman, shop steward, and foreman in the trade for 15 years. He was an officer from 1974 until 1979 and served as a delegate to the Bergen County Central Labor Union in northern New Jersey. He holds a bachelor's degree from Rutgers University and a master's degree in labor studies from that same institution. Currently, Mr. Casey is the director of Building Trades Programs at the Labor Education Service, Industrial Relations Center, University of Minnesota, and belongs to the University and College Labor Education Association.

Tony DeAngelis has a bachelor's degree in labor studies from Pennsylvania State University and a master's degree in industrial relations from the University of Minnesota. He co-authored the article "Steward Performance: A Behaviorally Anchored Description." While serving as a labor educator for the Labor Education Service at the University of Minnesota since 1974, Mr. DeAngelis has belonged to Minnesota Federation of Teachers, AFL–CIO, and the University and College Labor Education Association.